BLENDED BLESSINGS

Heavenly Carolina Cuisine

The Alpha

The Omega

Treasured
Recipes

Colorful
Menus

Seasonal
Blessings

Published By
First Presbyterian Church
Salisbury, North Carolina

Founded in 1821

BLENDED BLESSINGS

Proceeds from the sale of this cookbook will benefit the local and foreign missions and projects of the Presbyterian Women of First Presbyterian Church, Salisbury, North Carolina

For Additional Copies of:

BLENDED BLESSINGS

Please send $20⁰⁰ + $3⁰⁰ (U.S. Dollars) for Postage and Handling for each book ordered. Include your Name, Address and Phone Number. Please specify the Name and Address of any Gift Recipients. $10⁰⁰ of the Purchase Price qualifies as a Charitable Contribution. Make Checks Payable To:

Presbyterian Women

Mail All Orders To:

Blended Blessings Cookbook

c/o FIRST PRESBYTERIAN CHURCH
308 West Fisher Street, Salisbury, North Carolina 28144 USA

Cover Artwork

Cara Reische, a Spencer, North Carolina resident, began her studies in art in Junior High School. After graduating from the High School of the North Carolina School of the Arts, she spent a year in Italy, also making visits to other European countries. In 1990, having spent 3 1/2 years in the Illustrations Department at the Rhode Island School of Design, Cara graduated from college with a Bachelor of Fine Arts Degree. Now, a self-employed artist, Cara has clients from Mississippi to Alaska for whom she paints primarily commissioned portraits.

Drawings of Church Properties

Dan Norman and Frank Saunders

Color Photography

Beth Kluttz

Graphic Design

Phil Rogers and Peggy House – Omega Graphics, Kannapolis, North Carolina
Clipart Provided By Aridi Computer Graphics, Dallas, Texas
Joe Laib, Quick Copy/Print Shop, Salisbury, North Carolina

Hymn of Promise

Words and Music by Natalie Sleeth, Copyright 1986 By Hope Publishing Company,
Carol Stream, Illinois, 60188. Reprinted with Permission Under License № 5699

First Printing   4,000   1998

Copyright 1998 By:

First Presbyterian Church, Salisbury, North Carolina

International Standard Book Number – 0-9657293-0-3
Library of Congress Catalog Number – 97-061144

STARR★TOOF

Memphis, Tennessee, U.S.A.

First Presbyterian Church, Salisbury, NC

BLENDED BLESSINGS

IS PRESENTED WITH LOVE
TO THE
PAST, PRESENT AND FUTURE
MEMBERS OF
FIRST PRESBYTERIAN CHURCH,
SALISBURY, NORTH CAROLINA

Drawing of First Presbyterian Church, Salisbury, North Carolina by Dan Norman

Pastor's Introduction

The secret ingredient in cooking with BLENDED BLESSINGS is not contained in any exotic, rare, or imported herb or spice or in any single recipe, but in hearts warmed with the love of God, church, family, friends, and community.

The Bible tells us that the early church shared their meals with glad and generous hearts (Acts 2:46) and that Jesus Himself was known to them in the breaking of bread (Luke 24:35). When we gather to ask the Lord's blessing and share good food in fellowship with one another, we are nourished both physically and spiritually.

BLENDED BLESSINGS is a beautiful expression of the many blessings we share as members of First Presbyterian Church, Salisbury, NC. The rich heritage of our church, the bounty of food grown and raised in the Piedmont region of North Carolina, the warm hearts, the Southern traditions, and the hospitality of the people who live here are but a few of the blessings for which we are thankful.

The compilation of this cookbook was made possible by the efforts of the cookbook committee, our church family near and far, and people of the community. It is comprised of the blended ingredients of love, commitment, dedication, discipline, and long hard work, but the greatest of these is love.

The goal for this book is that its fruits will provide the means for the Presbyterian Women of First Presbyterian Church to reach out in love to those in need.

When you give this book as a gift, you are giving a gift of love, not only from you yourself, but also from our church family and all others who gave birth to it.

The Reverend Doctor Robert M. Lewis

Senior Pastor

Editor & Chairman
• Libby Gish •

Co-Editors
• Lynn Bertram • Carol Freed •

Editorial Executive Committee
• Lynn Bertram • Carol Freed • Collin Grubb • Jo Krider • Julie Steele •

Manuscript Computer Editor
• Jo Franklin •

Cookbook Committee Assistants & Recipe Proofing

Dottie Abramowski	Lisa Ganem	Helen Kichevski	Susanne Pierce
Susan Alexander	Libby Gish	Betsy Knauf	Diana Potts
Lynn Bertram	Dottie Goodnight	Jo Krider	Marilyn Smith
Betty Carli	Collin Grubb	Jan Lewis	Julie Steele
Cleo Dick	Ramona Humphries	Nancy Nolan	Pat Weber
Carol Freed	Tricia Johnson	Marcia Parrot	Donna Yale

Introduction
• Reverend Dr. Robert M. Lewis •

Church History & Presbyterian Women's History
• Jo Krider •

Editorial Consultant & Regional History
• Elizabeth Cook •

Heritage Recipes
• Jo Krider • Collin Grubb •

Colorful Menu Planning
• Lynn Bertram • Julie Steele •

Seasonal Blessings
• Lynn Bertram • Julie Steele • Reverend Dr. Robert M. Lewis •
• Sunday School Classes and Teachers • Reverend James Foil Jr. •

Research, Consumer Information & Web Sites
• Libby Gish •

Typists
• Jo Franklin • David Potts • Libby Gish •

Presbyterian Women Coordinating Team Members 1995 – 1999
Session Members of First Presbyterian Church 1995 – 1999
Presbyterian Women's Treasurer
• Joanne Eichelberger •

Presbyterian Women Moderators

Tessa Sansovich	Kay Paul	Deborah Messinger	Martha Lassiter
1998 – 1999	1997 – 1998	1996 – 1997	1995 – 1996

Church Staff

Reverend Dr. Robert M. Lewis
Senior Minister

Reverend James Foil Jr.
Associate Minister

Sophie Kivett
Director, Christian Education

Michael Quimby
Director, Youth

Flora Abernethy
Director, Music

Becky Lowery
Business Manager

Shirley Lewis
Church Secretary

Jane Welch
Director, Day School

Church Volunteer Receptionists

Cover Artwork
• Cara Reische •

Drawings
• Dan Norman • Frank Saunders •

Photography
• Beth Kluttz •

Graphic Design

Omega Graphics, Inc
Phil Rogers & Peggy House

Cherub and Letter Artwork
Courtesy of Aridi Graphics

QuickCopy/Print Shop
Joe Laib

Hymn of Promise
Lyrics Reprinted with Permission of Hope Publishing Company
with the Assistance of Flora Abernethy

Regional Map
Courtesy of Judy Newman Rowan County Convention & Visitors Bureau

Consultants
• Lorie Freed Reilly • Janet Rush •

Promotion & Marketing Committee Co-Ordinators
• Robin Perry • Martha Lassiter • Jan Williams •

Congregational Sales
• Deborah Messinger • Jackie Burleson •

Community & Businesses
• Tessa Sansovich • Tracy Smith •

Cookbook Kick-Off & Tasting Party Events
• Beth Pate • Carr Garner •

Advertising Brochure & Order Form
• Bob Bailey • Rochelle Redcay • Adair Doran •

Bookkeeping & Orders
• Sherry Jarret • Paula Troxler •

Media & Publicity
• Elizabeth Cook • Wendy Atkinson •

Starr*Toof
Consultant
Richard Anderson

Starr*Toof
Production Coordinator
Phyllis Cash

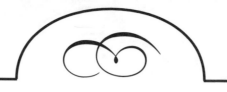

Sponsors

Session of First Presbyterian Church, Salisbury, North Carolina

Presbyterian Women, First Presbyterian Church, Salisbury, North Carolina

Lynn Bertram	Doris Brownlee	Carol Freed
Libby Gish	Collin Grubb	Mary Hudson
Jo Krider	Julie Steele	Louise Upchurch
	Wilburn Taylor	

Acknowledgment of Sponsors

The Cookbook Committee, on behalf of the Presbyterian Women of First Presbyterian Church, Salisbury, North Carolina, wish to express our sincere appreciation to **the Sponsors** whose support made the publication of *Blended Blessings* possible.

Acknowledgments

Blended Blessings is the result of the collective efforts of countless individuals who generously shared their culinary, creative, artistic, journalistic, and editorial talents; and promotional and marketing skills. We thank each one of you for helping us make *Blended Blessings* become a reality.

The Cookbook Committee gratefully acknowledges the participation and contributions of our church members, church staff, church families, friends and neighbors. We want to express our sincere appreciation and thanks to all of the many individuals who submitted, prepared, tasted and tested the recipes in *Blended Blessings*. We wish to thank our husbands, our children, and immediate family members whose love, patience and support during the last two years of our endeavor, enabled us to compile and complete this cookbook: We Extend A Heartfelt Thank You To Each Of You!

We regret that similarity of content and the limitation of space prevented us from including all of the over 1400 recipes that were submitted. We have attempted to compile a cookbook that offers variety, balance, and appeal, to people of all ages and cooking abilities.

A Very Special Thank You to Artist **Cara Reische**, for the Original Painting created for the cover of BLENDED BLESSINGS and to **Dan Norman**, for the Original Pen and Ink Drawing he created to depict First Presbyterian Church as it appeared in 1997, and to **Frank Saunders**, for the composite drawing of First Presbyterian Church properties.

Table of Contents

BLENDED BLESSINGS

— Recipe For A Cookbook —

Main Ingredient ....Cupfuls of LOVE

Leavening Agent ....FAITH

Measurement ....Over 1000 Heavenly Recipes from Talented Cooks, Caterers, and Restaurants

Seasonings ....Seasonal Blessings & Colorful Menus, Edible Food Crafts & Gifts, Buffet Food Bars, Strawberry & Heritage Sections

Dash Of ....History & Personal Commentary, Consumer Food Web Sites, Helpful Equivalents, Substitutions, Tips and Food Quantities for Cooking for a Crowd

Fill With ....Practical and Easy to Follow Guidelines for Planning Menus, Meals, and Entertaining; Local, Regional, Southern and International Recipes

Convenience ....Distinctive Symbols to Quickly Identify Heart Healthy, Children's, Strawberry, Feeding a Flock, & Food Craft Recipes

Directions ....Combine and Blend Ingredients with Care

Temperature ....Preheat with Warm Hearts of Church Members, Family, Friends and Neighbors

Nurture ....Until Well Done

Garnish ....Sprinkle with Original Artwork, Photography and Graphics

Yield ....BLENDED BLESSINGS – A Cookbook to Treasure, Serve Generous Portions to Family, Friends the Community and Those in Need

Key To Recipe Symbols

♥	*indicates*	Heart Healthy
🎈	*indicates*	Children's
🍓	*indicates*	Strawberry
🔔	*indicates*	Feeding A Flock
🧍	*indicates*	Food Crafts

Blessed Beginnings

History & Heritage
Heritage Recipes
Colorful Menus & Seasonal Blessings

First Presbyterian Church – Salisbury, North Carolina

First Sanctuary † 1826

Second Sanctuary † 1892

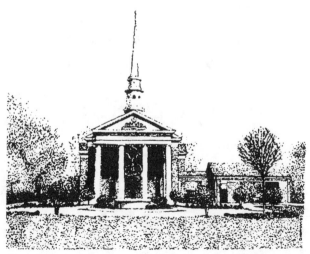

First Presbyterian Church † 1997

A Brief History of First Presbyterian Church

First Presbyterian Church of Salisbury, North Carolina, was organized with 13 members on August 4, 1821 by the Reverend Dr. Jonathan Otis Freeman.

Dr. Freeman, a teacher of the classics at the Salisbury Academy, served as minister until 1826 when the first church building was completed in the 200 block of West Innes Street on the corner of Innes Street and Jackson Street.

The lot on which the first church was built, had been given to the congregation by Rebecca Troy Caldwell, half-sister to Maxwell Chambers. At his death in 1855, Maxwell Chambers willed to First Presbyterian Church all the property on the square where the Church stood (except the Academy Building) and the entire 300 block of West Innes on which the manse, educational building and current Church stand today. The church purchased the Academy, built in 1838, from Nathaniel Boyden in 1871, completing the title to both the 200 and 300 square blocks of West Innes Street.

Lewis Utzman built a house in 1811 in the 300 block of West Innes Street on the corner of Jackson Street. Maxwell Chambers purchased this house in 1840 for use as a manse. The present manse was built in 1913, and the former manse was moved back, turned, and repositioned, to face Jackson Street. The former manse, now called the Utzman-Chambers House is preserved by Rowan Museum, Incorporated.

The Greek Revival Session House on the corner of the 200 block of West Innes Street and Jackson Street was constructed in 1855 over the graves of the Chambers family. The building was used for many years as a Sunday School for children.

The first Church, build in 1826, was torn down and the second Church was built on the same site. Completed in the fall of 1892, the second church was designed by Charles W. Bolton of Philadelphia and was cited as an outstanding architectural example of Romanesque Revival Style. The Church brick tower, known today as the "Bell Tower," was saved from demolition by the Historic Salisbury Foundation when the church was torn down in 1971.

John Erwin Ramsay, Elder of First Presbyterian Church, designed the Educational Building, which was completed in 1952 and the present church which is English Colonial architectural in style.

The first service in the present church, located on the corner of Fulton and Innes Street, was held on Easter ... April 6, 1969.

Sixteen Senior Ministers have served the church over the past 177 years. The present Senior Minister is the Reverend Dr. Robert M. Lewis and the Associate Minister is the Reverend James H. Foil Jr.

Compiled by Jo Krider

Based on *First Presbyterian Church, Salisbury,*
North Carolina and Its People, 1821 – 1995 by Jo White Linn

First Presbyterian Church Today

First Presbyterian Church is a growing and vibrant congregation with more than 1200 members and a median age of 40. It is a 7-day-a-week church with programs and opportunities for all ages. Worship services include two on Sunday morning and the Seeker's Service on Saturday night.

Believing we are "blessed to be a blessing," we provide support to Rowan Helping Ministries, the Homeless Shelter, Meals-on-Wheels, Habitat for Humanity, and numerous other local, national, and international ministries. Some of the foreign mission projects we are presently supporting are the Mwandi Medical Mission in Zambia, the border ministry in Mexico, and Rivers of the World. For the last several years, youth and adults have gone on mission trips to Africa and Mexico. We are generous in our support (the second leading church in our presbytery of 150 churches) of the Benevolence Program of the Presbyterian Church (USA).

In 1996, the church completed an expansion program that included the modernization of the educational building, including the installation of an elevator, and the building of a pedestrian plaza, a porte-cochere, a parking lot, and the landscaping of our campus. Most recently, Celebration Hall was completed on the lower level of the church and is used for the Saturday Seeker Service, receptions, retreats, Sunday School classes, and community events.

Programs that are ministering to growing numbers of people are the First Presbyterian Church Day School, Sunday School for all ages (16 classes), First Families, graded choirs, Presbyterian Women, Men's Prayer Breakfast, Middle School and Senior High youth groups, small groups, scout troops, and the Blessing Bunch.

The Strategic Planning Committee is now engaged in positioning our church for the first part of the new millennium. Many people are enthusiastic for a Family Life Center and an expanded Fellowship Hall.

We believe that the church must be purpose-driven and that a Great Commitment to the Great Commandments (Matthew 22:37 – 40) and the Great Commission (Matthew 28:19 – 20) will grow a Great Church. The purpose statement that is leading us forward is: To bring people to Jesus and MEMBERSHIP in his family, develop them to Christ-like MATURITY, and equip them for their MINISTRY in the church and MISSION in the world, in order to MAGNIFY God's name.

The Reverend Dr. Robert M. Lewis

Senior Pastor

History of Rowan County

"God is great and God is good," our children pray, little heads bent over plates of food, Each time we break bread, we remember God's generous bounty, a bounty that has poured forth here for many years in many ways.

The history of Salisbury and Rowan County is as rich and varied as the recipes in this book. Situated in the Piedmont of North Carolina, the area was first home to several native American tribes, including the Saponas and Catawbas. The natives tended to move around the state in migratory fashion, however. So when the first settlers started moving in, they found fertile, virgin territory – and little to keep them from making the best of it.

A beautiful region it was. Stretching out from the banks of the Yadkin River, the land was characterized by gently rolling hills with rich soil, durable granite, and an abundant supply of creeks and forests.

The Reverend Jethro Rumple, in his "History of Rowan County," described this land of plenty: 'The virgin soil brought forth bountifully. Herds of cattle and droves of swine fed at large, unrestrained by any stock law. Bears, deer, turkeys, wild geese and ducks abounded.'

And the rivers were so generously filled that 'the fisherman seldom returned without a heavy string of fish.'

Pioneer families flocked to this haven from several directions. Some came from South Carolina, following the Pee Dee and Santee rivers. But the two most popular routes came from the North: the Trading Path from eastern Virginia, and the Great Wagon Road that stretched all the way from Pennsylvania.

These routes brought a steady influx of English, Welsh, Scotch-Irish and German immigrants. The Scotch-Irish and Germans arrived in by far the greatest numbers. The mostly-Presbyterian Scots came first, around 1747, and settled in the western part of Rowan. The largely-Lutheran Germans followed soon after in the east.

Salisbury itself took shape in somewhat backwards fashion. A newly appointed county court decided in 1753 to situate a new courthouse for Rowan in an unsettled wilderness. The town grew up around it. By the time 13 people gathered to organize Salisbury Presbyterian Church in 1821 – now First Presbyterian – about 800 people lived within the town limits. (The 1820 Census counted 496 whites, 299 slaves and 13 free "colored" people.)

The temperaments of the Scotch-Irish and Germans shaped the character of the community. They brought with them a strong sense of practicality, independence and hard work – not without a streak of stubbornness. They were rock-solid.

They also farmed industriously and established a rural culture that thrived well past the mid-point of the 20th century.

The years brought many changes to the area – wars, the textile industry, highways in the place of wagon roads, housing developments in the place of cultivated fields. The population has gone from the hundreds to the thousands – some 25,000 in Salisbury, and more than 110,000 in Rowan. Near the close of the century, fewer than 1 percent of our people work on farms.

But, so far, no force or event has changed the area's essential nature: conservative, considerate and proud to preserve our hard-earned past.

The cooking style that evolved here and elsewhere in the South is truly a Blended Blessing of many influences. English, Scotch-Irish, German, Indian and African cultures come together in our kitchens. The flavors that emerge represent all parts of the Carolinas. From Ocean Drive to the Blue Ridge Mountains.

There's piquant pork barbecue, cooked long and slow over hot hickory coals and served with a vinegar-laced slaw. (You can get a pile of it at the Faith Fourth of July celebration.) Moravian sugar cookies are rolled to paper-thin perfection. Fried okra and squash taste as pop-in-your-mouth delicious as hot popcorn.

From apple-butter to zucchini bread, cooks here have always demonstrated skill at making the most of their crops. But some of our favorite treats get gobbled up plain on the spot: sun-warmed tomatoes from up Woodleaf ways; sweet, you-pick-'em strawberries from Patterson's Farm.

It is no wonder that George Washington once supped here during a tour of the region, or that Union General George Stoneman spared most private residences when his troops raided Salisbury – or even that the National Sportscasters and Sportswriters Association holds its annual convention here each spring. People who pass through Salisbury carry with them memories of warm greetings, good food and gracious hospitality. People who live here take pride in that tradition – and pass along these recipes to you.

"… and we thank Him for our food" – *and much, much more.*

Elizabeth G. Cook

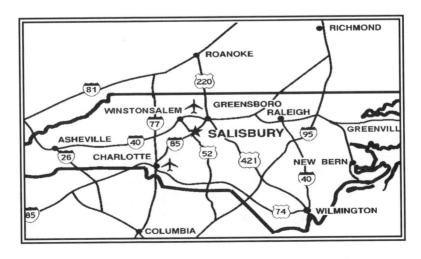

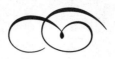

Presbyterian Women

Women's Work has always been an important part of First Presbyterian Church, Salisbury, NC. The Ladies Aide Society was organized in 1860 under the direction of the Reverend Dr. Jethro Rumple for the purpose of serving God, His Church, and fellowman with their time, talents and money.

The organization has seen tremendous growth through the years and its' name has been changed to "Women's Auxiliary," "Women of the Church," and today is known as Presbyterian Women.

The organization serves as the nurturing body of the church and cooperates with the Minister and the Session to help members of the church family and community. Organized into four groups, that meet monthly for Bible Study and fellowship: three of the "Circles" meet at the church, and one "Circle" meets in a members' home. The Presbyterian Women contribute to their budget in support of local and foreign missions and other church related projects.

In 1996, as part of the 175th Anniversary of our church, the Presbyterian Women launched a project to publish their first cookbook. The result of this effort is seen in BLENDED BLESSINGS. God has given each person different gifts; one is the GIFT OF COOKING. Included in this cookbook are recipes from some of the best present and former cooks from our church, families, and friends and our town and community. The purpose of the cookbook, is to record the treasured recipes and special blessings used when we share meals with family, friends, neighbors, and fellow church members and to provide additional funds to the Presbyterian Women's budget in support of its' missions and projects. We hope BLENDED BLESSINGS will inspire cooks everywhere who read its pages, use, share and enjoy its contents. The proceeds will be a BLESSING to God's children in need.

Presbyterian Women's Projects
Barium Springs Children's Home, Barium Springs, NC
Battered Women's Shelter, Rowan County, NC
Rowan Helping Ministries
TWAM (Teens With A Mission) Missions to Mexico
Presbyterian School of Christian Education, Richmond, VA

Presbyterian Women's Purpose
To Nurture our Faith Through Prayer and Bible Study,
To Support the Mission of the Church Worldwide
To Work for Justice and Peace, and
To Build an Inclusive, Caring Community of Women That Strengthens
the Presbyterian Church (USA) and Witnesses to the Promise of God's Kingdom.

Shrimp & Brown Rice

1½ pounds shrimp, peeled, deveined
2 medium onions, chopped
1 (9-ounce) can mushrooms, drained (or fresh)
Small amount chopped celery, with leaves (1 cup or less)

4 tablespoons butter
1 (10½-ounce) can mushroom soup
Salt and pepper
Sherry or white wine (small amount)
3 cups cooked brown rice

Sauté shrimp, onions, mushrooms and celery (if desired) in butter until shrimp are pink. Add soup, salt and pepper to taste and rice. Add small amount of sherry or white wine. Cook until hot.

Yield: 6-8 servings

CONTRIBUTOR: Mrs. Harry T. (Mary Putzel) Goldman, Jr. submitted this recipe of her mother's, Mrs. Charles Putzel (deceased).

COMMITTEE NOTE: *One of the best cooks in Salisbury, NC, Ellinor Ramsay Putzel grew up and was married in the Rowan Oak House. Mrs. Putzel was a life long member of First Presbyterian Church. Her daughter, Mary Putzel Goldman, said this was her favorite "home coming" meal.*

Ginny Williamson's Chicken Tetrazzini

4 tablespoons margarine, melted
4 tablespoons flour
2 cups milk
2 cups cooked cubed chicken
½-1 cup cooked and drained thin spaghetti, broken into 1-inch pieces before cooking

1 (4-ounce) can mushrooms, undrained
½ cup slivered almonds
⅔ cup Parmesan cheese
Salt and pepper
1½ cups crushed Ritz crackers
½ cup margarine, melted

Blend 4 tablespoons margarine and flour in saucepan. Warm over medium heat. Slowly pour in milk, stirring constantly until thickened. Remove from heat and mix together chicken, spaghetti, mushrooms, almonds, cheese and salt and pepper to taste. Pour into 9x13-inch casserole. Top casserole with a mixture of crackers and melted margarine. Bake at 350° for 30 minutes or until browned.

NOTE: *The Ritz cracker topping makes the casserole delicious!*

Yield: 6 servings

CONTRIBUTOR: Ginny Williamson

COMMITTEE NOTE: *Ginny Williamson is the wife of the late Rev. Dr. William W. Williamson, minister of First Presbyterian Church, Salisbury, NC, 1971-1978. She served as Elder of the church and President of the Women of Concord Presbytery.*

Chicken Marengo
A good company dish

1/2	cup flour	1	cup dry white wine
1	teaspoon salt	2	cups canned tomatoes
1/2	teaspoon freshly ground black pepper	1	clove garlic, minced or crushed
1	teaspoon dried tarragon	8	sliced fresh mushrooms, sautéed, or equivalent
8	boned chicken breasts (3 pounds)		amount canned, drained
1/4	cup olive oil		Chopped parsley
1/4	cup butter		Hot cooked rice

Preheat oven to 350°. Mix flour, salt, pepper and tarragon. Dredge chicken with seasoned flour; reserve remaining flour. In a large skillet, heat oil and butter. Add chicken and brown on all sides. Remove chicken to a heavy casserole dish. Add reserved flour to fat remaining in skillet. Using a wire whisk, stir in wine. When thickened, pour over chicken. Add tomatoes, garlic and mushrooms. Cover and bake 45 minutes. Sprinkle with parsley before serving with rice.

Yield: 8 servings

CONTRIBUTOR: Mrs. John G. Riley submitted this recipe of Mrs. W. Chapman Crawford (Arline).

COMMITTEE NOTE: *Mrs. John G. Riley is the daughter-in-law of Julia and John Riley, former members of First Presbyterian Church, Salisbury, NC.*

Gladys Miller's Chicken Pan Pie

1	(16-ounce) package frozen mixed vegetables	2	cups cooked chicken, chopped
1	(10 1/2-ounce) can chicken broth or broth made from cooking chicken	1	cup self-rising flour
		1	cup buttermilk
1	(10 1/2-ounce) can cream of chicken soup or mushroom soup	1	stick margarine, melted

Mix vegetables, broth and soup; simmer 5 minutes. Add chicken and place in bottom of Pyrex baking dish. Make a batter by mixing flour, buttermilk and margarine. Pour over chicken. Bake at 350° until brown.

Yield: 6-8 servings

CONTRIBUTOR: Becky Lowery submitted this recipe of Gladys Miller.

COMMITTEE NOTE: *Gladys Goodnight Miller was Treasurer of the Women of the Church, First Presbyterian Church, Salisbury, NC for 40 years and was the first woman to be elected Deacon. She was born September 10, 1907, daughter of Cabel Ransom and Essie Dale Sink Goodnight.*

"Wood Chuck" Chicken
A family favorite

1	(5-pound) cooked hen or chicken breasts, skinned and boned	6	hard boiled eggs, sliced
1/4	pound butter, melted	1	(2-ounce) jar pimentos, drained
2	tablespoons flour	1	(4-ounce) can mushrooms, drained (fresh, optional)
1	teaspoon salt		Cans of Chinese fried noodles, heated, or hot cooked, white rice
1	pint milk		
1	(16-ounce) box processed cheese		

Cut chicken into small pieces. Set aside. Combine butter, flour, salt and milk. Cook over medium to low heat until thick. Add cheese, cut up into small pieces, and cook until melted. Add eggs, pimentos, mushrooms and chicken. Heat thoroughly. Serve over heated fried Chinese noodles or hot cooked rice.

NOTE: *This is my mother's recipe. We serve this on special occasions at the children's request.*

Yield: 6-8 servings

CONTRIBUTOR: Marcia Reamer submitted this recipe of her mother's, Cornelia Sned (deceased).

COMMITTEE NOTE: *Cornelia Sned was a long-time Presbyterian and served as President of Women of the Church.*

🔔 Mama Delle's Cheese Dreams
A luncheon favorite

1	pound New York state cheese, grated (sharp)	1	teaspoon salt
1	pound American cheese, grated (mild)	1	teaspoon cayenne pepper
2	cups mayonnaise	1	unsliced loaf king-sized bread, chilled
		1	cup chopped pecans

Mix cheeses with mayonnaise until spreadable, like cake icing. Continue mixing as you add salt and pepper to taste. Trim crusts from bread. Cut bread lengthwise once, then cut each half into 8 chunks equaling 16 servings. With spatula, coat each side and top of each bread chunk with cheese mixture. Place on a baking sheet. Sprinkle top with chopped pecans. (At this point, Cheese Dreams may be frozen for later use.) Bake at 375° for 5 minutes or until hot. Serve immediately.

Yield: 16 servings

CONTRIBUTOR: Eleanor Hoey Bradshaw submitted this recipe of her mother's, Mrs. Franklin E. Hoey (deceased).

COMMITTEE NOTE: *Mrs. Hoey introduced this recipe to Salisbury, NC in 1945 and it has been served at parties for over 50 years.*

Welsh Rarebit
Wonderful luncheon dish

4	thick slices tomatoes	1/2	teaspoon salt
4	slices sandwich bread	1	(10³/₄-ounce) can cream of
1	cup half-and-half		mushroom soup
1½	cups canned whole	³/₄	pound grated sharp cheddar
	mushrooms, drained		cheese
4	drops Tabasco sauce	3	tablespoons sherry
1½	teaspoons Worcestershire		
	sauce		

Broil tomatoes; set aside. To make toast points, trim crusts from bread, toast, cut into triangles and set aside. In a double boiler, mix cream, mushrooms, Tabasco, Worcestershire, salt and soup. When mixture is hot, add grated cheese and sherry. Arrange 4 toast points on each plate. Top with a broiled tomato slice. Pour a generous amount of rarebit over tomato and toast. Serve with a green salad.

Yield: 4 servings

CONTRIBUTOR: Oliver Gilbert Scott submitted this recipe of Mrs. Margaret Craig Woodson (deceased).

COMMITTEE NOTE: *Mrs. Woodson was very generous with her time, talents and money for First Presbyterian Church, Salisbury, NC where she was a longtime member. This is one of her many recipes.*

Mrs. George B. Ferrier's Cucumber Salad

1	(3-ounce) package cream cheese	1	teaspoon cayenne pepper
1	cup cottage cheese	3	large cucumbers, peeled and grated
1/2	cup mayonnaise	2	(3-ounce) packages lime
1	teaspoon salt		gelatin
1	tablespoon white vinegar	1	cup boiling water

Blend the cream cheese and cottage cheese until creamy and smooth. Add mayonnaise, salt, vinegar, pepper and cucumbers. Dissolve the gelatin in boiling water and add to cheese mixture. Refrigerate until cool, stirring often. When mixture begins to thicken, spoon into individual molds.

Yield: 6 servings

CONTRIBUTOR: Eleanor Hoey Bradshaw submitted this recipe of Mrs. George B. Ferrier (deceased).

COMMITTEE NOTE: *Mrs. Ferrier was Anne Ramsay's mother and was a member of First Presbyterian Church, Salisbury, NC.*

♣ Cheese Straws

2 cups extra sharp cheddar cheese, grated	1/2 teaspoon salt
	1/4 teaspoon cayenne pepper
2 sticks margarine, room temperature	2 cups sifted flour
	1 tablespoon lemon juice

In a large bowl, combine all ingredients. Knead dough with hands to soften mixture, and form a ball. Divide dough into 3 portions. Roll each portion thin between sheets of floured wax paper. Cut into strips. Bake on a cookie sheet at 425° for about 12 minutes., watching constantly while baking to avoid overcooking. Remove from oven when lightly browned. Let cool slightly; transfer with a spatula to absorbent paper. When completely cooled, pack in air tight tins.

Yield: Over 2 pounds

CONTRIBUTOR: Jo White Linn submitted this recipe of Mrs. W. B. Strachan (deceased).

COMMITTEE NOTE: *This was one of the favorite recipes of Henrietta (McNeely) Strachan, who was born in, and lived in, the house that is now called the Dr. Josephus Hall House on South Jackson Street in Salisbury, NC. In 1891, First Presbyterian Church granted her a scholarship to the Presbyterian Academy. She joined First Presbyterian Church June 14, 1908 and contributed a recipe to the 1912 "Gem City Cook Book" published by the King's Daughters of First Presbyterian Church. She would not share this "receipt" as she called it, because it was her specialty.*

Frozen Fruit Salad

1 (16-ounce) container sour cream	6 blanched almonds or 1/4 cup chopped pecans
1/2 cup sugar	1 banana, diced
1 tablespoon lemon juice	4 marshmallows, diced
1 (30-ounce) can fruit cocktail, drained	

Mix sour cream, 1/2 cup sugar or more to taste and lemon juice. Add fruit cocktail, nuts, banana and marshmallows. Mix well. Freeze in an 8x8-inch glass dish. Soften slightly at room temperature before cutting into individual squares.

Yield: 6 servings

CONTRIBUTOR: Jo White Linn submitted this recipe of Mrs. Haden Holmes (deceased).

COMMITTEE NOTE: *Mrs. Holmes was the mother of Elizabeth Holmes Hurley (deceased). She joined First Presbyterian Church in 1909 and died in 1969.*

BLESSINGS

Butter Mayonnaise

3   **heaping tablespoons butter**
1   **tablespoon flour**
³/₄ **cup hot milk**
3   **eggs, beaten (light)**
1   **teaspoon dry mustard**

³/₄ **cup vinegar**
¹/₄ **cup water**
    Salt and pepper
    Juice of one lemon

Melt butter in double boiler. Add flour, milk, eggs, mustard, vinegar, water and salt and pepper to taste. Cook until thickened. Cool; add lemon juice and stir.

Yield: About 2 cups

CONTRIBUTOR: Jo White Linn submitted this recipe of Mrs. Stahle Linn, Sr. (deceased).

COMMITTEE NOTE: *Mrs. Stahle Linn, Sr., (Charlotte Brown Linn) was a life-long member of First Presbyterian Church, Salisbury, NC and mother of Stahle Linn, Jr.*

A Page from Long Ago

This recipe appeared in the Salisbury paper many years ago. "Served last week at a luncheon for Miss Blanche Robertson, bride-to-be, and was so good that guests asked for the recipe to be printed in "Sunday Potluck". Hostesses, Mrs. J. Ray Wilson and Mrs. James F. Hurley accommodated, so here is the recipe for 8 servings."

Stuffed Tomatoes

Cut off stem ends of eight tomatoes; scoop out centers. Turn tomatoes upside down to drain off juice; set the contents aside.

Fry 5 strips bacon crisp and lift from the grease. In the hot grease, first pouring off some if there is too much, sauté one medium onion, sliced thin, and one green pepper, diced. Add the tomato contents and cook this down a little. Then add 1 cup broken crackers or bread crumbs, 2 tablespoons tomato catsup, 1/4 cup sharp cheese (grated), red and black pepper and salt to taste, a dash of Worcestershire sauce and a pinch of sugar. Then add 3 whole eggs, beaten lightly and cook until the sauce is of stuffing consistency. Finally, add the crumbled bacon. Fill the tomato cups with this mixture. Top with bread crumbs. Bake in a moderate oven for 15-20 minutes, until they are heated through.

Yield: 8 servings

CONTRIBUTOR: Wilburn Taylor, reprinted with permission of *The Salisbury Post.*

COMMITTEE NOTE: *Mrs. Wilson (deceased) and Mrs. Hurley (deceased) were life-long Presbyterians. Miss Blanche Robertson is the daughter of Mr. and Mrs. Julian Robertson, Sr. (deceased).*

Easy Tomato Aspic

1	(14¹/₂-ounce) can original stewed tomatoes	Small amount chopped onion, celery, olives, green pepper and Worcestershire sauce
1	(3-ounce) box lemon gelatin	
3	tablespoons vinegar	

Blend tomatoes in blender. In a saucepan, heat tomatoes, add gelatin and stir until dissolved. Add vinegar, onion, celery, olives, green pepper and Worcestershire. Stir mixture and cool. Pour into molds and refrigerate until firm.

Yield: 6 servings

CONTRIBUTOR: Anne Hobson Murdoch

COMMITTEE NOTE: *This was a favorite recipe when prepared by Anne Murdoch, hostess for First Presbyterian Church in the 1970's.*

Grated Sweet Potatoes

2	large raw sweet potatoes, peeled and grated	¹/₂	cup sugar
		2	tablespoons butter, melted

Grate potatoes on coarse grater. Add sugar and butter; mix well. Bake immediately (do not let stand). Bake piled up loosely in shallow baking dish in 325° oven for 30 minutes. Should look like coconut but orange in color.

Yield: 4 servings

CONTRIBUTOR: Margaret McCall Copple submitted this recipe of her mother's Mrs. E. D. McCall (deceased).

COMMITTEE NOTE: *Mrs. McCall sent a recipe booklet to her friends for Christmas greetings in 1942. Her daughter, Margaret, liked this recipe the best. The McCall family were long-time members of First Presbyterian Church.*

🔔 Creamed Potatoes Delight

35	pounds Irish potatoes		Salt
1¹/₂	pounds butter, melted	1	cup finely grated onions
2	pints sour cream		(or onion salt)
1	pint half-and-half		

Cook potatoes until tender, reserving liquid for later use if needed. Whip peeled potatoes with electric mixer. Add butter, sour cream, half-and-half and salt to taste. Add enough potato liquid to make mixture very light and fluffy. Add onions last, stirring well. Serve very hot.

Yield: Serves 50 or more

CONTRIBUTOR: Collin Grubb submitted this recipe of Mrs. T. E. Rice (deceased).

Ruth Elliott's
Broccoli Casserole

2   (10-ounce) packages frozen
    broccoli spears, cooked
    according to package
    directions, drained
1   (10³/₄-ounce) can cream of
    chicken soup

2   eggs, beaten
1   cup cheddar cheese, grated
1   medium onion, chopped
1   cup mayonnaise
    Buttered bread crumbs

Place cooked broccoli spears in a greased 9x13-inch casserole. Cut broccoli into pieces. In another bowl, combine soup, eggs, cheese, onion and mayonnaise. Pour mixture over broccoli; top with bread crumbs. Bake at 350° for 30 minutes or until bubbly.

Yield: 8-10 servings

CONTRIBUTOR: Collin Grubb submitted this recipe of Ruth Elliott (deceased).

COMMITTEE NOTE: *Ruth Elliott was the popular hostess for First Baptist Church of Salisbury, NC for many years.*

🔔 Mrs. Rice's Baked Beans
A favorite at church picnics

1   (3-pound, 7-ounce) can
    baked beans
1   large onion, chopped
3   tablespoons vinegar

3   tablespoons sugar
1   tablespoon mustard
2   strips bacon (optional)

Mix beans and onion in a 2 1/2-quart baking dish. In a separate small bowl, mix together vinegar, sugar and mustard. Pour this mixture into beans and onions; mix well. Arrange bacon strips on top. Bake uncovered at 350° for 45 minutes.

Yield: 15 servings

CONTRIBUTOR: Jo Krider submitted this recipe of Mrs. T. E. Rice (deceased).

COMMITTEE NOTE: *Mrs. Rice (Bertha) was a long time member of First Presbyterian Church where she was the beloved church hostess in the 1950's. She was also the cook for the Salisbury Rotary Club.*

Coconut Pie

1	cup milk	2	eggs, beaten
1	cup coconut	2	tablespoons butter, melted
1	cup sugar	1	teaspoon vanilla
	Pinch of salt	1	(9-inch) unbaked pie shell
2	tablespoons flour		

Pour milk over coconut; set aside. Mix sugar, salt and flour together. Add eggs, butter, vanilla and coconut-milk mixture. Mix well. Pour in unbaked pie shell. Bake at 350° for 35 minutes.

Yield: 6 servings

CONTRIBUTOR: Collin Grubb submitted this recipe of Mrs. Annie Goodman (deceased).

COMMITTEE NOTE: *This was a specialty of Hilda Foreman's mother, Mrs. Annie Goodman (deceased), who was a member of First Presbyterian Church, Salisbury, NC.*

Lemon Pie

1	frozen pie crust, unbaked	7	tablespoons sugar
2	eggs yolks	1	tablespoon butter, melted
2	whole eggs		Juice of 1 large lemon

Beat 2 egg yolks and 2 whole eggs together. (Use the remaining 2 egg whites for the meringue.) Add sugar, butter and lemon juice, mixing well. Pour mixture into pie shell. Bake at 350° for 30 minutes.

MERINGUE:

2	egg whites	1/2	teaspoon cream of tartar
4	teaspoons sugar		

While pie is baking, beat egg whites until stiff, slowly adding cream of tartar and sugar. When pie is done, remove from oven and spread meringue over pie. Return pie to oven. Bake until meringue is light brown.

Yield: 6 servings

CONTRIBUTOR: Margaret McCall Copple submitted this recipe of Miss Clara Knox (deceased).

COMMITTEE NOTE: *Miss Clara Knox lived with her sisters Miss Margaret Knox and Miss Bertha Knox in the Knox house on West Bank Street in Salisbury, NC. They were life-long members of First Presbyterian Church and willed their antique piano to the church.*

B
L
E
S
S
I
N
G
S

♣ Ice Cream Pie
with Meringue Crust
This is a favorite dessert at our house.

MERINGUE PIE SHELL:

4   egg whites, room
     temperature
1/2 teaspoon cream of tartar

1   cup sugar
1/2 cup broken pecans

Preheat oven to 300°. Beat egg whites with cream of tartar until stiff; gradually add sugar 1 teaspoon at a time. Continue to beat in sugar, scraping sides of bowl with rubber spatula. Fold in nuts. Spread meringue evenly into two 9-inch pie pans. Meringue should extend 3/4-inch above edge of pan. Bake for 50-60 minutes. Turn off oven and crack open door; let cool in oven.

FILLING:

1/2 gallon vanilla ice cream

Cut slices of ice cream 3/4-inch thick. Soften slightly and spread to fill cooled meringue shells. Freeze immediately.

CHOCOLATE SAUCE AND WHIPPED CREAM TOPPING:

1 1/2 cups sugar
1   cup cocoa
1/4   teaspoon salt

1   cup minus 2 tablespoons
     boiling water
1   teaspoon vanilla
1/2 pint whipping cream

Stir together sugar, cocoa, salt and water to blend. Bring to a boil over medium heat. Continue to boil and stir for 3 minutes until thickened. Remove from heat; add vanilla. Pour sauce into a jar. Cool and refrigerate until ready to make topping. To complete pie, whip cream until stiff and gently fold in chocolate sauce. Spread chocolate sauce and whipped cream mixture on top of pie and return to freezer until ready to serve.

Yield: 16-18 servings

CONTRIBUTOR: Mary Elizabeth Coleman Harbison

COMMITTEE NOTE: *Mary Elizabeth Harbison is the daughter of Mrs. E. C. Coleman (deceased), both long-time members of First Presbyterian Church, Salisbury, NC. Mrs. Harbison is the wife of William Harbison, Supreme Court Justice, Nashville, TN.*

Mrs. Hennessee's
Devil's Food Cake
Heavenly cake filled with sherry or coffee

BATTER:

1	cup butter	2	teaspoons baking soda
2	cups sugar	3	cups cake flour
5	eggs	1	cup buttermilk
4	ounces chocolate (4 squares), melted		

Preheat oven to 350°. Grease and flour two 8-9-inch cake pans. Cream butter and sugar well. Add eggs one at a time, beating well after each addition. Add cooled, melted chocolate. Add soda to flour and fold into batter along with buttermilk. Pour equal portions of batter into 2 pans and bake 30-35 minutes. Cool slightly and carefully remove both layers from cake pans. Cool on wire rack.

FILLING:

1	cup butter, softened		Cocoa
1	(16-ounce) box powdered sugar	1/4	cup sweet cream sherry or 1/4 cup strong coffee

Combine butter, sugar, cocoa to taste and sherry or coffee in a bowl. Mix until smooth and creamy. Set aside.

FROSTING:

3	cups sugar	1/4	teaspoon baking soda
4	ounces chocolate (4 squares)	1/4	pound butter
1	cup evaporated milk		

Place sugar, chocolate, milk, soda and butter in a saucepan. Gradually bring mixture to a boil and boil for 8 minutes stirring constantly. Cool and beat to spreading consistency. Spread filling between cake layers. Frost top and sides of cake.

NOTE: *I am submitting this recipe for my mother, Mrs. Leslie Weisiger. This cake was a special treat at my house and it is worth the time and effort it takes. A package of devil's food cake mix may be prepared according to package directions and substituted for the cake batter. Fill and frost as above.*

Yield: 1 cake

CONTRIBUTOR: Katharine Weisiger Osborne submitted this recipe of Mrs. W. A. Hennessee (deceased) for her mother, Mrs. Leslie Weisiger.

COMMITTEE NOTE: *Mrs. W. A. Hennessee was a long-time member of First Presbyterian Church, Salisbury, NC and was an outstanding cook. Mrs. Leslie Weisiger is a long-time member of First Presbyterian Church, Salisbury, N.C.*

♣ Irene Barker's Mini Cheesecakes

1¹/₂-2	cups finely crushed graham cracker crumbs	4	eggs
3	(8-ounce) packages cream cheese	1¹/₂	teaspoons vanilla
		1¹/₂	cups sour cream
1	cup plus 2 tablespoons sugar	2	tablespoons sugar
			Maraschino cherries (optional)

Grease miniature cupcake tins with solid shortening. Fill each section with crumbs, patting crumbs on sides and bottoms of tin. Tap out the surplus crumbs. Beat cream cheese, 1 cup plus 2 tablespoons sugar, eggs and vanilla for 10 minutes until well mixed. Fill cups 3/4 full with filling mixture. Bake at 350° for 10 minutes. Cool. For topping: Cook 1 1/2 cups sour cream and 2 tablespoons sugar for 5 minutes over medium heat, stirring constantly. Cool mixture. Top baked cheesecakes with cooled sour cream mixture. Add small pieces of maraschino cherries to topping if desired.

Yield: 60 servings

CONTRIBUTOR: Collin Grubb submitted this recipe of Mrs. Irene Barker (deceased).

COMMITTEE NOTE: *Irene Barker was a long-time member of First Presbyterian Church, Salisbury, NC.*

Ice Box Cookies
A favorite at Christmas time

1	cup butter	3¹/₂	cups flour
2	cups brown sugar	¹/₂	teaspoon soda
2	eggs	¹/₂	cup chopped pecans
1	teaspoon vanilla		

Cream butter and sugar. Add eggs one at a time. Add vanilla. Sift together flour and soda. Add to mixture with pecans; mix well. On wax paper, shape into a roll with hands. Chill at least 2 hours. Slice cookies; bake on a cookie sheet at 350° for 8 minutes.

Yield: About 5 dozen

CONTRIBUTOR: Mary Katherine Clark submitted this recipe of her mother's, Evelyn Ingle.

COMMITTEE NOTE: *Evelyn Ingle is a long-time member of First Presbyterian Church. She shared her musical talents by singing in the choir and playing the piano for Rumple Bible class.*

Mary Hanford's Pecan Cookie

1/2	pound butter	1	teaspoon vanilla
6	tablespoons powdered sugar	2	cups nuts, finely chopped
2	cups flour		Powdered sugar, for rolling
1	tablespoon water		

Cream butter; add sugar, flour, water, vanilla and nuts. Dust hands with flour; mold dough into small oblong-shaped pieces. Place on greased cookie sheet and flatten slightly with a fork. Bake at 225° for 1 hour. Roll twice in powdered sugar.

Yield: 4 dozen

CONTRIBUTOR: Collin Grubb submitted this recipe of Mrs. John Hanford, Sr.

Christmas Candy

1	stick butter, room temperature (not margarine)	1	teaspoon vanilla
		25	or more pecan halves
1	(1-pound) box powdered sugar	1/4	cake paraffin
2	tablespoons evaporated milk	2	(1-ounce) squares unsweetened chocolate

Cream butter and sugar; add milk and vanilla. Knead candy dough with hands until mixture forms a ball. Refrigerate until firm. Pinch off pieces of dough to form small balls. Flatten tops slightly. Place on cookie sheet; chill again.

COATING:
Melt paraffin in double boiler; add chocolate. Stir until hot and melted. Do not overheat. If chocolate is overheated, it will not stick to the candy. With a toothpick, dip and roll candy balls in chocolate paraffin mixture. Place each ball of candy on a cookie sheet and immediately press top with a pecan. Cool in refrigerator.

NOTE: *This recipe has been used in our family at Christmas for many years.*

Yield: 25 or more servings

CONTRIBUTOR: Jo Kluttz Krider submitted this recipe of her mother's, Mrs. Charles H. Kluttz (deceased).

B
L
E
S
S
I
N
G
S

♣ Pink Lady Punch

1	quart bottle cranberry juice, chilled	1	quart bottle ginger ale, chilled
1	(46-ounce) can pineapple juice, chilled	1	pint container pineapple sherbet

Pour juices into punch bowl. Stir in ginger ale and slightly thawed sherbet just before serving.

Yield: 25 (5-ounce) servings

CONTRIBUTOR: Jo White Linn submitted this recipe of Mildred Seaber (deceased).

COMMITTEE NOTE: *Mildred Seaber was a life-long member of First Presbyterian Church, Salisbury, NC. She was the daughter of Mrs. W. B. Strachan and lived in the historic Dr. Josephus Hall House most of her life.*

♣ Tomato Juice Cocktail

1	case of 46-ounce cans tomato juice, chilled (1 can used for ice ring)	$3/4$	cup vinegar
		2	tablespoons salt
3	(36-ounce) cans V-8 juice, chilled	$1/2$	cup Worcestershire sauce
		1	(14-ounce) bottle ketchup
1	cup sugar		Tabasco sauce

Make an ice ring to keep beverage cold by pouring 1 (46-ounce) can tomato juice into a mold. Freeze until firm and ready to use. Mix together chilled juices, sugar, vinegar, salt, Worcestershire, ketchup and Tabasco to taste. Place ice ring, made with tomato juice, in punch bowl and pour liquid mixture over the ice ring.

Yield: 50-60 servings (5 ounces or more)

CONTRIBUTOR: Collin Grubb submitted this recipe of Mrs. T. E. Rice (deceased).

COMMITTEE NOTE: *Mrs. Rice prepared this beverage for Women of the Church meetings and other large crowds. Smaller portions may be prepared.*

♣ Anna Belle's Chow Chow

Elegant green tomato mustard pickle

1	cup salt	1	head cabbage, sliced
1	gallon water	3	(3-ounce) jars pickled onions, drained
24	green tomatoes, cut into eighths	2	(1-pint) jars sliced kosher dill pickles, drained
12	onions, sliced	3	(1-pint) jars pickled artichokes, sliced
8	green peppers, seeded, cut into strips	12	(1-quart) sterilized canning jars, with lids
1	cauliflower, broken into pieces		
1	bunch celery, sliced		

In large pot, make a brine from salt and water. Add tomatoes, onions, peppers, cauliflower, celery and cabbage. Let stand for 3-4 hours. Bring to a boil for 10 minutes or until tender. Drain thoroughly. Toss into vegetables the pickled onions, pickles and artichokes.

MUSTARD SAUCE:

10	cups sugar	4	quarts white vinegar, chilled
2	cups flour	6	ounces whole mustard seed
12	teaspoons dry mustard	6	ounces celery seed
2	teaspoons turmeric		

Mix sugar, flour, dry mustard, turmeric and 2 quarts vinegar in large pot, stirring until sauce forms a smooth paste. Slowly add remaining vinegar while stirring constantly. Add mustard seed and celery seed. Cook over medium heat for 30 minutes, stirring to prevent mixture from sticking. Cool; stir sauce into vegetable mixture to desired taste. Spoon mixture into jars and seal.

Yield: 12 quarts

CONTRIBUTOR: Virginia Wallace submitted this recipe of Mrs. Leo Wallace, Sr. (deceased).

COMMITTEE NOTE: *Mrs. Leo Wallace, Sr. (deceased), the mother of Leo Wallace, Jr., was a member of First Presbyterian Church. Her recipes were outstanding.*

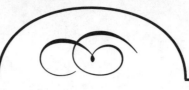

Baptism Lunch

Chilled Peach Soup

Cashew Chicken Salad

Broiled Tomato Cups

Mrs. George B. Ferrier's Salad

Sunshine Raisin Broccoli Salad

Corn Pudding

Mama Delle's Cheese Dreams

Old Fashioned Strawberry Custard Pie

Ginger Almond Tea

BLESSINGS

God gave this child to you to guide, to love, to walk through life beside.
A little child so full of charm To fill a pair of loving arms.
God picked you out because He knew
How safe His child would be with you.

Women's Elective Sunday School Class

Dear Lord, Thank You for the life of this precious child. Bestow Your
special blessings upon him, watch over him, and keep him in Your love.
Guide him so he may grow in grace and in the knowledge of Christ.
Be with those who nurture this child. Amen

Young Adult Sunday School Class

As you dedicate the little one God has given you,
May your child's life be blessed through your example …
Their spirit nurtured through your wisdom …
Their steps guided through your counsel …
Their heart comforted through Your love.

Unknown

Easter Sunday Lunch

Orange Souffle Salad

King Boras Salad

Roast Leg of Lamb with Pan Gravy

Easter Eggs on Rice

Carrots in Rosemary and Bourbon

Whole Wheat Spirals

Bird's Nest Macaroon Cookies

Broken Glass Tart

Apricot Slush

BLESSINGS

Oh God, thank you for your gift of eternal life. We know that through Christ's resurrection our sins are forgiven and your forgiveness is everlasting. As we break the bread, we will remember that your body was broken for us. As we drink the cup, we will remember that your blood was shed for us. When we look at the cross, we will remember that your sacrifice was for all of mankind. We are ever thankful for these everlasting gifts. Amen.

High School Sunday School Class

May every glorious promise borne on every springtime breeze
Refresh your soul and spirit as it puts your heart at ease.
For every golden daffodil on every sunny slope
Reminds us God gives Easter, and Easter gives us hope.

Unknown

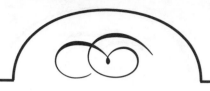

Confirmation

Pineapple Cheese Ball & Crackers

Quick Gourmet Caesar Salad

Family Favorite Sour Cream Lasagna

French Bread Monterey

Italian Cream Cake

or

Tiramisu

Betsy's Iced Tea

BLESSINGS

Lord, teach me all that I should know;
In grace and wisdom I may grow;
The more I learn to do Thy will,
The better may I love Thee still.

Unknown

God bless this student with all the
gifts that Heaven can bestow,
With kind and gentle nurturing and
strength to thrive and grow.
God bless this student with books to
read and new paths to explore,
With smiles to share and friends who
care and love for ever more.

Unknown

Graduation or Retirement Dinner

Golden Punch

Lake House Loafin' & Dippin'

Greek Pasta Salad

Grilled Chicken with Barbecue Sauce

Roasted Onions with Sage

Sauteed Peas and Snow Peas

Bread Sticks

A Different Strawberry Salad

Chocolate Swirl Cheesecake

BLESSINGS

Great God, in your purpose our lives are lived, and by your wisdom truth is found. We pray for graduates who have finished this step in their learning, and as they move to something new. By your grace take away anxiety or confusion of purpose and give them confidence as they follow Your plan for their lives. Amen.

Jim Foil, Associate Pastor

Your love for us never ends, Great God. When we retire, keep us alert to Your will for our lives. Give us energy to enjoy the world, and to care for others so often neglected by the busy. By Your grace, may we continue to walk in the footsteps of our risen Lord. Amen.

Jim Foil, Associate Pastor

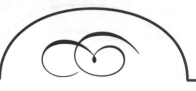

Wedding Reception

Star Caviar with Crackers

Cheese Straws

Toasted Pecans

Bacon Roll-ups

Marinated Shrimp

Hot Cheese Puffs

Vegetable Sandwich Spread

Party Ham & Cheese Sandwiches

Meringue Cookies

Cream Cheese Party Mints

Fresh Strawberries with Fluffy Fruit Dip

Italian Wedding Cake

Wedding Punch

or

Opalescent Pearl Punch

BLESSINGS

Oh Lord, grant that they may dwell in unity and love all the days of their lives, seeking one another's welfare, bearing one another's burdens, and sharing one another's joys; through Jesus Christ our Lord. Amen.

Dr. Robert Lewis, Pastor

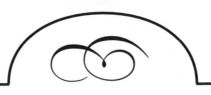

Summer Birthday Cookout

Rainbow Trifle Fruit Salad

Skeem Burgers

or

Beef Kabobs

Spinach-Bacon Deviled Eggs

Copper Pennies

Sour Cream Horseradish Potato Salad

Special Pork and Beans Casserole

Red Blush Cake

Orange Cookies

Fudge Brownies

Cheerwine Punch

BLESSINGS

Dear God, Thank you for birthdays to celebrate our friends and family.
Thank you for the chance to tell them how much we love them
and are glad they are here. And, thank you for the most
special birthday of all; the birth of Jesus. Amen.

Second and Third Grade Sunday School Class

If I were a butterfly, I'd thank you, Lord, for giving me wings,
And if I were a robin in a tree, I'd thank you, Lord, that I could sing,
And if I were a fish in the sea, I'd wiggle my tail, and I'd giggle with glee,
But I thank you, Father, for making me "me."

Unknown

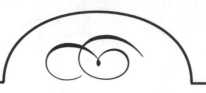

Teens With a Mission Mexican Supper

Guacamole

Shoe Peg Corn Dip

Layered Nacho Dip

Tortilla Chips

Spinach Salad

Grapefruit Ring

Mexican Chicken Enchiladas

Chiles Rellenos Casserole

Corny Cornbread

Key Lime Pie

Luscious Orange Mold Cake

Strawberry Sparkling Lemonade

BLESSINGS

Dear Heavenly Father, We lift your name up in praise and Thanksgiving. We ask you to be with the young people of our church as they do missions in Your name. We ask you to bless each of your children everywhere with Your protection and love. We thank you for all of the gifts that You've bestowed upon us. In Your blessed name we pray. Amen.

TWAM and Senior High Sunday School Class

Family Reunion
Gathering the Crowd

Gazpacho
Bone's Coleslaw
Baked Ham with Pineapple
Company Squash Casserole
Savory Corn on the Cob
Dill Casserole Bread
Fruit Pizza
Mock Baby Ruth Bars
Lemonade

BLESSINGS

Our Father, May our gathering together at this table be a time of strengthening the love between us. May it remind us of the place we hold in each other's lives. Renew the bond between us. Remind us that by sharing our joys and sorrows, God's love has strengthened our family. Thank you for the love with which this food was prepared. In Jesus' name, Amen.

Contemporary Christian Sunday School Class

God made the world a wonderful place,
Blessed with beauty and filled with grace.
He made for us the special home
With mountains, forests, and fields to roam.
Then to provide the finishing touch,
He gave us people who love us so much:
Parents who care, who guide and teach;
Children with tiny hands that reach;
Brothers and sisters to always share
The tears and laughter or just be there
God made families to help the world grow,
So His everlasting love would show.

Unknown

Thanksgiving Dinner

Cranberry Salad with Apples & Pecans
Dijon Crusted Turkey
Sweet Onion and Sage Dressing
Sweet Potato Casserole
Potato Gratin
Asparagus with Pimento Mock Hollandaise Sauce
Aunt Faye's Old Fashion Rolls
Robert's Favorite Pecan Pie
or
Pumpkin Chiffon Praline Pie
Delicious Cranberry Drink

BLESSINGS

Heavenly Father, We thank you for all the blessings you have given us. Your love has comforted us in our troubles and trials. It is everlasting and always there for us to use with your lending hand. You are there to care, understand and help us grow in fellowship with you Lord. Hear our words of thanksgiving. Amen.

Middle School Sunday School Class

Dear God, We thank you for all the things you give us. Thank you for our friends and our food. Help us to do what's right. Amen.

First Grade Sunday School Class

Bless our family gathered here.
Thank you for another year.
Grateful for the joy of living,
We thank Thee, Lord, for this Thanksgiving.

Unknown

Christmas Brunch

Honeyed Grapefruit Halves

Country Ham Reynolds' Method

Buttermilk Biscuits

Make Ahead Breakfast Strata

White Cheddar Cheese Grits

Amy's Christmas Morning Rolls

Holiday Wassail

or

Hot Scotch Cocoa

BLESSINGS

Happy Birthday Baby Jesus! We love you!

Two and Three Year Old Sunday School Class

Dearest Jesus, hear our prayer;
Keep us in your loving care.
You are gentle, meek, and mild;
You were once a little child.

Unknown

Heavenly Father, when we view the wonders of Thy world, we realize
they were created for our enjoyment, edification, and complete proof
that God is in His heaven, and all will be well. As Thy grateful servants,
may we share the blessings of Thy word and the gift of Thy Son, in
whose name we pray. Amen.

Fellowship Sunday School Class

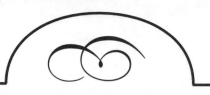

Christmas Dinner

Spicy Marinated Tenderloin

Mushroom Magic

Wild Rice Casserole

Broccoli with Sesame Sauce

Cranberry Mousse

Refrigerator Rolls

Bully Pudding

Holiday Fruit Cookies

Sparkling Eggnog

BLESSINGS

Dear God, Thank you for all the good things that happen at Christmas - for all the good food and presents and decorations. Thank you for Jesus being born to always take care of us and our families. Amen.

Four and Five Year Old Sunday School Class

It is more blessed to give than to receive.

Acts 20:35

Open House Afternoon Tea

Asparagus Sandwiches
Mushroom Caps
Quiche for a Crowd
French Quarter Cheese
Crab Imperial
Assorted Crackers
Pecan Tassies
Lemon Squares
Creamy Mocha Fudge
Coffee Ice Cream Punch
or
Pink Lady Punch

BLESSINGS

Oh God, do not let us get so busy in the activities of everyday life that we do not make time for those we love. Keep us from taking each other for granted, looking at each other but not really seeing, hearing each other but never actually understanding. May we live and grow together in love and peace all the days of our lives; through Jesus Christ our Lord. Amen

Dr. Robert Lewis, Pastor

Great and Almighty
Over us always
Desired by many
Salvation

Longing for
Overwhelming
Very kind
Everlasting love

Middle School Seventh and Eighth Grade Sunday School Class

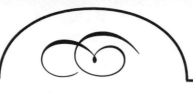

Blessings

Precious Gifts

God has given us morning,
Brightness and sun,
Food to be eaten and work to be done.
He has given us rainbows,
Flowers and song,
And the hand of a dear one to help us along.
He has given us blessings
To brighten our way
And always – the gift of another day

Johnny Apple Seed Blessing

The Lord's been good to me
And so I thank the Lord
For giving me
The things I need,
The sun and the rain
And the apple seed,
The Lord's been good to me! Amen

Traditional Irish Blessing

May the road rise to meet you
May the wind be always at your back,
May the sun shine warm on your face,
The rain fall softly on your fields.
And until we meet again,
May God hold you in the palm of His hand.

Blessing

Thank You for the world so sweet,
Thank You for the food we eat,
Thank You for the birds that sing,
Thank You, God, for everything! Amen

Blessing

God is great. God is good.
Now we thank Him for our food.
By His hands we all are fed.
Give us Lord our daily bread. Amen

The Doxology

Praise God, from whom all blessings flow;
Praise Him, all creatures here below;
Praise Him above, ye heavenly host;
Praise Father, Son and Holy Ghost. Amen

Appetizers
& Beverages

Hors d'oeuvre, Dips & Spreads

&

Bubbling Beverages

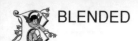

B
L
E
S
S
I
N
G
S

🔔 Asparagus Sandwiches

20	thin slices white bread	1	(12-14.5-ounce) can
3	ounces bottled blue cheese dressing		asparagus spears, drained, or 20 spears
1	egg	½	pound margarine, melted
1	(8-ounce) package cream cheese		

Trim crusts from bread. Flatten with rolling pin as thin as possible; cover to prevent bread from drying out. Blend dressing, egg and cream cheese. Spread mixture evenly on each slice of bread. Roll bread around each asparagus spear. Dip in margarine, coating thoroughly. Place on cookie sheet and freeze. When frozen, cut each roll into thirds. Bake at 400° until lightly brown. Serve immediately.

Yield: 60 bite size pieces   George-Anna Glenn

🔔 Bacon Crisps

1	pound thin sliced bacon	1	(16-ounce) box club crackers

For each appetizer, cut a strip of bacon in half, crosswise; wrap bacon lengthwise over cracker, tucking under ends of bacon. Place on a broiler pan and bake at 250°-275° for about 30 minutes, or until crisp. Place on paper towels to drain. Serve immediately or freeze and reheat.

NOTE: *Delicious. Can't eat just one!*

Yield: 40-50 servings   Mrs. J. D. Waggoner (Barbara)

🔔 Bacon Roll-Ups
Great appetizer!

¼	cup butter	1	egg, slightly beaten
½	cup water	¼	pound bulk sausage, mild or hot
1½	cup herb-seasoned stuffing mix	½-⅔	pound sliced bacon

Melt butter and water together; add stuffing. Add egg and sausage; blend thoroughly. Chill for 1 hour. Shape into oblong shapes about the size of a pecan. Cut bacon slices into thirds, wrap around formed shapes. Bake on a broiler pan at 375° for 35 minutes or until brown and crispy, turning over halfway through baking. Serve hot.

Yield: 3 dozen   Gayle Smerznak

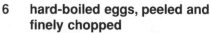

Caviar & Eggs

6	hard-boiled eggs, peeled and finely chopped	2	teaspoons lemon juice
⅓	cup butter or margarine, softened		Salt
			Sour cream for icing
⅓	cup mayonnaise	1	(2-ounce) jar caviar, drained
3	chopped scallions		Melba toast or crackers

In small bowl lined with plastic wrap, mix eggs, butter, mayonnaise, scallions, lemon juice and salt to taste. Chill 1 hour. Unmold upside down on serving plate. Remove plastic wrap; frost with sour cream, covering all surfaces. Cover with caviar. Serve with melba toast or crackers.

Yield: Serves 6-8   Suzanne Wallace Casey

Star Caviar Pie

	Butter	⅔	cup sour cream
6	hard-cooked eggs, chopped	1	(2-ounce) jar red caviar
3	tablespoons mayonnaise	1	(2-ounce) jar black caviar
⅔	cup minced onion		
1	(8-ounce) package cream cheese, softened		

Butter the sides and bottom of a springform pan or a glass dish. Mix chopped hard-cooked eggs and mayonnaise. Spread the mixture on the bottom of pan. Layer onion over the mixture. Beat cream cheese and sour cream until smooth and spread over onion layer. Cover and chill for several hours. Before serving, separately rinse each jar of caviar gently with cold water. Drain well. Spoon caviar onto cheese layer in a colorful star pattern, alternating red and black caviar. Serve with crackers.

Yield: 3-4 cups   Mrs. Edward H. Clement (Nancy)

♥ Quick Black Bean Dip

1	(16-ounce) can black beans, rinsed well and drained	1	(8-ounce) jar Pace medium picante sauce
1	(11-ounce) can white shoepeg corn, drained		

Mix in a bowl and serve with corn chips.

Yield: 4 cups   Lawana Ford

♣ Helen's Poor Man's Caviar

1	large eggplant (2 pounds)
1	cup finely chopped onion
6	tablespoons olive oil
½	cup finely chopped green pepper
1	teaspoon chopped garlic
2	large ripe tomatoes, peeled and chopped

½	teaspoon sugar
2	teaspoons salt
	Black pepper
2-3	tablespoons lemon juice
	Rye or pumpernickel bread rounds or sesame seed crackers

Preheat oven to 450°. Bake eggplant on center rack for 1 hour, turning once or twice until soft and skin is charred and blistered. Remove from oven. Cook onion in 4 tablespoons oil for 6-8 minutes until soft. Stir in green pepper and garlic. Cook 5 more minutes. Pour onion mixture into mixing bowl. Set aside. Remove eggplant skin with a sharp knife and using a food processor, chop eggplant finely until almost pureed. Add eggplant to mixture in bowl; stir in tomatoes, sugar, salt and pepper to taste, mixing well. Heat remaining 2 tablespoons oil in a medium pan and add eggplant mixture. Bring to a boil, stirring constantly. Reduce heat, simmer for 1 hour. Remove lid; cook another 1/2 hour until thick enough to hold its shape on a spoon. Stir in 2 tablespoons lemon juice. Chill. Serve on dark rye or pumpernickel bread rounds or sesame seed crackers.

NOTE: *This recipe comes from a friend whose mother is Russian.*

Yield: 4-6 cups   Karen Busby

Hot Cheesy Beef Dip

⅓	cup chopped pecans
1½	tablespoons melted butter
1	(2½-ounce) jar dried beef
1	(8-ounce) package cream cheese, softened
2	tablespoons milk

¼	cup finely chopped bell pepper
¼	cup finely chopped white onion
1	clove garlic, pressed
½	teaspoon white pepper
1	cup sour cream

Sauté pecans in butter 3-5 minutes; drain on paper towels and set aside. Finely chop beef in food processor or blender; set aside. Combine cream cheese and milk in mixing bowl; beat on medium speed until smooth. Stir in beef, bell pepper, onion, garlic and white pepper, mixing well. Stir in sour cream; spoon into greased 1-quart casserole dish. Sprinkle on pecans and bake at 325° for 25 minutes. Serve hot dip with assorted crackers.

Yield: 2 cups   Janie Matthews

🔔 Pineapple Cheese Ball

2 (8-ounce) packages cream cheese, softened	2 tablespoons finely chopped onion
1 (8.5-ounce) can crushed pineapple, drained	¼ cup finely chopped green pepper
1-2 cups chopped pecans	1 tablespoon seasoned salt

In a medium bowl beat cream cheese until smooth. Add pineapple, 1 cup pecans, onion, green pepper and seasoning salt. Refrigerate until firm. Form into a ball and roll in remaining pecans. Chill. Serve with your favorite crackers.

NOTE: *Jackie Burleson uses 1-1 1/2 cups pecans.*
Jan Williams uses 2 cups pecans.

Yield: 40 servings

Jackie Burleson
Jan Williams

🔔 Cheese Surprises

Crunchy cereal is the nut-like surprise ingredient

2 sticks margarine	⅛ teaspoon cayenne pepper
½ pound sharp cheese, grated	2 cups crispy rice cereal
2 cups unsifted flour	⅛ teaspoon salt
½ teaspoon baking powder	

Cream margarine and cheese. Add remaining ingredients. Mix well. Form into marble-size balls; flatten to 1/4-inch thickness. Bake on cookie sheet at 375° for 15 minutes. Cool on rack. Store in airtight tins.

Yield: 4 dozen

Betty Lomax

Kentucky Beer Cheese

1 pound sharp cheddar cheese	3 tablespoons Worcestershire sauce
1 pound medium cheddar cheese	6 drops Tabasco sauce
2 cloves garlic	1 teaspoon dry mustard
1 teaspoon salt	1 (12-ounce) can flat beer

Combine all ingredients, except beer, and feed through a meat grinder. Mix ground ingredients with beer. Chill. Serve at room temperature with crackers.

Yield: 2 cups

Nancy Pike

B
L
E
S
S
I
N
G
S

Brie with Brown Sugar & Almonds

1	(14-ounce) Petit Brie
3	tablespoons margarine
2	tablespoons light brown sugar

½	cup slivered almonds
	Apple, thin slices
	Pear, thin slices
	French bread, sliced

Place Brie in lightly buttered 9-inch quiche dish. Heat in oven, preheated to 300°, for 15 minutes or in microwave on high for 3-5 minutes. Melt margarine, stir in brown sugar and almonds. Pour over Brie. Broil until lightly toasted. Serve with apple and pear slices and French bread.

Yield: 10 servings   Lynn Bertram

Summer On The Patio Brie

1	large round of pumpernickel bread
4	large garlic cloves, minced

1	pound Brie, rind removed, sliced

Cut off the top of the bread loaf; hollow out center and reserve for dipping. In center of bread, put garlic and Brie. Replace top of bread and wrap in heavy foil. Bake at 350° for 1 hour. Serve with chunks of reserved bread for dipping.

Yield: 8-10 servings   Patty Bennett

Southwestern Dip

A neighborhood picnic favorite! Great for vegetarians!

3	cups shredded lettuce
1	(15-ounce) can black beans, rinsed, drained
½	cup chopped red or yellow sweet pepper
¼	cup sliced green onions
1	(8-ounce) carton sour cream or lowfat sour cream
2	jalapeño peppers, finely chopped

1	teaspoon grated lime peel
1	(8-ounce) jar chunky salsa
½	medium avocado, halved, seeded, peeled and chopped
⅔	cup shredded cheddar cheese
⅓	cup chopped ripe olives
1	tablespoon fresh chopped cilantro or parsley (optional)
1	(16-ounce) bag tortilla chips

Line 12-inch platter with lettuce. Stir together beans, peppers and onions. Spoon on top of lettuce, leaving a border. Dollop sour cream on bean layer. Sprinkle with jalapeños and lime peel. Drain excess liquid from salsa; stir in avocado. Spoon on top of sour cream; sprinkle with cheese. Top with olives; sprinkle on cilantro. Serve immediately or cover; chill for up to 6 hours. Serve with chips.

Yield: 8 cups   Beth Shafer

♣ French Quarter Cheese
A unique combination of flavors

1	(8-ounce) package cream cheese, softened
1	garlic clove, minced
1	tablespoon grated onion
4	tablespoons butter

¼	cup dark brown sugar
1	teaspoon Worcestershire sauce
½	teaspoon prepared mustard
1	cup finely chopped pecans

Combine cream cheese, garlic and onion with a fork. Shape into a 6x1-inch disk; place on a serving plate and refrigerate. Combine remaining ingredients in a saucepan, heating until butter melts. Cover chilled cheese with nut mixture. Wrap and chill. Serve at room temperature with crackers.

Yield: 10-12 servings   Dee Hopkins

♣ Jalapeño Pie
Easy and good

1	(11-ounce) can jalapeño peppers, sliced or whole, drain, remove excess moisture

1	pound grated cheddar cheese
4	eggs, beaten

Mash jalapeños flat to form a crust and cover bottom of greased 8-9-inch pie plate. Cover jalapeños evenly with cheese. Pour eggs over cheese. Bake at 350° for 30 minutes. Remove from oven. Cut into wedges to serve.

Yield: 10-15 servings   Elinor Reynolds

Bloody Mary Dip

1	cup of cream cheese with chives
¼	cup V-8 vegetable juice cocktail
2	teaspoons creamy horseradish sauce

1	teaspoon celery salt
1	teaspoon Worcestershire sauce
	Fine ground black pepper
	Hot pepper sauce

In a small bowl, blend cream cheese until fluffy with electric mixer. Gradually add remaining ingredients; adding pepper and pepper sauce to taste. Cover; refrigerate 2 hours. Serve with celery stick dippers.

Yield: 1 cup

Charleston Cheese
Favorite of men

1	(8-ounce) package cream cheese, softened	6	round buttery crackers, crushed
1	cup grated sharp cheese	8	slices bacon, cooked and crumbled
2	chopped green onions		
½	cup mayonnaise		

Combine cream cheese, grated cheese, onions and mayonnaise. Pour into greased quiche dish. Top with crackers. Bake at 350° for 15 minutes. Remove from oven and top with bacon. Serve with crackers.

Yield: 3 1/2 cups   Sandee Carrigan

Garlic Feta Cheese Spread

1	clove garlic, mashed	¼	teaspoon dried dill
¼	teaspoon salt	¼	teaspoon dried basil
¼	pound feta cheese, crumbled	¼	teaspoon thyme
¼	cup mayonnaise	¾	pound cream cheese
¼	teaspoon dried marjoram		

Mash the garlic clove with salt. Put feta cheese, mayonnaise, spices, cream cheese and garlic mixture into a blender or food processor. Process until well blended. Put in a crock or container with a lid. Refrigerate. Serve with crackers.

Yield: 1 1/2 cups   Diana Miller Rainey

Hot Crab Meat Appetizer
Simple and delicious!

1	(8-ounce) package cream cheese	½	teaspoon cream style horseradish
1	tablespoon milk	¼	teaspoon salt
1	(6½-ounce) can flaked crabmeat	⅛	teaspoon pepper
2	tablespoons finely chopped onion	⅓	cup sliced almonds, toasted

Combine all ingredients except almonds until well blended. Spoon into a 1-quart ovenproof dish. Sprinkle with almonds. Bake at 375° for 15 minutes. Serve with crackers.

Yield: 1 1/2 cups   Rochelle Redcay

Crab Appetizer

1	pound crabmeat, fresh	1	teaspoon Worcestershire
½	cup mayonnaise		sauce
½	stick butter		Juice from 1 lemon
2	tablespoons fresh chopped		Dash hot sauce
	parsley		Salt and pepper
2	teaspoons mustard	¼	cup bread crumbs
2	tablespoons sherry	6	large scallop shells

Mix crabmeat, mayonnaise, 1/2 of butter, parsley, mustard, sherry, Worcestershire, lemon juice, hot sauce, salt and pepper to taste and 1/2 of bread crumbs. Fill shells with mixture. Blend remaining butter and bread crumbs and lightly cover each serving. May be made ahead and refrigerated. Bake at 400° for 30 minutes. Serve hot.

Yield: Serves 6   Monica Farrington

Crab Imperial

2	tablespoons chopped onion	¼	teaspoon pepper
2	tablespoons chopped green	1	tablespoon sherry
	pepper	1	teaspoon dry mustard
3	tablespoons margarine,	¼	teaspoon Worcestershire
	melted		sauce
2	tablespoons flour	2-3	dashes Tabasco sauce
½	cup half-and-half	2	tablespoons Parmesan cheese
1	pound crabmeat	1-2	teaspoons parsley
½	teaspoon Old Bay seasoning		Paprika for garnish

Sauté onion and green pepper in melted margarine in skillet on low for 5 minutes. Combine flour and cream and cook on low 5 minutes. Add onion and green peppers and cook on medium until thick, about 2 minutes. Add remaining ingredients except paprika. Mix well and place in a 1-quart casserole. Garnish with paprika. Bake at 350° for 20-25 minutes. Serve hot.

Yield: Serves 4   Valinda Isenhower

Barbecued Shrimp

32	large raw shrimp, shelled,	1	cup honey-smoke barbecue
	deveined		sauce
		16	pieces of bacon, halved

Wrap each shrimp in bacon slices. Secure with toothpick. Brush or drizzle with sauce. Bake at 375° for 15 minutes; or until bacon is crisp.

Yield: 8 servings

Lake House "Loaffin & Dippin"

1	large loaf Hawaiian bread or 2 (16-ounce) loaves	16	ounces diced ham
16	ounces sour cream	6	scallions, cut up
8	ounces cream cheese	1	(4.5-ounce) can diced green chiles
2	cups grated cheddar cheese	¼	cup Worcestershire sauce

Preheat oven to 350°. Slice off top of bread loaf and set aside. Scoop out inside of bread, reserving pieces, being careful that loaf retains its shape. Mix sour cream, cheeses, ham, scallions, chiles and Worcestershire together. Fill hollowed bread loaf with mixture. Place top of bread on bread loaf; cover with foil. Bake for 1 1/4-1 1/2 hours. Serve with crackers or pieces of reserved bread.

Yield: 8 cups   Margaret Kluttz

♣ Poppy Seed Pick-Ups

1	(3-ounce) package cream cheese	1	(8-ounce) can crescent dinner rolls
2	teaspoons milk	1	egg, beaten
⅛	teaspoon garlic powder	1	teaspoon poppy seeds
½	cup chopped Spanish olives		

Combine cream cheese, milk and garlic powder; mix well. Stir in olives and set aside. Unroll dough to form four rectangles; press firmly to seal perforations. Spread cheese mixture evenly to edges of rectangles. Starting with short side, roll up jelly-roll fashion. Pinch edges to seal. Slice each roll into 8(1-inch) slices. Place cut side down on greased 14x15-inch cookie sheet. Brush with egg; sprinkle with poppy seeds. Bake at 375° for 12-14 minutes. Serve warm.

Yield: 32 slices   Linda Brown

♣ Bourbon Hot Dogs

1	cup ketchup	3	pounds hot dogs, cut into bite-size pieces
1	cup brown sugar		
1	cup bourbon		

Mix ketchup, brown sugar and bourbon. Place all ingredients in a 2 1/2-quart baking dish. Bake at 350° for 1 hour. Serve hot in chafing dish.

Yield: 30 servings   Helen "Pete" Miller-Dare

🔔 Sausage Rolls

2	cups flour	⅔	cup milk
⅓	teaspoon salt	1	pound ground hot sausage,
3	teaspoons baking powder		mashed in a bowl
5	teaspoons vegetable		
	shortening		

Mix dry ingredients. Cut in shortening. Add milk; mix. Divide dough into 2 parts. Roll each portion thin and dot each half with pieces of sausage. With a frosting spreader, distribute sausage thinly and evenly over dough. Roll up each portion; wrap individually in waxed paper. Freeze. Remove from freezer 40 minutes before using. Slice into 1/4-inch thick rolls and bake for 5-10 minutes. Serve hot.

Yield: 40 rolls   Janie Matthews

🔔 Hockey Pucks
Men love these

1	pound sausage	⅛	teaspoon oregano
1	pound ground beef	⅛	teaspoon basil
1	(1-pound) processed cheese		Party rye bread
	loaf		

Brown and cook sausage and ground beef together; drain well. While hot, fold in cheese, oregano and basil. Spoon a heaping teaspoonful of mixture onto a slice of bread. Broil for 3 minutes. Serve hot. Refrigerate if made ahead. Freezes well.

Yield: 50 servings   Una Pursel

Marinated Vidalia Onions

6	large Vidalia onions	½	cup vinegar
2	cups boiling water	1-1½	cup mayonnaise
1	cup sugar	2	teaspoons celery seed

Thinly slice onions and separate into rings. Place onions in a shallow dish and cover. Over medium heat, combine water, sugar and vinegar. Stir until sugar is dissolved. Pour hot mixture over onions and let stand covered overnight. Drain liquid. Add mayonnaise and celery seed. Toss onions in mixture to coat well. Chill; serve with crackers. Keeps for several weeks in the refrigerator.

Yield: 8 cups   Betsy Knauf

♣ Hot Cheese Puffs

2	eggs
½	pound Greek feta cheese, crumbled
1	(8-ounce) package cream cheese
¼	cup chopped parsley

¼	cup chopped green onions
½	teaspoon dried mint leaves
16	phyllo pastry sheets
1	cup butter or margarine, melted

Combine eggs and cheeses in blender container. Process until smooth. Add parsley, onion and mint; blend just until combined. Refrigerate for 1 hour, or until ready to use. Stack 2 pastry sheets on a work surface; brush with butter and cut into six 16x2-inch strips. For each pastry strip, place a rounded teaspoon of filling on the end of each strip. Fold one end corner over to opposite side covering filling and forming a triangle on top of dough strip. Continue folding strip into triangular shapes until the entire pastry strip has been folded into one triangle shaped puff. Stack, cut, fill and fold remaining pastry sheets. Arrange on ungreased cookie sheet. Bake at 375° for 20 minutes or until golden brown. Serve hot.

Yield: 48 puffs   Donna Goodman

♣ Ham & Cheese Squares

Great appetizer or brunch snack

1½	cups finely chopped boiled cooked ham
1	(8-ounce) carton sour cream
¼	cup shredded Swiss cheese
¼	cup crushed saltine crackers (8 crackers)

2	tablespoons butter or margarine, melted
1-2	teaspoons caraway seeds (optional)
6	eggs

In a medium bowl combine ham, sour cream, cheese, cracker crumbs, butter and caraway seeds (if desired). In mixing bowl beat eggs with electric mixer for about 6 minutes until thick and lemon colored. Fold and blend eggs into sour cream mixture. Pour into a greased 8x8-inch baking pan. Bake at 375° for 15-17 minutes until slightly brown. Cut into squares and serve hot.

NOTE: *One (10-ounce) box chopped spinach, cooked and drained, may be added to mixture before baking. For CHILI-CHEESE SQUARES or OLIVE-CHEESE SQUARES, omit caraway seeds, ham, and Swiss cheese, substituting cheddar or colby-jack cheese. Add 4-ounces drained, chopped green chiles or 4-ounces drained, sliced or chopped pimento-stuffed green olives. Bake as above. You may double this recipe and bake in a 10 1/2x15 1/2-inch jelly-roll pan until set.*

Yield: 12-16 servings

Mushroom Caps

Very good!

8	ounces bulk sausage	⅛	teaspoon garlic powder
¼	cup finely chopped onion	⅛	teaspoon pepper
¼	cup finely chopped green onion	½	cup sour cream
2	tablespoons chopped pimento	1	large container fresh whole mushrooms, washed, stems removed
1	teaspoon dried oregano		

In medium skillet, combine all ingredients except sour cream and mushrooms. Stir constantly over medium-high heat until sausage is browned. Remove from heat; drain. Stir in sour cream. Stuff mushroom caps with mixture. Place on broiler pan; broil 3-inches from heat for 3 minutes. Serve hot. Mushroom filling may be frozen.

Yield: 20 servings

Barbara Norman

🔔 Party Roll-Ups

3	(8-ounce) packages cream cheese or light cream cheese, softened	4	(12-inch) flour tortillas
1	(0.4-ounce) package dry ranch salad dressing mix (milk recipe)	1	(4-ounce) jar pimento, drained
		1	(4-ounce) can chopped green chiles, drained
2	green onions, minced		Thinly sliced turkey or ham Spinach leaves, rinsed, stemmed

Mix cream cheese, salad dressing mix and onions. Spread mixture on tortillas; sprinkle with pimento and chiles. Layer with meat and spinach leaves. Roll up tortillas and wrap in waxed paper. Store in tightly covered container. Chill at least 2 hours. When ready to serve rolls; cut off ends and cut crosswise into 1-inch slices to serve. Keep refrigerated.

Yield: 3 dozen

Betsy Knauf

Hot Cheese Dip

Quick and yummy

1	cup mayonnaise	1	small chopped onion
1	cup sour cream	6	slices bacon, cooked and crumbled
2	cups grated cheddar cheese		

Preheat oven to 350°. Mix ingredients; pour into a 10-inch or 8x8-inch casserole pan or dish. Bake 20 minutes. Cool 10 minutes. Serve with crackers.

Yield: 10 servings

Kathleen Boyd

Marinated Shrimp

4	quarts salted water	½	(3.5-ounce) bottle capers,
2	pounds raw shrimp		drained
1	cup tarragon vinegar	12	bay leaves
1	cup white wine vinegar	2	lemons, thinly sliced
⅓	cup sugar	4	medium onions, sliced into
2	cups salad oil		¼-inch thick rings
			Salt & pepper

Boil water in a large pot. Add shrimp; cook for 3 minutes or until pink. Peel and devein shrimp. Mix vinegars, sugar and oil together. Refrigerate for at least 24 hours. In a covered refrigerator container, place shrimp and completely cover with vinegar-oil mixture, lemon and onion slices, bay leaves, capers and salt and pepper to taste. Refrigerate for at least 24 hours. When ready to serve, remove shrimp, onions, lemon slices, bay leaves and capers from marinade with a slotted spoon; place in a clear glass bowl.

Yield: 6-8 servings

Art Gourmet,
Marilyn & Bob Smitherman

Hot Artichoke Dip

1	(8.5 ounce) can artichoke hearts, drained well	1	cup Parmesan cheese
1	cup mayonnaise	⅛	teaspoon garlic powder
			Paprika

Slice artichokes into small pieces and combine with mayonnaise, cheese and garlic powder. Mix thoroughly and spread in a 1-quart baking dish or quiche dish. Sprinkle with paprika. Bake at 350° for 20-25 minutes. Serve hot with water crackers or wheat thins.

NOTE: *May be made a day ahead and refrigerated. Bake when ready to use.*

Yield: 3 cups

Mary Wray Henshaw

Shoepeg Corn Dip

12	ounces shoepeg corn, drained	2	tablespoons green onions, chopped
1	cup sour cream	½	cup mayonnaise
4	ounces grated sharp cheese	¼	cup Parmesan cheese

Mix all ingredients in a bowl; chill. Serve with taco chips.

Yield: 4 cups

Sandee Carrigan

🔔 Party Ham & Cheese Sandwiches

¼	pound butter, room temperature	1	small onion, grated
2	teaspoons prepared mustard	1	package of 20 small party rolls, split horizontally
1	tablespoon poppy seeds	4-5	ounces boiled ham, sliced
2	teaspoons Worcestershire sauce	4	ounces Swiss cheese, sliced

Mix butter, mustard, poppy seeds, Worcestershire and onion. Spread mixture on both sides of rolls. Cut ham and cheese slices to fit rolls. Place small piece of ham and cheese on each roll. Wrap sandwiched rolls in foil and bake at 350° for 30 minutes, until cheese melts. These freeze well.

Yield: 20 sandwiches   Helen Sherrill

❤ Black Bean Dip

1¼	cups black beans, rinsed and well drained	2-4	hot jalapeño peppers
1¼	cups shoepeg white corn, rinsed and drained	¼-½	cup red onion, finely chopped
¼	cup red pepper, finely chopped	½	cup oil
		½	cup balsamic vinegar
¼	cup green pepper, finely chopped	1½	tablespoons Dijon mustard
		¼	cup fresh parsley, finely chopped

Toss all ingredients in a bowl and chill well before serving with crackers, chips or anything crunchy! Best when made a day ahead to allow flavors to blend.

Yield: 4½ cups   Carol Dunkley

❤ Fat Free Salsa Dip

1	(8-ounce) package fat free cream cheese	Vegetables for dipping
½	cup salsa or picante sauce	Lowfat chips for dipping

Mix cream cheese and salsa at medium speed until well blended. Warm mixture in microwave. Serve with vegetables or lowfat chips.

Yield: 1½ cup   Phyllis Gish

B
L
E
S
S
I
N
G
S

B
L
E
S
S
I
N
G
S

Layered Nacho Dip

2	(9-ounce) cans bean dip, mashed	1	(1-ounce) package taco seasoning mix
2	medium ripe avocados, peeled and seeded	1	cup chopped green onion tops
	Salt and pepper	1	tomato, chopped
1	tablespoon lemon juice	1	(8-ounce) package sharp cheddar cheese, grated
1	(8-ounce) carton sour cream		Tortilla chips
½	cup mayonnaise		

In sequence, spread and layer the following ingredients in the order listed, leaving a 1-inch border of bean dip around edge. When assembled, serve with tortilla chips.

Layer #1: Spread bean dip to edges of large circular tray.

Layer #2: Mash avocado and combine with salt and pepper to taste and lemon juice.

Layer #3: Combine sour cream, mayonnaise and taco mix.

Layer #4: Combine onions and tomatoes.

Layer #5: Top with grated cheese.

Yield: 8-10 servings   Lynn Hales

Hot Hamburger Dip

1	pound lean ground beef	1	teaspoon oregano
1	pound extra sharp cheese, shredded		Garlic salt
			Corn chips
1	(10¾-ounce) can tomato soup		

Brown ground beef; drain fat. Add cheese and soup and stir until cheese is melted. Add oregano and garlic salt to taste. Serve with nacho chips, king size corn chips or wheat crackers.

Yield: 5 cups   Mrs. Rob Eichelberger

Deviled Ham Dip

1	(4½-ounce) can deviled ham	1-2	tablespoons chopped onion
1	(8-ounce) package cream cheese, softened	2	tablespoons chopped, stuffed green olives
1	tablespoon ketchup		Parsley to garnish

Mix ham, cream cheese, ketchup and onions. Pour into a serving dish. Garnish with olives and parsley. Serve with crackers.

Yield: 8-10 servings   Becky Reitz-McKinley

Guacamole

1	cup fresh chopped tomatoes	¼	teaspoon cumin
¼	tablespoon fresh chopped jalapeño pepper	¼	tablespoon salt
½	cup chopped green chiles	¼	tablespoon black pepper
1	cup diced onion	1	ounce fresh lime juice
¼	tablespoon powdered garlic	6	ripe avocados, peeled, seeded, mashed

Mix all ingredients. Pour into clean canning jars. Avoid leaving air pockets in mixture. Must cover jar with plastic wrap before sealing with lids. Use within 2 days. Refrigerate but do not freeze. Serve as a dip or as an accompaniment to Mexican foods.

Yield: 3 cups   John and Lori Gray

Shrimp Dip
A *family favorite*

1	cup mayonnaise	1	tablespoon lemon juice
1	pint sour cream	⅛	teaspoon cayenne pepper
1	(8-ounce) package cream cheese	1	teaspoon sugar
1	tablespoon Worcestershire sauce	1	(12-ounce) package frozen cooked shrimp, thawed, chopped
⅛	teaspoon Tabasco sauce		Crackers
¼	cup chopped onion		

Mix all ingredients except crackers in a bowl. Chill at least 6 hours before serving with crackers.

Yield: 6 cups   Frances Binder

🍓 Berry Cheese Ring

1	pound sharp cheddar cheese, grated	1	cup chopped pecans
¾	cup mayonnaise	1	medium onion, grated
1	clove garlic, pressed	½	teaspoon Tabasco sauce
		1	cup strawberry preserves

Mix cheese, mayonnaise, garlic, pecans, onion and Tabasco. With hands, press cheese mixture (mixture will be sticky) into a 1 1/2-quart ring mold. Spread preserves on top of cheese mixture, filling mold. Chill. Serve with round wheat crackers.

Yield: 6 cups   Jane Gamewell

♣ Apricot Slush

1	**(46-ounce) can apricot nectar**
1	**(46-ounce) can unsweetened pineapple juice**
1	**(6-ounce) can frozen orange juice concentrate, thawed**

1	**(6-ounce) can frozen lemonade concentrate, thawed**
2	**(2-liter) bottles lemon-lime carbonated beverage, chilled**

Combine all fruit juices in a 4-quart plastic container; freeze. One hour before serving, remove mixture from freezer and thaw to a slushy consistency. It helps to break up mixture with a fork as it thaws. To serve, spoon slush mixture into a punch bowl and pour carbonated beverage over top, or spoon and pour equal portions of slush and carbonated beverage into individual glasses.

Yield: 7½ quarts   Carol Freed

● Floating Ice Rings

Bundt pan or any freezer-proof ring shaped container or gelatin mold.

Cold fruit juices, lemonade, punch liquids, distilled water or water that has been boiled

Assorted fruits: strawberries, grapes, melon balls, maraschino cherries, pineapple chunks, lemon and orange slices or fresh mint leaves

Pour 1/2-3/4-inch of cooled liquid into bottom of ring mold. Freeze until firm. Arrange choice of fruit or mint leaves on top of ice. Gently pour in additional liquid to partially cover fruit. Freeze until firm to keep fruit in place and embedded in ice ring. Fill the ice ring to within 1/2-inch of rim of mold by repeating the process to freeze the desired number of layers of fruits and liquids. Freeze until firm. When ready to serve, unmold by briefly dipping bottom of mold in warm water to loosen. Invert ice ring, decorative side up, and float in punch bowl.

NOTE: *Use boiled and cooled water; or distilled water to make an ice ring that is clear, not cloudy. For COFFEE ICE CUBES, fill ice cube tray compartments with coffee and freeze until firm. For DECORATIVE ICE CUBES to garnish iced beverages served in tall glasses, fill compartments with liquids or fruit juices. If desired, add your choice of mint, celery or basil leaves, or blueberries, cherries or strawberries. Freeze until firm. For children's parties, fill balloons with water; knot; freeze until firm. Float the COLORFUL ICE BALLOONS in a punch-filled bowl.*

🔔 Cheerwine Punch

3 (2-liter) bottles Cheerwine, chilled	**2 (46-ounce) cans sweetened pineapple juice, chilled**

Combine Cheerwine and juice in a punch bowl. Serve cold.

NOTE: *Cheerwine is a type of cherry flavored cola beverage bottled in Salisbury, North Carolina.*

Yield: 58 (5-ounce) cups

Tracy Smith
Alice Edwards

♥ Frosty Cappuccino Float

¼ cup coffee, vanilla or praline and caramel ice cream	**1 cup hot whole milk or skim milk**
1 (0.77-ounce) envelope instant cappuccino (amaretto, mocha or vanilla flavored)	

Place ice cream in large mug. Empty contents of cappuccino envelope into a Pyrex glass bowl or pitcher. Add 1 cup very hot (not boiling) milk to cappuccino mix. Stir gently. Pour cappuccino and milk mixture over ice cream. Serve immediately.

NOTE: *May use fat free ice cream or frozen yogurt.*

Yield: 1 serving

♥ Sugar Daddy Latte

⅔ ounce caramel flavored syrup for coffee	**½-¾ cup hot espresso**
½ ounce hazelnut flavored syrup for coffee	**⅓ cup milk, steamed and foamed**

Pour syrups into a large mug. Add espresso, filling mug to within 1-2 inches from rim. Top with foamed milk.* Serve immediately.

NOTE: *To make easy *STEAMED FOAMED MILK (for cappuccino and espresso) in the microwave, heat milk in glass container 50-60 seconds on high. Transfer to a blender container and process on low speed for 30 seconds until foamy. Gradually pour foamed milk over espresso, filling mug. Flavored syrups for coffee may be purchased at select coffee or gourmet specialty shops.*

Yield: 1 serving

The Daily Grind
Salisbury, North Carolina

🔔 Coffee Ice Cream Punch

6 tablespoons instant decaffeinated coffee	5 cups milk, chilled
1 cup hot water	1 quart ginger ale, chilled
1 cup sugar	1 quart vanilla ice cream, broken into small pieces

To make punch base, dissolve coffee in hot water. Add sugar; mix well and chill. When ready to serve, add milk, ginger ale and ice cream pieces to punch base. Serve in punch bowl.

NOTE: *Punch base yields 1 1/2 cups and may be made ahead and chilled.*

Yield: 24 (4½-ounce) servings   Virginia Wallace

🔔 Sparkling Eggnog
Delicious, light and bubbly

1 pint French vanilla or vanilla ice cream, softened	Almond flavoring
1 quart refrigerated dairy eggnog, (not canned) chilled	1 (28-ounce) bottle 7-Up, well chilled
	⅛ teaspoon ground nutmeg

In punch bowl, blend ice cream with eggnog by gently stirring and mashing ice cream. Add almond flavoring to taste. Just before serving, pour in 7-Up against side of punch bowl. Dust with nutmeg.

Yield: 15 (8-ounce) servings or
       25 (5-ounce) servings   Larry Gish

🔔 ❤ Golden Punch

2 (46-ounce) cans pineapple juice, chilled	1 (6-ounce) can frozen limeade
3 (6-ounce) cans frozen lemonade	Ice
	4 quarts ginger ale, chilled
4 (6-ounce) cans frozen orange juice	2 quarts soda water, chilled
	Fresh mint leaves (optional)
	Strawberries (optional)

Combine all cold juices in the order listed. Mix well; pour over ice in punch bowl. Add ginger ale and soda water just before serving. Garnish with fresh mint leaves or strawberries if desired.

NOTE: *A delicious non-alcoholic punch for wedding receptions.*

Yield: 75 punch cup servings   Lorraine Brownell

❦ Hot Scotch Cocoa

3   **cups water**
8   **ounces powdered cocoa mix**
6   **tablespoons butterscotch**
    chips or peanut butter

Miniature marshmallows (optional)

In a saucepan, bring water to a boil. Add cocoa mix and butterscotch chips or peanut butter. Stir until melted and mixture is hot. To serve, pour into 4 mugs and top with miniature marshmallows.

Yield: 4 servings

♩ Holiday Wassail

1   **orange, peeled; rind cut into**
    even strips
1   **lemon, peeled; rind cut into**
    even strips
1½ **teaspoons whole cloves**

3   **sticks cinnamon**
½   **cup sugar**
1   **gallon apple cider**
2   **cups orange juice**
1   **cup lemon juice**

Peel orange and lemon, being careful to keep rinds intact; insert cloves in each strip of rind. Combine rinds, cinnamon, sugar and apple cider in a large pot; bring to boil. Cover and reduce heat; simmer 10 minutes. Remove from heat; cool completely. To serve, add orange and lemon juices to mixture and cook until thoroughly heated. Stores well in refrigerator. Reheat before serving.

Yield: 5 quarts   Betty S. Carli

♩ Perky Punch

1   **(64-ounce) bottle cranberry-raspberry or cranberry-strawberry juice**
1   **(48-ounce) can sweetened pineapple juice**
1   **(64-ounce) bottle apple cider**
    Rum flavoring (optional)

1   **orange with rind, cut into eight pieces**
4   **sticks cinnamon, broken in half**
1-1½ **teaspoons whole cloves**
1-1½ **teaspoons whole allspice**
1   **(16-ounce) box light brown sugar**

Pour juices, cider and rum flavoring into a 30-cup electric percolator. In basket, place oranges, cinnamon sticks, cloves and allspice; crumble brown sugar on top. Perk punch 30 minutes until perking cycle or process is complete. Serve hot.

Yield: 24 (8-ounce) servings or
      32 (6-ounce) servings

♣ Opalescent Pearl Punch

Beautiful and elegant

1 **quart pineapple sherbet**	2 **(28-ounce) bottles Sprite,**
1 **(12-ounce) can frozen**	**chilled**
lemonade	
2 **(28-ounce) bottles 7-Up,**	
chilled	

Place sherbet and lemonade, slightly thawed, in punch bowl. Add ice cold 7-Up and Sprite immediately before serving.

NOTE: *A family favorite used for over 30 years for baby showers, wedding receptions and parties.*

Yield: 28-30 (5-ounce) cups   Libby Gish

Betsy's Iced Tea Punch

6 **small tea bags**	¾-1 **cup sugar**
8 **sprigs fresh mint**	½ **cup fresh lemon juice**
6 **cups boiling water**	½ **cup orange juice**

Steep tea and mint in water for 5 minutes. Remove tea bags and mint; add sugar and stir. Let tea cool. To prevent clouding, refrigerate tea mixture and then add juices when ready to serve.

NOTE: *If fresh mint is not available, mint tea bags may be substituted.*

Yield: 2 quarts   Liz Rankin

♣ Punch for a Bunch

2 **(0.12-ounce) packages unsweetened powdered cherry or strawberry drink mix**	1 **(46-ounce) can unsweetened pineapple juice, chilled**
2 **cups sugar**	1 **(12-ounce) can frozen lemonade, thawed**
2 **quarts water, chilled**	1 **quart ginger ale, chilled**

Mix together drink mix, sugar, water and fruit juices. Use part of this mixture to make an ice mold (see index for *FLOATING ICE RING*). When ready to serve punch, place ice mold in punch bowl and pour juices over ice; add ginger ale.

Yield: 34 (5-ounce) servings   Jane Dutton

♥ Delicious Cranberry Drink

Great to warm the winter chill

3	cups apple juice	10	whole cloves
4½	cups cranberry juice	½	cup brown sugar
3	sticks cinnamon, each broken in half	⅛	teaspoon salt

Mix all ingredients together in a large pot on the stove and heat thoroughly. Before serving, remove cinnamon and cloves.

Yield: 7½ cups   Rochelle Redcay

Orange Quencher

1	(12-ounce) can frozen orange juice concentrate	20	ounces cold water
1	banana, sliced	10	ice cubes

Combine all ingredients in blender container and process until well blended. Serve cold.

Yield: 6 servings   Robert Bertram

Lemonade

2	cups sugar	Juice of 2 oranges
2½	cups water	Zest of 1 orange
	Juice of 6 lemons	

Boil sugar and water together for 5 minutes to make a syrup; cool. Add juices and grated orange zest. Mix well. To serve, dilute 1 part syrup with 2 parts water and serve in tall glasses over ice.

Yield: 3½ cups syrup   Carr Garner

Post-Tennis Refresher

2	bananas, sliced	1	(8-ounce) carton plain or vanilla yogurt
1	cup orange juice		Ice cubes

Place bananas, juice and yogurt in blender container. Add enough ice cubes to bring mixture to the 3-cup level. Process until smooth. Pour into glasses to serve.

NOTE: *Frozen bananas make a thicker shake.*

Yield: 3 cups   Joyce Caddell

B
L
E
S
S
I
N
G
S

🍫 Banana Split Shake

1 large banana	4 maraschino cherries with
1 (6-ounce) container	stems
strawberry yogurt	Chopped nuts (optional)
2 cups chocolate ice cream or	Miniature chocolate bits
frozen yogurt	(optional)
Frozen whipped dessert	Chocolate syrup (optional)
topping, thawed	

Place banana, yogurt, and ice cream in blender container. Cover; process on high until smooth. Spoon into glasses. Top with a dollop of whipped topping and a maraschino cherry. Serve with a spoon and a straw. For additional garnish, top with chopped nuts, chocolate bits or drizzle with chocolate syrup.

Yield: 2-4 servings

🔔 ♥ Ginger Almond Tea

1 cup boiling water	1 tablespoon vanilla
5 regular size tea bags	1 teaspoon almond extract
1½ cups sugar	4 cups ginger ale or diet ginger
4 cups cold water	ale, chilled
¾ cup lemon juice	Ice

Pour boiling water over tea bags; cover, steep for 5 minutes. Gently squeeze and remove tea bags. Add sugar and stir until dissolved. Add cold water, lemon juice and extracts. Chill. Stir in ginger ale just before serving. Serve over ice and enjoy.

Yield: 10-12 cups   Jennifer W. Burks

♥ Friendship Tea

1 (15-ounce) jar powdered	1 (0.13-ounce) package
orange flavored drink mix	unsweetened powdered
1 cup sugar	cherry drink mix
1 cup unsweetened instant tea	2 teaspoons ground cinnamon
½ cup powdered lemonade mix	1 teaspoon ground nutmeg
	¼ teaspoon ground cloves

Mix all ingredients in a large bowl. Store in an air tight container. To use, mix 2 heaping tablespoons of dry mixture with 1 cup hot or cold water.

NOTE: *You may double the recipe and pour into small containers for Christmas gifts.*

Yield: 4½ cups mix   Carol McCubbins

Baskets
of Breads

Biscuits, Rolls, Muffins, Loaves,
Breads & Spreads for Tea
& Coffeecakes for Coffee

B
L
E
S
S
I
N
G
S

Sally Lunn

1	(¼-ounce) package yeast	⅓	cup sugar
¼	cup lukewarm water	3	eggs, well beaten
¾	cup lukewarm milk	1	teaspoon salt
½	cup butter	4	cups flour

Soften yeast in water; add milk and set aside. Cream butter and sugar; mix in eggs. Add salt to flour and stir into butter-sugar mixture, alternately with milk-yeast mixture. Beat well with hand mixer and turn into a buttered bowl. Let rise in a warm place until doubled. Beat again and pour into a buttered angel food cake pan or ring mold. Let rise again until doubled. Bake at 350° for about 45 minutes. Unmold and serve warm.

Yield: 6 servings   Elinor Swaim

Aunt Fay's Old Fashion Rolls

6	cups plain bread flour	2¼-2½	cups warm water
6	tablespoons sugar	½	cup cooking oil, plus oil
1	tablespoon salt		to coat dough
2	(¼-ounce) packages yeast		

Sift flour, sugar and salt; set aside. Dissolve yeast in water; gradually add to flour mixture, mixing well. Stir in cooking oil. Knead dough until elastic; shape into a ball. Rub oil on top and bottom of dough ball. Place in a bowl and cover with a clean towel. Let rise in a warm place for about 1 hour. Rising time may vary according to yeast used. Pinch off balls of dough (a little larger than golf balls) and place on greased baking sheet. Let rise 1 more hour. Bake at 375° until brown and hot. Baking time will vary according to size of roll.

NOTE: *Recipe may be halved.*

Yield: 6-8 dozen   Lawana Ford

🔔 Cheese Beer Bread

3½	cups self-rising flour	1	egg, beaten
⅓	cup sugar	1	(12-ounce) bottle of beer, or
2¼	cups shredded cheddar cheese		non-alcoholic beer

In a large bowl, stir flour and sugar together. Blend in cheese. Add egg and beer and mix thoroughly. Spoon equal portions of dough into 3 greased and floured 4 1/2x8-inch loaf pans. Bake at 350° for approximately 1 hour or until golden brown. Slice to serve. Freezes well.

NOTE: *For BEER BREAD, omit cheese. For HERB BEER BREAD, add 2/3 cup dried herbs, or desired amount of fresh herbs, to Beer Bread before baking.*

Yield: 3 loaves

♣ Easy Whole Wheat Bread

3	cups whole wheat flour	2¼	cups milk
1	teaspoon salt	¼	cup oil
¼	cup sugar or honey	1	egg
2	(¼-ounce) packages dry yeast	3	cups all-purpose flour

Combine 2 cups of the wheat flour, salt, sugar and yeast in mixer bowl. Heat milk and oil in saucepan over low heat until very warm (120°-130°). Add egg and milk mixture to flour mixture. Beat 30 seconds at low speed and 3 minutes at medium speed. By hand, gradually stir in remaining 1 cup of wheat flour and 3 cups all-purpose flour to form a soft dough. Turn out on a floured surface; knead until smooth and elastic, about 1 minute. Place dough in large greased or oiled bowl. Turn dough to grease all sides. Cover dough with plastic wrap and a towel. Let rise in a warm place (80°-85°) until light and doubled in size, about 45-60 minutes. Punch dough down. Turn back out onto floured surface and shape into loaves. Put in 2 large or 4 small greased loaf pans, and oil the tops of loaves. Cover again; let rise in warm place for 30-40 minutes. Bake at 325° until loaves brown and sound hollow when tapped. Cool on racks; rub tops with margarine.

Yield: 2 large or 4 small loaves   Carrie Brown

♣ Whole Wheat Spirals

2	(¼-ounce) packages dry yeast	¼	cup butter or margarine, plus melted butter for brushing tops of rolls
1¾	cups warm water (105°-115°)	1	egg, lightly beaten
½	cup sugar	2¼	cups whole wheat flour
1	teaspoon salt	2½-3	cups all-purpose flour

Dissolve yeast in water in a large bowl. Let stand 5 minutes. Add sugar, salt, butter, egg and whole wheat flour. Beat with electric mixer at medium speed for 2 minutes. Gradually stir in enough all-purpose flour to make a soft dough. Turn out onto a well floured surface; knead until smooth and elastic (about 5 minutes). Place dough in a well greased bowl, turning to grease top. Cover and let rise in a warm place (85°), free from drafts, for 1 hour or until dough is doubled in bulk. Punch dough down. Cover and let rise again, 45 minutes or until doubled in bulk. Punch dough down. Turn out onto a lightly floured surface and knead lightly 4-5 times. Divide dough in half; roll each portion into a 14x6-inch rectangle. Cut into twelve 7x1-inch strips. Roll each strip into a spiral and place in well-greased muffin pans. Brush rolls with melted butter. Let rise, uncovered in a warm place, free from drafts, 40 minutes or until doubled in bulk. Bake at 400° for 8 minutes; remove from pans and cool on wire rack. May be partially baked and frozen one month.

Yield: 2 dozen   Linda Brown

♣ English Muffin Bread

6	cups plain flour, or whole wheat flour	2	teaspoons salt
2	(¼-ounce) packages rapid rise yeast	½	teaspoon baking soda
1-1½	tablespoons sugar	2	cups milk
		½	cup water
			Cornmeal

In a mixing bowl, combine 3 cups flour, yeast, sugar, salt and soda. Heat milk and water until very warm (125°-130°). Add to flour mixture; blend. Add remainder of flour and blend. Mixture will be stiff. Spoon into two 4 1/2x8 1/2-inch loaf pans that have been sprinkled with cornmeal. Sprinkle top of loaves with cornmeal. Cover; let rise for 40-45 minutes in a warm place. Bake at 400° for 25 minutes. Remove from pans immediately and cool. To serve, butter bread slices and toast; serve with jam or preserves.

NOTE: *For WHOLE WHEAT ENGLISH MUFFIN BREAD, use whole wheat flour.*

Yield: 2 loaves

Corny Cornbread

2	eggs, beaten	1	(8.5-ounce) can cream style corn
½	cup corn oil		
1	cup sour cream	1	cup Ballard® Old South Cornbread Mix

Combine all ingredients. Mix well and pour into a greased 8x8-inch pan. Bake at 350° for 45 minutes or until brown.

NOTE: *This recipe came from Old Salem, North Carolina.*

Yield: 6 servings   Jo Krider

Lavosh
A thin, crispy bread

3	cups flour	4	tablespoons sesame seeds, toasted
½	teaspoon baking soda		
¼	cup sugar	1	stick butter, softened or melted
½	teaspoon salt		
1	tablespoon poppy seeds	1	cup buttermilk

Mix all the dry ingredients together. Add butter and buttermilk; mix well. On floured board, roll out dough as thin as possible. Place on an ungreased cookie sheet. Bake at 350° for 12 minutes. Cool and break into large pieces. Store in ziplock bag or airtight container.

NOTE: *May eat as a snack or serve in a bread basket with meals.*

Yield: 1 dozen pieces   Marty Kann

Glazed Lemon Tea Bread

6	tablespoons butter, softened	1	rounded teaspoon baking
1½	cups sugar		powder
2	eggs, beaten	½	cup milk
	Freshly grated lemon rind		Juice of one lemon
1½	cups flour		

Cream butter, 1 cup of sugar, eggs and lemon rind in a bowl. Stir well; adding flour and baking powder alternately with milk. Pour into a greased 9x5-inch loaf pan. Bake at 350° for 1 hour. Spoon a glaze made by mixing the remaining 1/2 cup sugar and fresh lemon juice on hot bread. Let bread stand, cool and absorb the glaze before slicing to serve.

Yield: 1 loaf   Pat Weber

Banana Bread

3-4	ripe bananas, mashed	1½	cups flour
¾	cup sugar	1	teaspoon baking soda
1	egg	1	teaspoon cinnamon
¼	cup margarine or butter, melted	½	teaspoon salt
		1	cup walnuts, chopped

Mix together bananas, sugar, egg and margarine. Combine flour, baking soda, cinnamon and salt and add to banana mixture. Add nuts. For bread, bake at 325° in 2 small or 1 large greased loaf pans for 1 hour. For *BANANA SNACK CAKE,* bake in 9x9-inch baking pan for 30 minutes. For *BANANA BREAD MUFFINS,* bake for 30 minutes in paper liners.

Yield: 1 loaf, 12 muffins, or 1 snack cake   Gail Langdon

The Best Banana Bread

½	cup butter	½	teaspoon salt
½	cup sugar	1	cup mashed bananas, overripe or ripe
½	cup brown sugar		
2	eggs	½	cup sour cream
1½	cups flour	1	teaspoon vanilla
1	teaspoon baking soda	½-¾	cup walnuts, chopped

In large bowl, combine butter, both sugars and eggs. Sift together flour, soda and salt. Mix dry ingredients with butter mixture. Add banana, sour cream and vanilla; add nuts and mix well. Pour in 9x5-inch ungreased loaf pan. Bake at 350° for 45-50 minutes. Cool. Slice to serve. Travels and freezes well.

Yield: 1 loaf   Teresa Gish Perry

Dill Casserole Bread

1	(¼-ounce) package dry yeast	1	tablespoon dry minced onion
¼	cup warm water	2	teaspoons dill seed
1	cup cottage cheese, warmed	1	teaspoon salt
1	egg	¼	teaspoon soda
2	tablespoons sugar	2¼	cups flour
1	tablespoon butter, softened, plus melted butter for topping		

Dissolve yeast in warm water and add cottage cheese. Add egg to cheese mixture. Mix together sugar, 1 tablespoon butter, onion, dill and salt; add to cheese mixture. Sift soda and flour together. Add gradually to cheese mixture; stir. Mixture will be stiff. Cover; let rise 1 hour in a warm place. Stir down and put into a greased 8-inch round casserole; let rise for 40-50 minutes. Bake at 350° for 45 minutes. Brush with butter. Cool on rack.

Yield: 8-10 servings   Carolyn C. Wilkerson

♣ Colonial Brown Bread

4	cups whole wheat flour	4	teaspoons baking soda
1½	cups all-purpose flour	1	teaspoon salt
2	cups brown sugar	4	cups buttermilk

Preheat oven to 350°. Grease 2 (9x5-inch) loaf pans. Lightly spoon flour into cup and level off when measuring. Gradually blend flours, sugar, baking soda and salt. Slowly add buttermilk until well blended. Pour into prepared pans. Bake 1 hour. Serve warm. Wrap in foil to re-warm in 350° oven.

Yield: 2 loaves   Kim Haldopoulos

French Bread Monterey

1	(16-ounce) loaf French bread	½	cup finely chopped onion
½	cup butter or margarine, softened	½	teaspoon Worcestershire sauce
1	cup mayonnaise		Paprika
½	cup grated Parmesan cheese		

Cut bread in half horizontally; spread butter evenly over cut surfaces. Place on a baking sheet, buttered sides up. Bake at 350° for 4-5 minutes. In a small bowl, combine mayonnaise, cheese, onion and Worcestershire sauce. Spread on bread halves and sprinkle with paprika. Broil 3-4 minutes or until lightly browned. Slice; serve hot.

Yield: 1 loaf   Patti Glassgow

♠ Refrigerator Potato Rolls

1½ cups warm water
1 (¼-ounce) package yeast
⅔ cup sugar
1½ teaspoons salt
⅔ cup soft shortening

2 eggs
1 cup lukewarm mashed potatoes
7-7½ cups flour, sifted

Dissolve yeast in water. Stir in sugar, salt and shortening. Add eggs and potatoes. Blend in flour; mix to form a soft dough. Knead on a lightly floured board until smooth and elastic. Place in a greased bowl. Cover with a damp cloth and place in the refrigerator. Punch down occasionally as it rises. Roll dough 1/4-inch thick. Using a biscuit cutter, cut out rolls and brush with butter. Fold and place on a greased cookie sheet. Let rise. Bake at 400° for 12-15 minutes.

NOTE: *Dough is excellent for making cinnamon buns, too.*

Yield: 6 dozen   Adair Doran

Broccoli Cornbread
Moist and delicious

3 eggs, lightly beaten
1 (6-ounce) carton cottage cheese
½ stick butter or margarine, melted
½ (10-ounce) box frozen chopped broccoli, thawed and drained

1 (8½-ounce) box cornbread mix
1 medium onion, chopped
½ cup shredded cheddar cheese

Combine eggs, cottage cheese and butter. Add broccoli, cornbread mix, onion and cheese; mix well. Pour into a greased 8x8-inch pan and bake at 350° for 45 minutes. (Test for doneness as you would a cake.) Freezes well.

Yield: Serves 8   Joanne Eichelberger

♥ Bread Sticks

¾ cup warm water
1½ teaspoons sugar
2 tablespoons cornmeal
1 tablespoon yeast
½ teaspoon salt

2¼ cups flour
½ stick margarine
Parmesan cheese (optional)
Seasonings (optional)

Combine water, sugar, cornmeal, yeast, salt and flour. Mix dough until it forms a ball. Knead a few times on a floured surface. Roll pieces of dough into 1 1/2-inch wide "snakes" with floured hands. Melt margarine in 9x13-inch pan. Roll breadsticks in margarine to coat all sides. Bake at 400° for 15-20 minutes. Sprinkle with Parmesan cheese or choice of other seasonings.

Yield: 2 dozen sticks   Pat Fromen

🔔 Buttermilk Biscuits

2	cups flour	1	teaspoon sugar
2	teaspoons baking powder	½	cup solid shortening
½	teaspoon baking soda	½	cup buttermilk
½	teaspoon salt		Melted butter

Mix flour, baking powder, baking soda, salt and sugar in mixing bowl. Cut shortening into flour mixture. Add 1/2 cup (more or less) buttermilk until dough can be easily picked up. Roll out dough onto a floured surface and cut to desired size, using a 2-inch cutter for large biscuits and a 1 1/2-inch cutter for small biscuits. Prick with fork and brush with melted butter. Bake at 400° for 15 minutes or until golden brown. Best when hot, but good cold for several days.

NOTE: *To freeze, bake until slightly brown at edges of biscuits; remove from oven. Cool and freeze on a baking sheet. Place frozen biscuits in ziplock bag and freeze again.*

Yield: 15-20 large or 30 small biscuits   Nancy C. Holshouser

Arline Crawford's Spoonbread

1	cup white cornmeal	2	cups buttermilk
1	teaspoon salt	2	eggs
1	tablespoon butter	½	teaspoon soda, dissolved in
1	cup boiling water		1 teaspoon water

Preheat oven to 400°. Mix cornmeal, salt and butter; add water and let sit 1 minute. Butter a 1 1/2-quart casserole. Beat buttermilk, eggs and soda and water mixture; add into the cornmeal mixture. Bake approximately 25 minutes. Serve hot.

Yield: 4-6 servings   Jane Gamewell

Virginia Spoonbread

2½	cups milk	1	teaspoon salt
½	cup cornmeal	2	tablespoons butter
3	eggs, yolks and whites separated		

Scald milk and sift cornmeal into it. Cook five minutes, stirring constantly. Remove from heat and add beaten egg yolks and salt; beat well. Beat egg whites. Fold into cornmeal mixture. Melt butter in casserole dish. Pour in mixture. Bake at 350° for 1 hour. Serve immediately with lots of butter.

Yield: Serves 6   Betty Lomax

Cheese Croissants

⅓   cup soft cream cheese with chives
⅓   cup shredded Monterey Jack cheese

1   (6-ounce) package of 6 frozen petite croissants, thawed and split lengthwise

Combine cheeses in mixing bowl. Spread 1 heaping tablespoon of cheese mixture between halves of each croissant. Place filled croissants on cookie sheet. Cover tightly with aluminum foil. Bake at 400° for 10-15 minutes until heated and cheeses have melted. Serve hot. May also be cooked in foil outdoors on the grill.

Yield: 6 servings

Amy's Christmas Morning Rolls

1   (25-ounce) bag frozen dinner roll dough
1   (3.4-ounce) package butterscotch pudding (not instant)

1   stick margarine
¾   teaspoon cinnamon
¾   cup brown sugar
1   cup chopped pecans

Arrange frozen dinner rolls in a greased tube pan. Sprinkle dry pudding mix over rolls. Melt margarine; add cinnamon, brown sugar and pecans; cook on medium heat until mixture is bubbly. Pour mixture over rolls. Cover tube pan tightly with foil and leave on countertop overnight. Bake the next morning in oven preheated to 350° for 30 minutes. Let stand 5 minutes before serving.

Yield: 10-12 rolls   Kaye Hirst

Blueberry Duffins
Cinnamon sugar coated mini muffins

1   (18.25-ounce) package blueberry muffin mix
2   tablespoons butter or margarine, melted

3   tablespoons sugar
½   teaspoon cinnamon

Mix and bake large or mini muffins as directed on the package. Cool in pan about 5 minutes, then remove. Dip tops of hot baked muffins in melted butter and then in a mixture of the sugar and cinnamon.

Yield: 12 medium or 24 small muffins   Peggy Rouzer

● Cinnamon Rolls

Children love them!

1	(¼-ounce) package dry yeast	1	teaspoon salt
¼	cup warm water	2	eggs
4½	cups flour	2	tablespoons butter
1	cup lukewarm milk	½	cup raisins
¾	cup sugar		Milk to brush on rolls
2	tablespoons cinnamon		

Stir yeast into water. Let stand for 5 minutes. Add dissolved yeast and 3 cups of flour to milk. Blend well. Cover and let rise in a warm place until double in size. Add sugar, cinnamon, salt, eggs, butter and 3/4 cup of flour to blend. Knead on slightly floured board, slowly adding remaining 3/4 cup flour, or more if necessary, until easily handled. Knead in raisins. Pull off pieces of dough the size of medium lemons and roll until 8 inches long. Wind into a coil. Place in buttered 9-inch cake pans. Cover and let rise until double. Brush tops with milk. Preheat oven to 375°. Bake for 25 minutes.

GLAZE:

¾	cup powdered sugar	4	teaspoons warm water
1	teaspoon vanilla		

Mix sugar, vanilla and water until smooth. Spread thinly on very hot rolls.

Yield: 16 rolls

Debbie Collins

♠ Glorious Morning Muffins

¾	cup brown sugar	1	cup chopped dates or raisins
1¾	cups sugar	1	(6-ounce) package frozen coconut
4	cups flour		
4	teaspoons baking soda	1	cup chopped pecans
4-5	teaspoons cinnamon sugar	6	eggs
4	cups grated carrots	1¾	cup vegetable oil
2	(8-ounce) cans crushed pineapple, drained, or 1 cup of shredded apple	4	teaspoons vanilla

Preheat oven to 350°. Sift together sugars, flour, baking soda and cinnamon sugar. Stir in carrots, pineapple, dates, coconut and pecans. Beat eggs with oil and vanilla; combine with flour and carrot mixture. Spoon batter into greased muffin tins filling to top of pan. Bake 30-35 minutes until muffin tops are springy to touch.

NOTE: *May use other fruits such as mashed or chopped bananas or chopped apples. For GLORIOUS MORNING COFFEE CAKE, may bake in three 8x8-inch pans.*

Yield: 30 large muffins or 27 pieces

B
L
E
S
S
I
N
G
S

Poppy Seed Loaves

1   (18.25-ounce) box butter
    pecan cake mix
1   (3.4-ounce) box instant
    toasted coconut pudding
1   teaspoon baking powder

⅛   cup poppy seeds
4   eggs
1½ cups warm water
½   cup oil

Mix cake mix, pudding mix, baking powder and poppy seeds in a mixing bowl. In a separate bowl, beat eggs. Add water and oil; mix well. Add egg mixture to cake mixture and blend well. Grease 2 large or 5 mini loaf pans. Pour in batter and bake at 325° for 25-30 minutes or until a toothpick inserted into center of loaves comes out clean. Let cool; turn out on waxed paper.

Yield: 2 large or 5 mini loaves   Patti Glassgow

Poppy Seed Loaf
Moist and yummy with coffee!

1   (18.25-ounce) box butter cake
    mix
½   cup sugar
¾   cup oil
¼   cup poppy seeds

1   (8-ounce) package cream
    cheese, softened
4   eggs
    Sugar to coat pan

Mix all ingredients together in a mixing bowl. Pour into a greased loaf pan that has been sprinkled with sugar, filling only half full. Bake at 350° for 45-50 minutes. For large loaves, bake 1 hour. For *POPPY SEED CUPCAKES,* fill paper-lined muffin tins half full. Bake at 350° for 20 minutes.

Yield: 1 loaf or 30 cupcakes   Rochelle Redcay

Pumpkin Muffins

2⅔ cups sugar
⅔   cup shortening
4   eggs, beaten
2   cups canned pumpkin
⅔   cup water
3⅓ cups flour

½   teaspoon baking powder
2   teaspoons baking soda
½   teaspoon cloves
1½ teaspoons cinnamon
⅔   cup nuts, chopped
1   cup dates, chopped

Cream sugar and shortening. Add eggs, pumpkin and water; mix well. Sift together flour, baking powder, soda and spices; add to pumpkin mixture. Mix well. Add nuts and dates. Bake in greased or paper-lined muffin cups at 350° for about 20 minutes. Muffins freeze well.

Yield: 12 muffins   Donna Yale

79

Chocolate Pumpkin Bread

½	cup butter, melted
1	cup canned pumpkin
2	eggs
½	cup water
1½	cups sugar
1¾	cups flour
¼	teaspoon baking powder
1	teaspoon baking soda
1	teaspoon cinnamon
½	teaspoon nutmeg
¼	teaspoon ground cloves
¼	teaspoon salt
½	cup dates
½	cup nuts
½	cup chocolate chips

Preheat oven to 350°. Beat together butter, pumpkin, eggs and water. Set aside. Sift together sugar, flour, baking powder, baking soda, spices and salt. Stir dates, nuts and chocolate chips into flour mixture, coating well. Combine dry ingredients with pumpkin mixture until well blended. Pour into greased 9x5-inch loaf pan. Bake for 1 1/4-1 1/2 hours. Freezes well.

Yield: 1 loaf   Susan Sember

♣ Brandon's Sour Cream Coffee Cake

2	sticks margarine or butter
1½	cups sugar
2	eggs
1	(8-ounce)carton sour cream
2	cups flour, sifted
1½	teaspoons baking powder
⅛	teaspoon salt
½	teaspoon baking soda
1	teaspoon vanilla
4	teaspoons cinnamon
¾	cup pecans, chopped
4	tablespoons sugar

Cream butter and sugar. Add eggs and mix well. Add sour cream and flour alternately. Add baking powder, salt, soda and vanilla. Mix together cinnamon, pecans and sugar. Pour half the batter into a well-greased Bundt pan. Sprinkle with the sugar mixture. Pour in other half of batter. Swirl a knife through the cake before baking. Bake at 350° for 40 minutes. Cool for 15 minutes. Remove from pan and glaze immediately.

GLAZE:

½	cup powdered sugar
2	teaspoons corn syrup
½	teaspoon vanilla

Dash of hot water
Shaved or finely minced
pecans, for topping

Mix ingredients for glaze and beat until very smooth. Glaze cake as soon as removed from pan and sprinkle with finely minced pecans.

NOTE: *Even better second day!*

Yield: 24 servings   Eleanor Hoey Bradshaw

🔔 Orange Poppy Seed Loaves
A hit with all ages

3	cups flour	1½	cups milk
2½	cups sugar	1	cup plus 2 tablespoons oil
1½	teaspoons salt	2	tablespoons poppy seeds
1½	teaspoons baking powder	1½	teaspoons vanilla
3	eggs	1½	teaspoons almond extract

Combine flour, sugar, salt, baking powder, eggs, milk, oil, poppy seeds and extracts; mix until smooth. Divide into 2 greased loaf pans. Bake at 325° for 1 hour. Cool.

GLAZE:

¼	cup orange juice	½	teaspoon almond extract
¾	cup sugar	½	teaspoon oil
½	teaspoon vanilla		

Combine juice, sugar, extracts and oil in a saucepan. Cook over low heat until mixture is a thin consistency. Cool and spoon over both loaves. Freezes well.

Yield: 2 loaves   Dottie Abramowski

🔔 Honey Bun Cake

1	(18.25-ounce) package yellow cake mix, with pudding	1	(8-ounce) carton sour cream
4	eggs	½	cup brown sugar
⅔	cup vegetable oil	1	tablespoon cinnamon
⅓	cup water	⅔	cup pecans

Combine cake mix, eggs, oil, water and sour cream; beat with mixer at medium speed. Set aside. Combine brown sugar, cinnamon and pecans. Pour half the batter into a greased and floured 9x13-inch pan. Sprinkle on half of sugar mixture. Repeat this procedure and swirl batter with a knife. Bake at 350° for 30-35 minutes.

GLAZE:

1	cup powdered sugar	½	teaspoon vanilla
2	tablespoons milk	3	tablespoons melted butter

Combine sugar, milk, vanilla and butter; mix well. Drizzle glaze over warm cake.

Yield: 24 servings   Marcia Parrott

🔔 Date Nut Brown Bread

2	cups water, boiling	2	tablespoons margarine
1	(8-ounce) package dates, pitted and chopped	2	eggs
½	pound raisins	4	cups flour
2	teaspoons baking soda	1	teaspoon salt
1	cup sugar	½	cup chopped pecans
1	cup dark brown sugar		Cream cheese
1	teaspoon vanilla		Orange juice

Pour boiling water over dates, raisins and baking soda. Stir and set aside to cool. Cream sugars, vanilla, margarine and eggs. Add flour, salt and nuts; mix well. Stir in fruit mixture. Fill 6 greased and floured vegetable tin cans about 1/2 full. Bake at 325° for 60 minutes. Using a can opener, remove the bottom of can and slide bread out through opening. Slice loaves; spread slices with cream cheese thinned slightly with orange juice and sandwich 2 slices together. Cut in halves or quarters to serve.

NOTE: *Mini loaf pans may be used in place of tin cans. Freezes well.*

Yield: 6 loaves   Fran Lawson

🔔 Markey's Coffee Cake

1	cup shortening	½	teaspoon salt
1½	cups sugar	1	teaspoon vanilla
2	eggs	14	ounces brown sugar
1	cup milk	4	teaspoons cinnamon
3	cups flour	1	cup pecans, chopped
3	teaspoons baking powder	1	stick butter, melted

Cream together shortening and sugar. Mix in eggs and milk. Sift together flour, baking powder and salt. Blend slowly into sugar mixture. Add vanilla and beat 1 minute at medium speed. Scrape beaters and bottom of bowl; beat at medium speed for 2 minutes. Combine brown sugar, cinnamon and pecans for topping. Spread half of batter into greased 8x13-inch glass pan. Sprinkle on half of topping; spread on remaining batter and cover with remainder of topping. Dribble melted butter over cake. Bake at 325° for 50-60 minutes.

NOTE: *Freezes well. Given to me by a student's mom in my first year of teaching.*

Yield: 12-16 servings   Beverly Mitchell

Overnight Coffee Cake

2	cups flour	2	eggs, beaten
½	teaspoon salt	1	cup buttermilk
1	teaspoon baking soda	1	teaspoon vanilla
1	teaspoon baking powder	½	teaspoon nutmeg
¾	cup margarine	1	teaspoon cinnamon
1	cup sugar	½	cup chopped nuts
1	cup brown sugar		

Sift flour, salt, baking soda and baking powder. In another bowl, cream margarine, sugar and 1/2 cup brown sugar. Add eggs and beat until fluffy. Blend in flour mixture alternately with buttermilk. Add vanilla and stir well. Pour into greased 9x13-inch metal pan. Combine remaining 1/2 cup of brown sugar, nutmeg, cinnamon and nuts; sprinkle over batter. Let stand covered in the refrigerator overnight. Bake at 350° for 35-40 minutes.

Yield: 24 servings

Betty I. Mickle

Lula's Coffee Cake

2	cups and 4 tablespoons sugar	2	cups sifted flour
2	eggs, well beaten	1	teaspoon baking powder
1	stick butter	1	teaspoon cinnamon
1	stick margarine	½	teaspoon salt
1	cup sour cream	1	teaspoon vanilla
		1	cup chopped nuts

Combine sugar, eggs, butter, margarine and cream well. Add sour cream, flour, baking powder and flavorings. Add 3/4 cup nuts. Pour into well greased tube pan. Sprinkle top with remaining 1/4 cup nuts. Bake for 1 hour in a 350° oven.

Yield: 12-14 servings

Gwen Webb

Applesauce Muffins

1½	cups unsweetened applesauce	1	cup flour
1	egg	2	teaspoons baking powder
2	tablespoons canola oil	¾	teaspoon baking soda
2	tablespoons honey	1	teaspoon cinnamon
1	cup whole wheat flour	½	teaspoon nutmeg

Preheat oven to 375°. In large bowl, beat applesauce, egg, oil and honey. In another bowl, stir together flours, baking powder, baking soda and spices; add to applesauce mixture. Stir until moist. Divide into 12 muffin cups. Bake for 20 minutes.

Yield: 12 muffins

Margaret Almeida

♣ Holiday Overnight Coffee Cake

⅔ cup margarine or butter
1 cup sugar
2 eggs
1 (8-ounce) carton sour cream
1 teaspoon vanilla
2 cups flour
1 teaspoon baking powder
½ teaspoon salt

½ teaspoon baking soda
½ cup candied green cherries
½ cup candied red cherries
½ cup raisins
½ cup brown sugar
½ teaspoon cinnamon
½ cup chopped pecans

Beat margarine and sugar with mixer. Add eggs, sour cream and vanilla, mixing well until light and fluffy. In another bowl, sift flour, baking powder, salt and soda. Combine flour and sugar mixtures. Add 1/3 cup each of red and green cherries, reserving remainder for topping. Add raisins and stir well. Pour batter into a greased 9x13-inch baking dish. In another bowl stir together brown sugar, cinnamon, pecans and reserved cherries. Sprinkle mixture evenly over top. Cover with foil and refrigerate overnight. The next morning, remove foil and bake at 350° for 35-40 minutes.

Yield: Serves 16   Di Potts

English Scones

3 sticks unsalted butter or
  margarine, softened
4 cups self-rising flour
4 tablespoons powdered sugar,
  plus sugar for dusting

2 teaspoons baking powder
¼ cup half-and-half
1 egg, beaten
2 pinches salt

Combine dry ingredients in a large mixing bowl. Knead butter into the dry ingredients with fingertips until mixture forms large crumbs. Add half-and-half gradually, mixing with fingers until dough is moist. Roll dough out to a 3/4-inch thickness on a floured board. Cut with a 2 1/2-inch biscuit cutter. Place on a lightly greased air-bake cookie sheet and brush with egg. Bake at 450° for about 15 minutes. Cool on rack for 5 minutes. Dust with powdered sugar and serve warm with butter and raspberry jam.

NOTE: *For RAISIN SCONES add 3/4-1 cup white raisins to moist dough before baking as above. For CHOCOLATE SCONES add 1/2 cup unsweetened cocoa, add 2 1/2 tablespoons powdered sugar and 1/2 cup mini-chocolate chips to basic recipe. Bake for 18-20 minutes. For GLAZED SCONES, mix 1 1/2 cups powdered sugar, 1 tablespoon melted butter, 1 teaspoon vanilla or almond extract and 1 teaspoon milk. Add more milk until glaze mixture is the consistency to drizzle on warm scones.*

Yield: 12-14 scones

♥ Blueberry Coffee Cake

½	cup butter, softened	½	teaspoon salt
1¼	cups sugar	1	cup sour cream, or non-fat
2	eggs	1	teaspoon vanilla
2	cups flour	1	cup blueberries
1	teaspoon baking soda	½	cup brown sugar
1	teaspoon baking powder	1	teaspoon cinnamon

Combine butter, sugar, eggs, flour, baking soda, baking powder, salt, sour cream and vanilla. Beat with mixer at medium speed. Fold in blueberries. Pour half of mixture into greased Bundt pan or 2 loaf pans. Mix brown sugar, remaining 1/4 cup sugar and cinnamon for topping. Spoon half of topping over blueberry mixture. Pour rest of batter into pan and spoon on remainder of topping. Bake at 350° for 40-50 minutes.

NOTE: *May use frozen blueberries or canned blueberries, drained and rinsed.*

Yield: 1 cake or 2 loaves   Jennifer Flynn

Golden Orange Muffins
Muffins with a twist

1¾	cups flour	1	cup buttermilk
⅓	cup sugar	3	tablespoons vegetable oil
¾	teaspoon baking soda	1	tablespoon grated orange rind
¼	teaspoon salt		
1	cup golden raisins	2	eggs

Combine flour, sugar, soda, salt and raisins in bowl; set aside. Combine buttermilk, oil, rind and eggs. Add to dry ingredients; stir until moistened. Spoon batter into muffin cups; sprayed with cooking spray. Bake at 375° for 25 minutes until golden. Remove; cool on wire racks. Freeze well.

Yield: 15 muffins   Virginia A. Clawson

Southern Muffin Biscuits

½	cup butter, softened	2-3	tablespoons sugar
2	cups all purpose biscuit baking mix	1	(8-ounce) carton sour cream

Preheat oven to 400°. Spray non-stick muffin tins with vegetable oil spray. Combine butter, baking mix and sugar in a large bowl using a pastry blender. Stir in sour cream. Blend until moist. Drop by spoonfuls into 12 muffin tins. Bake 20 minutes until lightly golden in color. Remove from pan and serve.

Yield: 12 muffins

Monkey Bread

5 tablespoons cinnamon	¾ cup butter
1¾ cups sugar	Vegetable oil or cooking spray
3 (10-ounce) cans flaky biscuits, each biscuit cut into 4 wedges	Plastic kitchen storage bag (1 gallon size)
½ cup chopped pecans	

In a plastic freezer bag, mix 3 tablespoons cinnamon and 3/4 cup sugar together. Place the biscuit pieces in plastic bag with cinnamon sugar mixture; shake bag to coat. Sprinkle pecans into a Bundt pan, oiled or sprayed with cooking spray. Layer the coated biscuits in pan on top of pecans. Melt the remaining 1 cup sugar and 2 tablespoons cinnamon and butter in a saucepan; mix until smooth. Pour syrup mixture over biscuits. Bake in a 350° oven for about 35 minutes. Invert warm bread over a plate and serve immediately.

Yield: 1 Bundt loaf

♣ Danish Puff Coffee Cake

CRUST:

1 stick margarine	2 tablespoons water
1 cup flour	

Blend ingredients for crust. Divide into 2 portions; press onto ungreased cookie sheet in strips 3x12-inches.

TOP LAYER:

1 stick margarine	1 cup flour
1 cup water	3 eggs
1 teaspoon almond extract	

Bring margarine and water to boil in a saucepan. Add extract and quickly beat in flour. Add eggs, one at a time, beating well. Spread half of this mixture on each of the strips of crust. Bake at 350° for 1 hour. Cool.

FROSTING:

4 tablespoons margarine	2 tablespoons milk
1 cup powdered sugar	Slivered almonds
¼ teaspoon almond extract	

Mix margarine, sugar, extract and milk together until smooth. Frost both baked coffee cakes and sprinkle with almonds.

Yield: 20 servings   Jean Johnsen

Microwave Cherry Caramel Ring

¼   **cup margarine**
½   **cup brown sugar**
1   **teaspoon cinnamon**
1   **(10-ounce) can refrigerated biscuits**

½   **cup pecan halves**
¼   **cup maraschino cherries, quartered**

Melt butter in 8-inch round casserole dish in microwave for 30-45 seconds. Mix sugar and cinnamon in small bowl. Roll each biscuit in butter; then in sugar mixture; set aside. Add leftover sugar and cinnamon to butter in dish, mix. Place a juice glass in middle of casserole; arrange cherries and pecans in a neat design in dish. Arrange biscuits around the glass, squeeze to fit if necessary, on top of cherries and pecans to form a petal shape. Bake in microwave on medium heat 8 minutes. Remove glass; invert onto serving plate; allow remaining syrup to drizzle over rolls.

Yield: 10 pieces   Janie Matthews

Peanut Butter & Jelly Banana Muffins

1¼ **cups flour**
¼   **cup whole wheat flour**
¼   **cup brown sugar**
1   **teaspoon baking powder**
½   **teaspoon salt**
¾   **cup buttermilk or lowfat milk**

½   **cup peanut butter**
½   **cup lowfat margarine, melted**
2   **medium ripe bananas, mashed**
1   **egg**
¼   **cup low-sugar jam**

Combine flours, sugar, baking powder and salt in a large bowl. In a separate mixing bowl combine buttermilk, peanut butter, margarine, bananas and egg; beat with electric mixer until smooth. Add to flour mixture, stirring just until moistened. Coat muffin pan with cooking spray or line with paper liners. Spoon mixture into muffin pan until 1/3 full; place 1/2 teaspoon of jam on top. Spoon batter mixture over jam until cup is 2/3 full. Bake at 400° for 20-25 minutes or until golden brown. Freeze well. Kids love them!

Yield: 16 muffins   Deborah Messinger

Cinnamon Biscuit Doughnuts

1   **(9.5-ounce) can of 10 biscuits**
    Vegetable cooking oil

1   **cup powdered sugar**
3   **tablespoons cinnamon**

Poke a hole in biscuit centers; brown in skillet in oil on medium high until puffy. Drain; shake each doughnut in plastic bag in mixture of sugar and cinnamon. Serve hot.

Yield: 10 servings

Friendship Bread Starter

DAY #1

When giving or receiving *FRIENDSHIP BREAD STARTER*, it is ready to make into bread OR set the bag aside at room temperature; OR do nothing to bag until Day #2, following the directions below to begin the 10 Day Process to multiply the STARTER. OR ON

DAY #1 — If you do not have a gift starter; make NEW STARTER with:

1	cup of flour	1	cup whole or skim milk
1	cup of sugar		

Using only a plastic or wooden spoon and either a plastic or glass mixing bowl: combine flour, sugar, and milk. Pour 2 cup mixture into gallon size ziplock bag; seal. Set aside at room temperature. As batter ferments and bubbles, the bag will become puffy. Open bag to release air as needed over the next few days, re-sealing each time.

DAY #2 through DAY #5 — Each day, knead the bag to mix the contents.

DAY #6

1	cup of flour	1	cup whole or skim milk
1	cup of sugar		

Feed the STARTER by adding the above flour, sugar, and milk to the STARTER in the bag, mix well. The volume of the mixture in the bag will now be 4 cups.

DAY #7 through DAY #9 — Each day, knead the bag to mix the contents.

DAY #10 — Empty bag mixture of STARTER into large glass bowl and add:

1	cup of flour	1	cup whole or skim milk
1	cup of sugar		

After adding the above flour, sugar, and milk, stir well. You now have six cups of STARTER. Pour 1-1 1/4 cups of the mixture into each of 4 (1-gallon sized) ziplock bags; seal. Keep one bag; give away the 3 remaining bags of the STARTER to friends along with recipes and instructions for *FRIENDSHIP BREAD* (Recipe on Page 89) and *FRIENDSHIP BREAD STARTER*. Use remaining STARTER in bowl to bake *FRIENDSHIP BREAD* following directions on Page 89.

Yield: 6 cups starter   Quick Copy Employees

Peachy Bread Spread

1	(8-ounce) package cream cheese, softened	½	teaspoon ground ginger
¾	cup peach preserves	2	teaspoons almond extract or liqueur
½	cup chopped pecans		

In a small bowl combine all ingredients; blend well. Refrigerate in air tight container for 8 hours to blend flavors. To serve, spread on muffins or tea breads.

Yield: 2 cups

Friendship Bread

1-1½	cup of *FRIENDSHIP BREAD* *STARTER* (Page 88)	½	teaspoon salt	
1	cup vegetable oil	1½	teaspoon baking powder	
1	cup sugar	½	teaspoon baking soda	
2	teaspoons of cinnamon	1	(5.1 ounce) large box of regular or instant vanilla pudding	
3	eggs			
½	cup whole or skim milk or sour cream; or half of each	1	cup chopped pecans or walnuts (optional)	
2	cups flour	½	cup raisins (optional)	
1	teaspoon vanilla		Cinnamon-Sugar mixture	

Preheat oven to 325°. In a large glass bowl, combine the *FRIENDSHIP BREAD STARTER* with the oil, sugar, cinnamon, eggs, milk, flour, vanilla, salt, baking powder and soda, and pudding. Add nuts and/or raisins if desired. Mix well. Grease a Bundt pan, 2 (9 1/4 x 5 x 2 1/4-inch) or 5 (5 3/4 x 3 1/4 x 2-inch) light colored aluminum loaf pans, or 24 muffin tins. Sprinkle pan interior with cinnamon-sugar mixture. Pour batter into pans. Sprinkle top of batter with additional cinnamon-sugar for a crustier top. Bake for 50-60 minutes or until done. Cool. Remove from pan.

NOTE: *For best results, avoid the use of metal utensils. Do not refrigerate starter. If using dark pan; reduce oven temperature to 300°. For flavor variety: substitute pistachio, banana, coconut, or chocolate pudding mixes. Starter may be frozen in plastic bags; thaw and re-ferment at room temperature (or until mixture begins to bubble) before using.*

Yield: 1 Bundt or 2 loaves,   Quick Copy Employees
       5 mini-loaves or 24 muffins

❢ Soft Pretzels

2½	cups warm water (110°-115°)	4	cups flour
1	(¼-ounce) envelope yeast	1	teaspoon salt
1	tablespoon sugar	1	egg, beaten

Mix water, yeast and sugar until yeast and sugar dissolve. Set aside for 5 minutes. Put flour and salt in a bowl. Add yeast mixture; mix well to form dough. On a floured surface, let children knead, play, identify and discuss the dough they form into letters, shapes, twists or numbers. Place on an ungreased cookie sheet. Brush tops with beaten egg and sprinkle with salt. Bake immediately at 425° for 12 minutes, or let rise and then bake.

NOTE: *Baking bread is a great educational opportunity for teaching word meanings, like "knead," "yeast," "dissolve" and "dough." Use a candy thermometer to demonstrate that water hotter than 130° kills yeast, water cooler than 110° will not activate yeast. Sugar is food for the yeast; too much salt inhibits yeast growth.*

Yield: 12 or more

♣ Cream Cheese Braids

1	cup sour cream	2	eggs, slightly beaten
½	cup sugar, plus 1 teaspoon	½	cup water, warm
1	teaspoon salt	2	(¼-ounce) packages yeast
1	stick margarine, melted	4	cups flour

Heat sour cream moderately. Stir in 1/2 cup sugar, salt and margarine. Cool to lukewarm; add eggs. Dissolve yeast in a mixture of 1/2 cup water and 1 teaspoon sugar. Add to sour cream and egg mixture; mix well. Add flour and stir well. Leave dough in large 3-4 quart mixing bowl (to allow for rising), after scraping sides of bowl with a spatula. Cover with plastic wrap and refrigerate overnight. The next day, divide dough into 4 equal portions. Roll out each portion on a floured board to form a rectangle (1/4-1/2-inch thick). Score the dough (do not cut through) to divide into 3 equal lengths. Make slits in dough perpendicular to scored lines at 1 1/4-inch intervals to form finger-like flaps, cutting only to the scored lines, leaving the center section of dough intact for filling.

FILLING:

2	(8-ounce) packages cream cheese, room temperature	1	egg Dash salt
¾	cup sugar	2	teaspoons almond extract or vanilla
1	egg		

Mix cream cheese, sugar, egg, salt and flavoring until smooth. Put 1/4 of mixture down the center section of each rectangle. Beginning at outer edge of rectangle, fold in the cut strips (or dough flaps) alternately to form a braid and to cover filling. Transfer to a cookie sheet. Cover and let rise about 1 1/2 hours until braid has doubled in volume. Bake at 350° for 12-15 minutes on top oven rack. Make glaze while braids are baking. Remove braids from oven.

GLAZE:

1	(1-pound box powdered sugar	2	teaspoons almond extract or vanilla
		4-6	tablespoons milk

Mix sugar, flavoring and milk until smooth and drizzle over each hot braid. Cool completely on cookie sheet. Warm before serving.

NOTE: *Braids may be frozen up to 2 months in plastic wrap and covered with aluminum foil.*

Yield: 4 braids, each braid serves 6   Ruth Philpott

Breakfast, Brunch & Lunch For a Bunch

Foods to Greet the Morning Sun,
& Mid-Day Meals Just for Fun

Breakfast Canapés

Great for morning bridge or coffee

MINIATURE WAFFLE SANDWICHES:

1   **(10-ounce) package sliced boiled ham**

1   **(6-ounce) package sliced Swiss cheese**

2   **sticks margarine, softened**

1½-2 **tablespoons raspberry or honey Dijon mustard**

3   **tablespoons poppy seeds**

1   **tablespoon Worcestershire sauce**

2   **(8.6-ounce) packages (each containing 8) frozen cinnamon toast mini waffles, thawed, each waffle separated to yield 64 mini waffles**

Cut stacked ham slices into quarters. Cut stacked cheese slices into eighths. Separate ham and cheese slices into 40 pieces of each. Mix margarine, mustard, poppy seeds and Worcestershire. Spread 1 teaspoon of mustard mixture on 32 mini waffles. Top with pieces of ham and cheese and remainder of mini waffles. Bake on a cookie sheet at 350° for 10 minutes. Serve hot.

MINIATURE WAFFLE TREATS:

¼   **cup chopped pecans**

¼   **cup cream cheese**

¼   **cup strawberry jam, or apple or cherry pie filling**

1   **(8.6-ounce) package frozen cinnamon toast mini waffles, separated into 32 pieces, thawed**

Blend pecans, cheese and jam in a small bowl and spread on each mini waffle. Bake on a cookie sheet at 350° for 10 minutes. Serve hot.

NOTE: *Other topping options: Brush waffles with melted butter, spread with creamed honey, maple spread or a mixture of cinnamon and sugar before baking, or spread waffles with egg salad or apple butter and bake as above.*

Yield: 32 sandwiches, 32 treats

♥ Breakfast Pizza

1   **(8-ounce) can crescent rolls**

1   **pound pork sausage**

1½ **cups shredded mozzarella cheese**

1½ **cups shredded cheddar cheese**

4   **eggs, beaten**

¾   **cup milk**
      Salt and pepper

Line a pizza pan with roll dough, pressing seams to seal. In skillet, brown, crumble and drain sausage. Spread sausage and cheeses over dough. Combine eggs, milk, salt and pepper to taste in bowl; mix until smooth. Pour over sausage and cheese. Bake at 375° for 20-25 minutes.

NOTE: *May substitute lowfat sausage and egg substitute.*

Yield: 8 slices

Nancy Penley

Cherry Pecan Sausage

1 (1-pound) roll mild whole hog country sausage

¾ cup cherry preserves
½ cup chopped pecans

In a bowl, combine and knead together the sausage, preserves and pecans. Form into patties or balls. Line a microwave baking sheet with 2 layers of paper towels. Cover with a towel and microwave for about 10 minutes. Serve hot.

Yield: 10 servings

Oatmeal Supreme

2 cups quick cooking oats
2 cups banana nut or lowfat granola with raisins
1 cup brown sugar
4 teaspoons cinnamon sugar

1 cup instant nonfat dry milk powder
Hot water
1 pint heavy whipping cream, milk, or skim milk

Mix oats, granola, brown sugar, cinnamon sugar and milk powder in a bowl. Store in a ziplock bag. When ready to serve, combine equal portions of oatmeal mixture and hot water in a glass microwavable bowl. Cover with plastic wrap. Cook on high for 2-3 minutes until thickened. Stir in cream to desired consistency. Serve hot.

NOTE: *For variety add 1/2 cup chopped pecans or chopped dates to dry mixture, or spoon apple butter, maple syrup or peanut butter and jam or preserves onto cooked cereal and stir to swirl.*

Yield: 8-10 servings

Grand Ham & Jam Cheese Biscuits

1 (17.3-ounce) can of 8 extra-large buttermilk biscuits, baked and split
10 ounces thinly sliced ham

6-8 (⅛-inch thick) slices colby jack cheese, cut into strips
⅔ cup strawberry preserves or jam

Layer ham and cheese on bottom biscuit halves. Spread preserves on inside surface of top halves of biscuits. Sandwich the 2 halves together and place biscuits on a cookie sheet. Cover with aluminum foil. Bake at 300° about 15 minutes. Serve hot.

NOTE: *May substitute peach preserves or SNAZZY JEZEBEL SAUCE. (See Page 416) for strawberry jam.*

Yield: 8 servings

B
L
E
S
S
I
N
G
S

Brunch Egg Casserole

2	cups seasoned croutons	2	cups whole milk or skim milk
1½	cups shredded sharp cheddar cheese	½	teaspoon salt
6	eggs, beaten or 1½ cups egg substitute	½	teaspoon dry mustard
		⅛	teaspoon onion powder
		⅛	teaspoon pepper

In a 10x6x1 3/4-inch baking dish, spread croutons and sprinkle with cheese. In a bowl, combine remaining ingredients; mix well. Pour over croutons. Bake at 350° for 25-30 minutes. Serve hot with salad and hot fruit.

Yield: 8-10 servings

Mary Sue Leonard

♥ Healthy Breakfast Casserole

	Light margarine spread	12	ounces shredded fat free cheddar cheese
9	slices white bread, crusts trimmed	1½	cups egg substitute
1½	teaspoons dry mustard	3	cups skim milk
	Salt	1½	cups crushed corn flakes

Spread margarine over bread. Cut bread into small cubes and place in 9x13-inch casserole prepared with cooking spray. Sprinkle mustard, small amount of salt and cheese over bread. In a bowl, beat eggs and milk slightly. Pour over bread and cheese. Cover and refrigerate overnight. Before baking, top with corn flakes. Place casserole in a pan of hot water in oven. Bake at 350° for 1 hour or until center is set. Serve immediately.

NOTE: *Recipe may be halved and baked in an 8x8-inch dish.*

Yield: 10-12 servings

Sybil P. Baker

Buttermilk Apple Pancakes

¾	cup powdered buttermilk	2	eggs, slightly beaten
2	cups sifted flour	¼	cup margarine, melted
1	teaspoon salt	2	cups water
1½	teaspoon soda	1-2	Granny Smith apples, peeled and grated
1	teaspoon cinnamon		

Sift together, buttermilk, flour, salt, soda and cinnamon. Add eggs, margarine and water. Stir lightly, just to moisten. Fold in apples. Mixture will be thick and lumpy. Spoon onto prepared griddle. Flip pancakes over when bubbles appear in center and edges are dry. Cook until lightly browned on both sides.

NOTE: *For plain BUTTERMILK PANCAKES, apples and cinnamon may be omitted.*

Yield: 10-15 pancakes

Lynn Bertram

Make Ahead Breakfast Strata

Great for Christmas morning

6	slices bread, crust removed, cubed	2	cups milk
1	pound pork or turkey sausage or diced canned ham	1	teaspoon salt
		1	teaspoon dry mustard
1	cup shredded cheese		Chopped green or red pepper (optional)
6	eggs		Chopped onions (optional)

Line a 9x13-inch baking dish with bread. Brown, crumble and drain sausage. Layer meat over bread. Next, layer cheese. Beat together eggs, milk, salt, mustard and add peppers and onions, if desired. Pour over cheese. Refrigerate overnight. Bake at 350° for 45 minutes. Serve hot.

NOTE: *Great served with baked apples and toast or bagels.*

Yield: 6-8 servings   Jamie Kimmer

Breakfast Granola Brownies

1	(18.25-ounce) package caramel cake mix	¼	cup corn syrup
2	eggs	½	cup honey
4	cups banana nut granola	½	cup peanut butter chips
½	cup crunchy peanut butter	¼	cup wheat germ

In a mixing bowl, combine cake mix, eggs, 3 cups of the granola, peanut butter, corn syrup, honey and peanut butter chips; blend well. Mixture will be stiff. With a spatula, spread mixture into a greased 10 1/2x15 1/2-inch pan. Sprinkle wheat germ and 1 cup granola over top of mixture and press into batter with finger tips. Bake at 350° for 25 minutes. When cool, cut into bars.

Yield: 50 bars

Cinnamon Syrup

1	cup light corn syrup	1	cup evaporated milk
2	cups sugar	1	teaspoon vanilla
½	cup water	1	teaspoon maple extract
2-3	teaspoons cinnamon sugar		

In medium saucepan, mix syrup, sugar, water and cinnamon sugar. Bring to a boil over medium heat; stir constantly. Boil 2 more minutes. Cool 5 minutes. Stir in milk and flavorings. Serve warm on pancakes or cold as dessert sauce.

Yield: 3 cups

♥ Spinach Omelet

FILLING:

1	(10-ounce) package frozen chopped spinach
½	cup chopped onion
¼	teaspoon salt
	Pepper
1	tablespoon margarine
⅛	teaspoon cinnamon

⅛	teaspoon nutmeg
1	(4-ounce) can mushrooms, stems and pieces, drained
⅔	cups firmly packed shredded Monterey Jack or Swiss cheese

Combine spinach, onion, salt, pepper, margarine, cinnamon and nutmeg in a microwave safe dish. Cook in microwave on high for 4 minutes. Stir and cook 4-5 more minutes. Drain; stir in mushrooms and cheese. Set aside.

OMELET:

6	eggs or 1½ cups egg substitute

	Salt and pepper
1	tablespoon butter

Beat together eggs, salt and pepper. In heavy 12-inch skillet over moderate heat, melt butter and coat sides thoroughly. Quickly pour egg mixture into skillet, sliding skillet back and forth rapidly over heat continuously, while spreading eggs over bottom of skillet as they thicken. Pour filling mixture over eggs; let stand over heat a few seconds to lightly brown bottom of omelet. Tilt skillet; run fork under edge of omelet, then jerk skillet sharply to loosen eggs from bottom of skillet. Fold 1/2 of omelet over onto other 1/2 using a spatula or fork.

SAUCE:

3	tablespoons fat free sour cream
1	teaspoon mayonnaise

½	teaspoon hot pepper sauce or Dijon mustard

Blend sour cream, mayonnaise, and hot pepper sauce or mustard well. Heat in microwave for 1 minute on high. Top hot omelet with sauce.

Yield: 2-4 servings

Joe Curtis

Easy Banana Pancakes
Dad's Saturday morning breakfast

2	bananas, mashed
2	cups all-purpose baking mix
1	cup milk

2	eggs
	Maple syrup or fruit topping

Mix all ingredients except syrup until blended. Pour 1/4 cupfuls of batter onto hot griddle. Cook until edges are dry. Turn; cook until golden. Serve with topping.

Yield: 15 pancakes

Rick Lewis

Green Chiles Breakfast Pie

2	cups cooked brown rice	2	tablespoons chopped pimento
1	(4-ounce) can chopped green chiles, drained	8	eggs
1	cup grated Monterey Jack cheese	1	teaspoon salt
1	cup grated sharp cheddar cheese		Garlic powder
			Lemon pepper
2	tablespoons chopped ripe olives		Worcestershire sauce

Combine rice, chiles, cheeses, olives and pimento in large bowl. Spray 9x13-inch casserole dish with nonstick cooking spray and press mixture into bottom and sides to form a crust. Beat eggs with your choice of seasoning ingredients listed, to taste. Pour over crust. Bake at 350° for 30 minutes or until set. Serve immediately.

NOTE: *May use the rice which comes in boiling bags. Crust may be made ahead and refrigerated.*

Yield: 6 servings   Luise Palmer

Eggs Isenhour for Two
Great for Sunday Brunch

2	tablespoons butter	2	English muffins, split
1½	tablespoons flour	4	eggs
¾	cup milk	1	tablespoon vinegar
½	teaspoon salt	4	slices fresh tomatoes
¼	teaspoon Tabasco sauce	½	cup sharp cheddar cheese, shredded
2	tablespoons sherry		
½	pound cleaned crabmeat, back fin or lump		

Melt butter over low heat in heavy saucepan. Gradually add flour, stirring constantly with whisk until smooth. Gradually add milk, stirring constantly while cooking on very low heat until mixture thickens. Remove from heat. Add salt, Tabasco, sherry and crabmeat. Set aside over a pan of hot water. Toast muffins on a baking sheet under broiler until warm and slightly browned. Poach eggs to desired doneness in salted water to which a tablespoon of vinegar has been added (to reduce the spreading of whites). Leaving muffins on baking sheet, cover each with tomato slice, then egg, followed by crabmeat mixture. Top with cheese; broil until cheese is melted. Do not brown. Serve hot.

Yield: 2 servings   Judy Isenhour

♥ Mint Frittata

2	medium white potatoes	8	eggs, lightly beaten, or
2	tablespoons safflower oil or		2 cups egg substitute
	nonstick vegetable spray	4	tablespoons fresh mint
2	tablespoons unsalted butter,		leaves, chopped
	melted	½	teaspoon salt
			Pepper

Boil potatoes until medium tender; dice into medium size chunks. Grease the bottom of a large ovenproof skillet with oil or nonstick spray. Brush melted butter around sides of pan to prevent frittata from sticking as it cooks. In same pan, sauté potatoes on moderate high heat until lightly brown. Preheat oven broiler. In a bowl, stir eggs, mint, salt and pepper together. Pour egg mixture into skillet. Stir slightly until mixture begins to set. Place under broiler until it puffs through and is barely brown. Run a knife around inside edge of skillet and flip frittata onto plate. Serve at once.

Yield: 4 servings   Linda Presutti

Zucchini & Cheese Omelet

3	zucchini squash (about 1¼ pounds), washed, stemmed, cut into ½-inch slices	Salt and pepper
		1 tablespoon butter
1	cup water	1 cup shredded mozzarella, or grated reduced fat sharp cheddar cheese
3	tablespoons salad oil	
5	eggs, well beaten	1 tablespoon Parmesan cheese

Preheat oven to 350⁰. Place zucchini into ovenproof frying pan. Add water, oil and salt; simmer about 15 minutes. Pour off liquid. In a bowl, beat eggs well, adding salt and pepper to taste. Dot zucchini with butter, keeping heat on low. When butter is melted, add eggs and cook on low until the eggs are slightly firm around the edges, but the top is still uncooked. Spread mozzarella (or cheddar) on top and place pan in oven and bake for about 10 minutes. Omelet will still not be done. Remove from oven, sprinkle with Parmesan, and place under oven broiler for about 5 minutes. Remove from oven and cool about 5 minutes. Cut into wedges to serve.

NOTE: *You may also add onions, green or red pepper, or mushrooms. Makes a great leftover when reheated in the microwave. This recipe came from Mrs. William Chapman Crawford (Arline), a noted Salisbury cook.*

Yield: 4-6 servings   Jane Gamewell

Overnight French Toast
Great holiday brunch treat

GLAZE:

1¼	cups brown sugar	1	(12-ounce) container
½	cup butter or margarine		cranberry-orange or
2	tablespoons light corn syrup		raspberry crushed fruit
	or honey		Nonstick cooking spray

Spray a 9x13-inch baking dish with nonstick spray; set aside. Combine sugar, butter and corn syrup in a saucepan. Bring to a boil, stirring to prevent sticking. Reduce heat to low and simmer several minutes. Stir in crushed fruit and pour the fruit glaze into prepared pan. Set aside.

EGG MIXTURE:

1	cup milk	1	teaspoon vanilla
6	eggs or 1½ cups	1	teaspoon salt
	egg substitute		

Beat egg mixture in bowl with electric mixer until well blended. Set aside.

FILLING AND BREAD:

1	(6-ounce) package	1	(16-ounce) loaf French bread,
	cream cheese (may use		cut into 1-inch slices
	reduced fat), softened		(about 16 slices)
⅓	cup chopped pecans		Maple syrup, optional

Blend cheese and nuts in a small mixing bowl. Spread 1 tablespoon mixture on 1 side of each slice of bread. Stack each slice vertically, top crust down, in 2 rows on top of glaze in baking dish. Pour egg mixture over top of bread. Cover with foil; refrigerate overnight. Preheat oven to 350° 1 1/2 hours before serving. Bake covered for 1 hour or until set. Let stand 5-10 minutes. For a nice presentation, invert onto a large serving platter, or serve from baking dish. Spoon on remaining glaze over toast. Serve hot with maple syrup, if desired.

Yield: 16 servings

Pecan Syrup with Apples

3	tablespoons butter or	½	teaspoon cinnamon sugar
	margarine, melted	⅛	teaspoon salt
¼	cup chopped pecans	2	cups thinly sliced peeled
1	cup maple syrup		apples

In medium saucepan, sauté nuts until brown; remove nuts. Add syrup, cinnamon sugar and apples to butter. Cover, simmer slowly for 10 minutes. Remove cover; simmer 5 minutes. Remove from heat; add nuts. Serve with pancakes.

Yield: 6 servings

♥ Omelet in a Bag
Great scout recipe!

2	**eggs**
	Salt and pepper
⅛	**cup diced ham**
⅛	**cup shredded cheddar cheese**
1	**ziplock freezer bag**

Break eggs into plastic bag. Add salt, pepper, ham and cheese. Holding bag, crunch together the top. Squeeze and knead the bag to mix ingredients in the bottom. To cook, seal bag and lower it into a pot of boiling water for 2 minutes, or longer depending on individual preference for doneness. Remove bag from pot; empty onto serving plate or eat from bag.

NOTE: *Add or substitute other fillings such as mushrooms, onions, cooked sausage, etc.*

Yield: 1 serving   Girl Scouts Junior Troop 24
Elizabeth Cook, Leader

Turkey Waldorf Salad

6	**cups turkey or chicken, cooked and cubed**
2	**Granny Smith apples with skin, cored and cubed**
1	**cup pineapple bits, drained**
4	**celery stalks, sliced**
½	**cup walnuts**
½	**tablespoon mayonnaise**
½	**cup whipping cream**
½	**teaspoon salt**
	Lettuce leaves
	Tomatoes, cut into wedges

Combine turkey, apple, pineapple, celery and nuts. Set aside. Mix mayonnaise, cream and salt; combine with chicken mixture. Serve on lettuce leaves with tomato wedges.

Yield: 4 servings   Claudia Sellers

Cashew Chicken Salad
Mild, light and fresh

6	**large chicken breasts, cooked and cut into 1-inch cubes**
4	**celery stalks, thinly sliced**
1	**small onion, finely chopped**
	Salt
½	**pint heavy whipping cream**
¼	**cup mayonnaise**
6	**ounces cashew halves**

Combine chicken, celery, onion and salt to taste; set aside. Whip cream until stiff; stir in mayonnaise. Add chicken mixture to cream mixture; mix well. Chill 1 hour or until ready to serve. Sprinkle with cashews just before serving.

Yield: 4 servings   Andrea Bullock

Candied Cinnamon Bacon

10-12	slices thin-sliced brown sugar Virginia cured bacon	6	teaspoons honey Dijon mustard
		1	cup light brown sugar
		3	teaspoons ground cinnamon

Preheat oven to 350°. Cut each bacon strip into thirds; spread 1 side of each bacon piece with mustard. In small bowl, mix sugar and cinnamon. Dip mustard coated side of bacon in the sugar mixture, to coat. Arrange bacon pieces in a single layer on a broiler pan rack. Bake for 25-30 minutes, until crisp and brown. Drain on paper towels. Serve at room temperature for brunch or as an appetizer.

NOTE: *For a SEASONED BACON variety, omit mustard, sugar and cinnamon; coat bacon with Parmesan cheese, coarse black pepper, ground pecans, or seasoned coating mix for pork or Italian bread crumbs.*

Yield: 30-36 pieces

Thai Beef Salad

Hot, cool, sweet, and tart, a unique blend of flavors

1	large head Boston lettuce, washed and separated	2	scallions, thinly sliced
1	(8-ounce) package rice stick noodles, soaked in hot water, drained	1	(16-ounce) beef flank steak or tenderloin, broiled medium rare, sliced thin
1	cucumber, peeled, seeded, sliced thin	½	cup chopped roasted peanuts
1	(8-ounce) package fresh bean sprouts		Fresh mint, cilantro sprigs for garnish

Line 6 dinner plates with lettuce leaves. Mound equal portions of noodles in center of lettuce leaves and arrange the cucumbers, sprouts and scallions around the edges. Pile steak slices in center and top with peanuts.

DRESSING:

¼	cup rice vinegar	1	tablespoon sugar
½	cup fish sauce or nam pla	1	finely minced garlic clove
	Juice of 1 fresh lime	½	cup finely grated carrot
1	teaspoon crushed red pepper		

Combine all ingredients in a jar. Cover with lid and shake to blend. Spoon dressing over salad and garnish with mint or cilantro before serving.

NOTE: *Nam pla, a fish sauce popular in Thailand, may be found in Asian specialty food shops. This luncheon specialty has been served at the Waterworks Visual Arts Center in Salisbury, North Carolina.*

Yield: 6 servings   Joan K. Ivan

B
L
E
S
S
I
N
G
S

Baked Chicken Sandwiches

16 slices white bread, crust
    trimmed
1 (4-ounce) stick margarine
¼ pound fresh mushrooms
2 cups diced, cooked chicken
    breast
3 hard cooked eggs, chopped

⅓ cup ripe olives, chopped
¾ cup mayonnaise
2 tablespoons onion, chopped
1 cup cream of chicken soup
1 cup sour cream
2 tablespoons sherry
    Paprika

Butter both sides of bread. Place 8 slices in 9x13-inch pan. Sauté mush-rooms in 2 tablespoons of the margarine. Cover bread with mushrooms, chicken, eggs, olives, mayonnaise and onions. Arrange remaining bread slices on top of mixture. Combine soup, sour cream and sherry; pour over sandwiches. Sprinkle with paprika. Bake at 325° for 30 minutes. Serve hot.

Yield: 8 servings

George Anna Glenn

Holiday Ham & Cheese Strata

12 slices white bread
¾ pound sharp cheese, sliced
1 (16-ounce) package frozen
    chopped broccoli, cooked
    and drained
2 cups diced cooked ham
3½ cups milk

2 tablespoons chopped Vidalia
    onions or instant minced onion
    rehydrated with ice water
½ teaspoon salt
¼ teaspoon dry mustard
    Shredded cheddar cheese for
    topping

Using the "cookie cutter" of the season, cut out and set aside 12 centers from bread slices. Place remains of bread in buttered 9x13x2-inch Pyrex dish. Top bread with sliced cheese; layer on broccoli and ham. Decorate top with bread cut-outs. Combine remaining ingredients and carefully pour over dish. Refrigerate 6 hours or overnight. Bake uncovered at 325° for 55 minutes or until done. Sprinkle with cheese during the last 5 minutes of baking.

Yield: 12 servings

Lana Hix Reavis

Sausage Stuffed Apples

10 Golden Delicious apples,
    seeded, cored

1 pound country pork sausage
2 cups apple cider

Cut slice from apple bottoms. With melon baller, scoop out apple, leaving a 3/4 inch shell; chop apple pieces; combine with sausage; stuff shells with mixture. Place in 9x13 baking dish. Pour cider on apples. Bake at 375° 40-50 minutes until apples are fork tender, baste often. Serve warm.

Yield: 10 servings

Chile Relleño Casserole

1	(7-ounce) can whole green chiles, drained	2	eggs
1	cup grated cheddar cheese	2	tablespoons flour
8	ounces plain yogurt or light sour cream	½	teaspoon chili powder
		⅛	teaspoon ground cumin
		½	cup chili salsa

Split chiles and open flat. Cover bottom of a greased 1-quart dish with 1/2 the chiles. Sprinkle with 1/2 the cheese. Repeat for a second layer. Beat together yogurt, eggs, flour, chili powder and cumin until smooth. Pour over chili-cheese layers. Bake at 350° for 30 minutes or until set. Pour salsa over casserole and bake 15 more minutes.

Yield: 4 servings   Laura Koontz

Cheddar Baked English Muffins

1	(2¼-ounce) can black olives, chopped	½	teaspoon curry powder
1½	cups sharp cheddar cheese, grated	1	clove garlic, minced or ½ teaspoon garlic powder
½	cup mayonnaise	⅛	teaspoon pepper
½	cup scallions, chopped	8	English muffins, split

Preheat oven to 450°. Combine all ingredients, except English muffins in medium bowl. May be prepared a day ahead, to this point. Cover and refrigerate. Spread mixture on English muffins and bake 10 minutes. Serve hot.

Yield: 8 servings   Margaret Almeida

Sue's Crab Muffins

Delicious luncheon dish or appetizer

	Juice of lemon wedge	8	ounces soft processed American cheese
1	(6½-ounce) can white crabmeat, drained	1½	teaspoons mayonnaise
1	stick margarine	½	teaspoon garlic salt
		6	English muffins, split in half

Squeeze lemon juice over crabmeat. Soften margarine and cheese at room temperature and mix with mayonnaise, garlic salt and crab. Spread mixture on muffin halves. Bake at 350° for 10 minutes then place under broiler until bubbly. Serve muffin halves hot, or cut each half into 4 pieces to make appetizers.

Yield: 12 lunch servings, or   Jean Messer Williams
      48 appetizers

Mediterranean Chicken Salad

1	whole chicken	2	tablespoons drained capers
1	medium onion, peeled and quartered	¾	cup imported black olives (optional)
1	bay leaf	⅓	cup extra virgin olive oil
2	carrots, peeled	¼	cup fresh lemon juice
3	cups fresh cut green beans	¾	teaspoon dried oregano
3	medium tomatoes, cut in wedges	¾	teaspoon dried basil
			Salt and pepper

Place chicken, onion, bay leaf, carrots and green beans in 5 cups of water in a large pot. Cover, bring to a boil; simmer on low heat for 50 minutes. Cool chicken. Remove chicken and green beans from broth. (Strain broth and save for soup after discarding onion, bay leaf and carrots.) Remove meat from bone; tear into pieces. Combine chicken with green beans, tomatoes, capers and olives. Toss with olive oil, lemon juice, oregano and basil. Chill.

NOTE: *Makes a great picnic or lunch dish. Even better after flavors blend in refrigerator for several hours.*

Yield: 6-8 servings   Tessa Sansovich

Spinach-Sausage Pie

FILLING:

1	pound Italian sausage, cooked until browned, crumbled	1	(8-ounce) can tomato sauce
1	(10-ounce) package frozen chopped spinach, thawed and drained	1	(4-ounce) can sliced mushrooms, drained
		⅓	cup fine, dry seasoned bread crumbs
		1	(2-ounce) jar pimento, drained

Combine all ingredients and set aside.

CRUST:

1	(16-ounce) loaf frozen whole wheat or rye bread dough, thawed	1	tablespoon melted butter

On a lightly floured surface, roll 2/3 of dough into an 11-inch circle. Place in greased 9-inch springform pan, patting dough 1 inch up on the sides of pan. Add filling. On the floured surface, roll remaining dough into a 10-inch circle. Cut into 10 or 12 equal wedges. Arrange wedges on top of filling, slightly overlapping edges and sealing ends to the bottom crust along edge of pan. Brush top with butter. Bake at 375° for 30-35 minutes or until crust is golden brown. Serve hot.

Yield: 6-8 slices   Amy Harrell Pullen

Salmon Quiche

1	small onion, minced
¼	cup butter or margarine
¼	cup flour
1	teaspoon salt
¼	teaspoon pepper
1	tablespoon lemon juice
1	(15-ounce) can red salmon, drained, boned and flaked, juices reserved, plus water
1	cup evaporated milk
2	eggs, slightly beaten
½	teaspoon dill weed
1	cup shredded cheddar or Monterey Jack cheese
1	cup frozen or cooked peas (optional)
1	(9-inch) frozen deep dish pie shell, thawed

Sauté onion in butter 2-3 minutes. Gradually blend in flour, salt and pepper, stirring constantly. Add lemon juice. Add enough water to reserved salmon juice to make 1 cup of liquid. Stir in milk. Gradually stir liquid mixture into onions. Cook, stirring until thickened. Add salmon, eggs, dill weed, cheese and peas, mixing well. Pour mixture into pie shell and bake at 400° for 30 minutes or until center is set. Let cool for 10 minutes before slicing to serve.

Yield: 6 servings   Phyllis M. Larson

Chicken & Pasta Salad

6	ounces rotini or other pasta twists
⅛	cup sesame seeds
½	cup oil
⅓	cup soy sauce
⅓	cup white wine vinegar
2	tablespoons sugar
½	teaspoon salt
¼	teaspoon pepper
3	cups chopped, cooked chicken, chilled
8	cups lightly packed and torn spinach leaves, rinsed and drained

Cook pasta until barely tender. Drain, rinse with cold water, drain again. Turn into a large bowl. In small frying pan, combine sesame seeds and 1/4 cup oil. Cook over medium low heat 2 minutes, stirring until seeds are golden. Cool. Combine sesame seeds, the remaining 1/4 cup oil, soy sauce, vinegar, sugar, salt and pepper. Pour over cooked pasta. Add chicken; toss gently. Cover; chill for at least 6 hours. Serve over spinach along with crunchy bread sticks.

Yield: 8 servings   Barbara Perry

Homemade Syrup

1	(1-pound) box light brown sugar
1	cup water
1	teaspoon maple flavoring

In pan, boil sugar and water 5 minutes to dissolve. Add flavoring. Serve warm.

Yield: 2 cups

Hot & Crunchy Chicken Salad

4	cups cooked, diced chicken	2	cups diced celery
4	hard boiled eggs, chopped	3	cups cooked rice
2	cups mayonnaise	½	cup slivered almonds
2	teaspoons Accent	2	(10½-ounce) cans cream of
4	tablespoons lemon juice		chicken soup
1	(2-ounce) jar pimento, chopped, drained	1	cup crushed potato chips

Combine all ingredients except potato chips. Pour into an ungreased 3-quart or 9x12-inch glass casserole dish. Top with crushed potato chips. Bake at 350° for 30 minutes, uncovered. May prepare ahead (omitting chips) and freeze. To serve, thaw, top with chips; bake as above.

Yield: 12 servings   Jan Broaddus Lewis

Crab Quiche

3	eggs, slightly beaten	1	(6½-ounce) can crabmeat, drained and flaked
1	cup sour cream	1	(3½-ounce) can French fried onion rings
½	teaspoon Worcestershire sauce	1	(9-inch) pie shell, baked
¾	teaspoon salt		
1	cup shredded Swiss cheese		

Combine all filling ingredients and pour into pie shell. Bake at 300° for 45-50 minutes. Serve hot.

Yield: 6 servings   Ginny Williamson

Spinach Pie

1	(10-ounce) package frozen chopped spinach, thawed and drained	3	eggs, lightly beaten
⅓	cup bacon bits	⅛	teaspoon salt
1	(15-ounce) container ricotta cheese	⅛	teaspoon pepper
1	cup shredded Swiss cheese	⅛	teaspoon nutmeg
1	cup grated Parmesan cheese	⅛	teaspoon sugar
1½	tablespoons minced onion	⅛	teaspoon hot pepper sauce
		⅛	teaspoon Worcestershire sauce
		1	(9-inch) pie shell, baked

Mix all filling ingredients and pour into pie shell. Bake at 350° for 30 minutes or until done and the center of pie is hot and set. Serve hot.

Yield: 6-8 servings   Carolyn McDonald

Tarragon Chicken Salad
Delicious! Everyone loves it!

3	pounds boneless chicken breasts	1	tablespoon crumbled, dried tarragon
1	cup heavy cream		Salt and pepper
2	celery ribs, sliced into 1-inch long pieces	½	cup sour cream
½	cup walnut or pecan pieces	½	cup mayonnaise

Arrange chicken breasts in single layer in pan; cover with cream. Bake in preheated 350° oven 20-25 minutes. Remove from oven; cool. Discard cream; shred chicken into bite-sized pieces. Add celery, nuts, tarragon, and salt and pepper to taste. Whisk sour cream and mayonnaise together; pour over chicken mixture. Refrigerate for several hours before serving.

Yield: 8 servings   Dot Gregory

Overnight Layered Chicken Salad

6	cups iceberg lettuce, shredded	¼	pound fresh or frozen snow peas, thawed and patted dry
¼	pound bean sprouts		
1	(5.8-ounce) can sliced water chestnuts, drained	2	cups mayonnaise
		1	teaspoon curry power
⅓	cup thinly sliced green onion	¾	tablespoon sugar
1	medium cucumber, thinly sliced	⅓	teaspoon ground ginger
4	cups cooked chicken, cut into 2-inch strips	½	cup peanuts
		16	cherry tomatoes, halved

In large bowl, layer lettuce, bean sprouts, water chestnuts, onions, cucumbers and chicken. Top with snow peas. In bowl mix mayonnaise, curry, sugar and ginger; spread over salad mixture, sealing edges. Cover and refrigerate overnight. To serve, garnish with peanuts, tomatoes; scoop out layered portions of salad and dressing ingredients.

Yield: 8 servings   Mary Ellen Turner

Salsa Baked Eggs

8	eggs	½	cup chunky salsa
3	tablespoons cream or milk		Shredded cheese
	Salt & pepper		

Break eggs into 8 greased baking cups; top evenly with cream. Season to taste. Top with salsa and cheese. Bake at 375° 15 minutes until set.

Yield: 8 servings

Skier's Cheese Souffle

8	slices country style white or whole grain bread, trimmed and cut into 1-inch squares	½	pound cheddar cheese, grated or shredded
½	pound bacon, fried very crisp, crumbled	6	eggs, beaten
		3	cups milk (whole, not skim), room temperature
		⅔	teaspoon salt

Lightly grease an 8x12-inch Pyrex dish or ovenproof soufflé dish. Layer bread on the bottom; and cover evenly with bacon and cheese. In a mixing bowl, beat eggs, milk and salt; and pour over bread, bacon and cheese. Cover; refrigerate overnight. When ready to serve, preheat oven to 325°. Uncover casserole; bake 45 minutes or until firm. Cut into squares to serve.

NOTE: *This is from an old friend and journalistic colleague, Heidi Martin, an editor and correspondent for the German fashion magazine, BURDA.*

Yield: Serves 4-6   — Ben Martin

Shrimp Tomato Aspic

4	envelopes unflavored gelatin	3	tablespoons bottled horseradish
¾	cup cold water		
1	(46-ounce) can tomato juice	2	cups cooked, small or chopped shrimp
3	tablespoons vinegar		Cold lettuce leaves
3	tablespoons grated onion		Mayonnaise
1	tablespoon sugar		Chopped olives (optional)
1	tablespoon salt		Chopped celery (optional)
¼	teaspoon cayenne pepper		

Soften gelatin in cold water. Heat juice, vinegar, onion, sugar, salt and cayenne pepper to boil. Simmer a few minutes. Add softened gelatin to hot juice; stir until dissolved. Add horseradish and shrimp. Mix well and cool. Pour into molds with equal quantities of shrimp in each mold. Refrigerate until firm. Unmold and serve on lettuce with mayonnaise.

NOTE: *For TOMATO ASPIC, omit shrimp and horseradish; add olives and celery.*

Yield: 12 servings   Jo Krider

Quick Bagels & Lox

½	cup cream cheese with salmon	¼	cup cream cheese and chives
2-4	teaspoons of lemon juice	6	bagels, halved, toasted

Combine cheeses and lemon juice to taste in bowl. Spread mixture on bagels.

Yield: 6 servings

Soups, Stews
&
Super Sandwiches

Meals by the Potful
& Quick Go-Betweens

❤ Blueberry Soup

5	cups orange juice	2	tablespoons cornstarch
2	cups fresh or frozen blueberries	2	tablespoons water
		1	teaspoon grated orange rind
3	tablespoons honey		Sour cream (optional)
¼	teaspoon cinnamon		Yogurt (optional)

Combine orange juice, blueberries, honey and cinnamon; bring to a boil in a 3-quart saucepan. Dissolve cornstarch in water and add to mixture to thicken. Remove from heat; add orange rind. Chill and serve with dollops of sour cream or yogurt.

NOTE: *It's great in the summertime with sandwiches. Try it for breakfast!*

Yield: 8 servings   Nell Bullard

❤ Chilled Peach Soup
Wonderful on a hot summer day!

1	quart frozen peaches or 8 fresh peaches, peeled, chopped and sprinkled with sugar, plus peach slices for garnish	2	pints sour cream or low fat sour cream or yogurt
		½	cup lemon juice
		½	cup orange juice
		½	cup pineapple juice
		¼-½	cup sherry (optional)

Blend peaches with sour cream in blender. Add juices and sherry, blending well. Refrigerate. Serve soup well chilled. Garnish with small slices of peaches if desired. Strawberries may be substituted for the peaches.

Yield: 8-10 servings   Anne Crawford

Vichyssoise

6	potatoes, peeled, diced	3	egg yolks
6	leeks, trimmed, sliced	1	cup heavy cream
4	(14½-ounce) cans chicken broth		Salt and pepper
		1	pint sour cream
1	quart milk	¼	cup chopped chives

Place potatoes, leeks and chicken broth in large saucepan. Simmer uncovered for 1 hour or until vegetables are tender. Place mixture in blender and blend until smooth. Stir in milk. In a bowl, beat egg yolks and cream. Pour into soup, stirring constantly over low heat until soup bubbles and thickens slightly. Season to taste. Chill and serve icy cold topped with sour cream and chopped chives.

Yield: 4 quarts   Mary V. Smith

♥ Easy Gazpacho
Wonderful for summer luncheons

1	(15-ounce) can tomato sauce	2-3	drops hot sauce
3	large ripe tomatoes, chopped		Juice of 1 lemon
1	medium onion, chopped	¼	cup bread crumbs
1	clove garlic, pressed	½	teaspoon cumin seed
1	tablespoon olive oil		Garnishes of diced
1	tablespoon vinegar		cucumber, tomato and
1	teaspoon Worcestershire sauce		bell pepper
			Sour cream

In a blender, process all ingredients except garnishes and sour cream. Chill. Serve soup cold; garnish top with diced vegetables and dollops of sour cream.

NOTE: *Great served with ham biscuits and fruit.*

Yield: Serves 5   Babe Nobles (Mrs. Al B.)

Gazpacho

2	medium cucumbers, peeled and coarsely chopped	2	teaspoons garlic, finely chopped
5	medium tomatoes, peeled and coarsely chopped	4	cups French or Italian bread, trimmed and coarsely crumbled
1	large onion, coarsely chopped	4	cups cold water
1	medium green pepper, seeded and coarsely chopped	¼	cup red wine vinegar
		4	teaspoons salt
		4	tablespoons olive oil
		1	tablespoon tomato paste

In large deep bowl, combine cucumbers, tomatoes, onion, green pepper, garlic and bread crumbs. Mix thoroughly. Stir in water, vinegar and salt. Ladle mixtures, about 2 cups at a time, into blender and process at high speed for 1 minute, until pureed. Pour puree into bowl and with whisk, beat in olive oil and tomato paste. Cover with plastic wrap; refrigerate at least 2 hours. Chill well. Before serving, whisk soup to blend. Serve cold in bowls.

GARNISHES:

1	cup (¼-inch) bread cubes, trimmed	½	cup cucumbers, peeled and finely chopped
½	cup onions, finely chopped	½	cup green peppers, finely chopped

Serve each garnish ingredient in separate bowls, as topping for gazpacho.

NOTE: *Soup may be prepared ahead and frozen, or may be kept covered in refrigerator for 3-4 days. Flavor is enhanced as it ages.*

Yield: 6-8 servings   Lillian Smith

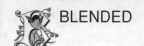

Dill & Cucumber Soup

2	English cucumbers, peeled, cut into 1-inch lengths	1	tablespoon dried dill weed
3	cups plain yogurt		Salt and pepper
1	cup chicken stock		Smoked salmon, finely chopped for garnish
¼	cup liquid honey		

In food processor, process 1/2 of cucumber pieces. Add 1/2 of yogurt, 1/2 of chicken stock, 1/2 of honey and 1/2 of dill weed. Process until very smooth. Transfer to bowl. Process remaining cucumbers, yogurt, stock, honey and dill weed and add to bowl, mixing well. Season to taste. Refrigerate for a minimum of 3 hours. Garnish with smoked salmon before serving. Serve cold.

Yield: 6 servings   Brenda Wood

Cabbage & Beef Soup
Great with corn muffins

1	pound lean ground beef	1	(28-ounce) tomato canful of water
½	teaspoon garlic salt		
¼	teaspoon garlic powder	1	(16-ounce) can kidney beans, drained
¼	teaspoon pepper		
2	stalks celery, chopped	½	medium head cabbage, chopped
4	beef bouillon cubes		
1	(28-ounce) can tomatoes, chopped		

In large Dutch oven, brown beef until done. Add other ingredients; bring to a boil. Reduce heat, cover; simmer 1 hour. Serve hot. Freezes well.

Yield: 3 quarts   Suzanne Brewer

Mushroom & Clam Bisque

½	pound chopped mushrooms	¾	cup cream
2	tablespoons butter		Salt and pepper
2	tablespoons flour		Parsley
2½	cups clam broth with minced clams		

Sauté mushrooms in butter. Gradually add in flour and stir until blended. Slowly stir in broth and clams. Simmer for 5 minutes; remove from heat. Add cream and heat thoroughly. Do not boil. Salt and pepper to taste. Garnish with parsley.

Yield: 3 cups   Dottie Abramowski

112

Oklahoma Soup

1	pound lean ground beef	1	(3-ounce) can chopped green chiles, undrained
3	(15-ounce) cans stewed tomatoes	1	(10-ounce) can beef consommé
1	(15-ounce) can kidney beans, undrained	1	(1-ounce) package taco seasoning
1	(15-ounce) can pinto beans, undrained	1	(0.4-ounce) envelope ranch dressing mix

Brown ground beef. Stir in tomatoes, beans, chiles, consommé, taco seasoning and dressing mix. Bring to a boil and simmer for approximately 1 hour.

NOTE: *Good hearty soup to serve with salad and garlic bread. May be prepared ahead and frozen.*

Yield: 8-10 servings   Helen "Pete" Miller Dare

Clam Chowder

½	pound streak of lean or salt pork	3	(6½-ounce) cans minced clams
2	(16-ounce) cans whole peeled tomatoes	4	potatoes, peeled, cubed
2	(16-ounce) cans water	2	whole onions, chopped
			Pepper

Cut streak of lean salt pork into small cubes and slowly fry in heavy skillet until crisp and brown. Drain well. Pour tomatoes and water into soup pot, add streak of lean and minced clams. Add potatoes and onions and pepper to taste. Cook on low heat until potatoes and onions are soft.

Yield: 6 servings   Betty Little

♥ Cabbage Soup

1	(46-ounce) can tomato juice	1	small head cabbage, shredded
4	beef bouillon cubes	2	tablespoons dried onion flakes
4	ribs celery, chopped		
¼	teaspoon garlic powder	¼	teaspoon pepper
	Dash chili powder	¾	pound cooked ground beef (optional)
2	teaspoons sugar		
½	cup water		

Combine all ingredients. Simmer for 1 hour. Serve hot. Freezes well.

Yield: Serves 8   Donna Yale

Sausage Soup

1	pound sausage, cooked and drained	1	(10-ounce) package frozen corn
2	(10¾-ounce) cans cream of potato soup	2	cups water
1	(10¾-ounce) can cream of celery soup		Salt and pepper

Combine sausage, soups, corn, and water and season to taste. Cook on low in a crock pot for 4 hours, stirring occasionally. Serve hot.

Yield: 4-6 servings   Kelley Rohrer

Aunt Barbara's Split Pea Soup

1	large onion, peeled	2	ribs celery
8	whole cloves	2	bay leaves
1	pound green split peas	1	large clove garlic
1	meaty ham bone	2	quarts water
2	carrots		Salt

Pierce the onion and insert 8 cloves. Bring all ingredients except salt, to a boil and simmer until very thick, about 1-2 hours. Remove ham bone, celery, carrots, onion with cloves, bay leaves and garlic. Strain soup. Salt to taste. Freezes well.

Yield: 4-5 servings   Julie Guion Steele

Onion Soup

5	cups thinly sliced onions	1	quart boiling water
4	tablespoons butter	1	quart beef bouillon
1	tablespoon olive oil	½	cup dry white wine or white vermouth
1	teaspoon salt		Salt and pepper
¼	teaspoon sugar		Parmesan cheese, grated
4	tablespoons flour		

Cook onions slowly in butter and oil in covered saucepan for 15 minutes. Uncover; raise heat to moderate and stir in salt and sugar. Cook for about 30 minutes, stirring often, until the onions have turned golden brown. Slowly sprinkle in flour and stir for 3 minutes. Remove saucepan from heat and blend in boiling liquids. Add wine and season to taste. Simmer 30 minutes or more, skimming surface as needed. Sprinkle with grated Parmesan cheese before serving.

Yield: 8-10 servings   Liz Rankin

♥ Vegetable Bean Soup

1½	cups elbow macaroni	1	teaspoon salt
3	tablespoons olive oil	½	teaspoon pepper
2	medium carrots, chopped	3	cups water
2	medium celery stalks, chopped	2	(16-ounce) cans white kidney beans, drained
1	medium onion, chopped	1	(15¼-19-ounce) can red kidney beans, drained
1	(14½-16-ounce) can tomatoes, with liquid	1	(10-ounce) package frozen chopped spinach
1	(13¾-14½-ounce) can chicken broth		Grated Parmesan cheese

Prepare macaroni according to package directions, omitting salt. Drain. In a 5-quart Dutch oven in hot olive oil, sauté carrots, celery and onions until tender. Add tomatoes with liquid, broth, salt, pepper and water. Heat to boiling; simmer uncovered 10 minutes. Mash one can of beans in small bowl. To soup mixture, add mashed beans and whole beans, macaroni and frozen spinach. Cook over medium-high heat until all ingredients are thoroughly heated. If necessary, add water to thin soup. Serve with grated Parmesan cheese.

NOTE: *This is a delicious lowfat soup, our favorite. Leftovers keep well in refrigerator.*

Yield: 6-8 servings   Joan Green

Gourmet Burger Vegetable Soup

½	cup chopped onion	1	(16-ounce) bag frozen mixed vegetables
2	tablespoons vegetable oil	1	(1-ounce) package dried onion soup mix
1½	pound ground chuck		
2	(16-20-ounce) cans stewed tomatoes	2	teaspoons sugar
1	(16-ounce) can tomato sauce		Salt and pepper
2	cups water		

Brown onions in frying pan with 2 tablespoons vegetable oil. Add ground chuck and brown. Stir. Place meat and onions in large soup pot. Add tomatoes, tomato sauce, water, vegetables, onion soup mix, sugar and salt and pepper to taste. Simmer about 2 hours. Serve hot.

NOTE: *To thin or thicken soup while simmering, you may add water, stewed tomatoes, lima beans or corn as desired. Good winter soup. Great for lunch served with grilled cheese sandwiches, salad and a simple dessert. Freezes well.*

Yield: 3 quarts   Edith Hinshaw

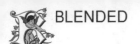

Super Corn Chowder

5   bacon slices
1   medium onion, thinly sliced and separated into rings
2   cups canned whole kernel corn, drained
1   cup cooked potatoes, diced
1   (10¾-ounce) can cream of mushroom soup
2½   cups milk
1   teaspoon salt
     Butter

Dash of cayenne pepper or ground white pepper
Chopped green onions (optional garnish)
Grated cheddar cheese (optional garnish)
Chopped fresh mushrooms (optional garnish)
Crisp croutons (optional garnish)

In a large skillet, cook bacon until crisp. Remove bacon from grease and drain on paper towels. Pour off all but 3 tablespoons of the drippings. Add onion rings and cook until translucent. Add remaining ingredients, except pepper and garnishes. Heat to boiling; reduce heat and simmer 3 minutes. Ladle chowder into serving bowls and crumble bacon on top. Dot each bowl of chowder with a small pat of butter. To season, sprinkle on your choice of cayenne or ground white pepper and garnish as desired.

NOTE: *Small crisp cornbread muffins are a nice accompaniment to serve with chowder.*

Yield: 6 servings   Dee Hopkins

Corn Chowder

½-1   pound potatoes
2   (14½-ounce) cans chicken broth
½   cup finely chopped onion
1   bay leaf
½   teaspoon tarragon
½   teaspoon thyme
1   tablespoon chopped parsley

1   (10-ounce) package frozen corn
½   cup half-and-half
     Salt and freshly ground pepper
     Finely grated cheese for garnish
     Crumbled bacon for garnish

Boil peeled, whole potatoes until tender; drain and cool. Cut into cubes to yield two cups and set aside. In a saucepan, combine broth, onion, bay leaf, tarragon, thyme and parsley; bring to a boil. Reduce heat; simmer 15 minutes. Strain herbs from broth. Add potatoes, corn and half-and-half. Cook until corn is done. Season with salt and pepper to taste. Serve with finely grated cheese and crumbled bacon on top.

Yield: 2 quarts   Kaye Daniel

Sausage Bean Chowder

1	pound pork sausage	1	bay leaf
2	(15-ounce) cans kidney beans	1½	teaspoons seasoned salt
1	(29-ounce) can tomatoes, with juice	½	teaspoon garlic salt
		½	teaspoon thyme
3	cups water	⅛	teaspoon pepper
1	large onion, chopped	1-2	cups diced potatoes
		½	green pepper, chopped

Cook sausage in a skillet until brown. Pour off fat. In large kettle, combine beans, tomatoes, water, onion, bay leaf, seasoned salt, garlic salt, thyme and pepper. Add sausage. Simmer, covered for 1 hour. Add potatoes and green pepper. Cook, covered 15-30 minutes or until potatoes are tender. Remove bay leaf before serving. Serve with a green salad and French bread.

Yield: 8 servings   Helen Whicker

Curried Cream of Chicken Soup

6	tablespoons unsalted butter	6	parsley sprigs
2	cups yellow onions, finely chopped	1	(2½-3-pound) chicken, cut up
		½	cup brown rice
2	carrots, peeled and chopped	1	cup half-and-half
2	tablespoons curry powder	1	(10-ounce) package frozen peas, thawed
5	cups chicken stock (without monosodium glutamate)		Salt and pepper

Melt butter in a pot. Add onions, carrots, curry powder; cook over low heat 25 minutes until vegetables are tender. Add stock, parsley, chicken and rice. Bring to a boil; reduce heat; cover. Cook on low heat 50 minutes. Cool chicken; remove and discard bones, dice chicken; set aside. Strain soup, reserving liquid, transfer solids to bowl of food processor fitted with steel blade. Add 1 cup of cooking liquid; process until smooth. Return soup to pot. Add half-and-half. Stir in 4 cups reserved stock, until soup is desired consistency. Add diced chicken and peas; simmer 15 minutes. Salt and pepper to taste.

Yield: Serves 6   Tessa Sansovich

Sherried Melon Soup

3¼	quarts cantaloupe or honeydew melon, cubed	¼	cup dry sherry
		¼	cup orange juice
¼	cup powdered sugar		Fresh mint for garnish

Process ingredients in blender until smooth; cover, chill 4 hours. Garnish; serve.

Yield: 6-8 servings

Antique Show Soup

2	pounds stew beef, cut into small pieces	1	(16-ounce) can corn
3	(28-ounce) cans tomatoes	1	(1-pound) can butter beans
3	large potatoes, peeled and diced	1	(1-pound) can okra
2	medium onions, chopped	1½	cups diced celery
½	bunch carrots, chopped		Salt and pepper
			V-8 juice or canned tomatoes (optional)

In a large container, cover meat with cold water and let stand in refrigerator overnight. In a large soup pot, bring the beef and water mixture to a boil. Cook gently until meat is tender. Skim off fat and return to a boil. Add tomatoes and potatoes and cook for 30 minutes. Add the remainder of ingredients. Cook, covered for several hours. Add V-8 juice, canned tomatoes, or water if liquid is needed.

Yield: 6 quarts   Sara Ann Spear

Baked Potato Soup
Yummy!

⅔	cup margarine, melted	12	pieces bacon, cooked and crumbled, reserve grease
⅔	cup flour		
6	cups milk	¾	teaspoon salt
3	green onions, chopped	1¼	teaspoons pepper
4	medium baking potatoes, baked	1¼	cups grated cheddar cheese
		8	ounces sour cream

Blend margarine and flour in Dutch oven on low-medium heat. Gradually add milk; stir constantly until thick. Sauté onions in small amount of bacon grease in separate pan. Remove potato pulp from skins; mash. To milk mixture, add salt, pepper, potatoes, onions, cheese and bacon. Stir until hot. Add sour cream; stir until mixed. Thin mixture with milk or water if needed. Serve hot.

Yield: 6-8 servings   Jayne Hubbard

Oyster Stew

1	quart oysters	3-4	slices bacon, cooked, crumbled
1	quart milk		Salt

Place oysters and juice in a large pot and heat until edges of oysters curl. Add milk and bacon and simmer about 30 minutes. Add salt to taste. Serve hot.

Yield: 4 servings   Mary Kay Zigmont

Grandmom Jinnie's Bean Soup

1 pound navy beans
Water
2 packages ham hocks (5 or 6)
2 medium onions, chopped
2 cloves garlic, crushed

1 (10¾-ounce) can cream of tomato soup
2 cups sliced carrots
Salt and pepper

Cover beans with water and soak overnight. Put ham hocks in large pot, cover with water and cook until meat falls off bones. Remove meat from bones. Discard bones and return meat to broth. Add onions and garlic. Drain beans and add to broth, making sure all ingredients are covered; if not, add more water. Add soup, carrots and salt and pepper to taste. Simmer on low heat 1 1/2-2 hours or until beans are done. May be frozen.

Yield: 6 servings

Karen Wood

Low Country She-Crab Soup

2 large onions, finely diced
1 cup clarified butter
2 cups flour
2½ quarts half-and-half
1 quart heavy cream
1½ teaspoons mace

1 cup sherry plus additional for topping (not cooking sherry)
Salt and pepper
1 pound fresh Atlantic Blue crabmeat, picked and cleaned

In a large pot, cook onions in butter until soft. Add flour; reduce heat to low, stirring constantly for 15 minutes. Add milk products and continue stirring. Add mace, sherry, salt and pepper to taste and crabmeat. Simmer for 30 minutes, stirring frequently. Serve hot in bowls; top with a dash of sherry.

NOTE: *This recipe is served at the Sea Captain House in Myrtle Beach, SC.*

Yield: 1 gallon

Swim Team Chili

Everyone loves this topping!

3 pounds lean ground beef
⅓ (2-ounce) bottle onion powder
2 teaspoons garlic powder

1⅓ tablespoons chili powder
¾ (14-ounce) bottle ketchup
Salt and pepper

Brown ground beef in large saucepan and drain fat. Add the remaining ingredients and season with salt and pepper to taste. Simmer for 20-30 minutes. Serve hot chili topping over hot dogs or hamburgers.

Yield: 4 cups

Carol Dunkley

Broccoli Blue Cheese Soup

Delicious and different!

2 cups broccoli (fresh or frozen) uncooked, finely chopped	Salt and pepper Seasoned salt (optional)
1 small onion, finely chopped	3 ounces crumbled blue cheese
3 cups chicken stock	⅛ teaspoon paprika
1 cup canned vegetable stock	1 teaspoon chopped parsley
2 cups milk or cream	

In a 3-quart stock pot, cook broccoli and onion in stock. Add milk, simmer; do not boil. Season with salts, pepper, and spices as desired. Add cheese just before serving, stir to melt. Top with paprika or parsley. Serve hot.

Yield: Serves 6   Lorraine Brownell

Easy Elegant Crab Bisque

1 (10¾-ounce) can cream of tomato soup	⅓ cup sherry Salt and pepper
1 (10¾-ounce) can split pea soup	6 ounces fresh crabmeat or 1(6-ounce) can lump crab, drained
1¼ cups half-and-half	

Combine soups and half-and-half. Heat thoroughly. Add sherry, salt and pepper to taste. Add crabmeat. Additional cream may be added, depending upon desired thickness. Cook on low heat for 10-15 minutes until hot, but not boiling.

NOTE: *Wonderful served in small portions as an accompaniment to a meal.*

Yield: 6 servings   Mrs. Clyde Terry (Shirley)

Chili

1½ pounds very lean ground beef	½ cup chopped olives
1 medium to large onion, chopped	¼ cup sweet pickle juice
3 (15-ounce) cans stewed tomatoes	1 (1-ounce) envelope chili powder mix
4 (15-ounce) cans kidney beans	6 slices bacon, fried crisp, crumbled
	Tomato juice (optional)

Brown beef with onion in a 6-quart pan. Add all ingredients and simmer for 2 hours. If mixture becomes too dry, add tomato juice. Serve hot, in bowls.

Yield: 8 servings   Inez M. Overton

Anguillan Mussel & Mushroom Soup
A Caribbean specialty

1	cup sliced portabello mushrooms	2	teaspoons sage powder
½	cup chopped shallots	½	teaspoon nutmeg
1	tablespoon light olive oil	½	teaspoon cayenne
1	tablespoon butter, unsalted	1	teaspoon Dijon mustard
2	medium cloves garlic, chopped	1	cup dry white wine
3	tablespoons fresh parsley, chopped	1	cup chicken stock from bouillon
2	tablespoons fresh rosemary leaves	1	cup half-and-half
		1	cup whole milk
		2	dozen mussels in shells, washed and whiskered

In bottom of deep saucepan, sauté mushrooms and shallots in oil and butter until clear. Do not allow onions to brown. Add garlic and continue to sauté slowly. Add parsley, rosemary, sage, nutmeg, cayenne and Dijon; blend for 1 minute. Add wine and stock. Stir in half-and-half and milk slowly with a whisk. Simmer for 5 minutes. Add mussels in shells, cover and steep on low heat for 10 minutes or until mussels have fully opened. Remove mussels and cut from the shells; discard shells. Return mussels to the mixture. Simmer, covered, on low for 20 minutes.

Yield: Serves 4-6   Anna Mills and Bill Wagoner

Chili Beans

2	tablespoons oil	2	(20-ounce) cans tomato sauce
2	pounds lean ground beef	1	cup water
3	tablespoons chili powder	1	tablespoon flour
1	green bell pepper, seeded and chopped	2	(15-ounce) cans pinto or kidney beans
1	large onion, chopped		Grated cheese for garnish
2	teaspoons salt		
1	teaspoon sugar		

In a Dutch oven, heat oil and brown meat; drain well. Stir in chili powder, green pepper, onion, salt, sugar, tomato sauce and water. Cook for 1 1/2 hours over medium heat. Mix flour with beans and add to meat mixture. Cook for another 1/2 hour. Serve with grated cheese.

Yield: 2 quarts   Kaye Daniel

♥ Red Beans & Rice

1	large onion, coarsely chopped
1-2	green, red or yellow peppers, seeded, coarsely chopped
	Oil
1	(16-ounce) can stewed tomatoes
3	ounces tomato paste

½	teaspoon Cajun Creole seasoning
1	(15-ounce) can black beans, drained
1	(15-ounce) can dark red kidney beans, drained
1	pound lowfat smoked sausage, sliced
	Yellow or white rice, cooked

Sauté onion and pepper in oil until almost soft. Add tomatoes and tomato paste. Stir in seasonings to taste. Add beans. Simmer 15-20 minutes to blend flavors. Brown sliced sausage. Serve beans over hot rice. Top with sausage.

Yield: Over 2 quarts   Charlotte Hall

♣ Taco Soup

2	pounds ground fresh turkey or lean beef
2	cups chopped onions
1	(1¼-ounce) envelope taco seasoning mix
1	(0.4 ounce) envelope ranch salad dressing mix
4	(10-ounce) cans Ro-Tel tomatoes

4	cups canned tomatoes, crushed
1	(15-ounce) can pinto beans
1	(15-ounce) can red kidney beans
1	(15-ounce) can white shoepeg corn
4	cups shredded cheddar cheese

Brown turkey and onions in large saucepan; drain. Add taco seasoning mix, salad dressing mix, tomatoes, beans and corn; mix well. Simmer for 2 hours. Serve in soup bowls and top with cheese. Serve hot with taco chips.

NOTE: *For a milder version, omit Ro-Tel tomatoes; substitute 1 (32-ounce) can crushed tomatoes and 8 ounces chopped green chiles, drained.*

Yield: 16 servings   Fran Tannehill

Easy Onion Soup

2	(10-ounce) cans French onion soup, heated
4	slices French bread, toasted

1	cup shredded Swiss cheese
	Parmesan cheese

Pour soups into ovenproof bowls. Top with bread and cheese. Bake at 375° 10-15 minutes until cheese melts. Sprinkle with Parmesan.

Yield: 4 servings

White Chili

Great for winter evenings

4	large chicken breasts, cooked and cut up	2	(15.5-ounce) cans white navy beans, drained
1	clove garlic, minced	2	(15.5-ounce) cans Northern white beans, drained
1	medium onion, chopped		
2	tablespoons olive oil	2	(15.5-ounce) cans white shoe peg corn, drained
1	teaspoon cumin		
1	teaspoon salt	1	(4-ounce) can chopped green chiles
2	chicken bouillon cubes, dissolved in 1½ cups water		

In a large pot, sauté chicken, garlic and onion in olive oil. Add remaining ingredients. Simmer for 30 minutes. Serve hot.

Yield: 6-8 servings   Susan Ward

Knife & Fork Soup

1½	pounds smoked sausage, cut into bite-size pieces	6	cups boiling water
1	cup carrots, sliced	1	(14-ounce) can tomatoes
1	cup celery, diced	1	(1-pound) package frozen hash brown potatoes with onions
1	(1-ounce) envelope dry onion soup mix		
1	tablespoon sugar	1	(10-ounce) package frozen green beans
1	teaspoon salt	¼	teaspoon oregano leaves

In a 6-quart Dutch oven, combine sausage, carrots, celery, onion soup mix, sugar and salt. Add boiling water and stir. Bring mixture to a boil and simmer for 10 minutes. Add tomatoes, hash brown potatoes, green beans and oregano. Return to boiling; reduce heat and simmer 50 minutes. Serve hot.

Yield: 4-6 servings   Jeannette Colby

Iced Tomato Soup

6	medium tomatoes, peeled and seeded	2	cups half and half or cream
			Salt
1-2	large cucumbers, peeled and seeded		Black pepper or cayenne pepper
12	ounces plain yogurt	6	mint leaves

Blend tomatoes and cucumbers in blender. Add yogurt, cream; season to taste. Blend 2 minutes. Refrigerate 1-3 hours. Serve in glasses; garnish with mint.

Yield: 4-6 servings   Marie Fork

Italian Wedding Soup

1	gallon water
5	chicken breasts or parts
6-8	chicken bouillon cubes
1	pound ground beef
	Salt and pepper
1	tablespoon dried basil

½	cup dried parsley
1	(10-ounce) package frozen chopped spinach, or fresh
4-5	eggs, beaten
1	cup grated Parmesan cheese
1	(16-ounce) box egg noodles

Boil water, chicken and bouillon cubes for 20 minutes or until meat begins falling off bones. Remove from heat. Reserve stock, remove bones and discard, leaving meat in bite-size pieces. Make tiny 1/2-inch meatballs from ground beef seasoned with basil, parsley and salt and pepper to taste. Add to stock and cook for 10 minutes on medium heat. Add spinach and cook an additional 10 minutes. Carefully stir and scramble eggs into simmering soup, then slowly add cheese, stirring constantly. Simmer for 40 minutes to 2 hours, stirring at midpoint. Add noodles to soup 15 minutes before serving, stirring once after 7 1/2 minutes. Serve hot. Best made a day ahead.

NOTE: *This is from a wonderful Italian friend named Mary Alice.*

Yield: 8 servings   Karen B. DeGraaf

Crab & Broccoli Soup

6	tablespoons butter
1	cup onion, chopped
4	tablespoons flour
4	cups milk
4	cups half-and-half
6	chicken bouillon packets
12	ounces canned crabmeat, drained

15-20	ounces broccoli, cooked and drained, chopped
1	teaspoon salt
½	teaspoon ground pepper
¼	teaspoon cayenne pepper
½	teaspoon thyme

Sauté onions in butter in large soup pan until soft. Blend in flour. Gradually add milk and half-and-half. Stir and cook until thickened; add bouillon. Add crabmeat and broccoli, season with salt, peppers and thyme. Serve hot.

NOTE: *Delightful on a cold winter afternoon*

Yield: 8 cups   Debbie Lucas

Pesto Mayonnaise

1	cup mayonnaise
¼	cup prepared basil pesto

2	teaspoons lemon juice

Combine all ingredients in bowl. Cover; refrigerate. Use as sandwich spread.

Yield: 1 cup

♥ Caribbean Black Bean Soup & Rice

Very light

12	ounces black beans	½	teaspoon ground oregano
5	cups vegetable stock	2	bay leaves
2	tablespoons olive oil	1	teaspoon ground cumin
1	large onion, chopped	¼	cup lime juice
2	green peppers, seeded,		Salt
	chopped into ½-inch chunks	3	cups hot cooked rice
2	cloves garlic, minced	6	lime wedges for garnish

In large bowl, cover beans with water and soak overnight. Drain beans and place in large soup pot. Cover with vegetable stock. Bring to a boil. In large skillet, heat olive oil and sauté onions, green peppers and garlic. Add vegetables to beans. Add oregano, bay leaves and cumin. Cover and simmer until beans are tender and liquid is thick, about 1 hour. Remove bay leaves. Just before serving, add lime juice and salt to taste. Ladle into large individual bowls filled with 1/2 cup cooked hot rice. Garnish with lime wedges.

Yield: 6 servings   Julie Guion Steele

♥ Red Beans & Rice with Grilled Smoked Sausage

1	medium onion, coarsely chopped	1	(16-ounce) can red beans
2	stalks celery, coarsely chopped	1	(16-ounce) can diced tomatoes, with liquid
1	large green pepper, seeded, coarsely chopped	6	precooked smoked sausages, sliced diagonally
	Olive oil	4	cups hot yellow rice, cooked with a small amount of
1	teaspoon thyme leaves		turmeric for color and
	Coarsely ground pepper		fragrance
2	bay leaves		Sour cream
1	teaspoon red pepper flakes		Chopped fresh cilantro
1	tablespoon cumin		

Sauté onion, celery and green pepper in desired amount of olive oil. Add spices to taste. Add beans and tomatoes; simmer 30 minutes, stirring occasionally with wooden spoon. Sauté or grill sausage until slightly charred to release caramelized flavor. To serve, remove bay leaves, place rice in a bowl and top with several spoonfuls of red bean mixture. Arrange sliced sausage on top. Garnish with a dollop of sour cream and cilantro.

NOTE: *Lowfat sausage and lowfat sour cream may be substituted.*

Yield: 6-8 (4-5 ounce) servings   Marilyn Harrison
Sweet Meadow Cafe

125

Chicken & Andouille Jambalaya

Quick and easy!

1	yellow onion, chopped	1	(6-ounce) can tomato paste
1	green pepper, seeded, chopped	1	(14-ounce) can peeled and diced tomatoes with juice
2	tablespoons butter	1	cup long grain rice
1	(10-ounce) can chicken broth, plus water added to make 2 cups liquid	1-2	tablespoons hot sauce, or less, to taste
½	pound chopped chicken, cooked	1	teaspoon black pepper
		1	teaspoon red pepper
		1	teaspoon white pepper
½	pound andouille sausage or smoked turkey sausage	1	teaspoon garlic powder
			Salt

In large skillet, sauté onion and green pepper in butter until onion is translucent. Add diluted chicken broth and water and bring to boil. Add chicken, sausage, tomato paste, tomatoes and rice. Season with hot sauce, peppers, garlic and salt to taste. Stir; return to boil. Cover and simmer for 20-25 minutes, stirring frequently. Serve hot.

NOTE: *This is one of our favorites from New Orleans, LA. It may be served as a main or side dish*

Yield: 3-4 servings   David and Ellen Gish Dutton

Chilly Willy

1	pound lowfat ground beef	1	(16-ounce) can tomatoes, drained, then pureed
1	(1¼-ounce) package chili seasoning mix	4½	cups water
1	beef bouillon cube, crushed	1	(16-ounce) package rotini noodles, cooked and drained
1	(15-ounce) can kidney beans, drained or undrained		Grated medium sharp cheddar cheese

Brown beef. Add chili seasoning and bouillon; mix well. Place mixture in crock pot; add beans, tomatoes and water. Stir well. Cook all day on low setting of crock pot. When ready to serve, place desired amount of noodles in individual bowls. Ladle Chilly Willy (which will be soupy) on top. Cover with cheese.

NOTE: *Great with crusty French bread and green salad.*

Yield: 6-8 servings   Judy Ginn

Chicken Quesadilla

Quick, and great for teenagers!

5	(10-inch) flour tortillas	1	cup grated Monterey Jack
1	(6-ounce) can cooked white		cheese
	chicken, drained	1	(16-ounce) jar salsa
1	cup grated colby cheese		

Preheat oven to 340°. On half of each tortilla, sprinkle 1/5 of chicken and 1/4 cup of combined cheeses. Fold other half of tortilla over chicken and cheese. Repeat for each tortilla. Place quesadilla on a cookie sheet. Bake for 5 minutes; turn over and bake another 5 minutes. Cool 1 minute. Cut into wedges with a pizza cutter and arrange wedges on a plate. Serve with salsa.

Yield: 5 servings   Kathy Boyd

Crab Toast

1	stick butter, softened	½	teaspoon seasoning salt
1	(5-ounce) jar cheese spread	1	(7-ounce) can crabmeat,
1½	teaspoons mayonnaise		drained
½	teaspoon garlic salt	6-8	English muffins, split

Mix together butter, cheese spread and mayonnaise. Add salts and crabmeat. Spread on split muffins, cut into quarters. Freeze for 10 minutes. Broil until bubbly and crisp. Serve hot.

NOTE: *You may assemble these ahead and freeze on a cookie sheet. When frozen, place in a plastic bag. Return to freezer for later use. Defrosting is not necessary before broiling.*

Yield: 6-8 servings

Tuna Puffs

1	(7-ounce) can tuna, drained	1	tablespoon chopped green
1½	teaspoons mustard		pepper
¼	teaspoon Worcestershire	3	hamburger buns, split
	sauce	½	cup shredded cheddar
¾	cup mayonnaise		cheese
1½	teaspoons grated onion	6	tomato slices

Blend tuna, mustard, Worcestershire, 1/4 cup mayonnaise, onion and pepper. Spoon mixture onto bun halves. Mix remaining mayonnaise and cheese and spoon onto buns. Top with a tomato slice. Bake at 350° for 10 minutes. Broil for 2 minutes or until topping begins to puff. Serve hot.

Yield: 6 servings   Jan Broaddus Lewis

🔔 Tail Gate Sandwiches

1½	pounds shaved ham	1	small green pepper, seeded, diced
½	cup American cheese, diced	¼	cup mayonnaise
1	small onion, diced or 4 green onions, diced	2	tablespoons yellow mustard
		12	buns or rolls

Coarsely chop ham and cheese in food processor. In large bowl mix ham, cheese, onion, pepper, mayonnaise and mustard. Chill overnight. Fill buns with ham mixture and wrap in foil. Bake at 350° for 15 minutes. Pack in a large brown paper bag and place in insulated container to keep warm for 2-3 hours until ready to serve.

Yield: 12 sandwiches   June Eshelman

🔔 Bite - Size Sandwiches

1	cup margarine, softened	3	packages party rolls (20 rolls each), sliced
3	tablespoons Worcestershire sauce	1	pound of turkey slices
3	tablespoons mustard	¾	pound sliced Swiss cheese
1	medium onion, grated		

Mix margarine, Worcestershire sauce, mustard and onions. Spread on party rolls. Top with turkey and cheese. Wrap in foil. Bake at 400° for 10 minutes. May be assembled and frozen, then baked after thawing overnight in refrigerator. Serve hot.

Yield: 60 sandwiches   Jan Broaddus Lewis

Devonshire Sandwich

6	slices bread, toasted	2	(12-ounce) packages frozen Welsh Rarebit sauce, thawed
18	slices bacon, cooked crisp		Grated Parmesan cheese
1	pound sliced white turkey meat		

Line baking pan with toast. Top each toast slice with 3 bacon slices. Top bacon with turkey. Pour thawed sauce over sandwich and sprinkle with cheese. Bake at 450° in a 9x12-inch pan for 10-15 minutes, until cheese is bubbly and brown. Serve hot.

NOTE: *This recipe may also be prepared with crab, chicken, shrimp, tomato and asparagus. It originated in Pittsburgh, PA in 1934 and is still a favorite today.*

Yield: 6 servings   Joanne Eichelberger

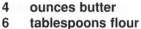
Kentucky Hot Brown

4 ounces butter	Salt and pepper
6 tablespoons flour	⅛ teaspoon nutmeg
3½ cups half-and-half	12 slices bread, toasted
10 tablespoons Parmesan cheese	12 slices turkey breast
	12 strips bacon, cooked limp
1 egg, beaten	6 slices tomato

To make a *MORNAY SAUCE WITH PARMESAN,* melt butter in saucepan; blend in flour. Add cream and 8 tablespoons of cheese. Cook stirring constantly until thick. Stir in egg, salt and pepper to taste and nutmeg. Remove sauce from heat. For each sandwich, place 2 slices of toast on oven-proof plate. Cover with turkey; pour sauce over turkey. Sprinkle with remainder of cheese. Top with bacon and tomato. Broil until brown. Serve hot.

Yield: 6 servings   Nancy G. Pike

Best Ever Wieners

8-10 chicken or turkey wieners	Sweet pickle relish
Mustard with horseradish	1 package hot dog buns
1 solid brick cheddar cheese, cut into strips	Canned or homemade chili
	Chopped onions
8-10 bacon strips	Hot sauce
Ketchup	Garlic powder (optional)

Boil wieners until they begin to split. Remove, partially slice lengthwise. Spread mustard on wiener; layer cheese on top. Wrap wieners and cheese with bacon. Serve with toothpick. Fry in a 9-10-inch heavy pan until crisp. Spread ketchup, mustard, relish on buns. Top weiners with chili, onions, hot sauce and garlic powder as desired. Serve while hot and juicy with beans, slaw and french fries. May reheat for 1 minute in microwave.

Yield: 8 servings   Ed J. Church, Sr.

Egg Salad Sandwich Spread

3 ounces cream cheese with chives	½ teaspoon dry mustard
	½ cup chopped celery
¼ cup mayonnaise	1 cup sliced ripe olives, drained
¾ teaspoon dill weed	1-2 tablespoon chopped green onion
½ teaspoon salt	
Dash lemon pepper	6 hard boiled eggs, chopped

Blend cream cheese, mayonnaise and remaining ingredients, fold in eggs.

Yield: 3 cups

Tomato Sandwich Filling

1	(8-ounce) package cream cheese	4	slices bacon, crisply cooked and crumbled
2	medium tomatoes, finely chopped	3	drops Worcestershire sauce Salt and pepper
1	tablespoon grated onion	6	slices sandwich bread, crusts removed

Mix cheese, tomatoes, onion, bacon, Worcestershire and salt and pepper to taste. Chill. Spread even amounts of mixture between bread slices. Cut each sandwich into thirds before serving.

NOTE: *For STUFFED CHERRY TOMATOES: Scoop out tomato pulp, invert shells to drain and stuff with above filling.*

Yield: 9 finger sandwiches   Annette Snider

Creamy Bacon Pimento Cheese

1	(8-ounce) package cream cheese	½-¾	teaspoon Worcestershire sauce
2	cups finely shredded sharp cheddar cheese	1	(7-ounce) jar chopped pimento, drained well
¼-½	cup mayonnaise		Salt and pepper
2	teaspoons cider vinegar	½-1	teaspoon sugar
½-1	tablespoon corn syrup	⅓	cup crumbled bacon

Combine cheeses in a large bowl. Blend with a fork or electric mixer until light and fluffy. Add mayonnaise, vinegar, corn syrup, Worcestershire, pimentos, and salt and pepper; sugar to taste. Stir well; add bacon. Keep refrigerated. Serve at room temperature with crackers or as a sandwich spread.

NOTE: *For PIMENTO CHEESE, omit bacon. To make JALAPEÑO PIMENTO CHEESE, substitute Colby Jack Cheese for cheddar cheese and substitute 1 to 2 (4-ounce) cans drained, diced green chiles for the bacon.*

Yield: 4-5 cups

Tiny Cucumber Sandwiches

1	(8-ounce) tub soft cream cheese with chives	2-3	teaspoons apple cider vinegar
¼	cup peeled, grated cucumber, drained	⅛	teaspoon paprika Salt
		24	thin slices bread, trimmed

Mix ingredients, salt to taste; spread between bread slices. Cut into tiny sandwiches. Refrigerate briefly, covered with damp paper towel. Serve.

Yield: 4 dozen

Colorful Vegetable Sandwiches

1	(8-ounce) package cream cheese, softened	¼	cup chopped green pepper
¼	cup mayonnaise	¼	cup chopped cucumber
2	cups shredded carrots	¼	cup chopped celery
¼	cup chopped onions	12	slices sandwich bread, crusts removed

Mix all ingredients except bread in a bowl. Spread mixture generously on 6 bread slices. Top with remaining bread. Serve.

Yield: 6 sandwiches   Jan Broaddus Lewis

Vegetable Sandwich Spread
A Presbyterian Favorite

2	tomatoes, chopped	1	(¼-ounce) envelope unflavored gelatin
1	cup chopped celery		
1	small onion, chopped	2	cups mayonnaise
1	bell pepper, seeded, chopped	1	teaspoon salt
1	cucumber, peeled, seeded and chopped		

Mix tomato, celery, onion, pepper and cucumber. Drain in a colander or on paper towels to remove excess liquid. Soften gelatin in 1/4 cup cold water; add 1/4 cup boiling water. Cool. Fold in mayonnaise and salt. Combine mayonnaise and vegetable mixtures; cover. Refrigerate overnight to allow flavors to blend before using as a sandwich spread.

NOTE: *I was recognized as a good cook at John Calvin Presbyterian Church in Salisbury, NC, using this recipe.*

Yield: 1 quart   Mary Brandon

♣ Beef Wrap Ups

	Cream style horseradish	10	(10-inch) flour tortillas
1	(8-ounce) tub whipped cream cheese	20	slices thin-sliced deli roast beef (about ½ pound)

In a small bowl, blend horseradish to taste with cream cheese. Spread mixture evenly and thinly on each tortilla. Arrange 2 pieces of beef on top. Fold in 2 edges of each tortilla, 1-inch towards center. Tightly roll up each tortilla. Wrap in moistened paper towels. Refrigerate overnight. Cut crosswise into 1-inch slices to serve.

Yield: 80 slices   Rick Anderson
                                                        The Sidewalk Deli

♣ Pineapple Ham Roll Ups

1	(8-ounce) tub whipped cream cheese	10	(10-inch) flour tortillas
½	(16-ounce) can crushed pineapple drained	20	(6-8-inch) thin round slices deli ham, about ½ pound

In a small bowl, blend cheese and pineapple. Spread mixture thinly and evenly on each tortilla. Arrange 2 slices ham on top. Fold in 2 edges of each tortilla, 1-inch towards center. Tightly roll up each tortilla. Wrap in moistened paper towels. Refrigerate overnight. Before serving, cut crosswise into 1-inch slices.

NOTE: *Delicatessen meats may be purchased from The Sidewalk Deli, in Salisbury, NC.*

Yield: 80 slices   Rick Anderson, The Sidewalk Deli

♣ Wrap & Roll Sandwiches

1	(4-ounce) package herb flavored spreadable cheese or cream cheese with chives, softened	4-6	ounces deli roast beef, sliced wafer thin (8-10 slices)
1½	teaspoons cream style horseradish sauce (optional)	12	spinach leaves, stemmed, rinsed and patted dry
2	(8-inch) flour tortillas	1	(7-ounce) jar roasted red peppers, rinsed and drained

Blend cheese and horseradish. Spread 1/2 of the cheese mixture thinly on each tortilla, covering to the edge. Arrange beef slices evenly over cheese. Arrange spinach leaves in a clock-like pattern around each tortilla. Arrange peppers over spinach leaves. Press sandwich ingredients with fingertips to slightly flatten. Tightly roll up sandwiches, starting from edge. Wrap tightly in plastic wrap. Refrigerate at least 1 hour before serving. Chill 4-8 hours to improve flavor. Cut each sandwich roll crosswise into 8-10 (3/4-inch) slices to serve, or serve whole.

Yield: 16-20 slices

Herbal Mayonnaise

½	cup mayonnaise or salad dressing	3	tablespoons fresh dill or 1 tablespoon dried dill or basil
½	cup dairy sour cream	2	tablespoons parsley
		1	clove garlic, minced

In a blender container; combine and blend ingredients until smooth. Cover container; refrigerate at least 1 hour before using as sandwich spread.

Yield: 1 3/4 cups

Feeding A Flock
of
Family or Friends

Large or Small Quantities of Food

For Friends or Neighbors Congregating,

For Picnics, Barbecues

& Festive Celebrating

♣ Spiced Round Roast

An old Christmas tradition

1	(6-8 pound) eye of round roast	1	ounce ground allspice
1½	ounces saltpeter	1	ounce ground cinnamon
1	cup salt	½	ounce ground nutmeg
2	cups dark molasses	½	teaspoon red pepper
1	ounce ground cloves		Water to cover roast while cooking

Mix saltpeter and salt; rub into beef well. Put into a heavy-weight ziplock bag. Mix molasses and spices; pour over beef. Place first bag inside another bag to secure against leaks. Place in refrigerator and turn every day for 10 days. When ready to cook, transfer meat from bag to a large pot, reserving molasses mixture. Cover roast with cold water and add 1 cup of the molasses mixture. Bring slowly to a boil. Cut back heat to simmer and continue to cook, 20 minutes per pound of roast. Cool roast in molasses and water mixture. Slice very thinly and serve cold.

Yield: 15-20 servings   Mary Ellen Turner

♣ Stew for a Large Gathering

3	pounds onions, diced	3	(28-ounce) cans crushed tomatoes
5	pounds potatoes, diced	⅓	cup oil
5	pounds chicken, boiled, boned and cubed, reserve stock		Salt and pepper
		3	teaspoons powdered chicken bouillion
5	pounds deer meat, boiled, boned and cubed		Cajun seasoning
3	(16-ounce) packages frozen cut corn		Louisiana hot sauce
		1	teaspoon curry
3	(16-ounce) packages frozen tiny lima beans	1	teaspoon nutmeg
			Seasoned salt
3	(16-ounce) packages frozen cut okra		Worcestershire sauce

In 2 large pots, boil each meat separately in 2 quarts of water. Cook until done. Reserve stock from cooking chicken. Discard bones, cube meat. Sauté onions in oil in 4-5 gallon pot over gas cooker. Add potatoes and sauté, stirring constantly until slightly softened. Add reserved chicken stock. Bring to boil; add both meats and remaining ingredients and seasonings to taste. Add water to cover. Cook to desired consistency, at least 2 hours or more. Serve hot.

Yield: 20-25 servings   Don Sayers

♣ Beef Stew

Great for a houseful of family or friends!

1½-2	pounds lean beef, cut into cubes	5	sliced carrots
	Water	8	stalks celery, sliced
3	tablespoons Worcestershire sauce	1	(2-pound) can crushed tomatoes
3	bay leaves	2	cups red wine
2	onions, sliced	1	bunch chopped parsley
		10	small red potatoes

In large stew pot, brown beef. Add water to fill pot half full. Add Worcestershire, bay leaves and onion. Cook on low for 1 hour. Meanwhile, cut vegetables and add to beef. Cook 1 more hour. Add tomatoes and wine and heat thoroughly; remove bay leaf. Better if refrigerated and served the next day. Serve hot.

NOTE: *Nice to freeze and have on hand.*

Yield: 10-12 servings   Rosalie Kizziah Laughlin

♣ Baked Ham with Pineapple

12-14	pound ham with bone, fully cooked	2	(12-ounce) cans beer
2	cups prepared mustard	1	(6-ounce) can pineapple rings, drained
2	pounds light brown sugar	6-8	maraschino cherries
8	ounces crushed pineapple, drained		

Preheat oven to 375°. Score across top surface of ham, cutting ½-1-inch deep, making a diamond pattern. On bottom of ham, make about twelve 2-inch deep by 1-inch across cuts randomly around the ham. Place ham in large roasting pan on roasting rack. Roast in oven for 18 minutes per pound or until internal temperature reaches 160°-170°. Remove from oven. Completely coat top surface with mustard and pack brown sugar onto ham coated with mustard. Top sugar with crushed pineapple. Pour beer into roasting pan; return ham to a 400° oven and roast for another 30-45 minutes or until pineapple and brown sugar have caramelized. Remove from oven and let rest for 15-20 minutes. Garnish with pineapple rings and cherries. Slice, to serve.

Yield: Serves 22-26   James Pierson
                                                    Executive Chef
                                          Country Club of Salisbury

Stuffed Potato Bar

8   large baking potatoes,
    washed and scrubbed well
2   (8-ounce) tubs margarine,
    softened
2   (8-ounce) cartons sour cream
2   cups chopped fresh
    mushrooms
2   heads iceberg lettuce, rinsed,
    cored, drained and shredded
3   large tomatoes, chopped
1   (16-ounce) bottle chunky
    mild salsa, heated
2   cups grated mozzarella or
    Colby-jack cheese
2   cups sliced mushrooms,
    sautéed in butter
2   cups sliced ripe olives,
    drained

2   pounds bacon slices, cooked
    and crumbled
1-2 cups finely sliced green
    onions or chives
2   cups frozen western style
    guacamole, thawed
2   pounds ground chuck,
    cooked, drained and heated
    with 2 (16-ounce) jars of mild
    chunky salsa or seasoned
    with 2 (1.5-ounce) packages
    of taco mix, prepared
    according to package
    directions (adding a pinch of
    sugar)
4   cups chili with meat and
    beans, heated
    Salt and pepper

Pierce potatoes with a fork and arrange evenly spaced in a microwavable dish. Cover with plastic wrap. Cook on high for 20 minutes or until done, rotating dish once during cook cycle. Cut a crisscross on top of each potato, pushing both ends of potato to fluff up pulp. Place potato bar ingredients in attractive containers and serve hot potatoes buffet-style. Each guest may stuff potatoes as desired.

Yield: Serves 8

🔔 Chicken à la King

28   ounces margarine (7 sticks)
½   cup onion, minced
5   cups flour
1½   tablespoons salt
1   teaspoon pepper
3   quarts chicken stock
2¼   quarts milk

18   cups diced cooked chicken
¾   cup chopped green pepper
4   ounces chopped pimento or
     red pepper
1   pound sliced mushrooms,
     sautéed

In a very large pot, sauté onions in margarine. Stir flour, salt and pepper into margarine and cooked onions. Add chicken stock and milk, stirring constantly. Cook over medium heat until thick. Carefully fold in chicken, green pepper, pimento and mushrooms. Heat thoroughly before serving over biscuits, toast, rice or mashed potatoes

Yield: 50 (⅔ cup) servings   Donna Yale

🔔 Skeem Burgers

5	pounds extra lean ground chuck	5	tablespoons Worcestershire sauce	
1	cup applesauce	1	(0.9-ounce) package dry onion soup mix	
1	cup finely ground Ritz® crackers	¼	teaspoon garlic powder	
5	teaspoons Accent	½	cup apple cider	
3	teaspoons Tabasco		Salt	

Mix ingredients and add salt to taste. Refrigerate overnight. Form into 20-25 patties. Grill; serve.

NOTE: *A favorite recipe from a now-closed Thomasville, NC eating establishment.*

Yield: 20-25 servings   Christine Cline

Sausage Wild Rice Casserole

½	cup wild rice, rinsed 3 times	½	teaspoon pepper, coarsely ground
½	cup white rice, cooked according to package directions	1	(4-ounce) jar pimento, drained
1	pound pork sausage	1	(6-ounce) can water chestnuts, drained and chopped
½	pound hamburger	½	cup chicken broth
½	cup chopped green pepper	1	(10½-ounce) can cream of mushroom soup
½	cup chopped onion		
¼	cup minced celery	1	cup shredded sharp cheddar cheese
1	cup chopped, fresh mushrooms, or 1 (7-ounce) can, drained	1	teaspoon dried parsley flakes

Cover wild rice with 2 cups boiling salted water and simmer for 30-45 minutes (it should be slightly crunchy). Drain excess water; set aside. Combine the wild and white rice. Brown sausage and hamburger in skillet, stirring to crumble. During last few minutes of cooking time, add pepper, onion and celery to sauté. Drain well to remove grease. Combine rice, sausage mixture, mushrooms, pepper, pimento, water chestnuts, chicken broth, soup, cheese and parsley in a large bowl. Spoon into a greased 2-quart dish. Bake at 350° for 1 hour. Serve hot.

Yield: Serves 6-8   Jeannette Colby

Hamburger Macaroni Casserole

1	pound lean hamburger	2	cups cheddar cheese, grated
1	medium onion, finely chopped	1	(14-ounce) package macaroni and cheese dinner mix, prepared according to directions on the box
1	cup mushrooms, sliced		
1	(10¾-ounce) can cream of mushroom soup		

Preheat oven to 350°. Brown hamburger, onion and mushrooms in skillet. Drain. Put half of hamburger mixture in a 1 1/2-quart casserole sprayed with non-stick cooking oil. Layer with half the macaroni and cheese mixture, half the soup and half the grated cheese. Repeat layers, beginning with hamburger and ending with grated cheese. Bake 30-40 minutes, until casserole is bubbling. Serve hot.

Yield: 6-8 servings   Pennie Martin

♣ Lasagna

1	pound ground beef	1	teaspoon sugar
¾	cup chopped onion	1	teaspoon garlic powder
2	tablespoons olive oil	½	teaspoon oregano leaves
1	(14.5-ounce) can whole tomatoes, undrained	½	(16-ounce) package uncooked lasagna noodles
2	(6-ounce) cans tomato paste	1	pound ricotta cheese
2	cups water	8	ounces grated Mozzarella cheese
1	teaspoon parsley, chopped		
½	teaspoon pepper	1	cup grated Parmesan cheese
2	teaspoons salt		

In a large heavy pan, lightly brown beef and onions in oil. Pour tomatoes into blender container and process until chopped. Add tomatoes, tomato paste, water, parsley, salt, sugar, garlic powder, pepper and oregano to beef mixture. Simmer uncovered for 30 minutes, stirring occasionally. In a 9x13-inch baking pan, spread 1 cup of meat and tomato mixture. Then alternate layers of uncooked lasagna noodles, sauce, ricotta cheese, Mozzarella cheese and Parmesan cheese, ending with sauce, Mozzarella and Parmesan. Bake 40-50 minutes until bubbling and lightly browned. Cool for 15 minutes before serving.

Yield: 10-12 servings   Tami Nianouris

Family Favorite Sour Cream Lasagna

2	(8-ounce) cartons sour cream	1½	(8-ounce) cans tomato sauce
2	(3-ounce) packages cream cheese	1	teaspoon sugar
1	finely chopped onion	1	teaspoon salt
2	pounds ground beef, cooked and drained	1	(8-ounce) package lasagna noodles, cooked and drained
		1	cup grated cheddar cheese

Mix sour cream, cream cheese and onion; chill mixture 4-8 hours, allowing flavors to blend. Simmer beef, tomato sauce, sugar and salt for 30 minutes. Arrange noodles, half of sour cream mixture, and half of beef mixture alternately in layers in a 9x12-inch glass or aluminum pan. Repeat layers; top with cheese. Bake at 350° for 45 minutes. Serve hot. Freezes well.

Yield: 8 servings   Beth Pate

♣ ♥ Lowfat Lasagna

1	pound lean ground beef	15	ounces part skim or no-fat ricotta cheese
¼	teaspoon salt		
1	(26-ounce) jar spaghetti sauce	¼	cup grated Parmesan cheese
		¼	cup egg substitute
1	(14-ounce) jar Italian style diced tomatoes	1½	cups shredded part skim Mozzarella cheese
¼	teaspoon pepper	10	uncooked lasagna noodles

Brown beef in skillet; add salt. Stir in spaghetti sauce, tomatoes and pepper; set aside. In bowl, combine ricotta and Parmesan cheeses and egg substitute. Spread 2 cups of sauce mixture on bottom of 9x13-inch pan; arrange; press 4 noodles in single layer. Spread on ricotta mixture. Sprinkle with 1 cup of Mozzarella; top with 1 1/2 cups sauce; pressing in remaining noodles. Top with remaining sauce. Bake 45 minutes at 375°. Sprinkle with remaining Mozzarella; cover lightly with foil; bake 15 minutes to melt cheese. Serve hot.

Yield: 10-12 servings   Anne Thurston

Quick Pizza Casserole

2	pounds ground chuck, cooked, crumbled, drained	4	cups pizza cheese
		3	cups milk
2	(14-ounce) jars pizza sauce	1½	cups biscuit mix
1	tablespoon sugar	4	eggs

Spoon beef into 4-quart dish. Top with mixture of pizza sauce, sugar and cheese. Pour mixture of remaining ingredients on top. Bake 30 minutes at 400°.

Yield: 8-10 servings

Lasagna Swirls
Great for book club or bridge luncheons

LIGHT TOMATO SAUCE:

1	large onion, chopped	2	tablespoons olive oil
2	cloves garlic, minced	2	teaspoons dried whole basil
3	tablespoons butter or margarine, melted	2	teaspoons dried Italian seasoning
2	(28-ounce) cans crushed tomatoes in tomato puree	¼	teaspoon salt
1	(15½-ounce) can tomato sauce	¼	teaspoon pepper
2	tablespoons sugar	⅛	teaspoon sweet red pepper flakes

To prepare sauce, sauté onion and garlic in butter until tender. Add tomatoes, tomato sauce and remaining ingredients. Simmer 10-15 minutes; set aside.

ROLLS:

2	(10-ounce) packages frozen chopped spinach, thawed and drained	1	(8-ounce) package cream cheese, softened
1	(16-ounce) carton ricotta cheese	½	teaspoon dried whole basil
		¼	teaspoon salt
2	cups shredded Mozzarella cheese	¼	teaspoon pepper
		¼	teaspoon dried whole oregano
1½	cups grated Parmesan cheese	1	(8-ounce) package lasagna noodles, cooked and drained

Combine spinach, ricotta and Mozzarella cheese, 1 cup of the Parmesan cheese, cream cheese, basil, salt, pepper and oregano in a large bowl. Stir well. Spread 1/2 cup of spinach mixture on each noodle; starting at narrow end, roll up jelly roll fashion. Place rolls, seam side down, in a 9x13-inch glass baking dish. Pour sauce evenly over rolls; sprinkle with remaining 1/2 cup Parmesan cheese. Bake at 350° for 35 minutes. Serve hot.

Yield: 5-10 servings   Denise Somers

🔔 Creamy Rice Salad

1	(8-ounce) package cream cheese	2	cups white rice, cooked, drained, cooled
2	tablespoons powdered sugar		
1	tablespoon mayonnaise	1	(6-ounce) jar of maraschino cherries, drained
1	(10.5-ounce) bag mini marshmallows		
		1	cup heavy whipping cream, whipped
1	(16-ounce) can crushed pineapple, drained	¼	cup chopped pecans

Cream cheese, sugar and mayonnaise until smooth; fold in remaining ingredients. Pour into 9x13-inch dish. Chill. Cut into squares to serve.

Yield: 18 servings

♣ Favorite Broccoli Casserole
Great for church and large family gatherings

Non-stick cooking spray
4 (10-ounce) packages chopped broccoli, cooked, drained
2 (10¾-ounce) cans cream of mushroom soup
½ cup mayonnaise

3 beaten eggs
4 teaspoons minced onion
Salt and pepper
Ritz® crackers, crumbled
2 cups grated sharp cheddar cheese

Coat 10x13-inch glass baking dish with non-stick cooking spray. Place broccoli in baking dish. Mix soup, mayonnaise, eggs, onion, and salt and pepper to taste. Spread over broccoli. Top with crumbled crackers and cheese. Bake at 350° for 40 minutes. Serve hot.

Yield: 16 servings   Dianne Agner

♣ Spinach Lasagna

1 medium onion, chopped
4 tablespoons olive oil
1 pound chopped fresh spinach or 1 (10-ounce) package frozen spinach, thawed and drained
1 cup pesto sauce
4 cups ricotta cheese

1 cup grated Parmesan cheese
Salt and pepper
4 cups Italian tomato sauce
1 pound Mozzarella cheese, shredded
1 (16-ounce) box pre-cooked lasagna noodles

Preheat oven to 350°. Sauté onion in 2 tablespoons olive oil until soft. Add chopped spinach and sauté briefly. Transfer mixture to large bowl; add pesto, ricotta and 1/2 cup Parmesan. Blend well; add salt and pepper to taste. Divide ricotta mixture, tomato sauce, Mozzarella and noodles. Oil two (9x13-inch) baking dishes. Using the divided ingredients, layer noodles, 1/3 ricotta mixture, 1/2 cup tomato sauce, 1/3 of Mozzarella. Repeat layering ending with noodles. Top with 1 tablespoon olive oil, remaining tomato sauce and Parmesan. Repeat procedure for second baking dish. Cover prepared dishes with foil; bake 60 minutes or until hot and bubbly. Serve hot.

NOTE: *May be frozen, uncooked, after assembling. Adjust amounts of noodles and sauce to your preference.*

Yield: 18-20 servings   Jeanne H. Moore

♣ Grandma's Casserole
Young people like this easy recipe

2 pounds ground chuck	1 quart whole tomatoes,
1 cup onion, chopped	chopped
1 green bell pepper, seeded	1 (15-ounce) can tomato sauce
and chopped	1 (8-ounce) package egg
2 teaspoons seasoned salt	noodles, uncooked
½ teaspoon ground black	1 (8-ounce) package grated
pepper	Mozzarella cheese

Brown meat. Add onion, bell pepper, salt and pepper. Stir until mixed well. Add tomatoes and sauce. Bring to boil, lower heat and simmer for 15 minutes. Pour half of the meat mixture into glass 9x13-inch pan. Spread with uncooked noodles. Pour remaining mixture over noodles, covering well. Sprinkle cheese on top. Bake at 350° for 45 minutes. Serve hot.

Yield: 10-12 servings   Barbara Norman

♣ Low Country Shrimp Boil

4 gallons sea water or salted	Lots of black pepper
water	2 pounds cubed, Hillshire
Crab boil seasoning	Farm® cooked smoked
(optional)	sausage
1 quart vinegar	1 dozen ears fresh corn,
1 jar bay leaves, crushed	broken in half
6 lemons, thinly sliced	8-10 pounds shrimp in shells
6 large onions, thinly sliced	

On an outdoor gas cooker, in a very large pot, bring salt water to boil. Add crab boil seasonings if desired. Add vinegar, crushed bay leaves, lemons, onions and pepper. Boil vigorously for one hour. Add sausage and return to a boil. Add the corn and cook for 10-12 minutes. Finally, add shrimp in shells and allow to remain in mixture for only 1 minute. Remove all ingredients with a large sieve and place in bowls on a table with lots of newspapers and paper towels and prepared white and red sauces following directions below.

WHITE SAUCE:
For white sauce, combine quantities of mayonnaise, lemon juice, horse-radish, hot sauce and Worcestershire to taste.

RED SAUCE:
Combine 1/2 bottle ketchup, 1/2 bottle chili sauce, lemon juice, horseradish, and Worcestershire sauce to taste.

Yield: Serves a crowd!   Don Sayers

🔔 Bone's Slaw

2	heads of cabbage
2	(14.5-ounce) cans whole stewed tomatoes
2	green peppers, seeded and cut into pieces
½	small onion, cut into pieces

1	cup sugar
1	cup vinegar
	Salt and pepper
	Hot sauce, or crushed red peppers

Using a food processor, shred cabbage into large (not fine) pieces. Place tomatoes, green peppers and onion in a food processor and puree until peppers are no longer recognizable. In a large bowl, combine tomato mixture and cabbage. Add sugar, vinegar, salt, pepper and hot sauce to taste. Stir. Let stand in refrigerator at least one day before serving.

NOTE: *This is a good slaw to prepare ahead for a large group. It goes well with fish, barbecue or chicken. Recipe may be halved.*

Yield: 1 gallon, 30 servings   W. T. Hillard

🔔 Quiche For A Crowd

Makes a beautiful presentation. Worth the extra effort!

2⅔	cups flour
1¼	teaspoons salt
1	cup vegetable shortening
6-7	tablespoons ice water
1	(8-ounce) package cream cheese, softened
12	eggs
4	cups milk
⅓	cup grated Parmesan cheese

2	tablespoons chopped chives
2½	teaspoons salt
½	teaspoon dried oregano
¼	teaspoon pepper
6	ounces (1½ cups) Jarlsberg cheese, shredded
6	ounces (1½ cups) Gruyère cheese, shredded
	Fresh chives for garnish

Preheat oven to 375°. Stir flour and salt in medium bowl, cut in shortening to resemble coarse crumbs. Stir in 6-7 tablespoons ice water, a tablespoon at a time, until pastry holds together. Roll 3/4 of pastry into a rectangle 3-inches wider all around than a 9x13-inch pan. Line baking dish with pastry, trim to leave a 1-inch over-hang. Fold over-hang under and press firmly onto pan rim. Roll trimmings 1/8-inch thick; using a floured 1/2-inch canapé cutter cut out as many rounds as possible. Moisten edge of pastry rim with water and place rounds along rim, overlapping slightly. Press gently with fingers. Re-roll trimmings and cut more rounds if necessary. Using a large bowl, beat cream cheese with a mixer on low speed until smooth. Add eggs, 1 at a time, until blended well. Beat in milk and next 5 ingredients. Sprinkle cheeses evenly over bottom of pie crust. Pour egg mixture over cheeses. If desired, arrange fresh chives on top in a pretty fan-shaped design. Bake 45 minutes or until knife inserted in center comes out clean. Serve hot.

Yield: 12 main dish servings   Vickie M. Wallace

B L E S S I N G S

♥ ♦ Mexican Fare for the Heart

2   (16-ounce) cartons nonfat
    sour cream
2-3 (8-ounce) jars green and red
    taco sauce
¼   cup finely minced onion

2   (4-ounce) cans chopped
    green chilies
4   cups cooked chicken, cubed
2   cups nonfat grated cheddar
    cheese

Mix sour cream, taco sauce, onion and chilies together in a large casserole. Add chicken and stir well. Spread cheese over top and bake at 350° for 25 minutes, until cheese melts. Serve hot.

NOTE: *Requested by teens and college students frequently!*

Yield: Serves 8   Karen Busby

Tamale Pie

1   pound ground beef
2   onions, chopped
⅓   cup chopped green pepper
1   (8-ounce) can tomato sauce
1   (12-ounce) can whole kernel
    corn
⅛   teaspoon celery salt

Salt and pepper
Garlic
½   cup cornmeal mixed with 1
    cup water
1   (3.8-ounce) can black olives,
    sliced
1½ cups grated cheddar cheese

Brown beef with onion and green pepper. Add tomato sauce, corn, celery salt, seasonings to taste and cornmeal mixed with water. Cook on low heat until mixture thickens. Remove from heat, add olives and pour into 3-quart baking dish. Bake at 350° for 30 minutes. Sprinkle cheese on top; bake 5 minutes more. Serve as an entrée with corn chips and salsa.

Yield: 6 servings   Ruth Philpott

Skewered Hot Dogs

20 (12-inch) wooden skewers
20 beef or lowfat frankfurters
1   cup honey mustard

2   (8-ounce) cans refrigerated
    crescent dinner rolls
2   tablespoons brown sugar
1½ teaspoons curry powder

Insert 6 skewers into franks. Unroll; form dough into 2 rectangles; press, seal perforations. Cut into 20 (8-inch) strips; brush 1 side with combined mixture of mustard, sugar and curry powder. Wrap franks spiral fashion with strips (coated side in). Bake on ungreased pan at 375° for 10-12 minutes until light brown. Serve with remaining mustard mixture.

Yield: 20 servings

♣ Salad Bar Buffet

3	heads iceberg lettuce, rinsed, cored	4	yellow or zucchini squash, thinly sliced, chilled
1	bunch Romaine lettuce, rinsed, cored	1	pound fresh mushrooms, stemmed, sliced thin, chilled
2	bunches spinach, stemmed, rinsed well	2	bunches radishes, stemmed, thinly sliced, chilled
1	head red cabbage, rinsed, cored, thinly sliced	3	(10-ounce) packages frozen peas, rinsed in cold water to thaw
2	Bermuda onions, peeled, sliced very thin	2	(16-ounce) cans garbanzo beans, rinsed, drained and chilled
	Florets from 2 heads cauliflower, chilled	1	pound fresh bean sprouts
	Florets from 2 heads broccoli, chilled	2	(16-ounce) cans ripe olives, sliced and chilled
1	dozen hard-cooked eggs, shelled and chopped, chilled	2½	pounds bacon, cooked and crumbled
3-4	large tomatoes, cut into thin wedges (or use cherry tomatoes, halved)	2	(6-ounce) boxes Caesar salad croutons
4	seedless cucumbers, thinly sliced, chilled	1	cup sunflower kernels (with black and white hulls removed)
6-8	cups finely shredded Swiss cheese		Salad seasonings
6-8	cups finely shredded cheddar cheese	8-10	cups or 64-80 ounces assorted regular or low-fat salad dressings, served in carafes
4-5	cups raw carrots, finely shredded, chilled		Club crackers
2½-3	cups ham or turkey cut into thin strips, chilled		

Rinse and drain lettuce, spinach and cabbage; wrap with paper towels. Refrigerate in sealed plastic bags to keep crisp. After vegetables, meats, cheese and eggs are prepared, tear lettuce and spinach into small pieces and thinly slice cabbage. Arrange all ingredients buffet-style on table in serving bowls, along with seasonings, croutons, sunflower kernels and salad dressings.

NOTE: *All ingredients listed may not be consumed but will provide a variety of choices.*

Yield: 16-20 servings

🔔 Orange Congealed Salad

1 (6-ounce) package orange gelatin	2 (8½-ounce) cans peaches, drained, diced, reserving juice
1 (3-ounce) package orange gelatin	4 large bananas, sliced
2 cups boiling water	1 cup chopped nuts (optional)
1 (20-ounce) can crushed pineapple, drained, reserving juice	

Dissolve gelatins in boiling water. Combine reserved juices to make 1 cup of liquid and add to hot gelatin mixture. Add fruit and nuts. Place in greased 9x13-inch dish. Refrigerate to congeal until firm.

TOPPING:

1 (8-ounce) package cream cheese, softened	½ cup sugar
1 (8-ounce) container sour cream	1 teaspoon vanilla
	½ cup chopped nuts (optional)

Cream cheese, sour cream, sugar and vanilla together until smooth. Spread on top of congealed salad. Sprinkle with nuts. Cut into squares to serve.

Yield: 24 servings   Peggy Rouzer

Beef à la Deutsch

1 pound ground beef	1 (15-ounce) package thin egg noodles, cooked and drained
1 (8-ounce) can tomato sauce	
1 clove garlic, minced	1 (3-ounce) package cream cheese, cubed
2 teaspoons sugar	
1 (16-ounce) can tomatoes, undrained	1 cup sour cream
Salt and pepper	6 green onions, chopped
	1½ cups grated cheddar cheese

Brown meat, drain. Add tomato sauce, garlic, sugar, tomatoes, salt and pepper to taste. Simmer, covered 45 minutes. Combine noodles with cream cheese. Add sour cream and onions. Grease 3-quart baking dish. Layer meat, noodles and cheddar cheese alternately. Bake, uncovered at 350° for 35 minutes. Serve hot.

NOTE: *Best when assembled uncooked, refrigerated overnight, then baked.*

Yield: 4-6 servings   Debbie Collins

♥ Aunt Bernice's Refrigerator Slaw

2	medium cabbage heads, chopped or shredded to make 1 gallon	1	(14.5-ounce) can or 1 pint canned tomatoes (drained)
1	pint chow-chow, sweet or hot	3	teaspoons salt
2	cups sugar	1	teaspoon black pepper (omit if using hot chow-chow)
1	cup vinegar	2	bell peppers, seeded and chopped

Mix all ingredients and place in a large covered glass jar or bowl in the refrigerator. Great on hamburgers, hot dogs, barbecued pork or chicken. Keeps 3 weeks in the refrigerator. Flavor improves after 3 days. Serve cold.

NOTE: *A family favorite. We always ask Aunt Bernice to bring it to family picnics.*

Yield: 6 quarts   Jamie Kimmer

🔔 Spinach - Bacon Deviled Eggs

1	dozen hard-boiled eggs, peeled	2½	tablespoons apple cider vinegar
½	cup chopped, fresh spinach	1	tablespoon sugar
¼	cup lowfat mayonnaise	2	teaspoons pepper
¼	cup cooked and crumbled bacon	¼	teaspoon salt Paprika

Cut eggs in half lengthwise. Reserving egg white halves, scoop out yolks. Mash yolks in a bowl with fork and add remaining ingredients, except for paprika. Mix well. Spoon egg mixture into egg white halves. Sprinkle with paprika. Refrigerate until ready to serve.

NOTE: *May substitute bacon bits for cooked bacon to reduce fat and cholesterol.*

Yield: 24 halves   Deborah Freed

🔔 ♥ Richard's Barbecue Slaw

75	pounds cabbage, chopped	2	gallons canned whole peeled tomatoes, chopped fine, with liquid
1	gallon distilled white vinegar		
4	pounds sugar	1	quart tomato juice
1	(6-ounce) can black pepper		
1	gallon tomato cubes		

Combine ingredients in storage container. Refrigerate; serve.

Yield: 12 gallons   Richard Monroe
        (35 servings per gallon)   Richard's Bar-B-Que

Deviled Eggs

6	large hard boiled eggs		Dash vinegar
½	teaspoon salt	1	tablespoon chopped sweet
½	teaspoon dry mustard		pickle relish
¼	teaspoon white pepper		Paprika
3	tablespoons mayonnaise		

Peel eggs and cut in half lengthwise. Slip out yolks. Mash yolks with fork. Mix in salt, mustard, pepper, mayonnaise and vinegar. Add pickle relish. Fill egg whites with mixture. For a pretty garnish, sprinkle paprika over eggs with fingertips. Refrigerate until ready to serve.

Yield: 6 servings   Janie Golden

Cowboy Beans
An all in one meal

1½	pounds ground beef	1	(15-ounce) can lima beans
½	pound bacon	½	cup ketchup
1	large onion, chopped	½	cup brown sugar
1	(15-ounce) can pork and beans	1	teaspoon mustard
1	(15-ounce) can kidney beans	2	teaspoons cider vinegar

In a skillet, brown ground beef, bacon and onion; combine with remaining ingredients. Cook in crock pot on low for 4-6 hours. Serve hot.

NOTE: *Great served with corn muffins*

Yield: 6 servings   Robin Perry

♠ California Gold Rush Beans
Best baked beans ever

8	bacon slices	1	(15-ounce) can kidney beans, drained
1	large chopped onion		
1	(15-ounce) can garbanzo beans, or chick peas, drained	1	cup brown sugar
		1	tablespoon Worcestershire sauce
1	(15-ounce) can butter beans, drained	⅔	cup barbecue sauce
1	(15-ounce) can barbecue baked beans	6	ounces sharp cheddar cheese, cubed

Sauté bacon with onion until crisp. Combine all ingredients and bake 350° for 1 1/2 hours. Serve hot.

Yield: 12 servings   Lois Loeblein

♣ Liz Gentry's Barbecue Beans
Delicious!

3	medium onions, chopped	1	(16-ounce) pinto beans, drained
4	strips bacon, cut in pieces	½	cup sugar
½	pound ground beef	¾	cup brown sugar
1	(15-ounce) can lima beans, drained	1½	cups ketchup
2	(16-ounce) cans pork and beans, drained	¼	teaspoon vinegar

Brown onions, bacon and ground beef. Drain excess grease. Add remaining ingredients and place in a 3-quart casserole. Bake uncovered at 350° until bubbly, about 30 minutes. Serve hot.

Yield: 8-12 servings   Kaye Hirst

♣ Aunt Cathy's Baked Beans

1	pound lean ground beef	¾	cup brown sugar
1	large onion, chopped	½	cup ketchup
1	large green pepper, seeded and chopped	½	cup water
1	(20-ounce) can pork and beans	1	tablespoon mustard

Brown beef and drain. Sauté onion and green pepper. Add meat and remaining ingredients. Pour into 2-quart casserole and stir. Cover and bake in oven at 350° for 20-30 minutes. Serve hot.

Yield: 10-12 servings   Sondra Komada

♣ Special Pork & Bean Casserole
Wonderful for picnics

2	(31-ounce) cans pork and beans, drained in a colander	2	tablespoons bourbon whiskey
1	large sweet apple, peeled, cored and diced	1	cup Kraft® Old Fashioned Barbecue Sauce
¾	cup white raisins	6	slices bacon

Put drained beans in a 2-quart baking dish. Add all ingredients except bacon and mix. Top casserole with bacon. Bake uncovered at 350° until bacon is crisp, about 30-40 minutes. Spoon off fat before serving. Serve hot.

NOTE: *Good with fried chicken, salad or cole slaw.*

Yield: 16 servings   Bert W. Oestreicher

B
L
E
S
S
I
N
G
S

♣ Jeter's Deli Shrimp Salad

1	(8-ounce) package cream cheese	1	teaspoon chopped fresh dill, or ½ teaspoon dried dill
1	tablespoon clover honey	2	tablespoons chopped fresh chives or 1 tablespoon dried chives
1	tablespoon Dijon mustard		
1	tablespoon Tabasco sauce		
1	tablespoon lemon juice, freshly squeezed	2	teaspoons seasoned salt
1	cup mayonnaise	3½-4	pounds (about 70-90 count) cooked, peeled shrimp

In a food processor, blend cream cheese, honey, mustard, Tabasco, lemon juice and mayonnaise. Transfer to large bowl. Add dill, chives and salt; mix well. Add shrimp; blend with dressing mixture. Chill 4 hours before serving.

Yield: 16 servings   Jeter Pritchard, Jeter's Deli

Stromboli

1	(2-pound) package frozen bread dough, thawed	1	pound Swiss cheese, thinly sliced
1	pound Genoa salami, thinly sliced	2	(9½-ounce) jars prepared pepper salad, drained
1	pound baked ham, thinly sliced	1	egg, beaten

Roll out each loaf separately to form 2 (1/4-inch thick) rectangles. Divide the meats and cheese evenly between the 2 loaves, alternating layers. Pour 1 jar of the salad down the center of each loaf, lengthwise. Loosely roll dough jelly roll fashion. Tuck ends to seal. Lay seam side down on a cookie sheet; brush tops with beaten egg. Bake at 350° for 30-40 minutes until golden brown. Let cool. When ready to serve, slice into 1-1 1/2 inch slices.

NOTE: *Freezes and travels well, unsliced. A favorite for picnics, parties or tailgating.*

Yield: Serves 8-10   Karen Morris

Hot Apple Cider Mix

1½	cups packed brown sugar	1	cup vanilla ice cream, softened
2	teaspoons cinnamon sugar	4	tablespoons butter, softened

Combine; blend ingredients until smooth. Pour into plastic container. Freeze until firm. To serve, spoon teaspoons of mixture into cups of hot apple cider. Stir. Keeps well in freezer.

Yield: 2 cups mix

♣ Overnight Rolls or Bread

1	cup vegetable shortening	2	(¼-ounce) packages yeast
1½	cups, plus 1 teaspoon sugar	6½	cups lukewarm water
3	teaspoons salt	18-20	cups flour

Grease a large mixing bowl. Mix shortening, 1 1/2-cups sugar and salt with an electric mixer until fluffy. Mix in yeast that has been dissolved in 1/2 cup lukewarm water and that has 1 teaspoon sugar added. Add 6 cups lukewarm water and mix. Add 18-20 cups flour. Knead well and let rise 2 hours. Punch down. Let rise another 2 hours. Shape into fairly large rolls or bread loaves. One dozen rolls should fit into a 9-inch round cake pan. Be sure all pans and rising bowls are well greased. Cover and let rise overnight. Bake the next morning in a 350° oven for 20 minutes. Serve hot.

NOTE: *This dough may be mixed and baked on the same day by increasing the yeast to 3 packages. I usually substitute about 4 cups of whole wheat flour for 4 cups white flour. This dough is also great for cinnamon rolls. Freezes well.*

Yield: 8 dozen rolls or 7-8 loaves   Ruth Philpott

♣ Butterscotch Dessert

FIRST LAYER:

1	cup flour	1	cup chopped walnuts or pecans
1	stick margarine, melted		

Preheat oven to 350°. Mix flour, margarine and nuts until crumbly. Press on bottom of 9x13-inch pan. Bake for 15 minutes. Cool.

SECOND LAYER:

1	(8-ounce) package cream cheese, softened	1	(16-ounce) container frozen whipped topping, thawed
1	cup sugar		

Beat cream cheese and sugar until well blended. Combine with half of the whipped topping. Spread evenly on top of crust.

THIRD LAYER:

2	(3.4-ounce) boxes instant butterscotch pudding mix	3	cups cold milk
			Remaining whipped topping

Mix pudding with milk and beat 3-4 minutes with electric mixer on low speed. Spread evenly over cream cheese layer and top with remainder of whipped topping. Chill. May be prepared ahead. Keeps well in refrigerator until ready to serve.

NOTE: *Lemon or chocolate instant pudding may be substituted.*

Yield: 15 servings   Lois Loeblein

Heavenly Crowd Cake

CAKE AND CREAM CHEESE FILLING:

1	(18.25-ounce) box yellow cake mix	3	tablespoons sugar
1	(8-ounce) package cream cheese	3	tablespoons milk

Make cake according to package directions. Bake in a 10 1/2x13 1/2-inch jelly roll pan at 350° for 15-20 minutes. Cool in pan. Blend cream cheese, sugar and milk in a bowl until smooth; set aside.

PUDDING FILLING:

2	(4-ounce) boxes instant vanilla pudding	3	cups milk

Blend pudding mix and milk in a bowl until smooth; set aside. To assemble cake, spread cream cheese filling on top of cooled cake. Next, spread pudding filling evenly over the top of cream cheese filling.

TOPPING:

1	(15¼-ounce) can crushed pineapple, drained	½	cup chopped nuts
1	(12-ounce) container frozen whipped dessert topping, thawed	1	cup flaked coconut
			Maraschino cherries

To complete cake, carefully spread pineapple over pudding filling. Spread whipped topping over pineapple. Sprinkle top with nuts and coconut; dot with cherries. Refrigerate until ready to serve.

Yield: 18-20 servings   Nancy McMurray

Cream Cheese Pound Cake

1½	cups butter, softened	6	large eggs
1	(8-ounce) package cream cheese, softened	1½	teaspoons vanilla extract
3	cups sugar	3	cups all-purpose flour
		⅛	teaspoon salt

With electric mixer at medium speed, cream butter and cream cheese. Gradually add sugar; beating for several minutes. Add eggs one at a time beating well after each addition. Add vanilla; mix. Combine flour and salt; add gradually to butter mixture, beating at low speed. Pour batter into a greased and floured 10-inch tube pan. Bake at 300° for 1 1/2 hours. Cool 10-15 minutes; remove from pan. Cool on wire rack.

Yield: 12 servings   Jackie Burleson

🔔 ♥ "To Die For"
Chocolate Cheesecake

CHOCOLATE CRUMB CRUST:

	Non-stick vegetable spray	⅓	cup cocoa
1½	cups graham cracker crumbs	½	stick melted margarine
½	cup powdered sugar		

Preheat oven to 300°. Spray a 10-inch springform pan with non-stick spray. Combine all ingredients for crust and press into pan. Set aside.

FILLING:

3	(8-ounce) packages cream cheese	1	(14-ounce) can sweetened condensed milk
1	(12-ounce) package semi-sweet chocolate chips	2	teaspoons vanilla
		4	eggs, slightly beaten

Beat cream cheese until fluffy. Melt chocolate chips over low heat (being careful not to burn), stirring constantly. Add milk to cream cheese and beat until smooth. Add melted chips, flavoring and eggs; mix well. Pour into springform pan. Bake for 1 hour and 25 minutes, or until edges are slightly puffed, and center is soft and moist. Cool completely before removing outer rim of springform pan to serve. Refrigerate or freeze.

NOTE: *May use 1 teaspoon of vanilla and 1 teaspoon of almond extract instead of the 2 teaspoons vanilla. May be made by using lowfat or fat free sweetened condensed milk, lowfat chocolate chips, lowfat cream cheese and egg substitute to reduce fat content. Surprisingly, the texture and flavor are very good.*

Yield: 16-20 servings   Shirley (Mrs. Clyde) Terry

🔔 Peanut Butter Pie
A great make ahead dessert

1	cup crunchy peanut butter	3	(9-inch) chocolate cookie crumb pie shells, purchased or homemade
2	cups powdered sugar		
1	cup milk		
1	(8-ounce) package cream cheese	18	ounces frozen whipped dessert topping, thawed
½	cup finely chopped nuts (optional)		

Combine peanut butter, sugar, milk, cream cheese and nuts in a large bowl. Beat on low speed until well blended; then beat on medium speed 1 minute. Fold in whipped topping; fill pie shells. Refrigerate or freeze before serving.

NOTE: *A great make ahead dessert. You may refreeze uncut portions of pie.*

Yield: 18-24 servings   Judy Moore

🔔 Chocolate Peanut Butter Balls

1½ cups crunchy peanut butter
2   cups margarine
1   teaspoon vanilla
2½ (16-ounce) boxes powdered
    sugar

1   (12-ounce) package
    chocolate chips
1   (4-ounce) cake paraffin wax

Melt peanut butter and margarine over low heat. Stir in vanilla and remove from heat. Add sugar and mix well. Shape into 1-inch balls. Place on a cookie sheet and freeze for 10 minutes. Melt chips and wax on very low heat in double boiler. Dip each ball into chocolate with a spoon; place on wax paper. Cool; serve.

NOTE: *May prepare ahead. Freezes well.*

Yield: 200 small or large candies   Anne H. Sugg

🔔 🎈 Porcupine Dessert

A specialty served at Christmas

½   gallon chocolate ice cream,
    softened
1   quart raspberry sherbet

½   gallon coffee ice cream
    Toasted almonds for garnish

In a 5-quart melon shaped bombe mold or a bowl, line the bottom half with chocolate ice cream, leaving center hollowed out. Freeze until firm. Fill hollowed center in mold with softened sherbet. Freeze mold again until firm. Soften coffee ice cream and fill frozen mold to top. Freeze again until ice creams are firm.

CHOCOLATE SAUCE WITH COFFEE:

1   (8-ounce) package
    semi-sweet chocolate
    morsels

½   cup strong brewed coffee

Before serving, make chocolate sauce by heating morsels and coffee in top of double boiler until morsels are melted. Blend until smooth. Keep warm over simmering water in double boiler until ready to serve. Remove mold from freezer and invert onto a serving plate or tray. Place a hot dampened dish towel on top of mold to loosen. Remove mold and decorate top of dessert with toasted almonds arranged and inserted on end into "body" of porcupine to resemble porcupine quills. When ready to serve, slice portions at the table and pass hot chocolate sauce for topping.

Yield: 18-20 servings   Elizabeth Hardin Taylor (Mrs. Edward T.)

154

Sundae Every Day

ICE CREAM OR FROZEN YOGURT:

Vanilla

Chocolate

Neapolitan

Cherry or Berry

Butter Pecan

Rocky Road

BOWLS OF FRUIT:

Sliced bananas

Pineapple tidbits

Fresh or frozen strawberries

Maraschino cherries

HEATED SAUCES:

Hot fudge

Butterscotch

Caramel

Peanut butter

Fruit syrups, pourable fruits or

Chocolate syrup

TOPPINGS:

Mini-chocolate chips

Mini M&Ms

Chopped nuts or granola

Toasted coconut

Crushed peppermint candy

Chopped peanut butter cups

Chopped cookies or brownies

Whipped cream or dessert

topping, thawed

Arrange your choice of ingredients and amounts in shallow serving bowls. Provide necessary utensils and let guests "create their own special dessert". For a group party, ask each guest to bring one ingredient. Fun for all ages!

Yield: As desired

🔔 Cookies & Cream Freeze

Junior Women's Club favorite

28	Oreo® cookies, crushed	1	teaspoon vanilla
¼	cup soft margarine	4	squares semi-sweet chocolate
½	gallon vanilla ice cream, softened	6	tablespoons margarine
½	cup cold brewed coffee	1	(16-ounce) container frozen whipped topping, thawed
1	cup sugar	1	cup chopped pecans, walnuts
1	(5-ounce) can evaporated milk		or almonds (optional)

Mix crumbs with margarine; spread into 9x13-inch pan. Freeze. Mix ice cream with coffee. Spread on top of crust; freeze again. Mix sugar, milk, vanilla, chocolate and margarine in a saucepan. Boil 1 minute. Cool. Pour over ice cream and refreeze. Mix whipped topping and nuts, if desired; spread on top of chocolate. Cover and refreeze. Cut into squares; serve.

Yield: 25 servings

Elizabeth G. Cook

🔔 Holiday Fruitcake

1	pound butter
1	pound brown sugar
1	cup honey
10	eggs
4	cups flour, sifted
2	teaspoons baking powder
¾	teaspoon salt
1	teaspoon allspice
2	teaspoons cinnamon
½	cup light cream
2	tablespoons lemon juice

1	cup apricot nectar
3	pounds dried apricots
1½	pounds dates, chopped or thinly sliced
1	pound seedless golden raisins
2	pounds pecans, whole or broken
½	cup brandy (optional)
⅛	cup Grand Marnier (optional)
	Non-stick cooking spray

Preheat oven to 350°. Cream butter, sugar and honey in a large bowl. Add eggs, one at a time, beating well after each. Sift together flour, baking powder, salt, allspice and cinnamon. Fold half of flour mixture into batter. In a small bowl, cream lemon juice and apricot nectar. Stir into batter, mixing well. In the remaining flour mixture, dredge the apricots, dates, raisins and pecans. Add to batter and stir to blend. Grease and flour four (9 1/2x5-inch) loaf pans or five (8 1/2x4 1/2-inch) disposable pans sprayed with non-stick cooking spray. Bake for 3 hours or until done. Cool in pans before removing. Refrigerate until Christmas. Slice to serve.

NOTE: *The flavor and moistness are enhanced by sprinkling with 1/2 cup brandy, mixed with 1/8 cup Grand Marnier, wrapping well and refrigerating. Cakes should cure at least a week, but may be made 3-4 months before the holidays. This cake is designed for those who dislike picking out all those little "red and green things". The cake contains a lot of fruit and nuts; the batter is there only to hold it all together.*

Yield: 32-40 servings   John A. Larson

Fix Fast Fruitcake

1	(18.25 ounce) box of spice cake mix
1	(3.4 ounce) box of instant lemon pudding mix
⅔	cup apricot nectar
¼	cup apricot brandy, plus 3 tablespoons for frosting

½	cup vegetable oil
4	eggs
1	cup golden raisins
1	cup candied fruits (pineapple and cherries) chopped
1	cup pecans, chopped
1	cup sifted powdered sugar

In large bowl, combine and beat for 2 minutes the cake mix, pudding mix, nectar 1/4 cup brandy and the oil. Add eggs 1 at a time, beating well after each addition. Stir in the raisins, fruits and nuts. Bake in a greased and floured Bundt pan at 350° for 50-60 minutes. When cool, frost with a spreadable mixture of 3 tablespoons of brandy and powdered sugar.

Yield: 12 or more servings

♣ Aunt Clara's Fruitcake

1	pound red candied pineapple	½	pound shelled black walnuts
1	pound green candied pineapple	1	pound shelled pecans
1½	pounds yellow candied pineapple	½	pound shelled English walnuts
		4	cups plus 2 tablespoons flour
¾	pound candied citron	1	teaspoon ground cinnamon
¼	pound crystallized ginger	1	teaspoon ground cloves
1	pound dates	½	teaspoon nutmeg
½	box dark raisins	½	teaspoon ground ginger
½	box white raisins	¾	teaspoon ground mace
1½	pounds red candied cherries	1	pound butter
1	pound green candied cherries	1	pound sugar
½	pound candied lemon rind	12	eggs, beaten
½	pound candied orange rind	1	tablespoon lemon extract
2	pounds mixed candied fruit	1	cup grape or scuppernong wine

Preheat oven to 225°. Grease 2 large tube pans and 1 or 2 (9x5-inch) loaf pans; line each with greased and floured brown paper. Reserve some pineapple, cherries and whole nuts for decorating cake tops. Dice fruits; chop nuts. Mix well. Add just enough flour to fruit mixture to coat fruit. Add spices to remaining flour; sift. Cream butter and sugar; add eggs, mix well. Add lemon extract and flour mixture; mix well. Combine batter and fruit, adding and mixing small portions at a time until all is well blended. Add wine; blend. Spoon into pans. Bake for 4-4 1/2 hours. Decorate the cake tops before cakes are done. Cake is moist and ready to slice and eat the next day.

NOTE: *Mrs. John Paris won many blue ribbons at the Forsyth County Fair for this cake. The recipe was requested and published often at Christmas in Winston-Salem, NC newspapers. I make it every other year. We enjoy one; I freeze the other for the next Christmas. It is just as good the second year. If you like fruit-filled cake, you will enjoy this one.*

Yield: 34 or more servings   Lawana Ford

Spinach Muffin Quiches

1	pound mild pork sausage	2	cups shredded cheddar cheese
1	cup mayonnaise	1	cup Colby Jack cheese
1¼	cups buttermilk Bisquick	1	(8-ounce) can chopped mushrooms, drained
2	tablespoons cornstarch		
½-⅔	cup finely chopped onion	1	(10-ounce) box of frozen chopped broccoli or spinach, cooked and drained
4	eggs		
1	cup milk or half and half		

Combine ingredients; mix well. Pour into greased mini or regular sized muffin tins or 2 pie plates. Bake at 350° until set. Freezes well.

Yield: 24 muffins, 48 mini muffins; or 2 pies

QUANTITY FOOD PREPARATION FOR 50

Quantities suggested are average. For 25 servings, divide amount by 2.
Adjust amounts according to adult or children's appetites.

Food	Serving Unit	Quantity
Ice.	(¹/₂-1 pound/person)	25-50 pounds
	(4-8; 7 pound bags)	
Lemonade or Tea.	(10 ounces/person)	3-4 gallons
Soft Drinks	(14 ounces/person)	50 (14 ounce cans)
Punch	(5-7 ounces/person)	3 gallons
Coffee (1 pound)	(5 cups grounds)	3 gallons perked
Tea	(48 teabags)	3 gallons steeped
Cookies, Bars, Cupcakes,		
Mini Desserts, Doughnuts	(1-2/person)	5-10 dozen
Pies.	(1 slice/person)	10 pies = 60 slices
Cakes	(1 piece/person)	1-12x20" sheet
		2-10x13" sheets or
		4-9" layer cakes
Ice Cream, Custards, Puddings	(6 ounces/person)	2¹/₂ gallon
Biscuits/Muffins/Rolls/		
Buns/Toast/Croissants.	(1-3 pieces/person)	4-12 dozen
Coffeecake	(1-3 pieces/person)	3-5 Bundt cakes
Potato/Tortilla Chips.	(1 ounce/person)	10 (6 ounce bags)
Bread for Sandwiches	(2 slices/person)	6-8 (1 pound loaves)
Tea Sandwiches	(2-3/person)	28 whole sandwiches
		quartered = 112 pieces
Egg, Tuna, Chicken Salad or Pimento		
Cheese for filling sandwiches.	(3 ounces/person)	5 quarts
Deli Cold Cuts (Meat & Cheese)	(3 ounces/person)	10 pounds
Sliced tomatoes.	(3-4 ounces/person)	10-12 pounds
Cooked Vegetables, Baked Beans, Scalloped		
or Mashed Potatoes, Canned Yams,		
Pasta or Bean Salads	(6 ounces/person)	2¹/₂ gallons
Jello, Fruit Salad, Fruit Cocktail,		
Cranberry or Applesauce	(1¹/₂ cups/person)	6¹/₂ quarts
Coleslaw	(4 ounces/person)	6-7 quarts
Lettuce for Tossed Salad.	(2¹/₂ ounces/person)	8-10 heads
Salad, Tossed	(1¹/₂ cups/person)	4¹/₂ gallons
White or Sweet Potatoes	(5 ounces/person)	18 pounds
Peaches or Pear Halves	(1 half/person)	7 (29 ounce cans)
Grapes	(10/person)	6-8 pounds
Strawberries	(2/person)	4 pounds
Pineapples or Cantaloupes	(6 chunks/person)	10 (3-4 pound)
Watermelons for Salad.	(6 chunks/person)	6 (4-5 pound)
Grits, Noodles, Rice, cooked	(1 cup/person)	3 gallons
Chicken Salad as Side Dish.	(¹/₂ cup/person)	6¹/₂ quarts
Chicken for Salad,		
Pot Pies or Casseroles	(6 ounces/person.	2¹/₂ gallons
Crudite (for Dipping)		
Broccoli, Squash, Cauliflower.	(3 pieces;person)	12-16 dozen pieces
Cauliflower, Broccoli or Carrots		
as Vegetables	(6 ounces/person)	15 pounds
Asparagus/Broccoli Spears	(6/person)	15 pounds
Nuts, Mixed	(1-2 ounces/person)	1-3 pounds
Seafood Molds	(2 ounces/person)	3¹/₂ quarts
Cheese Balls or Paté.	(2 tablespoons/person)	2 (1 pound balls) or 4 cups
Cheese Cubes	(1 ounce/person)	3 pounds
Dips.	(3 tablespoons/person)	4-5 cups
Meatballs/Chafing Dish	(3 per person)	150
Ground Beef, Turkey, Lamb,		
Ham, Stew Beef	(6-8 ounces/person).	20-25 pounds
Boneless Beef, Beef Tenderloins,		
Ham, Fish, Lamb, Pork, Turkey	(6-8 ounces/person)	18-25 pounds
Bone-In Beef, Ham, Pork, Lamb, Turkey	(12-16 ounces/person)	36-50 pounds
Chicken for Frying	(10-20 ounces/person)	14-26 fryers
Bacon	(2 slices/person)	96 slices (6 pounds)
Sausage	(2 patties/person)	96 patties (12 pounds)
Eggs, Scrambled	(2/person)	9 dozen
Eggs, Deviled	(2 halves/person)	5 dozen

Elegant Meat Entrees

Beef, Game, Ham & Lamb

&

Pork & Veal with Appeal

Bobotie

A South African dish

1	large onion, chopped	1	tablespoon chutney
	Oil or unsalted butter	1	tablespoon apricot jam
1	tablespoon curry powder		(optional)
1	teaspoon salt	1	pound lean ground beef
	Slightly less than	2	regular slices white bread, or
	1 tablespoon sugar		1 sliced thick
1	tablespoon vinegar	1	cup milk
	Pepper	2	eggs
2	tablespoons raisins	2	bay leaves
1	teaspoon ground turmeric		Cooked, hot rice

Prepare a water bath by putting water in a pan that can accommodate a 1 1/2-2-quart baking dish. Place in oven at 350°. Sauté onion in small amount of oil. Add curry and stir well. Add salt, sugar, vinegar, pepper to taste, raisins, turmeric, chutney and jam. Mix and cook a few minutes. Add meat and mix together. Soak bread in milk; drain off milk and reserve. Mash the bread with a fork and add to meat mixture with 1 beaten egg. Mix well and turn into casserole. Add sufficient milk to reserved milk to make 3/4 cup. Beat remaining egg and mix with milk. Season with a little salt and pepper to taste and pour mixture over the meat mixture. Stick 2 bay leaves, upright in mixture. Stand dish in water bath (water approximately halfway up side of dish) and bake at 350° for 30-40 minutes. Serve with rice.

NOTE: *May serve with brown bread and butter, a green salad and fresh fruit.*

Yield: 3-4 servings

Mrs. John G. Riley (Jane)

♣ Spicy Marinated Tenderloin

2	cups port wine	2	teaspoons Tabasco
2	cups soy sauce	2	tablespoons minced or
1	cup olive oil		chopped garlic
2	tablespoons freshly ground,	1	(5-6 pound) whole beef
	coarse black pepper		tenderloin, trimmed
2	tablespoons dried thyme		

Combine wine, soy sauce, oil, pepper, thyme, Tabasco and garlic. Place beef in a large 3-quart glass dish. Tuck thin tail of beef under roast. Pour marinade mixture over beef. Refrigerate 6 hours or overnight, turning occasionally. To bake, preheat oven to 450°. Place beef in roasting pan on rack in oven. Immediately reduce heat to 400°; roast 40-50 minutes. Roast will be medium rare. Remove from oven; allow to sit 10 minutes before slicing to serve.

NOTE: *For a wonderful BEEF MARINADE, prepare only half of above mixture to marinate beef filets or steaks.*

Yield: 10-12 servings

Frances Binder

Beef Wine Goulash
Friends love this dish!

3	sticks margarine
4	pounds lean, trimmed beef rump roast, cut into 1½-inch cubes
3-4	cups finely chopped onion
4	cloves fresh garlic, minced
2	teaspoons sweet paprika
1	(8-ounce) can tomato sauce
2	tablespoons ketchup
1	teaspoon salt
1	teaspoon ground black pepper
1	(10½-ounce) can beef broth
1	cup red wine (½ cup burgundy cooking wine, plus ½ cup red table wine)
5	bay leaves
½	teaspoon garlic powder
	Cooked hot rice

Melt half the margarine in a 6-quart pot. Add meat and a little water; brown meat for about 1/2 hour, until water evaporates. Transfer meat to another pot with enough water to simmer for 1 hour. Stir occasionally. Add remaining margarine to the 6-quart pot and sauté onion for about 1 hour, gradually adding water and mashing onions occasionally. Add garlic, paprika, tomato sauce, ketchup, salt, pepper, broth, wine, bay leaves and garlic powder. Cook on medium heat 15 minutes. Add meat and cook about 1 hour on low, stirring occasionally. For taste, add more red wine if desired, but sauce must be thick. Discard bay leaves. Serve over hot rice. Freezes well.

Yield: 8-10 servings   Tanja Kishev

Tofu Mushroom Stroganoff

2	tablespoons margarine
1	medium onion, chopped
10-12	fresh mushrooms, washed and sliced
	Fresh minced garlic
	Salt and pepper
2	tablespoons chopped chives
1¼-1½	pounds tofu, drained on paper towel, sliced into 13x¾x½-inch strips
1	cup sour cream
½	cup soy sauce
1-2	tablespoons sherry
	Egg noodles, cooked

Melt 1 tablespoon margarine in a large saucepan. Add onion, mushrooms and garlic to taste. Sauté until tender. Add salt, pepper and chives; blend well. Remove mixture from pan and set aside. Fry tofu on both sides in remaining margarine and some more garlic until golden brown. Add mushroom and onion mixture to tofu in pan. Add sour cream, soy sauce and sherry to taste, just before serving. Cook a few minutes until blended and mixture is hot. Serve over egg noodles.

NOTE: *If sauce is too thick, add more sour cream. Tofu is a soybean cheese, rich in protein and makes a good substitute for meat.*

Yield: Serves 4   Kerry Kribbs

♥ After Church Stew

1½	pounds lean stew beef, cut into 1½-inch cubes	1	(10¾-ounce) can French onion soup
4	medium carrots, quartered and cut into 3-inch lengths	1	(10¾-ounce) can tomato soup
2	stalks celery, sliced	1	(10¾-ounce) can water
2	large onions, quartered	3	tablespoons quick cooking tapioca
4	medium potatoes, peeled and quartered	⅓	cup red wine
½	teaspoon salt	1	bay leaf
½	teaspoon dried basil	1	(10-ounce) package frozen mixed vegetables
¼	teaspoon pepper		

Mix all ingredients except frozen vegetables. Place mixture in 4-quart casserole dish. Bake covered at 325° for 3 1/2 hours. Test meat; it should be tender. Twenty minutes before serving, cook or microwave frozen vegetables and stir into hot stew. Remove bay leaf. Serve hot.

NOTE: *All ingredients may be assembled the day before and refrigerated. In the morning, place casserole in a 325° oven for 3 1/2 hours. Stew will be cooked and ready to eat after church. You may add any fresh vegetables such as raw sweet potatoes, quartered; various squash; cut green beans; red and green peppers, quartered; or fresh mushrooms to stew during the last 1 1/4 hour of cooking.*

Yield: 4 servings   Carol Freed

Confetti Meat Loaf

1¼	pounds ground beef (or half beef, half turkey)	¼	cup tomato or spaghetti sauce
1	medium zucchini, shredded (moisture squeezed out)	2	tablespoons seasoned dry bread crumbs
1	medium carrot, shredded	3	tablespoons chopped fresh parsley
2	cloves garlic, pressed or minced	1	teaspoon thyme leaves
1	egg, lightly beaten		Salt and pepper
			Chunky tomato salsa

Preheat oven to 325°. Mix beef, vegetables, garlic, egg, sauce, crumbs, herbs, salt and pepper to taste, until evenly blended. Shape into an oval loaf about 9 inches long. Place on a rack in a baking pan. Bake for 1 hour, 15 minutes. Let stand for 10 minutes. Slice and serve with chunky tomato salsa.

NOTE: *For an optional topping on meat loaf, combine 1 tablespoon dark brown sugar, 3 tablespoons ketchup and 1 teaspoon spicy mustard. Spread over meat loaf and bake as above.*

Yield: 1 meat loaf   Moffit Swaim Churn

Easy Beef Burgundy

1   (0.9-ounce) envelope dry
    onion soup mix
2   (10¾-ounce) cans cream of
    mushroom soup
2   (4-ounce) cans mushrooms,
    undrained

1   clove garlic, minced
1   bay leaf
½   cup burgundy wine
3   pounds cubed beef
    Hot cooked noodles or rice

Combine soups, mushrooms, garlic, bay leaf, wine and beef. Mix well. Bake in large covered casserole at 350° for 3 hours. Serve hot over noodles.

Yield: 8-10 servings   Sandy Callison

Sweet & Sour Beef

½   cup flour
2   teaspoons salt
    Pepper
4-5 pounds cubed beef
2   cups sliced onion
3   tablespoons vinegar

4   tablespoons soy sauce
¾   cup water
¾   cup ketchup
2   tablespoons Worcestershire
    sauce
½   cup sugar

Mix flour, salt and pepper to taste. Roll meat in seasoned flour to coat. Arrange in lightly greased 12x14-inch casserole. Cover with onions. Mix vinegar, soy sauce, water, ketchup, Worcestershire and sugar; pour over meat. Bake at 325° covered, for 3 hours. Serve hot.

Yield: Serves 8   Peggy Maness

Swiss Steak

    Salt and pepper
2   pounds cubed steak
    Flour
    Oil
¼   teaspoon garlic powder
1   cup coarsely chopped onion
1   cup coarsely chopped celery

¼   teaspoon salt
1   (16-ounce) can tomatoes with
    juice
1   tablespoon sugar
½   cup coarsely chopped bell
    pepper

Salt and pepper each piece of meat. Coat with flour; brown in hot oil and place meat in 8x12-inch greased baking dish. Sprinkle meat with garlic powder. Cover with onions and celery. Sprinkle with salt. Add tomatoes; sprinkle with sugar. Cook covered at 350° for 1 hour, 15 minutes. Uncover, add bell pepper. Cook uncovered for 30 more minutes. Serve hot.

Yield: 6-8 servings   Robbin Curtis

Horseradish Beef

2	pounds round beef, cubed	1	teaspoon curry
¼	cup flour	1-1½	teaspoons molasses
1	tablespoon salt	½	teaspoon ginger
¼	tablespoon pepper	1	cup water
2	tablespoons oil	1	cup sour cream
2	onions, sliced	2	tablespoons creamy
1	tablespoon Worcestershire sauce		horseradish sauce

Preheat oven to 350°. In plastic bag, shake meat in mixture of flour, salt and pepper. Brown coated meat in hot oil over medium heat. Add onions, Worcestershire, curry, molasses, ginger and water; stir. Cover; bake 2 1/2 hours or less until meat is tender. Combine sour cream and horseradish. Cool beef mixture slightly to prevent curdling; before adding and stirring in the sour cream mixture. Serve hot.

Yield: Serves 6   Sara DeLapp

Ranch Roast

1	(1-2 pounds) sirloin tip roast Salt	6-7	Anaheim peppers, canned or fresh
1	cup ranch salad dressing	2	medium onions, quartered
½	teaspoon hot pepper sauce		

Preheat oven to 350°. Line roaster pan with foil. Salt roast lightly and place in pan. Combine dressing and pepper sauce and cover roast. If using fresh peppers, blister peppers under broiler, peel and cut into 2-inch slices. Top meat with peppers and onions. Seal foil. Bake at 350° for 3 hours for a large roast and at 325° for a small roast. Serve hot.

Yield: 4-6 servings   Robbin Curtis

Mini Freezer Meat Loaves

1½	pounds lean ground beef	1¼	teaspoons salt
1	egg, beaten	¼	teaspoon garlic salt
¼	cup chopped onion	1	tablespoon Worcestershire sauce
1	teaspoon sage		
¼	teaspoon pepper	3	slices soft bread, torn into small pieces
¼	teaspoon dry mustard		
¼	teaspoon celery salt	¾	cup milk

Combine all ingredients. Form into 6 mini-loaves. At this point, loaves may be frozen. To serve, thaw in refrigerator. Bake at 350° for 1 hour.

Yield: 6 mini-loaves or 1 large loaf   Dorothy Garrison

Steak au Poivre

BROWN SAUCE: (Must be prepared ahead.)

4	pounds beef bones (neck bones, etc.)	3	bay leaves (fresh, if available)
1	whole onion, quartered	2	cloves garlic, unpeeled
2	stalks celery, cut into 2-inch sections	2	teaspoons thyme
2	carrots, cut into 2-inch sections	½	teaspoon salt
		½	teaspoon pepper

Bake ingredients in roasting pan at 350° for 2 hours; transfer ingredients to large stock pot, scraping solids that may have stuck to pan. Add 3 quarts water; bring to boil. Reduce heat; simmer 6 hours. Strain mixture, reserving liquid. Cool sauce; discard bones and vegetables. Sauce may be poured into ice cube trays to freeze. Store cubes in a ziplock bag to use as needed. May be frozen up to 4 months.

FOR EACH SERVING:

1	(8-ounce) strip steak or filet	3	tablespoons heavy cream
½	cup cracked peppercorns	4	tablespoons brandy or cognac
¼	cup brown or bordelaise sauce		

Preheat oven to 350°. Spread peppercorns evenly in shallow dish. Press both sides of steak into peppercorns to coat. Sear steak 1-2 minutes on both sides in oven-proof skillet over high heat; place in oven; cook to preferred temperature (8 minutes for rare, 12 minutes for medium rare, 18 minutes for well done). Be careful of pepper fumes when opening oven. Remove skillet from oven; place on medium heat. Pour brandy over steak; ignite. Remove steak; place in a serving dish. Add *BROWN SAUCE* and cream to skillet; heat thoroughly; pour over steak. Serve immediately.

NOTE: *To make BORDELAISE SAUCE, add 1 tablespoon red wine for every cup of brown sauce. Boil, reduce heat; simmer 1/2 hour to reduce volume 1/3.*

Yield: 1 serving

Anthony Vitellozzi
General Manager, La Cava Restaurant

Bride's Stroganoff

1	pound ground chuck	2	(6-ounce) cans mushrooms, drained
½	teaspoon crushed garlic		
1	package dry onion soup mix	1	cup sour cream
1	(10-ounce) can cream of mushroom soup	¼	cup wine or water

Brown meat and garlic in skillet; drain. Stir in soup mix, soup and mushrooms. Simmer 15 minutes. Stir in sour cream and wine. Simmer 5-10 minutes. Serve over rice or noodles.

Yield: 4 servings

Transpacific Flank Steak

¾	cup oil	1	clove garlic, crushed
¼	cup soy sauce	1½	teaspoons ground ginger
2	tablespoons honey	1	green onion, chopped
2	tablespoons red wine vinegar	1½-2	pounds flank steak

Combine oil, soy sauce, honey, vinegar, garlic, ginger and onion. Pour mixture over steak that has been placed in a large ziplock, bag and place bag in a shallow pan. Marinate in refrigerator at least 5 hours, turning several times. May be frozen at this point, until needed; defrost before grilling. Grill 2 inches above coals or under a broiler for 4-5 minutes per side. To serve, slice steak thinly, diagonally across the grain of meat.

Yield: 4 servings   Beth Pate

♣ Baked Corned Beef with Glaze

4-6	pounds corned beef brisket	1	stalk celery with leaves, sliced
¼	cup water		
2	tablespoons pickling spice	1	carrot, sliced
1	orange, sliced	1	tablespoon prepared mustard
1	onion, sliced	1⅓	cups brown sugar, packed

Place meat on baking dish lined with a large sheet of heavy foil. Pour water over beef, sprinkle with spices and arrange orange and vegetable slices on and around beef. Lightly seal meat in foil, turning up ends of foil. Bake at 325° for 4 hours. Cool slightly; remove oranges and vegetables and spread with a mixture of the mustard and brown sugar. To glaze, leave foil open and bake at 375° for 20 minutes.

Yield: 8-12 servings   Evelyn Harrison

Venison Roast

3-4	pound venison or beef roast	2	tablespoons Worcestershire sauce
4	slices bacon, cooked, reserve fat		
		1	(10½-ounce) can golden mushroom soup
1	teaspoon lemon pepper	½	cup chopped dill pickle

Brown roast in bacon fat and sprinkle with lemon pepper. Transfer roast to Dutch oven. Combine Worcestershire, soup and pickles; pour over meat. Cover and bake 2 1/2-3 hours at 325°-350°. Roast makes its own gravy. Serve hot venison sliced, topped with gravy and crumbled bacon.

Yield: 6-8 servings   Phyllis Steimel

Beef Kabobs

1½-2 pounds boneless sirloin
      steak, cut into 1½-inch cubes
2   bell peppers, seeded, cut
      into 1½-inch pieces
24   medium mushrooms, washed
6   medium onions, peeled and
      quartered
24   cherry tomatoes, washed

24   whole small red potatoes,
      washed and boiled 6 minutes
      or 2 small zucchini squash
      cut into 1-inch rounds
6-7   (15-inch) metal skewers or
      wooden skewers soaked in
      water for 30 minutes

Prepare beef cubes and refrigerate until ready to marinate. Prepare vegetables and refrigerate in a covered container until ready to use.

KABOB MARINADE:

⅓   cup olive oil
¼   cup light soy sauce
⅓   cup Burgundy wine
1   tablespoon grated fresh
      ginger
¼   cup brown sugar

3   garlic cloves, crushed or
      minced
2   tablespoons balsamic vinegar
4   tablespoons ketchup
2   tablespoons fresh minced
      parsley leaves

Combine marinade ingredients in a shallow glass or plastic dish. Add beef cubes, stir to coat; cover. Refrigerate at least 4 hours, stirring and turning beef 3-4 times. Remove beef, reserving marinade. Divide beef cubes and vegetables into 6 equal portions and thread beef and vegetables alternately on skewers. Grill 4-5 inches from heat source for 15-20 minutes for medium doneness, turning and basting often with marinade. Remove kabobs from skewers and serve on a platter, with hot cooked rice if desired.

NOTE: *JAPANESE ORIENTAL GINGER DRESSING (See salad dressings) makes a great marinade. Lamb, poultry, fish or other vegetables may be used.*

Yield: 4-6 servings

Forgotten Roast Beef

1   (3-pound) chuck roast
4   carrots, sliced
2   onions, sliced
4   potatoes, peeled, cut into
      chunks

2   packages of beefy onion dry
      soup mix
1   (10-ounce) can cream of
      mushroom soup
      Water, sherry or wine

Arrange roast and vegetables on foil-lined roasting pan; sprinkle with soup mix. Spoon on mushroom soup, thinned with water to desired consistency. Wrap foil tightly; seal. Cook 3 hours at 325°.

Yield: 4 servings

Beef Brisket

B
L
E
S
S
I
N
G
S

1 beef brisket, any size, allow 6-8 ounces per person	Seasoned salt
Meat tenderizer	¼ cup Worcestershire sauce
Garlic salt	3 tablespoons liquid smoke
Celery salt	Small new potatoes, whole or halved (optional)

Sprinkle both sides of brisket with tenderizer. Sprinkle with garlic, celery and seasoned salts. Combine Worcestershire and liquid smoke and pour over roast. Cover and bake at 225° for 6-8 hours. About 3 hours before roast is done, potatoes may be added. Serve hot.

Yield: 1 roast   Perdita Brantley

Beef Brisket with Potatoes On the Half-Shell

4-4½ pounds whole beef brisket	2 bay leaves
Salt and freshly ground pepper	6-8 Idaho potatoes, uniform in size
2 cups water, or as needed	Watercress or parsley for garnish
3 sprigs fresh thyme, or 1 teaspoon dried	

Preheat oven to 450°. Wipe brisket with clean, damp cloth and season with salt to taste. Brown in a deep roasting pan, 30-35 minutes, until golden brown. Add 2 cups or just enough water to keep the bottom of roast from sticking and burning. Sprinkle roast with pepper to taste. Add thyme and bay leaves; cover and reduce heat to 325°. Cook another 2-2 1/2 hours or until meat is tender. Meanwhile, scrub potatoes and cut in half lengthwise. About 35-40 minutes before meat is done, lay potatoes skin side up, cut side down, around the brisket. Season meat juices and potatoes with salt to taste if needed. Allow potatoes to cook in meat drippings in roasting pan. About 15 minutes before potatoes are done, raise heat to 425°; remove cover and baste with juices. Test meat for tenderness with a thin skewer. To serve, remove bay leaves and place brisket on a warmed platter; surround it with potatoes and garnish. Slice the meat as it is served, as brisket dries out quickly. Serve with sauce boats of skimmed pan juices and *SOUR CREAM-HORSERADISH SAUCE.*

SOUR CREAM-HORSERADISH SAUCE:

1 cup sour cream	3 tablespoons prepared horseradish
Salt to taste	

Combine all ingredients in a small bowl. Transfer to a sauce boat and serve.

Yield: 6-8 servings   Dee Hopkins

Raisin Sauce

Great on ham!

1	cup raisins	¼	teaspoon salt
1	cup water	⅛	teaspoon pepper
5	whole cloves	1	tablespoon margarine
¾	cup brown sugar	1	teaspoon Worcestershire
1	teaspoon cornstarch		sauce

Cover the raisins with 1 cup water in a saucepan and add cloves. Simmer 10 minutes. Mix sugar, cornstarch, salt and pepper. Add to raisin mixture and cook until slightly thickened. Remove and discard cloves. Add margarine and Worcestershire to raisin mixture. Stir well until margarine melts. Store sauce in refrigerator.

Yield: 1 cup

Miriam L. Williams

Fluffy Horseradish Sauce

2-3	tablespoons creamy horseradish sauce	¾	teaspoon sugar
⅓-½	cup mayonnaise	2	cups whipped heavy cream or frozen extra creamy whipped topping, thawed
1-2	teaspoons lemon juice		

In a bowl, blend horseradish sauce, mayonnaise, lemon juice and sugar. Fold in whipped cream. Refrigerate. Serve sauce with beef.

Yield: 2½ cups

Barbecue Sauce

2	tablespoons brown sugar	¼	teaspoon pepper
2	tablespoons cider vinegar	1	teaspoon prepared mustard
4	tablespoons lemon juice	1	cup ketchup
3	tablespoons Worcestershire sauce	2	tablespoons butter
		1	medium onion, chopped

Combine sugar, vinegar, lemon juice, Worcestershire, pepper, mustard and ketchup. In a medium pan, melt butter and sauté onions. Add ketchup mixture and bring to a boil. Use as a sauce for chicken, pork or beef.

Yield: 1½ cups

Donna Cauble

Beef Sir Wellington
Worth the effort

2½	pounds ground sirloin	½	teaspoon salt
3	tablespoons white wine Worcestershire sauce		Dash of pepper or lemon pepper
3	tablespoons Worcestershire sauce	1-2	(7-ounce) cans sliced mushrooms, drained (optional)
3-6	tablespoons water		
1	clove garlic, crushed, or ¼ teaspoon garlic powder	8	dashes of liquid smoke Vegetable cooking oil
1	tablespoon fresh parsley, snipped	2	(17¼-ounce) packages frozen puff pastry dough
⅛	teaspoon dried tarragon, crushed	1	egg white, slightly beaten

Preheat oven to 450°. Combine beef, Worcestershire sauces (and a small amount of water to moisten), and the garlic, parsley, tarragon, salt and pepper. Add mushrooms if desired. Divide mixture into 8 round, flattened portions; top each patty with a dash of liquid smoke. Brush both sides of patties with oil. Brown in a hot skillet for about 5 minutes on each side. Remove from heat; set aside. On a slightly floured surface, roll out and cut pastry sheets to form eight 7x7-inch squares. Place 1 patty in the center of each pastry square. Brush the edges of pastry with beaten egg white. Fold pastry over meat and pinch edges to seal. Brush tops with egg white. Cut out and apply excess pastry decoratively, if desired. Place on a baking sheet. Bake for 10 minutes. Reduce heat to 400° and bake another 10 minutes or until pastry is golden brown. Let stand 5 minutes before serving.

GOLDEN TARRAGON SAUCE:

3	egg yolks	¼	teaspoon salt
½	cup butter or margarine, melted	½	teaspoon dried tarragon, crushed
2	tablespoons lemon juice	1	teaspoon parsley, snipped
2	tablespoons hot water		

Beat egg yolks in a glass bowl with wire whisk until fluffy. Add butter, lemon juice, hot water, salt, tarragon and parsley. Cook on high in microwave for 1 1/2 minutes, stirring every 30 seconds until thickened. Remove from oven and whisk again. Pour sauce into a gravy ladle and serve over hot *BEEF SIR WELLINGTON ENTRÉE.*

NOTE: You may substitute 8 (4-5-ounce) beef filets for the ground sirloin or you may serve the sauce on the cooked beef patties without pastry wraps. GOLDEN TARRAGON SAUCE is also wonderful served over broccoli.

Yield: 8 servings

Stir Fry Beef & Broccoli

1	pound boneless round steak	3	tablespoons vegetable oil
⅓	cup soy sauce	4	cups broccoli florets
½	cup water	1	large onion, cut into 8
2	tablespoons brown sugar		wedges
1	clove garlic, crushed		Hot cooked rice
1	teaspoon ground ginger		(approximately 1 cup,
1	teaspoon cornstarch		uncooked)

Partially freeze steak and slice across grain into 3x1/4-inch strips. Marinate steak 1 hour in marinade made by combining soy sauce, 1/4 cup of the water, brown sugar, garlic, ginger and cornstarch. Drain steak, reserving marinade. Pour oil in preheated wok or large non-stick frying pan. Stir fry steak until just browned; remove and set aside. Add broccoli, onion and remaining 1/4 cup water. Cover and reduce heat. Cook 3-5 minutes until broccoli is crisp tender. Stir in steak and marinade. Cook 1 minute stirring constantly until thickened. Serve over rice.

Yield: 4-6 servings   Ann S. Koontz

Crock Pot Beef Barbecue

A yummy fix - ahead casual dish

1	(2-2½-pound) boneless chuck roast, trimmed	½	teaspoon dry mustard
1	medium onion, chopped	1	teaspoon beef bouillon granules
¾	cup cola beverage	½	teaspoon chili powder
¼	cup Worcestershire sauce	¼	teaspoon ground red pepper
1	tablespoon apple cider vinegar	½	cup ketchup
2	cloves garlic, minced	2	teaspoons margarine
			Buns or rolls

Combine roast and onion in a 4-quart slow cooker. Combine cola, Worcestershire, vinegar, garlic, mustard, bouillon, chili powder and pepper. Reserve 1/2 cup of cola mixture and place in refrigerator. Pour remaining mixture over roast. Cook, covered, on high for 6 hours or until roast is very tender. Drain and shred roast. Combine reserved 1/2 cup cola mixture with ketchup and margarine in small saucepan. Cook over medium heat, stirring constantly until thoroughly heated. Pour over shredded roast and stir gently. Serve on buns or rolls.

Yield: 6 servings   Nancy Anderson

Honey Grilled Tenderloins

2 (¾-pound) pork tenderloins, trimmed
½ cup low sodium soy sauce
5 cloves garlic, halved

2 tablespoons brown sugar
3 tablespoons honey
2 teaspoons dark sesame oil

Butterfly tenderloins by cutting each lengthwise to within 1/4-inch of other side. Place in shallow container. Combine soy sauce and garlic; pour over tenderloins. Cover; refrigerate at least 3 hours, turning occasionally. Remove tenderloins, discard marinade. Combine brown sugar, honey and oil in a small saucepan. Cook over low heat, stirring constantly, until sugar dissolves, keeping warm to prevent thickening. Place tenderloins on grill rack coated with cooking spray over medium coals (350°-400°). Brush with honey mixture. Cook 20 minutes until meat thermometer registers 160°, basting frequently with honey mixture and turning once.

Yield: 6 servings   Dee Hopkins

Pasta with Sausage & Peppers
Viva Italia!

1½-2 pounds sweet Italian sausage
3 tablespoons olive oil
1 cup finely chopped onion
3 sweet red peppers seeded and cut into medium julienne
1 cup dry red wine
1 (27-ounce) can Italian tomatoes, including juice
½-1 cup water
1 tablespoon dried oregano

1 teaspoon dried thyme
Salt and freshly ground pepper
Dash of dried red pepper flakes
1 teaspoon fennel seeds
½ cup chopped, fresh Italian parsley
6 cloves garlic, minced
2 pounds pasta of choice, cooked and drained

Prick sausage links all over with fork tines and place in 1/2-inch water in a 4-quart pot. Simmer on medium heat for 20 minutes. As water evaporates, sausage will begin to fry in it's own juice. Turn occasionally; cook 10 minutes. Remove sausage and drain on paper towel; discard fat. Set pot on low heat. Add olive oil and onions; cook until tender, about 20 minutes. Add peppers, raising heat, and cook uncovered, 5 minutes, stirring often. Add wine, tomatoes with juice, water, oregano, thyme, salt and pepper to taste and red pepper flakes. Bring to a boil; reduce heat and simmer, partially covered, for 30 minutes. Meanwhile, slice sausage into 1/2-inch rounds. When sauce has simmered 30 minutes, add sausages and fennel seeds; simmer uncovered, 20 minutes. Add parsley and garlic; simmer 5 minutes. Pour over pasta and serve.

Yield: Serves 6   Claire Mitchell Allen

♠ Ham with Raspberry Cherry Glaze

1	(3-4-pound) boneless, fully cooked ham, skin removed	¼	teaspoon ground cloves
1	(21-ounce) can dark, sweet cherry pie filling	1½-2	tablespoons black raspberry wine vinegar
1½	teaspoons cinnamon sugar	2	(12-ounce) jars cherry preserves

Preheat oven to 325°. Place ham in an aluminum foil lined roasting pan and bake for 1 hour. While ham is baking, prepare *RASPBERRY CHERRY GLAZE.* In a saucepan, combine pie filling, cinnamon sugar, cloves, vinegar and preserves. Simmer 10-15 minutes until liquid reduces and mixture thickens. Set aside until ready to use. Remove ham from oven and spoon on some of glaze mixture. Bake ham another 30-45 minutes, spooning glaze over ham every 15 minutes. Slice, serve and pass with remaining glaze.

Yield: 10-12 servings

Southern Pork Chops

4	pork chops	1	(28-ounce) can whole or chopped tomatoes, undrained
1	large onion, chopped		
1	cup rice, cooked as directed		
	Salt and pepper		

Brown chops and remove to Dutch oven or heavy baking pan, reserving drippings. Brown onion in drippings, adding water if necessary.) Season chops and rice with salt and pepper to taste. Mix rice with onions; spoon over chops. Pour tomatoes over all. May assemble in morning and bake that night. Cover; bake at 325° for 40 minutes.

Yield: Serves 4

Lollie Wesner Streiff
Elizabeth Boyle Wesner

Easy Barbecued Pork

1	pork roast	1	(28-ounce) can tomatoes, diced
1	(10-ounce) bottle soy sauce		
1	(10-ounce) bottle Worcestershire sauce	1	cup brown sugar
		1	onion, diced

Place roast in a Dutch oven. Mix soy sauce, Worcestershire, tomatoes, sugar and onion and pour over meat. Cover and bake at 350° for 4 hours.

NOTE: *Allow 3/4-1 pound of pork per person for bone-in roast; or allow 6-8 ounces of pork per person for boneless roast.*

Yield: 1 pork roast

Carolyn McDonald

Tuscan Herbed Pork Roast

1½	tablespoons chopped, fresh rosemary	½	teaspoon pepper
2	large cloves garlic, minced	3½	pounds pork tenderloin
1	teaspoon salt	3	tablespoons olive oil
		½	cup dry white wine

Preheat oven to 450°. Mix rosemary, garlic, salt and pepper. Rub mixture on tenderloin. Position meat in roasting pan and brush with oil. Place in oven; immediately reduce heat to 325°. After 15 minutes, add wine and baste with drippings. Cook 20-30 more minutes until meat thermometer reads 170°. Let meat rest 10-15 minutes before carving. Meanwhile, deglaze pan with water, boiling it down to a syrupy glaze. Slice meat thinly and serve hot or cold with glaze.

NOTE: *May serve with ROASTED ROSEMARY POTATOES (see Page 248).*

Yield: Serves 6-8   Monica Farrington

Oriental Baby Back Ribs

3-3½	pounds baby back ribs	¾	cup sugar
½	cup ketchup	1	garlic clove, minced
½	cup soy sauce	1	1-inch piece gingerroot, peeled and minced
½	cup dry sherry		

Put ribs in a large dish, meaty side down. Whisk ketchup, soy sauce, sherry, sugar, cloves and ginger together. Pour mixture over meat and marinate 4 hours or overnight. Preheat oven to 325°. Line bottom of broiler pan with foil and fill with 1-inch of water. Remove ribs (reserving marinade liquid) and place on a rack over the water. Drain marinade into saucepan and bring to a boil. Reduce heat; simmer for 3 minutes. Remove pan from heat. Bake ribs for about 45 minutes, basting occasionally with marinade.

Yield: 6 servings   Valinda Isenhower

Marinated London Broil

¼	cup soy sauce	1	tablespoon Worcestershire sauce
⅔	cup oil		Pepper
¼	cup vinegar or wine	1	clove garlic, crushed
1	tablespoon dry mustard	1	flank steak or London broil

Combine all ingredients except meat. Pour mixture over steak and marinate 6-8 hours or overnight, turning meat periodically and piercing with a sharp fork. Grill, broil or cook steak as desired, basting with marinade while cooking.

Yield: 1⅓ cups   Adair Doran

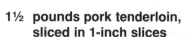

Pork Medallions

1½	pounds pork tenderloin, sliced in 1-inch slices
4	tablespoons olive oil
2	tablespoons balsamic vinegar
5	ounces thinly sliced prosciutto (Italian ham), chopped

1	pound fresh spinach, rinsed and chopped coarsely
1	pound plum tomatoes, chopped coarsely
½	teaspoon salt
¼	teaspoon fresh ground pepper

In a 2-quart sauté pan, brown pork slices in 2 tablespoons of olive oil; toss with vinegar. Remove from pan. Set aside and keep warm. In same pan, sauté prosciutto in remaining 2 tablespoons oil. Add spinach, tomatoes, salt and pepper. Cover and simmer for 10 minutes. Add pork; heat through before serving. Great with mashed potatoes.

Yield: Serves 4   Lisa Ganem

Cre's Rosemary Pork Loin Roast

1	(3-4 pound) pork loin
1	tablespoon rosemary leaves
	Salt
	Garlic salt

	Fresh ground black pepper
1	(8-ounce) jar apricot preserves, tested

Sprinkle pork generously with rosemary, salt, garlic salt and pepper to taste. Place pork in roasting pan. Bake in oven preheated to 400° for 20 minutes to brown roast. Reduce heat to 325°, bake 2 hours. Remove from oven; cover roast with preserves. Serve hot.

Yield: 8-10 servings   Sara Cook

🔔 Country Ham Reynolds' Method

1	country ham (Boneless Ham — allow ½ pound per person)
	(Bone-in Ham — allow 1 pound per person)

Scrub ham well. Place in tepid water in a 5-gallon lard tin to soak 8 hours or overnight. Pour off water; cover with fresh water. Bring to rolling boil (may take 1-2 hours). Boil for 15-20 minutes, uncovered. Remove from heat; cover with lid. Meanwhile, arrange in a little red wagon: layer of blankets and thick layer of newspapers. Place ham in lard tin with lid on top; wrap with newspapers; tie to secure. Over wrap blankets; tie to secure. Roll wagon carrying ham into a back room; let stand overnight. Next day, roll wagon back into kitchen, undo wrappings, open tin; enjoy! A tender ham!

NOTE: *In the late 1700's the Reynolds family, as Quakers from Illinois, learned from the Indians who baked hams on the ground, wrapped in leaves.*

Yield: 1 ham   Patsy and Ozzie Reynolds

Grilled Lamb with Rosemary

3 tablespoons fresh lemon juice
3 tablespoons extra virgin olive oil
2 tablespoons chopped fresh rosemary
1 tablespoon chopped fresh thyme

1 tablespoon minced garlic
1 teaspoon freshly ground pepper
1 (5-pound) leg of lamb, boned, butterflied and trimmed
Salt

Mix lemon juice, oil, herbs, garlic and pepper in a large shallow dish. Add lamb, rubbing well with oil mixture. Let stand at room temperature for 1 hour. Prepare grill. Sprinkle lamb with dash of salt. Grill over hot coals for 20 minutes on each side. Slice diagonally to serve.

NOTE: *Prepared lamb may be refrigerated overnight, uncooked. Return lamb to room temperature before grilling.*

Yield: 10 servings   Dottie Abramowski

Roast Leg of Lamb with Pan Gravy

1 (5 pound) leg of lamb, half boned or bone in
12 cloves garlic, peeled
⅓ cup herbes Des Provence or mixed dried herbs

½ cup flour, seasoned with salt and pepper
12 large sprigs fresh rosemary

Preheat oven to 450°. Trim exterior fat from roast, leaving a little fat for flavor. Cut small incisions all over meat surface with a sharp knife; insert garlic in each. Rub roast surface with herbs, then seasoned flour. In a roasting pan, set roast on a bed of 1/2 the rosemary and strew the remainder of rosemary on top. Roast in oven for 10-15 minutes. Reduce heat to 400°; cook about 40 minutes or until done. Remove from oven; let rest 15 minutes before carving. Serve with gravy.

PAN GRAVY:
Juices in pan from roasting meat

1 cup wine, white or red
⅓ cup flour (approximately)

After removing the roast and rosemary from the pan, set pan on top of stove burner. Deglaze the crusty bits from pan with a spatula by adding a little wine over a very low heat. Then gradually add flour, whisking constantly, until gravy is a pale brown. Gradually whisk in wine until desired consistency is reached. Serve with roasted lamb.

Yield: 5-6 servings   Lee Clement Piper

Lamb Patties with Mint Sauce

3½	pounds ground lamb		Dash of fresh ground white pepper
1¾-2	cups soft bread crumbs		
1	cup white wine Worcestershire sauce	1	tablespoon butter or margarine
¼-½	teaspoon salt	¾	cup sour cream or yogurt
½	teaspoon crushed dried rosemary	2-3	teaspoons sugar
½-¾	teaspoon crushed dried thyme	1	(10-ounce) bottle mint sauce, contents heated
½	teaspoon garlic powder	1	(10-ounce) bottle mint jelly, melted (optional)

In a mixing bowl, combine lamb, bread crumbs, 1/2 cup Worcestershire, salt, rosemary, thyme, garlic and pepper. Shape into eight (3-4-inch) patties, (3/4-1-inch) thick. In a skillet, melt butter on medium heat. Cook patties 4 at a time by sautéing for 6-8 minutes on each side. Baste with remaining 1/2 cup Worcestershire sauce. Serve lamb with a warm *MINT SAUCE* made by blending sour cream, sugar and mint sauce; or serve patties simply with mint jelly.

Yield: 8 patties, 1¼ cup sauce

Veal Marsala

6	(8-ounce) veal cutlets, pounded	1	cup chicken broth
	Oil	⅓	cup Marsala wine
2	tablespoons flour	1	teaspoon lemon juice
1	cup mushrooms, sliced	¼	teaspoon salt
½	cup red or green pepper strips	¼	teaspoon pepper
½	cup onion slices	1	cup cooked fettuccine or any pasta, drained

Coat veal with flour and sauté in small amount of oil. Remove veal from pan and set aside. Sauté vegetables. Add broth, wine, lemon juice, salt and pepper; cook until tender. Add vegetable mixture to veal; place in an ovenproof dish. Bake at 400° for 15-20 minutes. Serve over pasta.

NOTE: *Recipe works well with pork or chicken cutlets. My teenage son's favorite entrée.*

Yield: 6 servings   Kaye Hirst

177

Peppercorn Beef Tenderloin

1 (5-6 pound) beef tenderloin, trimmed Nature's Seasonings salt	Garlic powder Black peppercorns, crushed

Preheat oven to 450°. Rub tenderloin with desired amount of seasoning salt and garlic powder and cover meat completely with peppercorns. Place in roasting pan and bake 15 minutes for rare, 30 minutes for medium. Turn oven off; do not open door. Let roast remain in oven for 45 minutes; time may vary according to oven, size of roast, and desired doneness. Thinly slice and serve with *HORSERADISH SAUCE.*

Yield: 6-8 servings

HORSERADISH SAUCE:

⅓	cup mayonnaise	⅓ cup horseradish
⅓	cup sour cream	

Combine all ingredients; refrigerate until ready to serve.

Yield: 1 cup

Sara Cook

Cranberry Ketchup

1 (16-ounce) can jellied cranberry or whole berry sauce	1 tablespoon minced fresh ginger
¾ cup sugar (white or light brown) sugar	⅛ teaspoon ground allspice
¼ cup white or apple cider vinegar	⅛ teaspoon fine ground black pepper
	1 tablespoon flour
	1½-2 tablespoons water

Combine sauce, sugar, vinegar, ginger, allspice and pepper in medium saucepan. Blend flour with water until smooth; add to cranberry mixture. Bring to boil; stir constantly, reduce heat and simmer 5 minutes until thick and bubbly. Store covered in refrigerator. Serve with meat or with crackers and cream cheese.

Yield: 2 cups

Plenty of Poultry

Classic Chicken Choices

&

Turkey for the Platter

Easy Chicken Cordon Bleu

10-12 boneless chicken breasts
6   strips bacon, cut in half
12   slices dried beef
1   (10¾-ounce) can cream of
       mushroom soup

1   (10¾-ounce) can cream of
       chicken soup
1   (8-ounce) package cream
       cheese, softened

Wrap each chicken breast with a piece of bacon and a slice of dried beef; arrange in 9x13-inch baking dish. Mix soups and cream cheese; pour over chicken. Bake at 325° for 1 hour or until done. Serve over white rice.

Yield: 12 servings   Crystal Vanhoy

New Year's Chicken

3½ cups cooked chicken or
     turkey, cubed
1   pound hot sausage, cooked
     and crumbled
1   (6-ounce) box long grain and
     wild rice

2½ cups chicken broth
2   (10¾-ounce) cans cream of
     mushroom soup
1   cup dry herb stuffing mix
     Melted butter

Combine chicken and sausage. Prepare the rice according to package directions using broth instead of water. Combine chicken, sausage, rice and soup; stir and place in a large baking dish. Sprinkle with herb stuffing mix that has been tossed with melted butter. Bake for 30 minutes at 375°. Serve hot.

Yield: 10 servings   Pat Fromen

Chicken, Artichoke &
Country Ham Casserole

8   thin slices country ham
8   slices bacon
8   chicken breast halves, boned
    and skinned

1   (14-ounce) can artichoke
    hearts, drained and quartered
1   (10¾-ounce) can cream of
    mushroom soup
½   pint sour cream

Place ham slices in bottom of a large casserole dish. Wrap bacon around each chicken piece and place on top of ham. Arrange artichoke hearts around chicken. Mix soup and sour cream and spread over all. Refrigerate until needed, then bake uncovered at 275° for 3 1/2 hours. Serve hot.

NOTE: *May be assembled and refrigerated a day ahead. Bake as directed; serve.*

Yield: Serves 8   Susan Kluttz

🔔 Surprise Chicken Casserole

1	hen, large fryer, or 4-5 chicken breasts	1	onion, chopped fine
1	(10¾-ounce) can cream of celery soup	1	(10-ounce) package tiny frozen lima beans, thawed
1	(10¾-ounce) can cream of mushroom soup	1	(8-ounce) package herb stuffing mix
		1	stick margarine or butter

Stew chicken in water until done. Reserve 2 1/2 cups of broth from stewing chicken; remove and discard chicken skin and bones. Cut chicken into bite-sized pieces to equal 4 cups and set aside. Stir together chicken broth, celery soup and mushroom soup in large saucepan and heat. To assemble, melt margarine in the bottom of a large (12x15-inch) shallow casserole or two medium (9x12-inch) dishes. Make layers as follows: 1) half of stuffing mix sprinkled over the margarine, 2) lima beans (the surprise ingredient), 3) onions. Top onion layer with the chicken. Pour soup mixture over chicken and top with remaining stuffing. Bake 35 minutes at 400°. Serve hot.

Yield: 12-15 servings   Melda M. Killion

Chicken Divan Divine

3	whole boneless chicken breasts, cooked and halved	1½-2	teaspoons Dijon mustard Salt and pepper
2	(10-ounce) packages frozen broccoli spears	½	cup fresh grated Parmesan cheese
2	(10¾-ounce) cans cream of chicken soup	1	cup crushed sesame cheese cracker tidbits
1	cup mayonnaise		Paprika
1	(8-ounce) carton sour cream		Butter
1	cup grated sharp cheddar cheese		Mushrooms (optional)
1	tablespoon fresh lemon juice		Slivered almonds (optional)

Cut chicken into bite-sized pieces and set aside. Cook broccoli in microwave in a glass 3-quart greased dish until each spear is hot, thawed and almost done. (About 10-15 minutes for 2 packages.) Drain; arrange spears to cover casserole dish. In a bowl, mix soup, mayonnaise, sour cream and cheddar cheese; add lemon juice, mustard and salt and pepper to taste to make sauce. Sprinkle half of parmesan cheese over broccoli. Next, layer the chicken. Sprinkle with remaining Parmesan. Pour sauce over chicken and broccoli. Bake at 350° for 35-45 minutes. Top casserole with crushed crackers and paprika, dot with butter and bake 10-15 more minutes. Serve hot.

NOTE: *You may add sautéed fresh sliced or canned mushrooms, drained, or slivered almonds. Recipe may be doubled and may be frozen.*

Yield: 6-8 servings

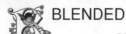

B
L
E
S
S
I
N
G
S

♥ Favorite Grilled Chicken

½	cup extra-virgin olive oil	¼	cup lemon juice
1	(0.6-ounce) envelope Italian salad dressing mix	4	boneless, skinless chicken breasts, halved

Prepare a hot grill. Combine oil, dressing mix and lemon juice in a small bowl. Pour mixture over chicken; arranged in a large dish. Let stand for 5 minutes. Grill chicken 10-12 minutes, turning occasionally, until done; serve.

Yield: 4-8 servings   Betsy Knauf

Almond Rice Chicken Casserole

1	tablespoon chopped onion	1	cup cooked chicken pieces
3	tablespoons butter or margarine	¾	cup almonds, slivered
¼	cup flour	1	teaspoon salt
1	cup chicken stock		Dash pepper
½	cup milk	2	cups cooked rice
½	cup cream	1	cup grated cheese

Sauté onions in butter or margarine. Stir in flour. Add chicken stock and milk gradually. Cook, stirring until thick. Add cream, chicken, almonds, salt and pepper. Bring to boil; mix together with rice. Turn into a 2-quart greased casserole dish. Cover with cheese; bake for 20 minutes at 400°. Serve hot.

Yield: 6-8 servings   Susan Mesimer

♣ Betsy's Chicken Casserole

1	(6-ounce) package long grain and wild rice, cooked according to package directions	1	(2-ounce) jar chopped pimentos, optional
		1	cup mayonnaise
3	cups chopped, cooked chicken	1	(8-ounce) can sliced water chestnuts, drained
1	(10¾-ounce) can cream of celery soup	2	(16-ounce) cans french-style green beans, drained
½	cup diced onion	1	(2.8-ounce) can french fried onions

Combine all ingredients except french fried onions. Pour into 2 1/2-3-quart casserole. Bake at 350° for 20 minutes. Cover with french fried onions; bake 20 minutes more. Serve hot.

NOTE: *May be prepared a day ahead. Freezes well prior to baking.*

Yield: Serves 10-12   Mrs. Frank S. Parrott

Easy Chicken & Wild Rice Casserole

1 **pound boneless chicken breasts**	1 **(4-ounce) can sliced mushrooms, with liquid**
1 **(6-ounce) package long grain wild rice mix with seasonings**	**Chopped onions (optional)**
1 **(10¾-ounce) can cream of mushroom soup, undiluted**	**Chopped celery (optional)**

Sauté chicken breasts until done. Cook rice according to package directions. Slice chicken and mix with cooked rice, soup and mushrooms. Bake at 350° for 30 minutes. Serve.

NOTE: *Chopped onions and celery may be sautéed along with the chicken and added to this dish.*

Yield: 4-6 servings   Katharine Osborne

♥ Family Favorite Chicken Tetrazzini

1 **chicken, stewed, boned and cut into pieces**	1 **(10¾-ounce) can cream of chicken soup**
1 **(2-ounce) jar pimentos, drained**	1 **cup milk**
1 **(3.4-ounce) can mushrooms plus liquid**	1 **cup grated Parmesan cheese**
	1 **(8-ounce) box spaghetti, cooked and drained**
	¼ **cup butter, melted**

Combine all ingredients; pour into buttered 11x7-inch casserole dish. Bake, uncovered, at 400° for about 30-45 minutes, until bubbly and brown. Serve.

NOTE: *I modify this original recipe using lowfat ingredients such as skim milk, low sodium soup and lowfat margarine. Freezes well.*

Yield: 6-8 servings   Barbara S. Bumgarner

Honey Dijon Grilled Chicken

¼ **cup olive oil**	¼ **cup honey**
½ **cup vegetable oil**	3 **tablespoons white vinegar**
½ **cup Dijon mustard**	6-8 **boneless chicken breasts**
¼ **cup whole grain mustard**	

Whisk all ingredients except chicken, together. Use mixture to marinate chicken overnight. Grill over hot coals 5-7 minutes per side, basting each side once while cooking; serve.

Yield: 6-8 servings   Tricia Johnson

Chicken Diablo

B
L
E
S
S
I
N
G
S

½	stick butter	1	teaspoon salt
½	cup honey	1	teaspoon curry powder
¼	cup Dijon mustard	4-6	pieces boneless chicken

Melt butter in shallow baking dish. Stir in honey, mustard, salt and curry. Roll chicken in dish, coating both sides. Bake at 350° for 45 minutes; serve.

Yield: 4-6 servings   Kathryn Baker

Chicken Tetrazzini

3	tablespoons chopped green pepper	1	teaspoon salt
		2	cups milk
3	tablespoons chopped onion	2	cups chopped, cooked chicken
1	(4-ounce) can sliced mushrooms, undrained	1	(10-ounce) package flat egg noodles, cooked and drained
½	cup margarine		
½	cup flour	2	cups grated cheese

Cook pepper, onion and mushrooms in margarine until soft. Blend in flour and salt. Stir in milk until mixture is smooth and thickened. Stir in chicken. Place noodles in a 9x13-inch casserole dish. Pour chicken mixture over noodles and stir until blended. Bake at 350° for 25 minutes. Top with cheese during the last 5 minutes of baking. Serve hot.

Yield: 4 servings   Charlotte Hall

Chicken Chimichangas

1	cup cooked chicken, diced	8	(8-inch) flour tortillas
⅓	cup sliced green onions	1	(8-ounce) package shredded
¾	teaspoon cumin		Monterey Jack and cheddar
½	teaspoon dried oregano		cheese
¼	teaspoon salt		Vegetable cooking spray
1	(16-ounce) jar salsa		Sour cream

Combine chicken (may use 3 (5-ounce) cans chicken, drained), onion, cumin, oregano, salt and 2/3 cup of the salsa. Cook on medium heat 5 minutes, stir often. Spoon 2 tablespoons of mixture on each tortilla; sprinkle evenly with 1/2 of the cheese. Fold tortillas to enclose filling. Place folded side down in a lightly greased 13x9-inch baking pan. Bake at 475° for 10 minutes. Pour remaining salsa over tortillas; sprinkle with remaining cheese. Bake 5 minutes. Top with dollops of sour cream. Serve hot.

Yield: 8 small or 4 large servings   Michelle Cook

Peachtree Chicken Fettuccine

Looks festive and is easy to make

½	pound fresh mushrooms, sliced	1	(8-ounce) fettuccine, cooked according to package directions, drained and kept warm
1	small sweet red pepper, seeded, cut into thin strips		
1	small onion, chopped	½	cup whipping cream
1	clove garlic, crushed	½	cup grated Parmesan cheese
½	cup plus 2 tablespoons butter or margarine, melted	2	tablespoons chopped fresh parsley
3	cups chopped, cooked chicken	¼	teaspoon ground white pepper

Sauté mushrooms, peppers, onion and garlic in 2 tablespoons of the butter in a large skillet over medium heat until vegetables are tender. Add chicken and cook until thoroughly heated. Set aside and keep warm. To make sauce, combine whipping cream and the remaining 1/2 cup of butter in a small saucepan. Cook over low heat. Stir in Parmesan cheese, parsley and white pepper. To serve, pour sauce over hot fettuccine; add chicken mixture. Toss until fettuccine is thoroughly coated. Serve hot.

Yield: 6-8 servings   Millie Gurley

Chicken Casserole

CREAM CHEESE CRUST:

1	(8-ounce) package cream cheese, softened	2	sticks butter or margarine, softened
		2	cups self-rising flour

Mix cream cheese, butter and flour. Chill dough in refrigerator 1 hour. Flouring hands often, pat out 2/3 of dough to form the bottom and sides of crust in a 9x12-inch dish. Shape remaining dough into patties for a top crust.

FILLING:

3½	pounds stewed and cooked chicken cooled, reserve 1 cup of broth	1	(10½-ounce) can cream of celery soup
			Salt and pepper
1	(10½-ounce) can cream of mushroom soup		

Bone and cut chicken into bite-sized pieces. Mix chicken with the soups, broth and salt and pepper to taste. Pour over crust; top with dough patties. Bake 45 minutes at 350°. Freezes well. Thaw; bake and serve.

NOTE: *Adding cooked frozen veggies adds color and flavor. Crust may be made and refrigerated a night or day ahead. Let dough sit at room temperature until workable.*

Yield: Serves 6-8   Jennifer C. Seifert

Mexican Chicken Enchiladas

A Teens With A Mission specialty

4 large chicken breasts, cooked and diced
1 medium chopped onion
1 (4.5-ounce) can chopped mild green chiles, drained
1 (10.5-ounce) can cream of chicken soup

1 pint sour cream
1 pound shredded mozzarella cheese
8-10 flour tortillas
Sliced ripe olives (optional)
Taco sauce (optional)
Salsa (optional)

Mix chicken, onion and chiles. In separate bowl, mix soup, sour cream and cheese. Grease a 9x13-inch pan; place a thin layer of tortillas on the bottom. Add half of chicken mixture, then half of sour cream mixture. Repeat layers. Bake at 375° for 30 minutes. Let stand 10-15 minutes before cutting and serving. Serve with olives and taco sauce or salsa if desired.

NOTE: *May be prepared ahead and refrigerated, or if frozen, thaw and bake an additional 15 minutes. It may be made with lowfat soup and non-fat sour cream. This recipe is served with tacos, Spanish rice, snickerdoodles and lime sherbet as a fund raising dinner for our annual TWAM trip to Mexico.*

Yield: Serves 4-6   Helen Kichefski

♣ Chicken Enchilada Casserole

Salt and pepper
4 chicken breasts
2 (10½-ounce) cans cream of chicken soup
½ teaspoon oregano
¼ teaspoon ground cumin
¼ teaspoon ground sage
¼ teaspoon chili powder
2 cloves garlic, pressed

Oil
1 package of 12 corn tortillas
2 (4-ounce) cans chopped mild green chiles, drained
1 pound longhorn cheese, grated
¼ pound Monterey Jack cheese
2 large chopped onions

Lightly salt and pepper chicken; enclose tightly in foil and bake at 350° about 50-60 minutes until chicken is very tender. Cool, skin and bone chicken, reserving broth. Combine soup, broth and seasonings. In a large skillet, heat small amount of oil. Dip each tortilla in hot oil until soft. Drain well on paper towels. Grease bottom of a 2 1/2-quart baking dish and place 3 tortillas evenly over the bottom, overlapping slightly. Place approximately 1 breast of chicken (broken into bite-sized pieces) over tortillas. Top chicken with 1/4 of chiles. Combine cheeses. Top chiles with 1/4 of cheese mixture, sprinkle 1/4 of onion over cheese, then pour 1/4 soup mixture over the top. Repeat process to make 3-4 layers. Top with remaining cheese and onions. Bake at 375° for 1 hour. Serve hot.

Yield: 10-12 servings   Ruth Philpott

Bridge Club Chicken

A winner!

6	tablespoons butter	1	teaspoon lemon juice
6	tablespoons flour	½	teaspoon onion powder
1	teaspoon salt	2	cups chicken breasts, cooked
	White pepper		and chopped
1½	cups chicken broth	6	baked puff pastry cups, or
1	cup half-and-half		toast cups
¼	cup sherry		

Make cream sauce with butter, flour, salt, pepper, broth, cream, sherry, lemon juice and onion powder. Cook, stirring until thick. Add chicken and heat thoroughly. Serve over toast or in puff pastry cups.

NOTE: *If desired, add mushrooms, ripe olives and pimento. My bridge club's favorite for over 30 years.*

Yield: 6 servings

Sue Hayworth

Sweet & Sour Chicken

6-8	boneless chicken breasts, with or without skin	1	(1-ounce) envelope dry onion soup mix
1	(8-ounce) bottle Russian dressing	¼	cup water
1	(8-12-ounce) jar apricot preserves	1	(20-ounce) can chunk pineapple, drained

Preheat oven to 350°. Place chicken in baking pan. Combine dressing, preserves, soup mix and water. Pour mixture over chicken; cover with foil. Bake 1 hour; uncover, add pineapple and bake 15 more minutes. Serve hot.

Yield: 6-8 servings

Vickie M. Wallace

Pizza Chicken

1	(14-ounce) jar pizza sauce	6-8	ounces mozzarella cheese, shredded
6	boneless, skinless chicken breasts		

Preheat oven to 350°. Spray casserole dish with non-stick spray and pour enough pizza sauce to cover bottom. Lay the chicken breasts in the dish and sprinkle with cheese. Pour on remaining pizza sauce, covering the chicken. Bake covered for 45-60 minutes until chicken is done. Serve hot.

Yield: 6 servings

Fredna Farris

Indian Curried Chicken with Green Rice

6 tablespoons margarine, melted	¼ teaspoon ground ginger
½ cup minced onion	2 chicken bouillon cubes, dissolved in 2 cups hot water
1 tablespoon curry powder	2 cups milk
6 tablespoons flour	4 cups cooked chicken
1½ teaspoons salt	1 teaspoon lemon juice
1½ teaspoons sugar	

Sauté onion and curry powder over low heat in margarine; blend in flour, salt, sugar and ginger. Cook slowly until smooth and bubbly. Remove from heat; add bouillon and milk; return to heat; boil 1 minute, stir constantly. Add chicken and lemon juice. Heat through; set aside and keep warm.

GREEN RICE:

10 ounces cooked chopped spinach, drained	⅔ cup milk
2 eggs, slightly beaten	1 teaspoon salt
4 tablespoons soft margarine	1 teaspoon thyme
1 tablespoon Worcestershire sauce	3 cups cooked rice
½ cup chopped onion	Bacon bits, crushed pineapple, toasted almonds, coconut, pickles, chutney, chopped egg, raisins, for garnish
1 cup shredded sharp cheddar cheese	

Combine all ingredients for *GREEN RICE* and mix well. Pour into a 2-quart baking dish. Bake at 350° for 20-25 minutes. Remove rice from oven. Serve warm chicken over rice and top with your choice of garnishes.

Yield: Serves 8

Ann Brownlee

Easy Roast Turkey

1 (16-pound) fresh turkey, giblets removed, washed	2 teaspoons each of crushed rosemary, sage and poultry seasoning
2-4 tablespoons soft butter or vegetable oil	2 large sweet onions, quartered
½ teaspoon salt	3 cups dry red wine
½ teaspoon white pepper	1 (19x23½-inch) large oven cooking bag

Place turkey in bag, breast side up, in roasting pan; rub turkey with butter, coat well. Sprinkle seasoning inside and on turkey. Place onions in body cavity. Pour wine into bag; close; punch holes in top; bake on bottom oven rack at 350° 3-3 1/2 hours. Juices make great gravy.

Yield: 16-18 servings

Easy Chicken Pot Pie

2   (9-inch) prepared frozen
    unbaked pie crusts, thawed
4-5 chicken breasts or 1 whole
    chicken, cooked, boned and
    cut up

2   (10-ounce) boxes frozen
    mixed vegetables, cooked
2   (10½-ounce) cans cream of
    chicken soup
    Salt and pepper

Place 1 pie crust in bottom of a deep 9 or 10-inch pie pan. Mix chicken, vegetables, soup, and salt and pepper to taste; pour into pie shell. Top with second crust; seal edges together and crimp crust edges. Cut slits in crust top to vent. Bake according to package directions for a 2-crust pie. Serve hot.

Yield: 8-10 servings   Melda M. Killion

Never Fail Chicken & Dumplings

1½ cups flour
½   teaspoon salt
3   tablespoons shortening
1   egg
5   tablespoons water

3⅔ cups chicken broth from
    cooked chicken or 2 (14½-
    ounce) cans chicken broth
3-4 cooked chicken breasts, or
    3 cans cooked chicken

To make dumplings, mix flour, salt, shortening, egg and water. Roll dough into thin sheets. Cut into strips. (A pizza cutter works well.) Bring chicken broth to a boil in a 4-quart pot. Drop dough strips one at a time into boiling broth. Add chicken and cook until dumplings have absorbed broth and are no longer like dough, and are done. Serve hot.

Yield: 4 servings   Sharon Hampton and Harold Mesimer

Sweet - Sour Chicken Tenders
Unusual combination, but very tasty!

1   (16-ounce) can whole
    cranberry sauce
1   (8-ounce) bottle French salad
    dressing

1   (1-ounce) envelope dry onion
    soup mix
1   (4-5-pound) bag non-breaded
    chicken tenders

Mix cranberry sauce, dressing and onion soup mix. Marinate chicken in mixture overnight or at least 8 hours. Bake chicken in marinade mixture uncovered in a 9x13-inch casserole dish at 350° for 45 minutes, stirring once during cooking. If it appears to be getting dry before it has cooked the full 45 minutes, cover for the remainder of cooking time. Serve with rice.

Yield: Serves 8   Lois Carter

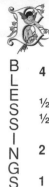

Uncle Louie's Chicken Cacciatore

4	large chicken breasts, boneless and skinless	6	large mushrooms, sliced
½	cup flour	10	green olives, sliced
½	cup olive oil (or any low fat oil)	10	black olives, sliced
		1	teaspoon capers (optional)
2	medium carrots, peeled and diced	2	(16-ounce) cans whole peeled tomatoes, with liquid
1	large red bell pepper, cored, seeded and julienned		Salt and pepper
		1	tablespoon fresh rosemary, chopped
1	large green bell pepper, cored, seeded and julienned	¼-1	cup dry white wine
1	large yellow onion, peeled and julienned	1	cup grated Parmesan cheese

Preheat oven to 400°. Toss chicken in bowl with flour and pat off excess flour from each piece of chicken. Brown chicken on both sides in a large frying pan with 1/2 the oil; remove to a roasting pan, leaving the oil in frying pan. Heat frying pan again and sauté carrots for 3 minutes. Add red and green peppers and onion, sautéing until onion is translucent. Place vegetables on top of chicken in roasting pan. Heat frying pan again, add remaining oil and sauté mushrooms, olives, and capers for 3 minutes. Add tomatoes; simmer for 5 minutes. Add salt and pepper to taste and pour mixture over chicken. Sprinkle with rosemary and drizzle the desired amount of wine over all. Cover roasting pan with foil; bake for 20 minutes. Uncover, add Parmesan cheese and bake uncovered for 15 minutes. Turn chicken twice in vegetable sauce while cooking. May eat as is, but Uncle Louie's serves this over linguine.

NOTE: *Uncle Louie's Restaurant is in Spencer, NC.*

Yield: 4 servings

Joseph and Leslie Cataldo

♥ Grilled Jalapeño Chicken

½	cup lime juice	2	tablespoons soy sauce
¼	cup honey	3	cloves garlic, minced
2	tablespoons fresh cilantro leaves, chopped		Salt and pepper
		6	chicken breasts
3	fresh jalapeños, seeded and chopped		

Combine all ingredients except chicken; process in blender. Place chicken in shallow container. Reserve 1/4 cup of marinade mixture; pour remainder over chicken. Refrigerate for 8 hours. Center a pan of water in bottom of grill; surround with charcoal. Place chicken on rack. Grill 1 hour, turning every 15 minutes. Warm reserved marinade; pour over cooked chicken to serve.

Yield: 6 servings

Mary V. Smith

Chicken Fajitas

FAJITA MARINADE:

2	tablespoons lemon juice
1	tablespoon Worcestershire sauce
⅛	teaspoon salt

¼	teaspoon pepper
¼	teaspoon cumin
2	cloves garlic, minced
1	tablespoon coriander

Combine marinade ingredients in a bowl; pour mixture over chicken. Cover and refrigerate for 30-60 minutes.

FAJITAS:

	Nonstick cooking spray
1	teaspoon canola oil
¼	green pepper, chopped
¼	onion, chopped
1	carrot, chopped

4	boneless, skinless chicken breasts, sliced diagonally or 1 pound chicken tenders that have been marinated
¼	tomato, chopped
4	(6-inch) tortillas
8	tablespoons salsa

Coat non-stick skillet with cooking spray; add oil. Allow to heat at medium high for 2 minutes. Add pepper, onion and carrot; stir-fry for 2 minutes. Remove vegetables and set aside. Add chicken to skillet and stir-fry 3-5 minutes. Return vegetables to skillet, add tomatoes; stir-fry 1 minute. Divide ingredients between 4 tortillas; spread 2 tablespoons of salsa over each. Roll up and serve.

Yield: Serves 4

Deborah Messinger

Tarragon Chicken

3	whole chicken breasts, skinned
1	onion
1	carrot
1	teaspoon fresh or dried tarragon, plus tarragon sprig for garnish

½	cup white wine
	Water
5	tablespoons butter
3	tablespoons flour
	Salt and pepper
1	egg yolk, beaten
3	tablespoons cream

Place chicken, onion, carrot, tarragon and wine in a 2-quart saucepan. Add enough water to cover; cook until tender. Remove breasts and keep warm. Strain broth. Cook until liquid is reduced to 2 cups. Melt 3 tablespoons of the butter. Stir in flour and salt and pepper to taste. Gradually add 2 cups broth. Stir until smooth. Stir in the remaining 2 tablespoons butter. Combine egg yolk and cream; stir into hot sauce. Serve sauce over chicken. Garnish with tarragon sprig.

Yield: 4-6 servings

Jean Owen

Chicken Wellington with Lemon Dill Sauce
Always a hit with guests!

8	boneless, skinless chicken breasts	8	thin slices reduced fat boiled ham
8	slices Swiss cheese	1	(17.25-ounce) package puff pastry sheets

Pound chicken breasts with mallet to flatten. Wrap each breast with slice of cheese and then a slice of ham. Cut puff pastry sheets into quarters to form 8 rectangles. With a rolling pin, roll each pastry piece out a bit larger than each breast. Place breast in center of dough and wrap like a package. Seal edges and place folded, sealed edges down on ungreased jelly roll pan. Bake 1 hour at 350°. Serve with Lemon Dill Sauce.

LEMON DILL SAUCE:

2	tablespoons margarine	2	cups low fat lemon yogurt
1	cup sliced fresh mushrooms	3	teaspoons grated lemon rind
6	tablespoons flour	½	teaspoon salt
1	cup chicken broth	1½	teaspoons dried dill weed
⅓	cup white wine		

Sauté mushrooms in melted margarine until soft. Add flour gradually, stirring constantly. Add broth, stirring constantly over medium heat until mixture is thick and smooth. Add wine, yogurt, lemon rind, salt and dill weed, stirring until blended and hot, but not boiling. Serve sauce in a dish with ladle.

NOTE: *To reduce fat, you may use 1 package phyllo dough to replace puff pastry, by cutting sheets into quarters, 5 sheets layered per breast. Spray sheets individually with butter-flavored cooking spray before wrapping chicken and proceed as above. LEMON DILL SAUCE is also good served with vegetables.*

Yield: Serves 8

Carol Freed

♥ Barbecue Chicken

½	cup horseradish powder	3	tablespoons Worcestershire sauce
½	cup mustard		
½	ounce chili powder	1	tablespoon salt
½	cup vinegar	2	cloves garlic, minced, or
1	tablespoon lemon juice		1 teaspoon garlic powder
1	cup brown sugar	¼	cup ketchup
		2	whole chickens

Mix horseradish powder, to taste, with remaining sauce ingredients. Pour over chickens. Cover and bake at 350° for 1 1/2 - 2 hours. Slice and serve.

Yield: 2 chickens

Becky Davis

Chicken Breast with Dill

1	teaspoon dill weed		Salt and pepper
¼	cup Parmesan cheese	4	boneless chicken breasts
2	cups bread crumbs	½	stick butter or margarine,
1	teaspoon parsley		melted

Preheat oven to 350°. Mix dill, cheese, crumbs, parsley, salt and pepper to taste. Dip chicken in melted butter; coat with dill mixture. Place chicken breasts in ungreased baking dish; drizzle remaining butter over top of chicken. Bake 30-40 minutes until lightly browned. Serve hot.

Yield: Serves 4   Margaret Kluttz

Chicken Cayenne

1	stick (½ cup) margarine or butter, melted	1	teaspoon salt
½	cup vinegar	1	teaspoon pepper
1	tablespoon lemon juice	⅛	teaspoon cayenne pepper
		6-8	chicken thighs

Mix all ingredients together except chicken. Pour mixture over chicken to coat. Marinate 4-6 hours in the refrigerator, turning often. Grill chicken over low flame 40-45 minutes. As chicken cooks, baste with marinade that has been warmed in microwave, turning chicken as it browns. Serve hot.

Yield: Serves 4   Bill Haggerty

Fajita in a Pita

⅓	cup Italian salad dressing	1	medium onion, sliced into rings
⅓	cup soy sauce		
4	(4-ounce) chicken breasts	2	pita bread rounds, cut in half, or flour tortillas
1	red pepper, cored, seeded, cut into slices	½	cup picante sauce
1	yellow pepper, cored, seeded, cut into slices	¼	cup sour cream
			Shredded sharp cheese

Combine Italian dressing and soy sauce; pour over chicken. Marinate at least 30 minutes. Remove chicken, reserving marinade. To cook chicken, grill or stir-fry in a hot, greased skillet. Cut the cooked chicken into strips and keep warm. Sauté peppers and onion in a skillet coated with oil; add 3 tablespoons marinade and cook until crisp-tender. Add chicken; toss to mix. Stuff mixture into pita halves or wrap in tortillas and add picante sauce, sour cream and cheese as desired.

Yield: Serves 4   Adair Doran

B
L
E
S
S
I
N
G
S

Southern Oven - Fried Chicken

Margarine or non-stick butter flavored cooking spray	2 eggs, beaten
6 chicken breasts with bone	¼ cup milk or buttermilk
2 teaspoons salt	6 cups crispy rice cereal, crushed
1 teaspoon black pepper	1 teaspoon garlic powder
⅔ cup flour	

Preheat oven to 400°. Grease a non-stick jelly roll pan with margarine or spray. Season the chicken with salt and pepper. Shake the chicken in plastic bag filled with the flour. Dip each piece in a mixture of the egg and milk; then coat with a mixture of cereal and garlic by shaking in a plastic bag. Place chicken on rack in broiler pan. Drizzle with melted margarine or spray chicken with butter flavored cooking spray. Bake skin side down for 30 minutes. Turn carefully and bake another 20-30 minutes.

Yield: 6 pieces

♥ Coriander Chicken

6 tablespoons soy sauce	¼ teaspoon turmeric
1 tablespoon honey	Cayenne pepper
1 teaspoon finely ground coriander seed	4 pounds boneless chicken breasts
2 teaspoons ginger	

Mix all ingredients together, except chicken. Use mixture to marinate chicken for 2 hours in refrigerator before grilling (brings out the best flavor) or baking. Bake at 325° until done, broiling chicken on each side the last few minutes for color. Serve hot.

Yield: Serves 6   Jennifer C. Seifert

♥ Lemon Herb Broiled Chicken

2 tablespoons canola oil	½ teaspoon salt
1 tablespoon lemon juice	¼ teaspoon pepper
½ teaspoon rosemary or tarragon, crushed	1 pound boneless chicken breast halves, skinned

Mix oil, juice, herbs, salt and pepper. Marinate chicken in mixture at room temperature for no more than 30 minutes, turning once. Broil chicken for 10 minutes, or until thoroughly cooked, turning once. Serve hot. Leftovers freeze well.

Yield: 4 servings   Dorothy Garrison

Chicken Piccata

6	boneless, skinless chicken breast halves	½	cup plus 6-8 tablespoons chilled butter
¼	teaspoon salt	¾	cup dry white wine or cooking vermouth
⅛	teaspoon white pepper	1	tablespoon lemon juice
⅓	cup flour	2	teaspoons minced parsley

Pound chicken until thin. Mix salt and pepper with flour. Dip both sides of chicken in flour mixture, shaking off excess. Heat 3 tablespoons butter in large fry pan over medium heat. Quickly sauté a few pieces of chicken at a time, turning to lightly brown on both sides. Add 3-5 tablespoons butter as needed. When all chicken is done, place on serving platter. To pan, add wine and lemon juice. Heat through, remove from heat; add parsley and 1/2 cup chilled butter. Quickly blend with a small whisk until it reaches a creamy texture. Pour sauce over chicken and serve immediately.

NOTE: *If preparing ahead, place cooked chicken in baking dish, keep hot in a warm oven, and prepare sauce just before serving.*

Yield: 6 servings   Joanne Eichelberger

Chicken Marsala

4	chicken breasts, cut in strips	¼	teaspoon pepper
1	cup mushrooms, sliced	8	ounces fettuccine, cooked al dente, rinsed and drained
¼	cup chopped onion		
2	tablespoons butter	¼	cup Parmesan cheese, grated
1	cup Marsala wine	1	cup mozzarella cheese, grated
1	cup heavy cream		
¼	teaspoon salt		

Preheat oven to 350°. Sauté chicken, mushrooms and onion in 1 tablespoon butter. When chicken is tender and browned slightly, add wine. Cover skillet and simmer until most of the liquid is cooked away. Scald cream, then add 1 tablespoon of the butter, salt and pepper; stir. In a 2-quart casserole, sprinkle fettuccine with Parmesan. Pour cream over fettuccine and add chicken mixture. Sprinkle with mozzarella and bake approximately 20 minutes until cheese is bubbly and browned slightly. Serve hot.

Yield: Serves 6   Nell Bullard

Snoops Chicken

1	(2¼-ounce) jar dried beef	1	(10¾-ounce) can cream of mushroom soup
6	chicken breasts, halved and boned	1	(8-ounce) container sour cream
	Pepper	5½	ounces water
6	slices bacon		Hot cooked rice

Preheat oven to 325°. Grease the bottom of a 9x13-inch baking dish. Arrange pieces of dried beef to cover bottom and sides of dish. Pepper chicken breasts to taste and wrap each in a piece of uncooked bacon. Place wrapped chicken on top of chipped beef. Mix soup, sour cream and water in a bowl. Pour over chicken. Cover dish tightly with foil. Bake 2 hours. Remove foil the last 30 minutes to brown chicken slightly. Serve on a bed of rice.

NOTE: *This is a family favorite from my mother, Donna Bailey, known as "Snoops". May use lowfat ingredients when possible. Makes great leftovers!*

Yield: 4-6 servings   Sarah Beth West

♥ Oven Fried Sesame Chicken

2	tablespoons low-sodium soy sauce	¼	teaspoon salt
4	(6-ounce) chicken breast halves, skinned	¼	teaspoon pepper
3	tablespoons sesame seeds		Vegetable cooking spray
2	tablespoons flour	1	tablespoon reduced-calorie margarine, melted

Preheat oven to 400°. Place soy sauce in a shallow dish; add chicken, turning to coat. Remove chicken from sauce, discarding sauce. Combine sesame seeds, flour, salt and pepper in a large ziplock heavy duty plastic bag. Add chicken; seal bag and shake to coat chicken with sesame seed mixture. Place chicken in a 9x13-inch baking dish, coated with cooking spray. Drizzle margarine over chicken. Bake for 45 minutes or until done. Serve.

NOTE: *The children in my family love this and call it Sesame Street Chicken.*

Yield: 4 servings   Mary Roakes

Chili Apricot Sauce

½	cup mayonnaise	2	tablespoons dry onion soup mix
¼	cup chili sauce	2-3	tablespoons apricot jam

Heat, simmer, and stir ingredients 10 minutes in saucepan. Serve with chicken drummettes.

Yield: 1 cup

Super Chicken for Super People
Makes a wonderful company dish!

6	boneless, skinless chicken breasts	2	(1-ounce) packages dry onion-mushroom soup mix
5	Roma tomatoes	1	(14½-ounce) can clear chicken broth
5	large mushrooms	1½	teaspoons cornstarch
1	(14½-ounce) can artichoke hearts, drained, quartered		Orzo or rice

Preheat oven to 350°. Rinse chicken; pat dry. Place chicken in a single layer in a 9x13-inch baking pan sprayed with non-stick spray. Slice 4 tomatoes and 4 mushrooms and layer on chicken. Layer artichokes in pan. Sprinkle with 1 1/2 envelopes soup mix. Pour 1/3-1/2 cup broth over all, cover with foil and bake for 45 minutes. For sauce, chop the other tomato and mushroom; combine with the remainder of broth and soup mix in a saucepan. Bring to boil; mix cornstarch with a little water and add to sauce to thicken. Serve over orzo or rice.

NOTE: *Good served with a green vegetable or salad.*

Yield: 6 servings   Luise Petie Palmer

♥ Campout Chicken at Home

2	large skinless, boneless chicken breasts	2	small onions, thinly sliced
	Salt and pepper	2	carrots, cut into julienne strips
	Spicy mustard	4-6	mushrooms, sliced
2	small red potatoes, thinly sliced	2	tablespoons butter
			Paprika

Preheat oven to 350°. Sprinkle chicken with salt and pepper to taste. Spread each breast half lightly with mustard. Set aside. On a large square of heavy-duty foil, alternate slices from 1 potato and 1 onion so they overlap slightly. Repeat with remaining onion and potato on another foil square. Sprinkle half of carrot strips over 1 aluminum foil square and the remainder of carrots over the other. Divide mushrooms between the 2 foil squares. Cut butter into small pieces and sprinkle over vegetables. Lay chicken on top of each pile of vegetables. Sprinkle both liberally with paprika. Seal foil and place packets on cookie sheet. Bake 30 minutes or more until chicken is done and vegetables are tender. Serve immediately.

Yield: 2 servings   Mary Wray Henshaw

B
L
E
S
S
I
N
G
S

♥ Swiss Chicken Cutlets

2 slices lowfat Swiss cheese, halved	1 tablespoon unsalted butter or margarine, melted
4 chicken cutlets, ¼-inch thick	½ cup reduced-sodium chicken broth
2 tablespoons flour	¼ cup dry white wine
½ teaspoon pepper	¼ teaspoon dried oregano

Place 1 cheese slice on each cutlet. Start at short end; tightly roll up cutlets jelly roll fashion; tie with string. On wax paper, toss cutlet in flour and pepper to coat. Sauté chicken in skillet until golden 3 minutes, turn often. Add broth, wine and oregano. Increase heat to a boil, reduce to medium-low; simmer 10-15 minutes until cooked and sauce has thickened. Serve with rice.

Yield: 4 servings   Liane Elias

♥ Chicken & Snow Pea Stir - Fry

¾ cup chicken broth	1½ cups sliced celery
¼ cup soy sauce	¼ pound fresh snow pea pods, trimmed
2 tablespoons cornstarch	4 large mushrooms, sliced
1 teaspoon sugar (optional)	3 green onions, sliced
1 tablespoon peanut or vegetable oil	½ cup slivered almonds, toasted
2 chicken breast halves, skin, bone, cut into ¼-inch strips	Hot cooked rice

Combine chicken broth, soy sauce, cornstarch and sugar if desired; set aside. Pour oil into wok or large skillet preheated to medium-high; add chicken. Cook, stirring constantly for 4 minutes or until chicken is almost done. Add celery, pea pods, mushrooms and onions, stirring constantly for 3-4 minutes. Stir in toasted almonds, then broth mixture, stirring constantly until mixture thickens. Boil 1 minute, stirring constantly. Serve over rice.

Yield: 2 servings   Maxine Bowman

Low Fat Turkey Gravy

4 cups turkey broth and defatted pan juices from cooking turkey	4 tablespoons water
4 tablespoons cornstarch	Salt and pepper

Refrigerate broth, solidify fats; remove top layer; discard. Combine cornstarch and water in small bowl. In large saucepan over medium heat, boil broth. Stir in a mixture of cornstarch and water; cook until thick. Season to taste.

Yield: 4 cups

♣ ♥ Wine Smoked Turkey

1	(10-14-pound) turkey, thawed	2	tablespoons pepper
5-7	teaspoons salt	2	tablespoons Worcestershire
⅓	cup nonfat margarine		sauce
1	gallon burgundy wine	4	cups water-soaked mesquite
½	(8-ounce) bottle lemon juice		chips
2	tablespoons marjoram	1	gallon white wine

Wash turkey; pat dry. Rub with salt and margarine. Combine burgundy, lemon juice, marjoram, pepper and Worcestershire; set aside. Prepare grill or smoker with charcoal and 4 cups water-soaked mesquite chips. Pour wine in drip pan over coals. Place turkey upside down on grill, with meat thermometer inserted 2-inches in breast. Baste turkey and cavity each hour with sauce. Cook turkey until thermometer reaches 160°. Cool; carve. Two turkeys may be smoked at a time on large grill.

Yield: Serves 8-10

Hap Roberts

Turkey Croquette

1	(8-ounce) package cream cheese	3	cups cooked turkey or chicken, cubed
4	teaspoons butter, melted	2	(8-ounce) tubes refrigerated
¼	teaspoon salt		crescent rolls
⅛	teaspoon pepper	¾	cup seasoned croutons,
4	tablespoons milk		crushed
4	tablespoons chopped onion		

Preheat oven to 350°. Mix cheese and 2 teaspoons of butter. Combine salt, pepper, milk, onion and turkey with cheese mixture. Separate crescent dough into 8 rectangles: place on a cookie sheet and seal perforations together. Spoon 1/2 cup meat mixture into center of each rectangle of dough. Fold all opposite corners to center and pinch together. Brush tops with remaining 2 teaspoons butter; dip into crumbs to coat. Bake for 20 minutes; serve.

Yield: Serves 8

Barbara Safrit

Cranberry Marinade

1	(8-ounce) can cranberry sauce	1	teaspoon Worcestershire
2	teaspoons brown sugar		sauce
1	teaspoon honey mustard		

Heat ingredients in pan; stir until smooth. Use to marinate chicken. Grill.

Yield: 1 cup

Turkey Hash with Mustard Sauce

HASH:

3   cups cooked dark turkey meat, finely chopped
1   cup cooked white turkey meat, finely chopped
1   cup boiled, unpeeled, Idaho potatoes, chilled
½   small onion, chopped
2   tablespoons chopped parsley
¼   cup butter
1   egg, beaten (optional)

Mix turkey and potatoes that have been peeled and finely chopped. (If mixture does not hold together, add 1 beaten egg.) Form mixture into 4 patties. In a 5-inch skillet, bring 1 tablespoon butter almost to smoking point. Add 1 patty and cook 4-5 minutes, until brown. Turn, brown other side. Place in warmed oven while preparing remaining portions.

MUSTARD SAUCE:

1½   cups chicken stock, heated
¼   cup beef stock, heated
1   tablespoon butter
1   tablespoon flour
¼   cup brown mustard
1   tablespoon dry mustard
     Salt
     Freshly ground pepper

Heat stocks to almost boiling. In a small saucepan make a roux by melting butter and whisking in flour. Cook 2-3 minutes. Add roux to stock, whisking constantly, and season with mustards and salt and pepper to taste. To serve, spoon sauce over patties.

NOTE: *The success of this recipe depends on the Idaho potatoes; prepare them in advance, do not overcook. MUSTARD SAUCE is marvelous on broccoli.*

Yield: Serves 4   Lorraine Brownell

♠ ♥ Dijon Crusted Turkey

1   (12-15-pound) turkey
½   cup butter or margarine, melted
¼   cup Dijon mustard
⅓   cup orange juice
1   teaspoon garlic powder
½   teaspoon rosemary

Remove giblets from front and back cavities of turkey. Rinse inside and outside of turkey thoroughly with cold water; drain and pat dry with paper towels. Combine butter and mustard. Stir in orange juice, garlic powder and rosemary; brush over turkey. Roast, uncovered, at 325° 10-12 minutes per pound or until meat thermometer inserted in center of inner thigh registers 175°, basting turkey frequently with Dijon mixture. Cover turkey loosely with foil if it browns too quickly. Let stand 15 minutes before carving.

Yield: 16-20 servings   Lee Allen

Crock Pot Doves

½   pound sliced bacon
12 dove breasts
     Non-stick vegetable spray
1   (10½-ounce) can cream of
     mushroom soup

1   teaspoon minced onion
1   tablespoon white wine
     (optional)

Partially cook bacon. Wrap each breast with bacon. Spray crock pot with non-stick spray and place breasts in pot. Mix soup, onion and wine (if desired); pour over breasts. Cook on low for 10 hours until ready to serve.

Yield: Serves 4   Phyllis Steimel

Grilled Chicken with Barbecue Sauce

First prize winning recipe in a 1997 national contest

¾   cup chopped onion
¼   cup vegetable oil
¾   cup ketchup
⅓   cup lemon juice or vinegar
3   tablespoons sugar

3   tablespoons Worcestershire
     sauce
3   tablespoons mustard
½   teaspoons salt
½   teaspoon pepper
2   whole chickens (or parts)

Heat oil in small saucepan over medium heat. Cook onions in oil about 5 minutes until soft. Add remaining sauce ingredients and simmer 20 minutes. Use for basting chicken while grilling. Cooking time will depend upon size and choice of chicken parts used and intensity of heat. Makes enough sauce to baste 2 whole chickens, cut up.

Yield: 2-3 cups sauce for 2 chickens   Bonnie B. Shaw

Lemon Chicken Tenderloins

1½ pounds of chicken breast
     tenderloin strips
1   tablespoon butter
½   cup white wine

½   cup bottled Italian salad
     dressing
1½ cups mayonnaise
¼   cup fresh lemon juice or frozen
     lemon juice from concentrate

Saute chicken in melted butter for 10 minutes, over medium heat until browned. Add wine; cook to reduce liquid to 1/3 cup. Add salad dressing. Place chicken in Pyrex dish; pour liquid over chicken. Cover; bake 350° for 30-40 minutes, basting often. Remove from oven; cool slightly. Place chicken strips in covered container; refrigerate until chilled or overnight. Combine mayonnaise and lemon juice. Spoon *LEMON MAYONNAISE* over chilled chicken. Serve.

Yield: 4 servings

♣ Sweet Onion & Sage Dressing

5	(10-ounce) packages frozen chopped onions, thawed	2	eggs, slightly beaten
1	(12-ounce) bottle 7-Up	2	large loaves eggbread, cut or torn into ¾ to 1-inch pieces
2	cups diced celery	1	teaspoon crushed dried sage
2	apples, peeled, cored and diced or 1 (21-ounce) can sliced apples, chopped	1	teaspoon salt
		½	teaspoon pepper
1	pound mild pork sausage, cooked, drained, crumbled		Chicken broth (optional)

Simmer onions in Dutch oven in 7-Up until tender and liquid is reduced. Add celery and simmer 10 minutes. In a large bowl, combine onion, celery and 7-Up mixture, apples, sausage, eggs, bread cubes and seasonings. Add chicken broth if stuffing is too dry. This mixture will stuff 1 large turkey plus a medium sized casserole or bake all of dressing in two greased, 3 1/2-quart casseroles at 325° for 1 to 1 1/4 hours. Cool slightly; serve.

Yield: Serves 16-20

Sour Cream Gravy

4	tablespoons turkey or other meat drippings, cooled	4	tablespoons instant shake and blend flour
2	(8-ounce) containers sour cream		Salt
1	cup sliced fresh mushrooms, sautéed (optional)		Freshly ground pepper
			Milk (optional)

In pan, combine meat drippings with sour cream and mushrooms, if desired. Sprinkle flour over mixture; bring to a boil, stirring constantly. Reduce heat; simmer for 2 minutes. Season to taste with salt and pepper. Thin with milk or other liquid if necessary. Serve in gravy boat.

NOTE: *Water, wine, beef or chicken broth may be substituted for sour cream.*

Yield: 2 cups

Sherried Gravy

½-1	stick margarine, melted	2	cups chicken broth
3	tablespoons flour	½	cup sherry or apple cider
½	pound sliced mushrooms		

Blend margarine, flour, mushrooms, broth, sherry; salt and pepper to taste in saucepan. Stir, cook until smooth. Serve with poultry or rice.

Yield: 3 cups

Seafoods to Savor

Fresh Fish from the Waters

&

Shellfish from the Sea

Shrimp & Grits

GRITS:

1	cup grits, quick or regular	1	teaspoon salt
4½	cups water	4	tablespoons butter

Bring salted water to a boil in a saucepan. Slowly add grits to water, continuously stirring with a whisk. Reduce heat to low until occasional bubble breaks surface. Continue cooking for 30-40 minutes, stirring frequently to prevent scorching. Beat in butter. Keep in a warm place or in top of double boiler over simmering water until ready to serve.

SHRIMP MIXTURE:

1	pound raw shrimp, peeled and deveined	2	cups sliced mushrooms
	Dash olive oil	1	cup diced green onion
6	slices bacon, cooked and crumbled		Dash white wine
		1	stick butter
½	cup Roma tomatoes, seeded and diced		Paprika
			Salt and pepper

Rinse shrimp and pat dry. Heat oil in heavy saucepan. Add shrimp and cook for 1 to 1 1/2 minutes. Add bacon, tomatoes, mushrooms and green onion. Cook, stirring constantly until done. Add wine and butter. Sprinkle on paprika, salt and pepper to taste. Spoon equal portions of grits onto 4 plates; spoon shrimp mixture over top.

Yield: Serves 4   Jeannie Jordan

Lobster or Shrimp Newburg

¾	pound cooked lobster meat or shrimp	⅛	teaspoon cayenne pepper
¼	cup butter or margarine	1	pint cream
2	tablespoons flour	2	egg yolks, beaten
1	teaspoon salt	2	tablespoons sherry
¼	teaspoon paprika		Toast points or steamed rice for 6

Cut lobster meat or shrimp into 1/2-inch pieces and set aside. In a 2-quart pot, melt butter and blend in flour, salt, paprika and pepper. Add cream gradually and cook until thick and smooth, stirring constantly. Stir a spoonful of hot cream sauce into egg yolks, then combine with remaining hot cream; continue stirring. Add lobster meat or shrimp. When mixture is hot, remove from heat and stir in sherry. Serve immediately on toast points or rice.

Yield: Serves 6   D. A. Errante

🔔 Rockefeller Shrimp & Rice

1	cup chopped onions
2	tablespoons butter
¾-1	pound raw shrimp, peeled, deveined and cut in half, lengthwise
1	(10¾-ounce) can condensed cream of mushroom soup
1	cup grated Swiss cheese
¼	cup sherry, or to taste
2	cups cooked white rice
1	(8-ounce) can water chestnuts, drained and chopped
2	(10-ounce) packages frozen spinach, cooked and drained
1	tablespoon lemon juice
¼-½	cups grated Parmesan cheese
	Salt and pepper

In a large saucepan, sauté onions in butter until tender. Add shrimp and cook until slightly pink, about 2 minutes. Add soup, Swiss cheese and sherry. Stir and heat mixture thoroughly. Add rice, water chestnuts, spinach, lemon juice and 2 tablespoons Parmesan cheese. Season with salt and pepper to taste. Pour into a greased shallow dish. Sprinkle remaining Parmesan cheese over the top of casserole. Bake uncovered at 350° for 25 minutes until hot and bubbly. Serve immediately.

NOTE: *This is a great luncheon dish. Try it with wild rice, too!*

Yield: 8-12 servings

Greek Shrimp

8	ounces uncooked vermicelli
1	pound medium shrimp, peeled and deveined
	Pinch of crushed red pepper flakes
¼	cup olive oil
⅔	cup (4-ounces) feta cheese
½	teaspoon crushed garlic
1	(14½-ounce) can tomato wedges, undrained
¼	cup dry white wine
¾	teaspoon dried whole basil
½	teaspoon dried whole oregano
¼	teaspoon salt
¼	teaspoon pepper

Cook vermicelli according to package directions, drain and keep warm. Sauté shrimp and red pepper flakes in 2 tablespoons olive oil for 1-2 minutes in a large skillet. Arrange shrimp in a 10x6-inch baking dish. Sprinkle with feta cheese; set aside. Add remaining oil to skillet. Sauté garlic over low heat. Add tomatoes with juice and cook 1 minute. Stir in wine, herbs, salt and pepper. Simmer uncovered for 10 minutes. Spoon tomato mixture over shrimp and bake uncovered at 400° for 10 minutes. Serve over vermicelli.

Yield: Serves 4   Rachel H. Ross

♥ Shrimp & Artichoke Hearts Linguine

Tastes too good to be healthy!

1	pound uncooked linguine	1	(9-ounce) package frozen
2	tablespoons olive oil		artichoke hearts or
1	pound large shrimp, shelled		1 (14-ounce) can, drained
	and deveined	1½	cups chopped, fresh plum
2	teaspoons minced garlic		tomatoes
½	teaspoon salt	½	cup chopped parsley
½	teaspoon pepper	2	tablespoons butter or
1½	cups chicken broth		margarine, melted
			Parmesan cheese

Cook linguine according to directions; drain and cover. In a large skillet, heat oil and add shrimp and 1 of the teaspoons of garlic, reserving the other. Cook over medium heat 3-5 minutes, stirring often. Remove shrimp with a slotted spoon, set aside. Add salt, pepper, chicken broth and remaining garlic to the skillet. Bring to a boil and cook 3-5 minutes until liquid is reduced slightly. Stir in artichokes and tomatoes and cook until artichokes are tender. To serve, add shrimp to mixture and cook 1 minute, until heated through. Remove from heat and stir in parsley and butter. Pour over pasta, toss to mix and sprinkle with Parmesan cheese; serve.

Yield: 8 servings   Tricia Johnson

Mrs. Whaley's Shrimp Pie

½	green pepper, chopped	1	(10¾-ounce) can tomato
1	onion, chopped		soup
1	cup celery, chopped	8	ounces grated sharp cheddar
1	stick butter		cheese
2	cups cooked and shelled	1	tablespoon Worcestershire
	shrimp		sauce
2	cups cooked rice		Hot sauce (optional)

Sauté peppers, onion and celery in butter until soft. Combine with shrimp, rice, soup, half of grated cheese and Worcestershire sauce. Place in a 2 1/2-quart greased casserole; bake at 350° for 20-25 minutes. Sprinkle with remaining cheese and return to oven for 15 minutes. Serve hot.

NOTE: *May be prepared earlier in the day and baked just before serving. This recipe is from Charleston, SC. Lynn has enjoyed serving this for several years and Allison adds hot sauce to taste as a seasoning.*

Yield: Serves 6   Lynn Fowler
                                                           Allison Ogden

Spiced Shrimp

Wonderful!

4	sticks butter	1	(2-ounce) can ground black
	Juice of 4 lemons		pepper
1	(16-ounce) bottle Italian salad	5	pounds raw shrimp, unpeeled
	dressing		(½ pound per person)

In a medium saucepan, melt butter and mix in lemon juice, Italian dressing and pepper. Heat, but do not boil. Pour butter mixture into a large roasting pan to cool. Place shrimp in pan and toss to combine with spicy butter mixture. Bake at 335° for 45 minutes; serve hot.

NOTE: *We serve this shrimp outdoors on a picnic table. Everyone peels his or her own shrimp.*

Yield: Serves 10

Marie Lomax

Buttery Pasta with Shrimp

¾	cup butter	½	teaspoon oregano leaves
1	cup chopped green pepper	¼	teaspoon pepper
½	cup chopped onion	1	(7-ounce) package spaghetti,
1½	pounds raw shrimp, shelled		cooked and drained
	and deveined	2	cups cubed tomatoes
1½	teaspoons garlic powder		Grated Parmesan cheese
½	teaspoon salt		

Melt butter in 3-quart saucepan over medium heat. Add pepper, onion, shrimp and spices. Cook and stir for about 5 minutes. Add cooked and drained spaghetti and continue cooking 3-5 minutes until mixture is heated through. Remove from heat and add tomatoes. Cover and let stand 1 minute. Cheese may be sprinkled on top when served.

Yield: 4 servings

Debbie Spears

Cajun Shrimp

2	tablespoons butter or	2	tablespoons Cajun seasoning
	margarine	1¼	pounds shelled raw shrimp
¾-1	cup wine, any kind		Hot cooked yellow, white,
1	tablespoon lemon juice		brown or wild rice

Combine butter, wine, juice and seasonings in a frying pan. Bring to a boil; add shrimp. Stir over medium heat until shrimp are pink in color. Simmer about 10 minutes on low heat. Serve over rice.

Yield: 4 servings

Judy Moore

Curry of Shrimp Suzanne

⅓ cup butter or margarine
3   tablespoons flour
1-2 tablespoons curry powder
½   teaspoon salt
¼   teaspoon paprika
     Nutmeg
2   cups light cream or
     half-and-half
3   cups cleaned, cooked shrimp

1   tablespoon finely chopped
     candied ginger
1   tablespoon lemon juice
1   teaspoon cooking sherry
1   teaspoon onion juice
     Dash of Worcestershire
     sauce
     Hot cooked rice

In a 2-quart saucepan, melt butter; blend in flour, curry powder, salt, paprika and nutmeg to taste. Gradually stir in cream. Cook until mixture thickens, stirring constantly. Add remaining ingredients. Heat through. Serve in a chafing dish with rice as an accompaniment.

NOTE: *May prepare ahead and refrigerate; bake in 400° oven until hot.*

Yield: Serves 4   Elizabeth Wiseman

Juanita's Boiled Shrimp

     Boiling water
1   tablespoon sugar
     Fresh small, medium or large
     shrimp, peeled, deveined,
     tails removed

     Cold water
1   fresh lemon, sliced
     Ice cubes

In a large enamel or stainless steel pot, bring enough water to cover shrimp to a rolling boil. Add sugar, then add shrimp and simmer. Stir and watch very closely. If using shrimp in a salad or shrimp cocktail, cook shrimp until done, (when they begin to turn pink). Remove shrimp from hot water and immediately immerse in a very cold water bath. Discard water when it begins to warm. Immerse shrimp again in fresh cold water. When cold, check to be sure that shrimp are well cleaned and deveined and that all bits of tail are removed. Rinse again. Keep shrimp cold in refrigerator, covered in water with ice cubes and lemon slices, until ready to serve. When using shrimp in a casserole or other hot dish, be sure all other ingredients are heated thoroughly before adding shrimp, which has been cooked just until barely pink, last; (to prevent overcooking and toughening shrimp). Then finish baking or heating the entrée.

Yield: 5-6 large shrimp per person
             for a shrimp cocktail
         6-7 medium shrimp per person
             for salads, entrées or casseroles   Juanita Williams

Pink Sauce for Shrimp

1	cup mayonnaise
½	cup ketchup
	Few drops Tabasco sauce

1½	teaspoons lemon juice
	Salt

Combine all ingredients and chill. Serve over shrimp or lettuce salad; or in combination with marinated artichoke hearts, celery and tomatoes. Keep refrigerated.

Yield: 1 1/2 cups   Evelyn Ribelin

Pasta with Broccoli & Clam Sauce

12	ounces pasta (shell or ziti)
½	large bunch broccoli, cut in bite-sized pieces
¼	cup olive oil
2	teaspoons minced garlic

1	(6½-ounce) can minced clams
¾	cup chicken broth
½	teaspoon salt
	Pepper
¼	teaspoon crushed red pepper

Bring a 1 1/2-2-quart saucepan of lightly salted water to boil. Add pasta and cook according to package directions. Add broccoli about 5 minutes before pasta is done. Cook until pasta and broccoli are still firm, but tender. Drain and set aside. Heat oil in a small saucepan. Add garlic and cook over medium-low heat 3-5 minutes, stirring often until tender. Stir in clams, chicken broth, salt, pepper to taste and red pepper. Bring to a boil; reduce heat and simmer for about 5 minutes. Toss drained pasta and broccoli with clam sauce. Serve.

Yield: Serves 4   Monica M. Alfonsi

Pasta with White Clam Sauce

3	tablespoons butter
¼	small onion, grated
2	large cloves garlic, minced
½	stalk celery, grated
¼	carrot, grated
2	tablespoons flour
3	tablespoons dry white wine

1	(6½-ounce) can minced clams, with liquid
1	cup half-and-half
	Dash of Tabasco sauce
2	tablespoons chopped parsley
8	ounces linguine, cooked and drained

Sauté onion, garlic, celery and carrot in butter for 5 minutes. Add flour and stir 3 minutes until mixture looks like satin. Add white wine and clams; stir. Add half-and-half and stir until smooth. Add Tabasco sauce and parsley. Cook linguine according to package directions and drain. Serve sauce over linguine.

Yield: 2 main dish servings or
       4 side dish servings   Valinda Isenhower

Mother's Crab Cakes

1	pound crabmeat, all shell bits removed
2	eggs, beaten slightly
2	tablespoons minced onion
2	tablespoons prepared mustard
1	teaspoon Worcestershire sauce
3	tablespoons mayonnaise
⅛	teaspoon salt
⅛	teaspoon pepper
	Progresso Bread Crumbs, Italian Style
	Butter

In bowl, mix crabmeat, eggs, onion, mustard, Worcestershire, mayonnaise, salt, pepper and sufficient bread crumbs to bind mixture together. Shape into 3-inch patties. Fry in hot butter until brown on both sides; serve.

Yield: 10 cakes   Joan Whitacre

Swiss Crab Casserole

¼	cup chopped onion
½	cup chopped celery
½	stick plus 2 tablespoons butter
¼	cup flour
1	teaspoon salt
2	cups milk
2	cups cooked rice
1	pound fresh crabmeat
2	cups shredded Swiss cheese
1	(4-ounce) can mushrooms, drained
⅓	cup black olives, sliced
¼	cup sliced almonds, toasted
⅓	cup dry bread crumbs

Sauté onion and celery in 1/2 stick of butter until tender. Blend in flour and salt. Add milk. Over medium heat, cook and stir mixture with a coiled spring whisk until it thickens. Add rice, crab, cheese, mushrooms, olives and almonds and blend ingredients together well. Pour mixture into a 2 1/2 or 3 quart casserole dish greased with vegetable or olive oil, or non-stick vegetable spray. Mix together the bread crumbs and the 2 tablespoons of melted butter and sprinkle on top of casserole. Bake at 350° for 30 minutes. Serve hot.

Yield: 6-8 servings   Juanita Williams

Simple Crab Au Gratin

2	cups crab
2	cups mayonnaise
2	teaspoons creamy horseradish
	Dash of Texas Pete
3	cups grated cheddar or Swiss cheese
	Buttered bread or cracker crumbs

Combine crab, mayonnaise, horseradish, Texas Pete. Spread mixture in greased 3 1/2-quart baking dish. Top with cheese and crumbs. Broil 10 minutes until heated through and cheese melts.

Yield: 6-8 servings

Crab Cakes à la Spooks

1	pound cooked crabmeat, cold	1	scant teaspoon seafood seasoning
25	saltine crackers, finely crushed	2	heaping teaspoons mayonnaise
2-2½	tablespoons mustard		

Mix all ingredients with a fork. Form 4 large or 6 medium crab cakes. Spray frying pan with non-stick cooking spray and pour a small amount of oil in pan, just covering the bottom surface. Bring pan to medium high heat. Place cakes in pan; fry until brown on both sides. Serve hot.

NOTE: *This is my mother-in-law, Mary Elizabeth "Spooks" Whittington's, recipe from Nassawadax, VA (the Eastern Shore). It is a family favorite!*

Yield: 4 large or 6 medium cakes   Sharon Whittington

Crabmeat Casserole

4	eggs	1	green pepper, seeded, finely chopped
2	whole pimentos, finely chopped	1	teaspoon dry mustard
½	teaspoon black pepper	2	pounds crabmeat
2	teaspoons salt		Paprika
1	cup mayonnaise plus extra for topping		

Beat eggs; add pimento, pepper, salt, mayonnaise, green pepper and mustard. Add crabmeat and mix with fingers. Put in greased 2-quart casserole dish and top with thin layer of mayonnaise. Sprinkle with paprika. Bake at 350° for 1 hour. Serve hot.

Yield: Serves 8-10   Jewel Ziprik

Oyster Pie

A South Carolina favorite for the holiday season

	Butter		Salt and pepper
½	box saltine crackers, crushed	1½	cups milk
2	eggs	1	pint oysters and liquid

Grease an 8x8-inch pan with butter. Mix together crackers, eggs, salt and pepper to taste, milk, oysters and liquid. Pour into pan. Bake at 375° for 25-30 minutes or until set. Good with turkey or roast chicken.

Yield: Serves 4-6   Cleo Catherine Dick

Irvin's Specialty Oysters

2	tablespoons butter or margarine	4	large tablespoons paprika
1	pint oysters	¼	teaspoon black pepper
¼	cup oyster liquid	½	teaspoons salt
3	teaspoons lime juice	4	thin slices white bread, toasted
6	teaspoons Worcestershire sauce	1	tablespoon chopped parsley

Heat a 10-inch frying pan; add butter, oysters, liquid, lime juice, Worcestershire, paprika, pepper and salt. Cook on medium high until oysters are plump and edges curl, about 10-12 minutes. Have ready 4 shallow soup bowls with 1 slice of toast in each. Put 4 large or 6 small oysters on each piece of toast and divide and spoon the pan juices over each dish. Sprinkle with parsley. Serve at once while hot as an appetizer or an entrée with salad. Do not freeze.

Yield: 4 servings   Bert W. Oestreicher

♥ Salmon Boats

3	medium-size, freshly baked potatoes, halved lengthwise	¼	cup finely chopped onion
8	ounces softened light cream cheese	1⅓	cup sliced, pitted ripe olives
½	cup light mayonnaise or salad dressing	½	teaspoon dill weed
		¼	teaspoon salt
		1	(6-ounce) can pink salmon, drained

Scoop out potato pulp, leaving shells intact. Spoon pulp into mixing bowl. Add cream cheese, mayonnaise, onion, olives, dill and salt; mix well. Carefully fold in salmon. Stuff mixture into potato skins. Bake at 350° for 15-20 minutes; serve.

Yield: 6 servings   Liane Elias

Quick Crab Quiche

2	(9-inch) pie shells, lightly baked	2	cups fresh lump crab meat
4	eggs, beaten	2-3	tablespoons chopped green onion
1	cup half and half or milk	4	cups shredded Colby Jack or Monterey Jack cheese
1	cup mayonnaise		Dash cayenne pepper
2	tablespoons cornstarch		

In large bowl beat eggs, cream, mayonnaise and cornstarch. Stir in crab, onion, cheese and pepper. Divide mixture; pour into 2 pie shells. Bake at 350° 30-40 minutes until light brown and center is set.

Yield: 12 servings

Broiled Flounder

3	pounds flounder filets	Lemon slices
1	(8-ounce) bottle Italian salad	Parsley
	dressing	Paprika
1	stick margarine, softened	

Marinate filets in dressing for several hours in covered container in refrigerator. When ready to cook, place filets skin side down on foil covered baking sheet; lightly spread margarine on top. Broil for 15-20 minutes until lightly browned. To serve, garnish with lemon, parsley and paprika.

Yield: Serves 6   Mrs. George Everhart

Anguillan Encrusted Grouper
A Caribbean specialty

1	cup flour	8	tablespoons butter
1	cup plain bread crumbs		Light olive oil for cooking
4	tablespoons cumin	4	(6-8-ounce) grouper filets,
4	tablespoons coriander		¾-1-inch thick
6	tablespoons sesame seeds		

Mix flour, bread crumbs, cumin, coriander and sesame seeds well in wide mixing bowl. Melt butter in wide shallow pan. Place filets into warm (not hot) butter, thoroughly turn to thickly coat. Roll each filet in dry mixture, thoroughly coating. Press crumb mixture into surface and roll once again. Do not shake off excess. Cook by either: 1) Baking in non-stick pan, preferably on elevated rack, at 325° for 15 minutes or until flaky. Broil a few minutes to create a toasty, crusty top, or 2) Sautéing rapidly in light olive oil, turning once until fish flakes with a fork, is brown and slightly crispy. Serve at once.

Yield: 4 servings   Anna Mills and Bill Wagoner

Louis Sauce for Seafood

½	cup mayonnaise	3	tablespoons finely chopped
¼	cup chili sauce		green pepper
1	tablespoon lemon juice	¼	teaspoon celery salt
3	tablespoons finely chopped	1	tablespoon creamy
	green onion		horseradish sauce
1	teaspoon Worcestershire	¼	teaspoon salt
2	tablespoons sweet pickle relish	¼	teaspoon pepper

Combine ingredients in bowl. Chill. Serve over cold seafood. Garnish with sliced tomatoes, avocados, or hardboiled eggs if desired.

Yield: 1 1/2 cups

B
L
E
S
S
I
N
G
S

Red Snapper & Peppercorns

4	eggs	2	cups finely chopped pecans
1	cup milk	1	cup raspberry peppercorns,
6-8	red snapper filets		crushed
3	cups flour	6	tablespoons butter

In a bowl, beat together the eggs and milk to make an egg wash. Dredge filets in flour, then dip in egg wash. Press crushed pecans and peppercorns into filets. Melt butter in skillet and sauté fish, turning once. Place in oven-proof dish and bake at 450° for 8 minutes; serve. Be very careful of peppercorn fumes while cooking. Serve with black beans and rice.

NOTE: *This recipe is from the "One-Eyed Parrot" restaurant in Charleston, SC.*

Yield: Serves 6-8 — Ruth Correll

Basil Champagne Cream Sauce

3	tablespoons margarine		Salt and pepper
¼	cup shallots	2½	tablespoons olive oil
1	teaspoon minced garlic	1¼	cups pine nuts or walnuts,
2	tablespoons peppercorns		coarsely chopped
2	cups dry champagne	1	cup packed fresh basil
2	cups whipping cream		

In a 2 1/2-quart saucepan, sauté shallots, garlic and peppercorns in margarine. Add champagne, whipping cream and salt to taste. In a food processor, finely chop pine nuts, basil, salt, pepper and olive oil. Add oil-herb-nut mixture to cream sauce and simmer on low heat for 10 minutes. Serve over grilled salmon.

Yield: 6 cups — Mrs. Fred Bachl (Susan)

Sole for the Soul

8	sole filets	1½	cups prepared or homemade
12	fresh scallops, rinsed		Hollandaise sauce
12	medium shrimp, shelled, cleaned		Paprika
			Puff pastry cut-outs (optional)
1	cup shredded Monterey Jack cheese		Buttered bread crumbs
			Parsley

Layer the filets, scallops, shrimp and cheese in a buttered baking dish. Spoon sauce over the fish. Bake at 450° for 30 minutes, or until fish flakes. Sprinkle with paprika. Top with pastry cut-outs or breadcrumbs during the last few minutes of baking. Garnish with parsley.

Yield: 4-6 servings

Scallops & Broccoli Linguine

4	cups fresh broccoli, stems and florets	1	pound scallops, rinsed and drained or ½ pound each shrimp and scallops
½	pound linguine		
¾	cup butter	2	teaspoons salt
2	teaspoons minced garlic	1	teaspoon pepper
		⅔	cup Parmesan cheese

Cut florets from stems. Peel broccoli stems and cut into 1/4-inch slices. Blanch broccoli florets and stem pieces in boiling, salted water for 5 minutes. Drain and refresh under cold water; drain again. Cook linguine in a large pot of boiling water according to package directions. Drain well and toss with 1/4 cup of the butter. Heat remaining 1/2 cup butter in a large skillet. Add garlic and sauté until soft. Add scallops, salt and pepper. Sauté 3 minutes or until scallops are opaque. Add broccoli and linguine and heat thoroughly. Add cheese and serve at once.

Yield: 4 servings   Dana Crocker

Casco Bay Maine Scallops

1	pound bay scallops	1	stick butter or margarine, melted
½	teaspoon pepper		
2	tablespoons lemon juice	1	cup crushed cracker crumbs
¼	cup honey		Hot cooked rice

Wash scallops in cool water; drain. Place in a 1 1/2-quart casserole dish. Sprinkle pepper and lemon juice over the top; drizzle with honey. Mix butter and crumbs; spread over top. Bake at 350° for 20-25 minutes. Serve with rice.

Yield: 8 servings   Diana R. Potts

Scallops with Mustard Sauce

2	pounds fresh scallops, rinsed and drained	1	cup mayonnaise
		¼	cup prepared mustard
1	pound fresh mushrooms	2	ounces shredded cheddar cheese
1	cup chopped onions		
2	tablespoons butter, melted		Paprika

Arrange scallops in a steaming rack; place over boiling water. Cover and steam for 10 minutes. Transfer scallops to lightly greased baking dish or individual shells. In a pan, sauté mushrooms and onions in butter or margarine until onion is tender. Set aside. In a bowl, combine mayonnaise and mustard; pour over scallops. Top with onion mixture. Sprinkle with cheese and paprika. Broil for 2-3 minutes about 5 inches from heat until cheese melts; serve.

Yield: 4-6 servings   Dorothy Garrison

Baked Seafood Casserole

½	pound pasteurized crabmeat	1½	cup finely chopped celery
½	pound cooked lobster meat	½	teaspoon salt
1	pound cooked and deveined shrimp	1	tablespoon Worcestershire sauce
1	cup mayonnaise	2	cups crushed potato chips
½	cup chopped green pepper		Paprika
¼	cup minced onion		

Mix crab, lobster, shrimp, mayonnaise, green pepper, onion, celery, salt and Worcestershire sauce together. Place in 2 1/2-quart casserole dish and completely cover with potato chips. Sprinkle with paprika and bake uncovered at 400° for 25 minutes. Serve hot.

Yield: 8 servings   Eleanor Finch

Seafood Linguine
Simple to prepare and great for guests

1	medium onion, chopped	1	teaspoon dried whole oregano
2	cloves garlic, minced		
½	cup green pepper, chopped	¼	teaspoon salt
⅓	cup fresh parsley, chopped	¼	teaspoon pepper
¼	cup olive oil	1	dozen cherrystone clams in shells (optional)
1	(15-ounce) can tomato sauce		
1	(28-ounce) can tomatoes, undrained and chopped	1	pound fresh medium-size shrimp, peeled and deveined
½	cup water	1	pound fresh lump crabmeat
1	tablespoon lemon juice	1	(12-ounce) package linguine
1	teaspoon dried whole basil		Parmesan cheese

Sauté onion, garlic, green pepper and parsley in hot oil in a Dutch oven. Add tomato sauce, tomatoes, water, lemon juice, basil, oregano, salt and pepper; simmer 20 minutes or until thickened, stirring occasionally. Scrub clams thoroughly, discarding any that have cracked or opened shells. Add clams to mixture; cover and simmer 5-10 minutes. Add shrimp and crabmeat; simmer additional 10 minutes or until clams open and shrimp turn pink. Cook linguine according to package directions; drain. Place on warm platter; top with sauce. Sprinkle with Parmesan cheese before serving.

Yield: 6-8 servings   Flora Lynn Abernethy

Vegetable Varieties

Fresh Vegetables From the Market

or

Home Grown Garden Harvest

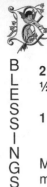

Asparagus Casserole

2 **cups cracker crumbs**	1 **(10¾-ounce) can cream of**
½ **pound grated cheddar**	**mushroom soup**
cheese	½ **cup chopped almonds**
1 **(14.5-ounce) can asparagus**	½ **cup butter, melted**
tips, reserve liquid	**Whole almonds, blanched**

Mix cracker crumbs and cheese. Set aside. Drain asparagus; save liquid and mix into soup. Layer a portion of crumb mixture in the bottom of a 1 1/2-quart casserole dish; add a layer of asparagus tips. Sprinkle with chopped almonds; cover with soup mixture. Repeat until all ingredients are used, ending with crumb mixture. Decorate with whole almonds. Pour melted butter over casserole. Cover dish. Bake at 350° for 20-30 minutes; serve hot.

Yield: Serves 8-10 Bonnie Shaw

Asparagus with Pimento
Mock Hollandaise Sauce

1 **pound (bunch) of fresh**	2 **tablespoons olive oil**
asparagus, rinsed, tough	2 **tablespoons water**
ends cut off and discarded	

Place asparagus in a 1 1/2-2-quart rectangular glass baking dish. Toss with oil. Add water. Cover with plastic wrap and microwave on high for about 7-9 minutes, until crisp tender. Cover and set aside while preparing sauce.

PIMENTO MOCK HOLLANDAISE SAUCE

⅓ **cup sour cream**	1 **(4-ounce) jar pimentos, well**
⅓ **cup mayonnaise or salad**	**drained, chopped (optional)**
dressing	1 **tablespoon fresh grated**
1½ **teaspoons fresh lemon juice**	**Parmesan cheese (optional)**

In a small bowl, blend sour cream, mayonnaise and lemon juice; stir in pimento. Spoon sauce evenly over asparagus. Sprinkle with Parmesan. Broil 2-3 minutes until puffy and lightly golden. Serve immediately.

Yield: 4 servings

Broccoli Casserole with Almonds

1	cup grated sharp cheddar cheese	2	eggs
2	(10-ounce) packages chopped broccoli, cooked and drained	1	teaspoon grated onion
		1	cup mayonnaise
		1	(3-ounce) package slivered almonds
1	(10¾-ounce) can cream of mushroom soup	¼	cup buttered bread crumbs (optional)

Combine cheese with hot cooked broccoli. Mix soup, eggs, onion, mayonnaise and almonds. Pour over broccoli and mix. Place in a 2-quart casserole dish. Sprinkle with bread crumbs. Bake at 375° for 30 minutes or until firm throughout; serve.

Yield: Serves 8-10   Mary Greene

Broccoli Puff

2	(10-ounce) packages frozen chopped broccoli	2	eggs, lightly beaten
		½	teaspoon salt
1	cup prepared biscuit mix	1	cup shredded cheddar cheese
1	cup milk		

Butter a 1 1/2-quart casserole or a 5 1/2-cup soufflé dish. Cook and drain broccoli; set aside. Beat biscuit mix, milk, eggs and salt until smooth. Stir in broccoli and cheese. Pour into prepared dish. Bake at 325° about 1 hour or until knife inserted into center comes out clean; serve.

NOTE: *Equally good using corn or spinach. A great way to get kids to eat their vegetables!*

Yield: 6 servings   Vickie M. Wallace

Broccoli with Sesame Sauce

1	large bunch broccoli	1	teaspoon sugar
2	tablespoons vegetable oil	2	tablespoons sesame seeds, toasted
2	tablespoons white vinegar		
2	tablespoons soy sauce		

Steam broccoli until crisp tender. Combine oil, vinegar, soy sauce, sugar and sesame seeds in a small saucepan; boil for 1 minute. Pour hot sauce over warm broccoli and serve.

Yield: 8 servings   Karen Morris

Stafford's Broccoli Supreme

1	(10-ounce) package frozen chopped broccoli or 2 cups fresh	2	eggs, slightly beaten
3	carrots, sliced	1	teaspoon lemon juice
1	(14-ounce) can artichoke hearts, drained and quartered	1	teaspoon Worcestershire sauce
1	(10¾-ounce) can cream of mushroom soup	1	cup sharp shredded cheese Bread crumbs Garlic salt
½	cup mayonnaise	¼	cup butter or margarine, melted

Cook broccoli in small amount of boiling water until just tender; drain and set aside. Cook carrots until tender; drain and set aside. Place artichokes in buttered 9-inch casserole dish. Combine soup, mayonnaise, eggs, lemon juice and Worcestershire; mix well. Combine soup mixture with broccoli and carrots. Pour over artichokes; sprinkle with cheese, bread crumbs and garlic salt. Pour butter over top. Bake at 350° for 25 minutes. Serve hot.

Yield: Serves 4-6   Sue Stafford

Brussels Sprouts Casserole

3	(10-ounce) boxes frozen Brussels sprouts, cooked	4	ounces sharp cheese, grated
1	tablespoon lemon juice Salt and Pepper	2	teaspoons dry mustard
½	stick butter	2	teaspoons Worcestershire sauce
2	tablespoons flour	¼	teaspoon Tabasco sauce
1	cup evaporated milk	2	cups buttered bread crumbs or crushed crackers
4	ounces mild cheese, grated		Paprika

Spread cooked sprouts in a 2-quart glass dish. Sprinkle with lemon juice and salt and pepper to taste. Melt butter in a saucepan; add flour and blend well. Gradually stir in milk and cook until bubbly and thickened. Add cheeses, mustard, Worcestershire and Tabasco; stir constantly until blended. Pour sauce over Brussels sprouts and top with buttered crumbs and paprika. Bake at 350° for 25-30 minutes until bubbly. Serve hot.

Yield: 8 servings   Mrs. Frank Parrott

♠ Creamy Butter Beans & Butter Peas

1	(10-ounce) package frozen chopped vegetable seasoning blend of onions, celery, peppers and parsley, thawed
5	tablespoons butter or margarine
1	(16-ounce) package frozen butter beans
1	(16-ounce) package frozen butter peas
6	slices bacon, cooked, drained, crumbled
2	cups water
2	teaspoons sugar
2	tablespoons apple cider vinegar
1	(8-ounce) carton garden vegetable cream cheese

Sauté vegetable seasoning blend in butter in Dutch oven until tender. Add beans, peas, bacon, water and sugar. Cover; simmer for 35 minutes, stirring often. Uncover; add vinegar and cream cheese. Stir; heat thoroughly. Serve hot.

Yield: 10-12 servings

♠ Cabbage Casserole

1	medium cabbage, sliced
1	medium onion, diced or sliced
	Salt
1	(8-ounce) can sliced water chestnuts, drained
1	(4-ounce) jar diced pimentos
1	(10¾-ounce) can cream of celery soup
	Grated cheddar cheese for topping
1	(2.8-ounce) can french fried onions

Boil cabbage and onion in salted water until tender. Drain; put in greased 3-quart baking dish. In layers, add water chestnuts, then pimentos, spreading each ingredient evenly. Pour soup evenly on top; sprinkle with cheese. Layer french fried onions evenly over top of casserole. Bake uncovered at 350° until bubbly, about 30 minutes; serve.

Yield: 10-12 servings

German - Style Red Cabbage

6	cups (about 1½ pounds) shredded red cabbage
½	cup water
¼	cup cider vinegar

½	medium apple, peeled and cubed
1	tablespoon sugar
1	teaspoon salt

Combine ingredients in a saucepan and cook until cabbage and apples are tender. Serve hot.

Yield: 4-6 servings

Mary Jane Reid

Sue's Company Carrots
Pretty and delicious

1	pound carrots, peeled
½	cup mayonnaise
1	tablespoon minced dried onion
1	tablespoon prepared horseradish

	Salt and pepper
¼	cup finely crushed crackers
2	tablespoons butter
	Parsley
	Paprika

Cut each carrot lengthwise into 3 strips and cook in salted water until fork tender. Drain, reserving 1/4 cup cooking liquid. Combine liquid with mayonnaise, onion, horseradish, salt and pepper to taste. Drain carrots on paper towels. Arrange carrots in shallow 9x13-inch casserole; pour mayonnaise mixture over carrots. Top with cracker crumbs; dot with butter. Sprinkle with parsley and paprika. Bake at 375° for 25 minutes. Serve hot.

NOTE: *Recipe may be doubled.*

Yield: 4-6 servings

Jean Messer Williams

Glazed Carrots

2	pounds carrots, peeled and sliced into 2-inch slices
1	teaspoon salt
3	tablespoons butter

3	tablespoons prepared mustard
¼	cup brown sugar
¼	cup chopped parsley

In a saucepan, cook carrots in salted water until tender, about 20 minutes. Drain; set aside. In small saucepan, cook butter, mustard and sugar until it forms a syrup. Pour over carrots; simmer for 5 minutes. Sprinkle with parsley and serve.

Yield: 6-8 servings

Debbie Spears

Carrots in Rosemary & Bourbon

4　large carrots, cleaned and
　　sliced
1　cup water
½　cup bourbon

½　teaspoon nutmeg
1　tablespoon rosemary
　　Salt

Combine in a 1 1/2-quart saucepan carrots, water, bourbon, nutmeg, rosemary and salt. Bring to a boil, stirring occasionally. Simmer 10 minutes. Drain and serve immediately.

Yield: 3-4 servings　　　　　　　　　Mrs. Fred Bachl (Susan)

Saucy Cauliflower

1　whole cauliflower, leaves
　　removed and cored
2　tablespoons water
½　cup mayonnaise
½　teaspoon garlic salt

½　teaspoon dill weed
1　teaspoon prepared mustard
¼　cup sour cream
　　Paprika

Place cauliflower stem side down in a 2-quart casserole dish. Add water; cover. Cook on high in the microwave for 8-10 minutes, until tender. Let stand for 5-10 minutes. Uncover. Spread with sauce made of mayonnaise, garlic salt, dill weed, mustard and sour cream. Sprinkle with paprika. Microwave 1 minute and serve hot.

Yield: Serves 8　　　　　　　　　　　Adair Doran

Carolina Collards

2　pounds collard or turnip
　　greens, washed, rinsed,
　　blemishes and tough stem
　　ends removed
¼-½　pound bacon strips,
　　quartered

¼-½ cup apple cider vinegar
2　tablespoons water
1　small onion, chopped
1½-2 tablespoons sugar

Stack collard leaves on top of each other. Roll up the bundle of collards tightly and chiffonade or cut crosswise into 1/2-inch slices. Set collard strips aside. Sauté bacon in a 6-quart Dutch oven until cooked, curled and translucent. Pour off and discard grease, leaving 2 tablespoons in pan. Toss collard strips in pan. Add vinegar, water, onion and sugar. Simmer uncovered for 15-30 minutes, stirring often until tender and done. Serve immediately.

NOTE: *Greens may be cooked longer if desired. Add water as needed. Bacon may be omitted. Cooking oil may be substituted for bacon drippings.*

Yield: Serves 2-4

Corn Casserole
A colorful, tasty side dish

1	large onion, chopped	1	(2-ounce) jar chopped
1	green pepper, seeded, chopped		pimento, drained
1	(16-ounce) can cream style	⅔	cup milk
	corn	1	egg, beaten
1	(16-ounce) can whole kernel	1	cup shredded cheddar cheese
	corn, drained	1	cup crushed saltine crackers

Sauté onion and green pepper in large non-stick skillet until translucent. Remove from heat and add corn and pimento. Stir in milk, egg, cheese and 3/4 cup of cracker crumbs. Mix well and pour into greased 2-quart baking dish. Top with remaining 1/4 cup crumbs. Bake at 350° for 20 minutes; serve.

Yield: Serves 8

Glenda Long

Savory Corn on the Cob

3	tablespoons mayonnaise	⅛	teaspoon pepper
1	large garlic clove, minced or	1	package frozen ears of corn
	mashed		on the cob (6 mini-ears)
1	teaspoon olive oil		Aluminum foil
1-1½	teaspoons liquid smoke		

In a small bowl, combine mayonnaise, garlic, olive oil, liquid smoke and pepper. Spread mayonnaise mixture onto ears of corn with a pastry brush. Wrap each ear of corn in a 6-inch square of aluminum foil Place foil-wrapped corn on a cookie sheet. Bake at 425°-450° for 1 hour. Unwrap; serve hot.

NOTE: *For SAVORY CORN WITH CHIVES, blend 1/2 (8-ounce) carton cream cheese with chives with 1 tablespoon melted butter and brush on corn instead of above mixture. Bake as above.*

Yield: 6 mini - ears

Corn Pudding

2	eggs	2	tablespoons melted butter
2	cups fresh corn or 1 (14¾-	2	tablespoons sugar
	ounce) can creamed corn	2	tablespoons flour
1	cup milk	1	teaspoon salt

Beat eggs well. Add corn, milk, butter, sugar, flour and salt. Mix well. Pour into a greased 1 1/2-quart casserole. Bake at 350° for 45 minutes or longer until done.

Yield: Serves 6

Jo Krider

Eggplant Parmesan

2   **very fresh eggplants, peeled
    and sliced into ½-inch slices
    Flour**
2   **eggs, beaten
    Seasoned bread crumbs**

4   **tablespoons cooking oil**
48 **ounces tomato sauce**
4   **cups shredded mozzarella
    cheese**

Dip each eggplant slice in flour, then egg and then bread crumbs. Fry in oil until fork tender. Drain well. In a 9x13-inch casserole dish, layer portions of tomato sauce, eggplant and cheese. Repeat layer, using the remaining portions of ingredients. Bake at 350° for 30-45 minutes. Casserole is done when cheese is melted. Serve hot.

NOTE: *Use very fresh eggplants in this recipe. They are very perishable and become bitter with age. For variety, add browned ground beef to the tomato sauce.*

Yield: Serves 6-8   Lynn S. Miller

Eggplant Soufflé

2   **small or 1 large firm eggplant**
2   **eggs**
7   **slices dry bread crumbled,
    3 slices in one bowl and
    4 slices in second bowl**
½   **cup milk**

½   **stick butter or margarine,
    melted**
1   **pound (4 cups) grated sharp
    cheese
    Salt and pepper**

Peel eggplant and cut into evenly sized chunks. Boil until tender, about 15-20 minutes. Drain well. Add eggs, bread crumbs from 3 slices of bread, milk, 1/4 stick margarine, 1 cup cheese and salt and pepper to taste. Mix well; place in a 2-quart baking dish. To make topping, mix remaining cheese and bread crumbs and butter. Sprinkle on top of eggplant mixture and bake at 375° for 30 minutes; serve hot.

Yield: 6-8 servings   Elizabeth Wiseman

Presbyterian Green Beans

1   **(50-ounce) can Hanover Blue
    Lake cut green beans,
    undrained**

2   **beef bouillon cubes**
1   **tablespoon sugar**
2   **tablespoons olive oil**

Place beans with liquid, bouillon cubes, sugar and olive oil in saucepan. Bring to boiling point, reduce heat and simmer for 1 hour before serving.

Yield: 6-8 servings

Lima Bean & Corn Casserole

¼   cup plus 3 tablespoons butter or margarine
¼   cup flour
1½ cups milk
½   cup grated cheddar cheese
1   teaspoon salt
¼   teaspoon pepper
¼   cup diced pimentos

1   (10-ounce) package frozen lima beans, cooked and drained
1   (10-ounce) package frozen corn, cooked and drained
½   cup green onion tops, chopped
2   cups bread cubes

In saucepan, melt 1/4 cup of butter; blend in flour and add milk gradually, stirring constantly. Cook until thick; simmer 2 or 3 minutes. Add cheese, salt, pepper and pimentos. Combine sauce with lima beans, corn and onion. Pour into a greased 11x7-inch baking dish. Melt remaining 3 tablespoons butter; mix with bread cubes and place on top of casserole. Bake at 350° for 30 minutes; serve.

NOTE: *May be frozen, but do not bake prior to freezing.*

Yield: 6 servings   Una Pursel

♠ Vegetable Casserole

1   (16-ounce) can white corn, drained
1   (14½-ounce) can french-style green beans, drained
1   (10¾-ounce) can cream of celery soup
1   cup grated sharp cheese
1   cup chopped celery

½   cup chopped bell pepper
½   cup chopped onion
1   cup sour cream
2½ cups crushed oval cracker crumbs
1   stick margarine, melted
1   (4-ounce) package slivered almonds

Mix together corn, beans, soup, cheese, celery, pepper, onion and sour cream. Pour into a 9x13-inch baking dish. Mix together cracker crumbs, margarine and almonds and sprinkle over vegetable mixture. Bake, uncovered at 350° for 45 minutes. Serve hot.

Yield: 12-16 servings   Martha Hix

♣ Mushroom Magic
Great with beef

3½ pounds fresh whole mushrooms, rinsed, stemmed and halved	1½ teaspoons salt
1½ cups butter or margarine	2 egg yolks
6 tablespoons Pillsbury's BEST® shake and blend flour	1 pint heavy cream
1 tablespoon dried tarragon, crushed	½ teaspoon paprika
	4 tablespoons lemon juice
	1 (16-ounce) box Ritz crackers, crushed
	4 dashes nutmeg

In a large Dutch oven, sauté mushrooms in 1/2 cup butter for 2-3 minutes. Add flour, tarragon and salt. Cover and cook over low heat for 10 minutes. Remove from heat. Beat egg yolks with 2 tablespoons cream. Stir paprika, egg yolks and cream mixture and the remainder of cream and lemon juice into the sautéed mushrooms. Pour into a 10x13-inch glass baking dish. Mix cracker crumbs with remaining 1 cup of butter and sprinkle over mushroom mixture. Cover and refrigerate overnight. Bake in a preheated 350° oven for 30 minutes or until bubbly. Cool slightly; serve.

NOTE: *Some of the crackers will be absorbed overnight by the cream and leave a crunchy topping when baked. Reduce the amount of butter and crackers in topping if desired.*

Yield: 12-16 servings

♥ Roasted Onions with Sage
Healthy and delicious

2 pounds red or yellow onions Salt	2 tablespoons balsamic vinegar
2-4 tablespoons virgin olive oil	1 teaspoon coarsely ground pepper
12 fresh sage leaves or 1 teaspoon dried sage or thyme	Finely chopped parsley Butter or oil for baking dish

Preheat oven to 375°. Peel onions and slice 1/2-inch thick; separate into rings. Combine salt to taste, olive oil, sage, vinegar and pepper; add onions and toss lightly. Butter a 2-quart gratin dish; add onion mixture. Cover with foil. Bake 30 minutes. Remove from oven, stir onions, re-cover and bake for another 15 minutes. Stir again; return to oven uncovered. Onions should be starting to brown. Bake for another 15 or more minutes, or until juices are reduced to a syrup and onions are done. Serve heaped in a bowl topped with parsley.

NOTE: *Serve with grilled steak, pork tenderloins or roast chicken. May use leftovers as a sauce for hamburgers or for pasta with broccoli florets added*

Yield: 4-6 servings   Jean Messer Williams

♣ Milly's Onion Casserole
Very tasty!

12	medium onions, sliced	2	(10¾-ounce) cans cream of
3¾	cups potato chips		mushroom soup
½	pound shredded cheese	½	cup milk
		⅛	teaspoon cayenne pepper

In a casserole dish, alternately layer the onions, chips and cheese until all portions are used. In a medium bowl, combine soup and milk, pour over casserole. Sprinkle with cayenne pepper. Bake at 350° for 45 minutes. Serve hot.

Yield: 10-12 servings   Kaye Hirst

Onion Tarts

4	medium onions, yellow or Vidalia, chopped		Salt and pepper
1	(10¾-ounce) can cream of celery soup	3	tablespoons soy sauce
		8	unbaked pastry tart shells
1½	cups grated sharp cheddar cheese	1	tube Ritz crackers, crushed

Mix onions, soup, cheese, salt and pepper to taste and soy sauce. Divide evenly into 8 unbaked tart shells. Top with crushed crackers. Bake at 325° for 45 minutes or until browned; serve.

Yield: 8 servings   Nancy Eason

French Onion Scallop
Great with beef

6	large yellow or Vidalia onions, diced and steamed	¼	teaspoon pepper
¼	cup margarine or butter, melted	1½	teaspoons Worcestershire sauce
¼	cup flour	6	slices Swiss cheese
½	teaspoon salt	6	slices French bread, buttered, crumbled or cubes
1½	cups milk		

In a greased 2 1/2-3-quart casserole dish, alternately layer the onions with a cheese sauce, made by combining margarine, flour, salt, milk, pepper, Worcestershire and cheese. Top with buttered bread crumbs. Bake at 350° for 30 minutes. Serve hot.

Yield: 6-10 servings   Ruth Meade

Creamed Onions with Peanuts
A family tradition from Williamsburg, VA

4	tablespoons butter, melted	2	cups milk
2	tablespoons flour	4	cups small sweet fresh
1/8	teaspoon ground black or		onions, cooked and drained
	white pepper	1/4	cup dried bread crumbs
1	teaspoon salt	1/2	cup coarsely chopped salted
1	teaspoon sugar		peanuts
1/8	teaspoon paprika		

In a small pan blend 2 tablespoons butter, flour, pepper, salt, sugar and paprika to make sauce. Slowly add milk while stirring constantly until creamy and smooth. In a bowl, pour sauce over onions. Pour mixture into a 1 1/2-quart glass baking dish. In a small bowl, toss bread crumbs with remaining 2 tablespoons of butter. Sprinkle crumb mixture and peanuts over onions. Bake at 375° for 20 minutes or until top is brown and crusty. Serve immediately.

Yield: 6 servings   Gena Hix Elias

Onions Howard

4	jumbo Vidalia onions	1	tablespoon mayonnaise
4	strips bacon	1½	teaspoons prepared
1	cup finely chopped fresh		horseradish
	mushrooms	1/2	teaspoon salt
1	cup sour cream		Pepper
2	ounces cream cheese,	1	cup finely grated cheddar
	softened		cheese

Remove brown skin layer from onions; carefully remove stem core. Scoop out 1/3 of onion being careful not to cut to bottom. Place onions in baking dish. Cook bacon until crisp and set aside. In bacon drippings, sauté mushrooms until soft and set aside. Mix together sour cream, cream cheese, mayonnaise, horseradish, salt and pepper to taste. Add mushrooms and cheese; mix well. Crumble 1 strip of bacon into each onion, then fill with sour cream mixture. Place 1/4 cup water around onions; cover and bake at 350° for 1 hour. Remove cover and bake 15 minutes more or until browned; serve.

NOTE: *Onions may be prepared a day ahead and stored in a tightly sealed container in refrigerator until ready to bake. This recipe was shared with me by friends Judy Newman and Charlotte Virtue.*

Yield: 4 servings   Sandy Lee

Sautéed Peas & Snow Peas with Tarragon

8	ounces fresh snow pea pods, washed	1	red bell pepper, seeded, cut into thin strips
3	tablespoons butter or margarine	3	tablespoons fresh tarragon or 1 teaspoon dried
2	(10-ounce) packages frozen green peas		Salt and pepper

Cook pea pods in boiling water for 1 minute; drain. Rinse under cold water; drain. Melt butter in large skillet on medium heat. Add pea pods, peas and peppers. Cook 3 minutes; stir in tarragon. Add salt and pepper to taste; serve.

Yield: Serves 8

Valinda Isenhower

Ratatouille

¼	cup oil	1	medium eggplant, cut into ½-inch cubes
2	small zucchini, sliced		
4	medium tomatoes, quartered	1	clove garlic, crushed
1	sweet onion, coarsely chopped	2	teaspoons salt
1	green pepper, seeded, chopped in large pieces	½	teaspoon freshly ground pepper

Place oil, vegetables, garlic, salt and pepper in a skillet. Cook and stir until heated through. Cover and cook on medium heat until crisp-tender, about 8-10 minutes. Serve hot.

Yield: 6-8 servings

Anne G. Lamson

Easy Spinach Casserole

½	(10-ounce) package frozen spinach, cooked and drained	1	tablespoon butter or margarine
1	pound cottage cheese	3	tablespoons flour
3	eggs, beaten	½	cup grated cheddar cheese

Combine spinach, cottage cheese, eggs, butter, flour and 1/4 cup of the cheddar cheese. Pour into greased 1-quart casserole and sprinkle remaining 1/4 cup cheese on top. Bake at 350°, covered, for 45 minutes. Bake another 15 minutes uncovered; serve hot.

NOTE: *May use more spinach, if desired*

Yield: 4 servings

Lynn Hales

Spinach & Artichoke Casserole

3 (10-ounce) packages frozen chopped spinach, cooked and drained
1 (8-ounce) package cream cheese
½ cup margarine
   Worcestershire sauce

   Salt and pepper
1 (14½-ounce) can whole artichoke hearts, drained and halved if desired
½ cup buttered bread crumbs or Italian bread crumbs

Mix spinach with cream cheese, margarine, a dash of Worcestershire and salt and pepper to taste, while hot. Place half of spinach mixture in bottom of a 2-quart casserole. Layer artichokes on top. Cover with remaining spinach. Sprinkle buttered bread crumbs on top. Bake at 350° for 30-40 minutes; serve.

NOTE: *May make ahead and refrigerate; increase cooking time. Delicious!*

Yield: 8 servings   Elizabeth M. Cooper

Cheesy Spinach Casserole

1 (10-ounce) package chopped spinach
½ cup water
1 teaspoon sugar
1 (10¾-ounce) can cream of chicken soup

1 cup shredded medium cheddar cheese
1 egg, beaten
2 slices bread, cubed
3 tablespoons butter, melted
⅛ teaspoon garlic salt
⅛ teaspoon paprika

Cook spinach in water with sugar in a saucepan. Drain thoroughly, pressing out all liquid from spinach. Combine spinach, soup, cheese and egg. Pour into greased 1 1/2-quart casserole dish. Toss the bread cubes in melted butter, garlic salt and paprika. Place on top of spinach and bake at 350° for 1 hour. Serve hot.

Yield: Serves 4-6   Ashley Bradshaw Shoaf

Curried Mayonnaise

¼   cup egg substitute
5   teaspoons lemon juice
1-1½ teaspoons curry powder
1   teaspoon Dijon mustard

1   clove garlic, crushed
¼   teaspoon salt
¼   teaspoon black pepper
¾   cup vegetable oil

In blender, process all ingredients except oil. Adding oil in a steady stream; blend again. Chill. Serve sauce with vegetables, meat, fish or poultry.

Yield: 1 cup

Mother's Spinach Soufflé

2	tablespoons butter	2	eggs, separated
2	tablespoons flour	1	(10-ounce) package frozen
1	cup milk		chopped spinach, cooked
¾	cup grated sharp cheese		and drained

In small saucepan, melt butter, add flour and mix well. Gradually add milk, stirring constantly until sauce comes to a boil. Remove from heat; add cheese, stirring until melted. Beat egg yolks and combine with spinach. Beat egg whites until stiff. Fold together beaten egg whites, spinach and cheese sauce. Pour into 1 1/2-quart baking dish. Place dish into a larger pan with 1 inch of water. Bake at 325° for 1 hour. Serve immediately.

Yield: 6 servings   Ruth Thabet

Acorn Squash with Toasted Almond Sauce

2	medium acorn squash, halved and seeded	⅓	cup slivered almonds
	Salt and pepper	⅓	cup sliced water chestnuts
¼	cup butter	1	teaspoon lemon juice

Preheat oven to 350°. Place squash halves, cut side down, in baking pan. Cover with foil; bake for 25-30 minutes. Turn squash cut side up; sprinkle with salt and pepper to taste. Bake covered until tender, about 20-30 minutes. In small skillet, melt butter; add almonds and cook until browned. Stir in water chestnuts and lemon juice. Cook until heated through. Serve hot squash, cut side up on a platter. Spoon almond mixture over squash.

Yield: Serves 4

Mornay Sauce

1	tablespoon butter or margarine	½	teaspoon chicken bouillon granules
1	tablespoon flour	⅛	teaspoon ground nutmeg
1	cup half and half	⅛	teaspoon salt
		½	cup shredded Swiss cheese

In small saucepan, melt butter over low heat. Add flour, cook and stir for 1 minute. Whisk in cream, bouillon, nutmeg and salt. Bring to boil over medium heat. Cook; stir 2 minutes. Remove from heat; stir in cheese until melted. Serve with, or over, vegetables, eggs, fish or shellfish.

Yield: 1 cup

Butternut Squash Casserole

2	cups cooked, mashed butternut squash	1	cup milk
3	eggs, beaten well	¼	teaspoon powdered ginger
⅓	cup sugar	¼	teaspoon coconut flavoring or 1 tablespoon flaked coconut
1	stick butter or margarine, melted		Buttered cracker crumbs

Preheat oven to 350°. In a bowl, mix squash, eggs, sugar, butter, milk, ginger and flavoring. Pour into greased 2-quart baking dish. Mixture will be thin. Bake 30 minutes; top with buttered crumbs. Bake 10 minutes until toothpick inserted in center comes out clean. Serve hot.

NOTE: *May be assembled ahead. Refrigerate until ready to cook. Freezes well.*

Yield: 6-8 servings   Catherine Hall

Company Squash Casserole

1	pound yellow squash, chopped	1	(3-ounce) can mushrooms, chopped and drained (optional)
1	medium onion, chopped		
3	tablespoons butter		
2	tablespoons flour	½	cup cracker crumbs or stuffing mix
1	cup milk		
5	slices American cheese, chopped	½	cup chopped pecans

Submerge squash and onions in boiling water in a saucepan. Cook 5 minutes. Drain and set aside. In heavy skillet, melt 3 tablespoons of the butter over low heat. Add flour; cook 1 minute, stirring constantly until thick and bubbly. Remove from heat. Add cheese; stir until melted. Combine squash mixture with cheese and mushrooms. Pour into lightly greased 1 1/2-quart casserole. Melt remaining 2 tablespoons butter in small saucepan and stir in crumbs and pecans. Sprinkle over squash. Bake at 350° for 30 minutes; serve.

NOTE: *This is a great way to prepare and serve seasonal fresh squash.*

Yield: 6-8 servings   Letty Kelly

Honey Mustard Sauce

4	tablespoons honey	1½	tablespoons lemon juice
4	tablespoons Dijon mustard	½	cup mayonnaise

Combine ingredients in saucepan; cook on medium heat; stir until smooth and hot. Drizzle over steamed asparagus.

Yield: 1 cup

233

♥ Spaghetti Squash with Tomato Vegetable Sauce

Fun to make! Good flavor and texture

1 large spaghetti squash	Salt and pepper

Cut squash in half lengthwise. Scoop our seeds; rinse. Place squash halves cut side down in large microwavable baking dish. Do not overlap squash halves. Add 1-inch water; cover and microwave 10 minutes. Drain. Prepare sauce while squash cools slightly.

TOMATO VEGETABLE SAUCE:

1 tablespoon olive oil	¼ cup shredded fresh
½ small eggplant, cut into 1-inch cubes	basil leaves
1 medium onion, coarsely chopped	2 cups marinara sauce
	Grated Parmesan cheese for garnish
1 red or green sweet pepper, seeded, chopped	

Place oil in skillet. Sauté eggplant, onion and peppers. Add basil and marinara sauce. Heat through. Hold squash over a serving dish and scrape out flesh into spaghetti-like strands with a dinner fork. Season with salt and pepper to taste. Pour tomato vegetable sauce over squash. Garnish with Parmesan cheese when serving, if desired.

Yield: 4 servings

Joan K. Ivan

Posh Squash

2 pounds yellow squash, sliced	½ teaspoon salt
1 cup mayonnaise	¼ teaspoon pepper
1 cup grated Parmesan cheese	½ cup soft bread crumbs
1 small onion, chopped	1 tablespoon margarine, melted
2 eggs, beaten	

Cook squash in boiling salted water to cover, for about 10-15 minutes, until tender. Drain squash and cool slightly; set aside. Stir together mayonnaise, cheese, onion, eggs, salt and pepper. Add squash and stir gently. Pour squash mixture into lightly greased 1 1/2-quart casserole. Combine bread crumbs and margarine; spoon over casserole covering squash. Bake at 350° for 30 minutes; serve hot.

Yield: Serves 6

Sally Brodie

🔔 Squash Casserole

1	stick butter, melted	1	(10¾-ounce) can cream of
1	(8-ounce) package dry		chicken soup
	stuffing	2	cups mashed, cooked
8	ounces sour cream		squash
2	medium carrots, grated		Crumbled cooked bacon or
1	small onion, finely chopped		imitation bacon bits
1	(2-ounce) jar pimento,		
	drained and cut up (optional)		

Pour butter over stuffing. Pour 3/4 of stuffing mixture in bottom of 8x12-inch Pyrex pan. In a large bowl, mix sour cream, carrots, onion, pimento, soup and squash. Pour over stuffing in casserole dish. Top with remaining stuffing mixture and bacon. Bake at 350° for 30 minutes. Serve hot.

Yield: 10-12 servings   Marcia Reamer

Green Tomato Casserole
Simple to prepare

4	green tomatoes, cut in thin		Salt and pepper
	slices	3	slices bacon, cooked and
1	cup shredded cheddar		crumbled
	cheese	⅓	cup fine bread or cracker
1	tablespoon butter or		crumbs
	margarine		

In baking dish, alternate layers of tomatoes, cheese, margarine, salt and pepper to taste. Top with bacon and crumbs. Cover casserole and bake at 400° for 1 hour; serve.

Yield: 4-6 servings   Phyllis S. Potter

Candied Tomatoes

¼	cup chopped onion	8	tablespoons brown sugar
2	tablespoons butter	¾	teaspoon salt
2	(16-ounce) cans diced	1	cup buttered bread crumbs
	tomatoes, undrained		

Brown onions in butter. Add tomatoes, 6 tablespoons of the brown sugar and salt. Place in casserole dish. Combine crumbs and remaining 2 tablespoons brown sugar; sprinkle on top of tomatoes. Bake at 350° for 20-30 minutes. Serve hot.

Yield: 8 servings   Michael Quimby

♣ Fried Red Tomatoes on Toast

8	slices bacon	½	teaspoon pepper
12	slices bread	4	large firm tomatoes, peeled
1	cup flour		and cut into ½-inch slices
1	teaspoon salt		Sugar

Cook bacon in a large skillet until crisp; drain well. Crumble and set aside. Reserve drippings in skillet. Cut each bread slice with a 3 1/2-inch round cookie cutter. Toast bread rounds on each side and set aside. Combine flour, salt and pepper; mix well. Dredge 12 of the largest tomato slices in flour mixture, reserving smaller slices for other uses. Heat reserved drippings over medium heat; add dredged tomato slices and cook until golden brown, turning once. Sprinkle sugar evenly over tomatoes. Place fried tomatoes on toast and sprinkle with bacon. Serve immediately.

Yield: 12 servings   Michelle Patterson, Patterson's Farm, Inc.

♣ ♥ Veggie Pizza

2	(8-ounce) cans crescent rolls	1	(1.5-ounce) package dry
2	(8-ounce) packages cream cheese, softened, or reduced fat		ranch dressing mix
			Fresh broccoli, cauliflower, carrots, onion, green, red, or yellow peppers, or stuffed green olives, chopped
1	cup mayonnaise, or reduced fat		

Press rolls onto 11x15-inch cookie sheet, seaming the pieces and perforations together to form a crust. Bake according to package directions. Cool completely. Combine cream cheese, mayonnaise and dressing mix. Blend until smooth and spread on crust. Cover crust with your choice of chopped vegetables. Serve cold. Slice into small squares.

Yield: 12-15 servings   Mary Kay Zigmont

Stuffed Artichoke Bottoms

2	(14-ounce) cans artichoke bottoms, drained	¾	cup ricotta cheese
2	eggs, beaten	¼	cup mayonnaise
½	cup fresh grated Parmesan cheese	20	slices pepperoni, chopped
			Buttered bread crumbs

In bowl, combine eggs, cheeses and pepperoni. Fill artichoke cups with mixture. Sprinkle with crumbs. Bake in 2 greased Pyrex dishes at 325° for 20 minutes, until cheese has melted. Serve hot.

Yield: 10 servings

Tomato Pudding

	Butter or margarine	6	tablespoons sugar, divided
4	slices bread	½	teaspoon salt
	Cooking oil	1	teaspoon sugar
5-6	medium tomatoes, peeled	8	ounces grated colby or
	and sliced into ¼-inch slices		Monterey-Jack cheese

Spread butter on bread; toast. When cool, break into large chunks. Grease bottom of 8x8-inch baking dish with oil or arrange in a single layer in a 3 1/2-quart dish; arrange half of toast chunks to cover bottom. Place half of tomatoes on top of toast, covering well. Sprinkle half of salt and half of sugar evenly on top. Sprinkle with half of cheese. Repeat layers once more, using the remainder of ingredients, ending with cheese and sugar on top. Bake at 350° for 15-20 minutes or until tomatoes are hot and cheese is melted; serve.

Yield: 4 servings   Hap Roberts

Cheese - Bacon Stuffed Tomatoes

4	medium, firm tomatoes	2	tablespoons chopped lettuce
12	slices bacon, cut up	2	tablespoons crushed cheese
½	cup chopped green pepper		crackers
½	cup chopped onion	4	teaspoons butter
1½	cups shredded cheddar cheese		

Preheat oven to 400°. Cut thin slice from top of each tomato; scoop out pulp and set aside. Drain tomatoes upside down on a rack. Cook bacon until almost done; drain. Add green pepper and onion; sauté until soft. Remove skillet from heat; blend in cheese, lettuce and tomato pulp. Fill each tomato cup with 1/4 of mixture. Sprinkle with cracker crumbs and dot each with 1 teaspoon butter. Place in buttered 9x13-inch baking dish. Bake for 25-30 minutes. Serve immediately.

Yield: 4 servings   Michelle Patterson, Patterson's Farm, Inc.

Spinach Stuffed Tomatoes

12	small firm tomatoes	Finely shredded Swiss or
2	(12-ounce) boxes frozen	Parmesan cheese
	Stouffer's spinach soufflé, thawed	

Cut off tomato tops; remove pulp. Invert shells; drain. Fill tomatoes with spinach. Sprinkle with cheese. Bake at 350° for 20 minutes in Pyrex dishes.

Yield: 12 servings

♨ Broiled Tomato Cups

½ cup sour cream
½ cup mayonnaise
¼ cup grated Parmesan cheese
1 teaspoon garlic salt
  Juice of 1 lemon

1 teaspoon chopped parsley
3 green onions, chopped
5-6 tomatoes, cut in half, crosswise

Combine sour cream, mayonnaise, cheese, garlic salt, lemon juice, parsley and onions; blend well. Top each tomato half with small amount of mixture. Broil tomatoes until bubbly; serve immediately.

Yield: 10-12 servings

Michelle Patterson
Patterson's Farm, Inc.

Cheese Vegetable Dish

¼ cup butter
4 tablespoons flour
2 cups milk
2 teaspoons salt
2 cups grated American cheese

2 cups diced, cooked potatoes
1 cup cooked green peas
1 cup diced, cooked carrots
1 small onion, minced

Melt butter in a saucepan; add flour and blend well. Add milk gradually, stirring constantly until sauce comes to a boil and is thickened. Remove from heat; add salt and cheese, stirring until cheese melts. Set aside. In buttered 2-quart casserole, arrange potatoes, peas, carrots and onions. Pour cheese sauce over. Bake at 350° for 30 minutes; serve.

Yield: 8 servings

Dorothy W. Smith

Savory Roasted Vegetables

2 garlic cloves halved
1 gallon assorted fresh vegetables (squash, eggplant, red, green or yellow bell peppers, red onions, plum tomatoes, carrots, potatoes, parsnips or turnips

3-4 tablespoons olive oil
2-3 teaspoons crushed basil, rosemary or Italian seasoning or 1-2 envelopes of Lipton's herb or onion soup mix
½ teaspoon salt
½ teaspoon black pepper

Preheat oven to 400°. Rub surface of large roasting pan with cut side of garlic. Cut vegetables into chunks of similar size. Toss vegetables in pan with oil and seasonings. Arrange evenly; bake 30 minutes. Turn, toss again, bake 30 more minutes until tender and brown.

Yield: 12 servings

Pasta, Potatoes, Grains & Rice

Bowls of Noodles, Grits and Rice,

&

Stuffed Potatoes You Bake Twice

Americanized Italian Tomato Sauce

6-8	links sweet Italian sausage	1	teaspoon garlic salt
12-16	small meatballs	1	teaspoon basil, crushed
2	(28-ounce) cans tomato	1	tablespoon sugar
	puree	1	pork bone or 1 pork chop
2	(28-ounce) cans crushed		
	tomatoes, strained		

Bake sausage and meatballs for 20 minutes on each side in a 350° oven. Combine tomato puree and tomatoes in a 4-quart pot; add seasonings, sugar, sausage, meatballs and pork bone. Simmer for about 2 hours, stirring occasionally. Add water if sauce becomes too thick. Remove pork bone. Serve over pasta.

NOTE: *Freezes well. The pork bone adds a sweet, mellow flavor.*

Yield: 8 servings   Lois S. Simone

♣ ♥ Light Pasta Sauce

3	large onions, chopped	1	tablespoon leaf oregano
2	large garlic cloves, minced	3	tablespoons leaf basil, crumbled
2	tablespoons olive oil	½	teaspoon crushed red pepper
1	teaspoon salt	1	teaspoon sugar
1	tablespoon black pepper	5	quarts tomatoes, pureed

In a 6-quart pot, sauté onions and garlic in oil; stir in seasonings. Add tomatoes and bring to a boil. Lower heat; simmer for 35 minutes, stirring frequently. Serve over pasta. Freezes well.

Yield: 5 1/2 quarts   Kaye Hirst

Rosemary Garlic Pasta

2	tablespoons olive oil	1	cup beef broth, simmered
6	tablespoons unsalted butter		and reduced to 1 tablespoon
4	(3-inch) pieces fresh	¾	pound angel hair pasta
	rosemary, snipped finely		Parmesan cheese, freshly
8	large garlic cloves, coarsely		grated
	chopped		

In a small saucepan, combine oil and butter. Add rosemary and garlic; cook over medium heat until garlic softens and browns lightly. Stir in reduced beef broth and set aside. Cook pasta according to package directions and drain. Mix hot pasta and broth mixture. Serve immediately with Parmesan cheese to taste.

Yield: 6 servings   Rachel H. Ross

Spaghetti Pie

8	ounces spaghetti	1	(8-ounce) can tomatoes,
2	tablespoons margarine or		chopped, reserve liquids
	olive oil	1	(6-ounce) can tomato paste
⅓	cup Parmesan cheese	1	teaspoon sugar
2	eggs, well beaten	1	teaspoon oregano
1	cup ricotta cheese	½	teaspoon garlic salt
1	pound ground beef	½	cup shredded Mozzarella
½	cup chopped onion		cheese
¼	cup chopped green pepper		

Cook spaghetti. Drain and add margarine. Stir in Parmesan cheese and eggs. Press spaghetti mixture into a buttered 12-inch pie pan. Spread ricotta cheese over bottom of spaghetti "crust". Brown meat with onion and green pepper. Stir in undrained tomatoes, tomato paste, sugar, oregano and garlic salt. Put meat mixture in crust. Top with cheese. Bake at 350° for 20 minutes. Cool briefly before cutting into wedges.

NOTE: *Freezes well.*

Yield: 4-6 servings   Martha Bostian

♥ Veggie Stuffed Shells

1	cup non-fat cottage cheese	20	jumbo pasta shells, cooked
½	cup mozzarella cheese,		and drained
	shredded		Vegetable cooking spray
¼	cup Parmesan cheese, grated	2	(14½-ounce) cans stewed
1	(10-ounce) package frozen		tomatoes with Italian spices
	spinach, thawed, well drained	1	(10-ounce) jar artichoke
2	green onions, minced		hearts, drained, quartered
½	teaspoon oregano	1	teaspoon flour
¼	teaspoon pepper		

Mix cheeses, spinach, onions, oregano and pepper in a bowl. Fill each pasta shell with 1 1/2 tablespoons of the mixture. Place shells in 9x13-inch pan coated with cooking spray. Bake uncovered at 375° for 15 minutes or until heated through. While shells are baking, heat tomatoes, artichokes and flour in saucepan until bubbly, simmering on low for about 15 minutes. Pour sauce over shells and serve hot.

Yield: 4-5 servings   Deborah Messinger

Ramsay Linguine

¾ pound linguine
8 ounces cold Brie cheese
⅓ cup extra virgin olive oil
3-4 large cloves garlic, minced
2 large shallots, minced
1 habanero or Scotch bonnet
   pepper, fresh or bottled, cut
   in half, seeded

4 red bell peppers, peeled,
   seeded and cut into ½-inch
   strips
1 cup sliced fresh mushrooms
½ cup fresh basil or coriander
   Salt and pepper

Cook linguine al dente in a large pot of boiling water; drain and keep warm. Use a wet knife to remove peel from Brie; cut into 1-inch chunks and set aside. Sauté garlic, shallots and habanero in oil over medium to low heat until garlic is fragrant, about 1 minute. Add bell peppers and cook for 5 minutes. Add mushrooms and sauté another 2 minutes. Remove and discard habanero pepper. Toss pasta with vegetable mixture. Add Brie chunks and toss again. Add basil and mix well. Season with salt and pepper to taste. Garnish with additional fresh basil.

NOTE: *Use caution when handling hot pepper. It can irritate the skin and eyes.*

Yield: 4 servings   Brenda Wood

Vegetable Fettuccine
with Alfredo Sauce

1 (8-ounce) package fettuccine
   noodles
1 cup heavy cream
¼ cup butter
¾ cup Parmesan cheese,
   shredded
¼ teaspoon black pepper
¼ teaspoon oregano

¼ teaspoon garlic salt
1 (16-ounce) can whole peeled
   tomatoes, drained and diced
1 small bunch broccoli,
   chopped
1 red bell pepper, seeded,
   sliced
1 tablespoon olive oil

Cook noodles according to package directions. Drain; set aside and keep warm. To make *ALFREDO SAUCE;* in medium saucepan, warm cream, then add butter. When butter is melted, stir in Parmesan cheese, pepper, oregano, garlic salt and tomatoes. In a separate pan, sauté broccoli and pepper in olive oil. Toss vegetables and pasta with sauce; to coat. Serve immediately.

Yield: 4 servings   Michael Quimby

PAX Manicotti

1	pound diced mozzarella cheese
1	cup cottage cheese
4	eggs, slightly beaten
¼	cup Parmesan cheese, grated, plus cheese for topping

¼	cup butter, softened
1	teaspoon salt
1	teaspoon pepper
1	(8-ounce) package manicotti pasta
1	(26-ounce) jar spaghetti sauce

Mix together mozzarella cheese, cottage cheese, eggs, Parmesan cheese, butter, salt and pepper. Stuff uncooked pasta with mixture and place in baking pan. Pour spaghetti sauce over stuffed shells and sprinkle with Parmesan cheese. Cover and bake at 350° for 45 minutes. Serve hot.

NOTE: *A favorite dish at my college eating house. "PAX" is Latin for "peace".*

Yield: 6 servings   Amy Harrell Pullen

Macaroni Cheese Deluxe

1	(7-ounce) package elbow macaroni
2	cups small curd, cream-style cottage cheese
1	cup sour cream
1	egg, beaten

¾	teaspoon salt
⅛	teaspoon pepper
8	ounces (2 cups) sharp processed American cheese, shredded
	Paprika

Cook macaroni according to package directions; drain well and set aside. Combine cottage cheese, sour cream, egg, salt and pepper. Add shredded cheese, mixing well; stir in macaroni. Pour into lightly greased 9-inch square pan. Sprinkle with paprika. Bake at 350° for 45 minutes or until bubbly.

NOTE: *Everyone loves it. It is a gourmet way of making macaroni and cheese.*

Yield: 6-8 servings   Elizabeth Joy Lewis

Spinach and Potato Pie

6	medium potatoes, peeled and shredded
1	medium onion, chopped
3	eggs, beaten
¼	cup margarine, melted

1	teaspoon salt
⅛	teaspoon pepper
1	pound fresh spinach, rinsed well and chopped

Preheat oven to 350°. Mix all ingredients except spinach. Spread 1/2 mixture in shallow baking dish. Layer spinach over potatoes and top with remainder of mixture. Bake for 30 minutes. Serve hot.

Yield: 6 servings   Jim and Daisy Nichols

♥ Potato Gratin

A good reduced fat side dish

1	clove garlic, halved
	Vegetable cooking spray
1	cup chopped onion
6	medium potatoes (about 2½ pounds), peeled and sliced ⅛-inch thick
¼	teaspoon salt
¼	teaspoon freshly ground pepper
¾	cup reduced fat shredded extra-sharp cheddar cheese
¼	cup grated fresh Romano cheese
1¾	cup low-sodium chicken broth
1	cup evaporated skim milk

Rub sides of shallow 3-quart dish with garlic halves; discard garlic. Coat baking dish and small non-stick skillet with cooking spray. In skillet, sauté onion over medium heat until tender; set aside. Arrange 1/3 of potato slices in prepared dish; sprinkle with 1/2 of the salt and pepper. Top with half the onions and cheddar and Romano cheeses. Repeat layers, ending with remaining potato slices. In small saucepan, bring broth and milk to boil over low heat. Pour over potatoes. Bake at 425° uncovered for 50 minutes or until tender. Let stand 5 minutes before serving.

Yield: 6 servings   Amy Brewer

Cheese Potatoes

Great for barbecues

1	medium chopped onion
4	tablespoons butter or margarine, melted
4	tablespoons flour
2	teaspoons salt
½	teaspoon dry mustard
	Paprika
½	teaspoon pepper
2	cups milk
8	medium potatoes (about 3 pounds), cooked, pared and diced
2	diced pimentos
1	pound processed American cheese

Sauté onion in butter in large saucepan for 5 minutes; remove from heat. Blend in flour, salt, mustard, paprika and pepper. Slowly stir in milk. Cook over medium heat, stirring constantly until sauce thicken and boils; boil for 1 minute. Stir in potatoes, pimento and cheese. Spoon into a 2-quart shallow, buttered baking dish. Bake at 350° for 40 minutes or until bubbly and brown. Serve immediately.

Yield: 8 servings   Elizabeth Boyle Wesner

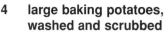

Twice - Baked Potatoes

4	large baking potatoes, washed and scrubbed	Minced spring onions (optional)
½	cup margarine, cut into pieces	Chives (optional) Sautéed mushrooms (optional)
¾	cup sour cream or light sour cream	Steamed broccoli florets (optional)
1	egg Milk (optional) Salt and pepper Bacon bits (optional)	Shredded Cheddar cheese (optional)

Wrap potatoes in aluminum foil. Bake at 400 - 425° for about 1 hour or until done. Leaving the foil wrapped shell intact and using an oven mitt to handle potatoes, carefully cut away a small lengthwise portion of top of potato. Scoop out the pulp and place in a mixing bowl. With hand mixer, blend the pulp, butter and sour cream; add egg. If mixture is too stiff, add a little milk. The addition of a second egg will make the twice-baked product even lighter in texture. Salt and pepper to taste. Stir in your choice of optional ingredients into potato mixture at this point. Fill potato shells with mixture. Bake at 350° for 25 minutes. Cheese may be sprinkled on top during the last 10 minutes of baking. Serve hot.

Yield: 4 servings   Liz Goodman

Potato Pancakes

2	pounds potatoes, peeled and grated	¾ teaspoon salt
¼	cup grated onion	⅛ teaspoon nutmeg
2	eggs, beaten	⅛ teaspoon pepper
2	tablespoons flour	Salad oil for frying Applesauce

Place potatoes in a large bowl of ice water and let stand for 15 minutes. Combine onions, eggs, flour, salt, nutmeg and pepper to taste. Mix well. Drain potatoes and pat dry with paper towel. Stir grated potatoes into egg and flour mixture. In a large heavy skillet, heat oil. Drop mixture in 1/4-cup portions into oil. Flatten out each pancake and fry until brown on both sides. Serve with applesauce.

NOTE: *May be served for breakfast, lunch or dinner.*

Yield: 6 servings   Mary Kay Zigmont

🔔 Confetti Party Potato Casserole

1 **(8-ounce) tub gourmet spreadable cream cheese, plain or with chives or garden vegetables**	1 **(10-ounce) package frozen chopped vegetable seasoning blend of onions, celery, peppers and parsley, cooked, drained and patted dry**
½ **cup garlic and herb flavored cream cheese spread, or plain cream cheese**	2½ **tablespoons butter, softened**
8 **ounces sour cream**	½ **teaspoon salt**
2 **(22-ounce) packages frozen mashed potatoes, thawed, or 6 pounds fresh potatoes, peeled, cooked, drained and mashed**	⅛ **teaspoon nutmeg**
	⅛ **teaspoon white pepper**
	1 **(4-ounce) bottle chopped pimentos, rinsed, drained and patted dry**
2 **cups buttermilk, whole milk or skim milk, heated**	8 **ounces shredded cheddar cheese (optional)**
2 **cups heavy cream or half-and-half, heated**	½ **cup grated fresh Parmesan cheese (optional)**

In a bowl, blend cream cheeses and sour cream; set aside. Pour hot milk and cream over potatoes in separate bowl. Whip with electric mixer until fluffy. Stir in cream cheese mixture. Stir in chopped vegetables. Blend in butter, salt, nutmeg and pepper; beat until fluffy. Fold in pimento. Spread mixture in two 2 1/2-quart glass baking dishes. Top with cheddar or Parmesan cheese if desired. Bake at 350° for 30-40 minutes. Serve hot.

NOTE: *Casserole may be prepared ahead, refrigerated overnight, then baked before serving. Increase or decrease amount of milk and cream for a thinner or thicker consistency. For PARTY POTATO CASSEROLE, use plain cream cheese, omit vegetables and pimento. Season to taste. Top with cheddar cheese and bake as above.*

Yield: 12-16 servings

Pittsburgh Potatoes

4 **cups potatoes, peeled and cubed**	4 **tablespoons flour**
1 **medium onion, chopped**	1 **teaspoon salt**
3 **pimentos, chopped**	¼ **teaspoon pepper**
4 **tablespoons butter**	2 **cups milk**
	1 **cup grated mild cheese**

Cook potatoes and onions in boiling water for 12 minutes. Drain; add pimentos. Spoon into 2-quart baking dish. Set aside. To make 2 cups of *WHITE SAUCE,* melt butter on low heat; add flour, salt, and pepper. Stir until well blended. Remove from heat. Gradually stir in milk and return to heat, stirring constantly until thickened. Pour white sauce over potato mixture. Top with cheese and bake at 350° for 20 minutes.

Yield: 6-8 servings   Joanne Eichelberger

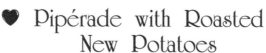

♥ Pipérade with Roasted New Potatoes

Simple, hearty and healthy

2	pounds small new potatoes, washed and scrubbed	2	large red peppers, sliced into ½-inch strips, seeded
	Salt and pepper, plus 1 teaspoon salt	¼	teaspoon dried or 1½ teaspoons of fresh thyme
	Paprika	¼	teaspoon dried or 1½ teaspoons of fresh marjoram
3	tablespoons olive oil		
3	cups thinly sliced red onion	¾	teaspoon fresh basil leaves, chopped
⅔	clove garlic, minced	1	(28-ounce) can plum tomatoes, chopped with juice
2	large green peppers, sliced into ½-inch strips, seeded		Parmesan cheese for garnish

Preheat oven to 450°. Sprinkle potatoes with salt, pepper and paprika to taste and roast for 30 minutes; turning once. Heat oil in skillet over medium heat; add onion and cook, stirring for 2 minutes. Add garlic; sauté 1 minute. Add peppers, thyme, marjoram, basil, tomatoes, 1 teaspoon salt and pepper to taste. Simmer, uncovered about 20 minutes, or until thick. To serve, spoon pipérade over roasted potatoes or hot cooked rice; sprinkle with Parmesan. Serve along with ham, beef or chicken.

Yield: 8 servings   Ruth Ann Coffey (Mrs. William)

Cheesy Scalloped Potatoes

3	tablespoons butter	¾	teaspoon salt
⅓	cup chopped green onion	¼	teaspoon pepper
¼	teaspoon ground red pepper	2½	pounds red potatoes, unpeeled, sliced ⅛-inch thick
1	clove garlic, minced		
2	cups whipping cream	1	cup shredded Swiss cheese
¾	cup milk	¼	cup grated Parmesan cheese

Melt butter over medium high heat in a Dutch oven. Add onion, red pepper and garlic; cook for 2 minutes, stirring constantly. Add cream, milk, salt and pepper, stirring well. Add potatoes and bring to a boil. Cook until tender, about 15 minutes. Spoon mixture into lightly greased 11x7-inch dish. Sprinkle with cheeses. Bake at 350° for 45 minutes or until golden brown and bubbly.

Yield: 8 servings   Jeannie Jordan

Roasted Rosemary Potatoes

2	pounds potatoes, washed, peeled, cut into 1½-inch chunks	1	tablespoon rosemary
			Salt and pepper
		4	tablespoons olive oil

Preheat oven to 425°. Lightly oil 15 1/2x10 1/2-inch jelly roll pan with 1 tablespoon olive oil. Arrange potatoes in single layer. Season with rosemary and salt and pepper to taste. Pour remaining oil over potatoes. Bake about 1 hour, turning once after 30 minutes. Serve golden brown.

NOTE: *Great with TUSCAN HERBED PORK ROAST (see Page 174) or chicken.*

Yield: 4-6 servings   Monica Farrington

Sweet Potato Casserole

3	cups mashed sweet potatoes	2	eggs, beaten
½	teaspoon salt	⅔	stick margarine, melted
½	cup milk	1	cup brown sugar
1	teaspoon vanilla	1	cup pecans, chopped
1	teaspoon rum flavoring	⅓	cup flour
1	cup sugar		

Mix potatoes, salt, milk, vanilla, rum flavoring, sugar, eggs and half of the margarine in a bowl. Spoon into a casserole dish. For a topping, combine brown sugar, pecans, flour and the remaining margarine; sprinkle mixture over the casserole. Bake at 350° for 35 minutes.

NOTE: *A family favorite*

Yield: 6-8 servings   Margaret Matthews

Sweet Potato Puff

4	large sweet potatoes, scrubbed, cooked, peeled and mashed	½	cup orange juice
		1½	teaspoons almond extract
½	cup orange marmalade or apricot preserves	2	tablespoons almond slivers, lightly toasted
¼	cup brown sugar	3	egg whites
			Non-stick cooking spray

In a large bowl combine potatoes, marmalade, sugar, juice and almond extract; beat with mixer until smooth. In a separate bowl, beat egg whites until stiff peaks form. Fold into potato mixture. Pour mixture into a 6-cup casserole dish which has been coated with non-stick spray. Sprinkle almonds over the top. Bake at 350° until puffy and set, about 40 minutes.

Yield: 6 servings

Southern Cheese Grits

3 cups water, boiling	¼-⅓ cup freshly grated Parmesan cheese
¾ cup regular (not quick-cook) grits	¼ cup half-and-half or heavy cream
1½ teaspoons minced garlic	White pepper
2 tablespoons butter	3-6 slices Smithfield bacon, cooked, crumbled
1½ cups (6-ounces) grated white cheddar cheese	

Stir grits into water in pan. Reduce heat, cover; simmer 15 minutes. Sauté garlic in butter until tender; add to grits. Mix in cheeses, cream, pepper to taste, stir until cheeses are melted. Pour into buttered 1 1/2-quart dish. Bake 30-35 minutes at 350° until edges are brown. Top with bacon.

Yield: 6 servings   Dee Hopkins

Hominy & Cheese Casserole

3 tablespoons margarine	1½ cups milk
3 tablespoons flour	2 (16-ounce) cans hominy, washed and drained
¼ cup minced onion	1 cup (4-ounces) shredded cheddar cheese
1 teaspoon salt	
¼ teaspoon chili powder	
Dash black pepper	

Melt margarine in saucepan over medium heat. Stir in flour until smooth. Add onions, salt, chili powder and pepper. Slowly add milk, stirring constantly. Cook until thick. Add hominy. Pour into 1 1/2-quart greased casserole and sprinkle with cheese. Bake at 325° for 10 minutes until hot and bubbly.

Yield: 6 servings   Daisy and Jim Nichols

Baked Tomato Risotto

2 medium zucchini, cubed	1 cup Arborio rice
1 (28-ounce) jar spaghetti sauce	2 cups (8-ounces) shredded mozzarella cheese
1 (14-ounce) can chicken broth	Yellow bell pepper slices (optional)
12 fresh mushrooms, sliced	

Preheat oven to 350°. Grease a 3-quart baking dish. Combine zucchini, spaghetti sauce, broth, mushrooms and rice; cover, bake 30 minutes; stir. Bake 15 to 20 minutes until rice is tender. Sprinkle cheese on top. Bake uncovered, 5 minutes, to melt cheese. Garnish with peppers. Serve hot with meat or poultry.

Yield: 4-6 servings   Marilyn Smith

Creamy Mushroom & Onion Wild Rice

2	(4.5-ounce) boxes Boil-in-the-Bag brown and wild rice, with seasoning packets	2	cups fresh mushrooms, rinsed, sliced; or canned, drained
2	quarts boiling water	¼-½	(10.5-ounce) can French onion soup, heated
¼	cup butter or margarine	1	(8-ounce) container sour cream

In a large saucepan, submerge both bags of rice in the boiling water for 10 minutes. Remove bags, drain off excess water, set aside. Sauté mushrooms in the butter. While rice is hot, spoon into a large casserole dish; stir in mushrooms and hot soup. Blend well. Stir in sour cream. Serve hot.

Yield: 8-10 servings

Wild Rice Casserole

¼	cup chopped onion	2	beef or chicken bouillon cubes
½	cup chopped celery		
1	tablespoon butter	1	(6-ounce) package long grain and wild rice with herb packet
2	cups boiling water		

Sauté onions and celery in butter in small skillet for about 5 minutes or until tender. Stir in boiling water, bouillon cubes and herbs. Pour mixture over rice and bake in a medium sized dish, covered with foil, at 350° for 40 minutes. Remove cover; bake an additional 15 minutes.

Yield: 4-6 servings   Mrs. Evelyn F. Harrison

Zesty Roasted Potatoes

6	medium red skin potatoes cut into chunks	3	tablespoons Dijon mustard
⅓	cup mayonnaise or salad dressing	½	teaspoon pepper
		2	cloves garlic, crushed Chopped fresh chives

Preheat oven to 425°. Arrange potatoes evenly in roasting pan. Brush a mixture of remaining ingredients (except chives) over potatoes Bake 30-40 minutes, until brown and tender, stirring often. Sprinkle with chives; serve.

Yield: 4 servings

Green Chili & Cheese Rice

1	cup chopped onion	½	teaspoon salt
¼	cup butter, melted	½	teaspoon pepper
1	cup rice, cooked as directed	2	(4½-ounce) cans green
2	cups sour cream		chiles, drained
1	cup cottage cheese	2	cups grated cheddar cheese

Sauté onions in butter and combine with rice, sour cream, cottage cheese, salt and pepper. Place half of rice mixture in 12x12-inch baking dish. Top with half of chiles and cheese. Repeat layer, ending with cheese on top. Bake at 375° for 25 minutes.

Yield: 6-8 servings   Becky Lowery

♣ Green Rice with Cheese

1	(6-ounce) package long grain wild rice	¼	cup butter, melted
2	(10-ounce) packages chopped spinach, thawed	1	tablespoon finely chopped onion
2	cups shredded Monterey Jack cheese	½	teaspoon salt

Cook rice according to package directions. Drain liquid from spinach and press with paper towel to absorb and remove moisture. In a large bowl, combine rice, spinach, cheese, butter, onion and salt. Transfer mixture to a 3-quart casserole dish. Bake at 350° for 35-40 minutes.

Yield: 12 servings   Frances Binder

St. Paul's Rice

A family favorite for over 25 years

1	pound mild sausage	1½	cups raw rice
1	medium green pepper, seeded, chopped	1	(4.5-ounce) box chicken noodle soup mix
1	stalk celery, chopped		(2 packages)
4½	cups water		

Preheat oven to 350°. Brown and drain sausage; crumble and set aside. Sauté pepper and celery until tender; set aside. In large pot, place water, rice and soup mix. Boil 7 minutes. Stir in sausage, pepper and celery. Pour into 2-quart dish, cover. Bake for 40-45 minutes.

Yield: 8 servings   Claudette Williams

Basic Rice Casserole

1	medium onion, chopped
3	stalks celery, chopped
¾	stick margarine or butter
1½	cups converted rice
2	(10¾-ounce) cans cream of mushroom soup
2	(10¾-ounce) cans consommé or beef broth
1	(⅜-ounce) jar sliced ripe olives, drained (optional)
1	(3-ounce) can sliced mushrooms, drained (optional)
1	(2-ounce) jar sliced pimentos, drained (optional)

Preheat oven to 375°. Sauté onions and celery in margarine. Mix rice, soups, broth, olives, mushrooms, pimentos and onion mixture. Pour into baking dish and cover. Bake for 30 minutes, stir. Bake 30 more minutes; stir. Serve hot.

NOTE: *A great accompaniment to a turkey or chicken dinner; or combine chopped turkey, chicken, ham or shrimp with the rice mixture before baking.*

Yield: 8-10 servings   Lois S. Simone

Easter Eggs on Rice

1	cup mayonnaise
1	cup sour cream
¼	cup milk
1½-2	tablespoons Dijon mustard
½	teaspoon salt
¼	teaspoon white pepper
2	tablespoons fresh lemon juice or white wine vinegar
2	(4-ounce) cans sliced mushrooms, undrained
2	cups hot cooked rice
8-10	hard-boiled eggs, shelled and sliced or quartered

To make *CREAMY MUSTARD MUSHROOM SAUCE,* mix together mayonnaise, sour cream, milk, mustard, salt, pepper, lemon juice and mushrooms in a saucepan. Cook over medium heat, stirring constantly for 5 minutes until warm. Do not boil. Spoon rice into an 11x7-inch baking dish. Arrange eggs on top of rice. Spoon creamy mushroom mixture over rice. Bake at 325° for 15 minutes.

NOTE: *A favorite springtime family tradition. This is a great recipe to use up extra dyed Easter eggs that have been kept in the refrigerator.*

Yield: Serves 4-6   Libby Gish

Baked Potato Topping

½	cup sour cream
¼	cup butter or margarine, softened
1	cup shredded cheddar cheese
2	tablespoons chopped green onion

Mix ingredients. Chill at least one hour before using. Keeps well.

Yield: 2 cups   Cleo Catherine Dick

Splendid Salads

Molded with Fruit,
Layered with Meat,
Shredded & Tossed,
Bowls of Crispy Greens

King Boras Salad
A family favorite

3-4 ripe tomatoes, peeled and quartered	⅓ cup feta cheese, crumbled
3-4 cucumbers, sliced	Salt and pepper
½ green pepper, seeded and sliced	¼ cup fresh lemon juice
	¼ cup olive oil

Assemble vegetables in a salad bowl, top with cheese and season with salt and pepper to taste. Just before serving, mix lemon juice and olive oil and pour over salad; toss.

Yield: 6-8 servings   Lois Carter

Scalded Lettuce Salad

1 bunch spring leaf lettuce, washed and dried	4-6 strips bacon, fried crisp and crumbled
1 small bunch spring onions, chopped	½-1 cup equal parts of vinegar and water
	⅛-¼ cup sugar

Tear lettuce into bite size pieces and add onions. Combine bacon (reserving some crumbs for garnish) with vinegar and water. Heat, and pour over lettuce and onion mixture. Garnish with bacon crumbs. Serve immediately.

Yield: 4-6 servings   Jim and Daisy Nichols

Spinach Salad

1 pound fresh spinach	1 hard cooked egg, chopped
5 leaves iceberg lettuce	1 large tomato, cut into wedges
3 green onions, chopped	1 cup prepared oil and vinegar dressing
2 stalks celery, chopped	
¼ pound fresh mushrooms, sliced	1 cup packaged herb-seasoned croutons

Tear spinach and lettuce into bite size pieces in a large bowl. Add onion, celery, mushrooms, egg and tomatoes. Toss spinach mixture with dressing and sprinkle with croutons before serving.

NOTE: *May use fat free salad dressing*

Yield: 8-10 servings   Maxine Bowman

Greek Salad

1	large head romaine lettuce, washed, dried and torn	1	(6-ounce) can pitted black olives, drained
1	large cucumber, sliced	1	(4-ounce) package feta cheese, crumbled
6	Roma tomatoes, halved lengthwise and sliced		

Place lettuce in large salad bowl. Top with cucumber, tomatoes, olives and cheese.

DRESSING:

1½	cups olive oil	½	teaspoon pepper
¼	cup white vinegar	1	tablespoon dried whole oregano
¼	cup lemon juice		
¼	teaspoon salt	2	small cloves garlic, minced

To make dressing, combine olive oil, vinegar, lemon juice, salt, pepper, oregano and garlic in a jar. Cover tightly, shake vigorously and chill at least two hours. Shake dressing again before serving with salad.

Yield: Serves 4-6   Laura Murph

🔔 Ramen Noodle Cabbage Salad
Brunch for a bunch!

2	(3-ounce) packages beef flavored Ramen noodle soup mix (Reserve both beef flavored seasoning packets to use in dressing.)	1	cup slivered almonds
		2	bunches green onions, diced
		1	(1-pound) bag shredded cabbage slaw mix from produce section
1	cup salted sunflower kernels, or seeds with black and white hulls removed	¾	cup oil
		⅓	cup sugar
		⅓	cup vinegar

Crumble and break the uncooked dry noodles into a large bowl. Combine with sunflower kernels, almonds, onions and slaw mix. To make dressing, mix together the oil, sugar, vinegar and the contents of the reserved flavoring packets from both soup mix packages in a small bowl. Toss dressing with the dry noodles and slaw mixture; refrigerate. Serve cold.

Yield: 12 servings   Elda Buxton

Layered Salad

1	head lettuce, chopped
1	cup chopped celery
¾	cup chopped spring onion
½	cup sliced stuffed green olives
1	(15-ounce) can peas, drained
1	tablespoon sugar

8-10 slices bacon, cooked, drained and crumbled
½ cup fresh grated Parmesan cheese
1 cup lowfat mayonnaise dressing
⅓ cup milk

In a bowl, layer salad in this order: lettuce, celery, onion, olives, then peas. Sprinkle sugar over top. Sprinkle with bacon and cheese. Thin mayonnaise with milk until spreadable. Pour over top of salad. Serve immediately or refrigerate overnight. Toss just before serving, if desired.

Yield: 8-10 servings   Jayne White (Mrs. Calvin J., Jr.)

Quick Gourmet Caesar Salad

Juice from 1 lemon
2 cloves garlic, minced through a garlic press
⅓ cup fresh Parmesan cheese, shredded, plus additional for topping
¼ cup Lawry's Classic Caesar Dressing with imported anchovies
½ cup croutons
1 bunch romaine lettuce
Wooden salad bowl

Create Caesar salad paste by squeezing lemon juice in a wooden bowl and rub salad bowl with lemon half to season. Add minced garlic, Parmesan cheese and Caesar dressing, stirring well. Add croutons, crunching up in paste to look like oatmeal. Toss lettuce with paste. Sprinkle with cheese before serving.

NOTE: *Adjust amounts of Parmesan cheese, croutons and dressing to taste.*

Yield: 4 servings   Janice Guion Threlkeld

Ocean Drive Slaw

1 medium cabbage, grated
2 medium white onions, diced
¾ cup sugar
¾ cup oil
1 cup vinegar
1 teaspoon salt
1 teaspoon dry mustard
1 teaspoon celery seed

Toss cabbage, onions and sugar in large bowl. To make dressing, bring to boil, oil, vinegar, salt, mustard and celery seed. Pour over cabbage mix and toss. Refrigerate and allow to age several days before serving.

Yield: 8-10 servings   Elizabeth Hardin Taylor (Mrs. Edward T.)

🔔 Moravian Slaw

2	cups water	2	green peppers, seeded and
2	cups white vinegar		cored
2	cups sugar	1	tablespoon salt
3	pounds cabbage	1	tablespoon mustard seed
2	medium white (or yellow) onions		(optional)

Combine and bring to boil the water, vinegar and sugar; set aside to cool. Chop fine in food processor the cabbage, onions and peppers; place in a large bowl. Add salt, mustard seed and stir. Pour dressing over cabbage mixture. Slaw is better when prepared a day before serving. Keeps in refrigerator with tight fitting lid for several weeks. Serve cold.

NOTE: *This recipe is a variation of a recipe from a Moravian cookbook.*

Yield: 2 quarts   Barbara Hendrix

🔔 Mountaineer Slaw

1	head cabbage, shredded	⅓	cup water
½	bunch celery, chopped	⅔	cup vinegar
½	whole green pepper, seeded and chopped	⅛	teaspoon mustard seed (optional)
1	medium size carrot, chopped	⅛	teaspoon salt (optional)
1	small onion, chopped		Tomato (optional)
1	cup sugar		

In a large bowl combine cabbage, celery, green pepper, carrot and onion; mix. Sprinkle vegetables with sugar; add water; add vinegar. Knead mixture by hand, gently bruising cabbage. Chill in covered glass container. Keeps in refrigerator for several weeks. Garnish with tomato when served. Serve cold.

NOTE: *An old family favorite recipe my mother (who died in 1958) used.*

Yield: 12 servings   Nancy Raynor

Green Pea Delight

1	cup finely shredded cheddar cheese	⅓	cup green onions, chopped
1	(8-ounce) can sliced water chestnuts, drained and coarsely chopped	¾	cup celery, coarsely chopped
		1	cup mayonnaise
		1	(10-ounce) box frozen green peas, thawed

Combine all ingredients in a bowl, except peas. Blend well. Fold in peas. Keep refrigerated. Serve cold.

Yield: 8-10 servings

🔔 ♥ A Different Bean Salad

2 cups green beans	1 cup baby lima beans
2 cups yellow wax beans	1 cup diagonally sliced celery
2 cups red kidney beans	1 onion, sliced and separated
2 cups black-eyed peas	into rings

Place all beans and peas in a colander; rinse under running water and drain. Place in a large plastic container with tight fitting lid; add celery and onions.

DRESSING:

½ cup sugar	½ teaspoon dry mustard
½ cup red wine vinegar	½ teaspoon dried tarragon
3 tablespoons olive or	½ teaspoon dried basil
canola oil	2 teaspoons dried parsley
¼ cup water	

Combine sugar, vinegar, oil, water, spices and herbs; mix well. Pour over bean mixture. Refrigerate 8-10 hours in a container with a lid, stirring mixture or inverting container often. Salad keeps for weeks refrigerated in sealed container. Serve cold.

NOTE: *My sister-in-law, Pat Tannehill, shared this family favorite with me.*

Yield: 16 servings   Fran Tannehill

Black Bean Salad

5 (15½-ounce) cans black beans, drained	2 ounces blue cheese, crumbled
	½ cup oil
¼ large red pepper, chopped	¼ cup red wine vinegar
5 small green onions, sliced	Salt and pepper

Combine beans, pepper, onions and cheese in medium bowl. Whisk oil and vinegar together; add salt and pepper to taste. Pour dressing over bean mixture; mix well. Refrigerate a few hours or overnight. Serve cold.

Yield: 8-10 servings   Nell Bullard

Marinated Cucumber Salad

1 cup sour cream	½ teaspoon salt
⅔ cup sugar	2 teaspoons onion, minced
⅓ cup cider vinegar	2 cucumbers, peeled, sliced

Toss all ingredients in bowl. Refrigerate. Serve cold.

Yield: 4-6 servings

♣ Pickled Black - Eyed Peas

5   (15-ounce) cans black-eyed
    peas, drained
3   (2¼-ounce) cans pitted black
    olives, drained and sliced
2½ cups sliced red onions
2   cloves garlic, pressed

2   cups salad oil
¾   cup red wine vinegar
1   tablespoon minced parsley
⅛   teaspoon Tabasco
    Salt and pepper

Combine the peas, olives, onion and garlic. Mix the oil, vinegar, parsley, Tabasco, salt and pepper. Pour over vegetable mixture and toss to blend. Refrigerate, covered, for at least 24 hours before serving.

NOTE: *Adjust amounts of garlic, oil, and salt and pepper to taste. Recipe is from my dear friend Doris Deal, who is a fabulous cook!*

Yield: 12-14 cups   Jane Gamewell

Green Bean Salad

1½ pounds fresh green beans
    Water
½   cup vegetable oil
½   cup white wine vinegar

2   tablespoons Dijon mustard
2   tablespoons honey
2   cloves garlic, minced
2   tablespoons fresh basil

Cook beans in water until barely tender, about 10 minutes. Drain and set aside. To make marinade, mix oil, vinegar, mustard, honey, garlic and basil in a blender. Pour mixture over beans and marinate overnight. Serve cold.

NOTE: *May substitute frozen green beans.*

Yield: 8 servings   Debbie Collins

Green Bean & Corn Salad

1   (16-ounce) can green beans,
    drained
1   (11-ounce) can yellow corn,
    drained
1   (2-ounce) jar chopped
    pimento with liquid

1   small onion, chopped
2   large stalks celery, chopped
1   cup sugar
1   cup white vinegar
½   cup vegetable oil

Combine beans, corn, pimento, onion and celery in a bowl. To make marinade, mix sugar, vinegar and oil; blend thoroughly. Pour over vegetables. Refrigerate 4-24 hours. Drain marinade before serving cold.

NOTE: *Great with fried chicken.*

Yield: 4-6 servings   Donna Cauble

♥ Quick & Easy Mint Pea Salad

2	(10-ounce) packages frozen peas, uncooked	1	bunch coarsely sliced green onions
⅓-½	cup gourmet weight control mayonnaise	½	teaspoon lemon juice Finely minced fresh mint leaves
¼	teaspoon coarse ground black pepper		

Break up frozen peas in a mixing bowl. In a separate bowl, mix mayonnaise, pepper, onions, and lemon juice and mint to taste. Add peas. Blend well. Chill salad until ready to serve to allow flavors to blend.

Yield: 2 3/4 cups   Tom Tucker
Tucker's Wholesome House Cafe

Pickled Refrigerator Broccoli

4	cups broccoli florets	½	teaspoons curry powder
⅔	cup cider vinegar		Salt and pepper
⅓	cup olive oil	½	medium red pepper, seeded,
¼	cup mustard		cut into ¼-inch strips,
2	tablespoons honey		1-inch long

Blanch broccoli in boiling water for 2-3 minutes. Drain and transfer to a glass container. To make marinade, whisk together vinegar, oil, mustard, honey, and curry; add salt and pepper to taste. Pour marinade over broccoli and lay pepper strips on top. Cover and allow to cool. Refrigerate 48 hours. Keeps for weeks in a covered container in refrigerator. Serve cold.

Yield: 6-8 servings   Linda Presutti

Sue's Broccoli & Grape Salad

4	cups broccoli florets	1	tablespoon white vinegar
2	cups red seedless grapes	¼	cup sugar
½	small red onion, chopped	½	cup sliced almonds
½	cup salad dressing	½	cup bacon pieces

Combine broccoli, grapes and onion in salad bowl. Mix salad dressing, vinegar and sugar; pour over broccoli mixture and chill. Before serving, add almonds and bacon.

Yield: 8-10 servings   Brenda Hutcherson

Sunshine Raisin Broccoli Salad

6	cups chopped fresh broccoli, with stems, blanched, drained and cooled
1	cup raisins
½	pound bacon, fried crisp and crumbled
⅓	cup coarsely chopped red onion
¼	cup sugar
2	tablespoons cider vinegar
1	cup mayonnaise
¼	cup roasted sunflower seeds (without black and white hulls)

Layer broccoli, raisins, bacon and onion in 2 1/2-quart serving bowl. Mix sugar, vinegar and mayonnaise together in small bowl. Spread dressing to edge of bowl, covering onions and sealing salad. Sprinkle sunflower seeds on top. Cover and refrigerate to chill well. Just before serving, toss thoroughly.

Yield: 8 servings   Marianna H. Swaim

Sweet & Sour Broccoli

1	bunch broccoli, chopped
1	purple onion, chopped finely
⅔	cup shredded cheddar cheese
	Crumbled bacon
1	cup mayonnaise
½	cup sugar
2	tablespoons vinegar
	Salt and pepper

Mix vegetables, cheese and bacon. To make dressing, combine mayonnaise, sugar and vinegar. Add salt and pepper to taste. Combine dressing with salad. Chill several hours before serving.

Yield: Serves 4-6   Cindi Graham

Carrot Raisin Salad

1	(2-pound) bag whole carrots, peeled and shredded
1	cup pineapple tidbits, drained
½	cup sugar
2	celery stalks, finely chopped
⅔	cup raisins
1½	cups mayonnaise

Combine all ingredients in a mixing bowl. Knead mixture with gloved hands to blend and mash pineapple. Keep refrigerated. Serve cold.

Yield: 10 (5-ounce) servings   Pocket's Restaurant

♥ Celery Victor

20 (4-inch) celery stalks, leaves removed	1 bay leaf
1 cup chicken bouillon	½ teaspoon thyme
1 cup water	2 tablespoons fresh parsley

Remove strings from celery; cut into 4-inch sections. Arrange celery in a rectangular glass dish. Combine bouillon, water, bay leaf, thyme and parsley; pour over celery. Cover with plastic wrap; microwave on high for 10 minutes. Test for tenderness. Increase cooking in 5 minute increments until celery can easily be pierced with a sharp knife. Let cool in poaching liquid. Drain.

MARINADE DRESSING:

¼ teaspoon salt	2 tablespoons wine vinegar
1 teaspoon GREY POUPON mustard	6 tablespoons olive or salad oil
2 scallions, finely chopped or ½ teaspoon chopped onion	Fresh ground pepper

Mix salt, mustard, scallions, vinegar, and oil in a bowl; add pepper to taste. Pour mixture over celery; and marinate in refrigerator for at least 2 hours.

GARNISH:

4 teaspoons capers	2 teaspoons chopped fresh parsley
4 teaspoons chopped pimento	

Remove celery from marinade with slotted spoon and serve at room temperature by stacking 5 stalks on each of 4 salad plates. Garnish each serving with 1 teaspoon capers, 1 teaspoon pimento and 1/2 teaspoon fresh parsley.

NOTE: *A delightful change from green salads. May prepare ahead, marinate overnight; serve at each place setting to welcome guests to the dinner table. For a single serving, use 1/4 of each garnish ingredient, and only 5 (4-inch) celery stalks.*

Yield: 4 servings   Cynthia Capps Pitt

Creamy Pistachio Salad

1 (3-ounce) box pistachio instant pudding	1½ cups mini marshmallows
	1 cup chopped pecans
1 (15-ounce) can crushed pineapple with juice	2 cups frozen dessert topping, thawed

In bowl, combine pudding, pineapple, marshmallows and nuts; mix well. Fold in topping; stir. Pour into 2-quart dish. Refrigerate. Serve on lettuce.

Yield: 6 cups

♣ Marinated Vegetable Salad

1	pound carrots, sliced and cooked	1	cucumber, sliced
1	green pepper, cut into rings	2	stalks celery, diced
2	onions, sliced, separated into rings	1	cup cauliflower, bite-size pieces

Place vegetables in a plastic container.

MARINADE:

1	(10½-ounce) can tomato soup, undiluted	1	tablespoon Worcestershire sauce
1	cup sugar	¼	teaspoon salt
¾	cup vinegar	1	teaspoon pepper
¼	cup oil	1	teaspoon prepared mustard

Mix all ingredients well and pour over vegetables. Marinate overnight in refrigerator. Serve cold.

NOTE: *Keeps about 3 weeks in an air tight container in refrigerator.*

Yield: 10-12 servings   Marcia Parrott

♣ Double Layer Tomato Aspic

2	(3-ounce) packages lemon gelatin	1½	teaspoons salt
1	cup boiling water	1⅔	cups tomato juice
2	cups cottage cheese	1	cup finely chopped celery
½	cup mayonnaise	1	(6-ounce) jar marinated artichoke hearts, drained and quartered
1	teaspoon grated onion		
¾	cup chopped green pepper		

Dissolve 1 package of gelatin in 1 cup boiling water. Cool. Combine cottage cheese, mayonnaise, onion, green pepper and 1/2 teaspoon salt. Mix with cooled gelatin. Pour into 12x18-inch glass or china dish. Refrigerate for about 1 1/2 hours until mixture is firm. Dissolve second package of gelatin in 1 cup of tomato juice, heated. Add 2/3 cup cold tomato juice and remaining salt. Add celery. Pour on top of congealed first layer. Place artichoke hearts on top and refrigerate. Ready to serve when aspic is set.

Yield: Serves 12   Stella Gillespie

♥ Tomato Aspic in a Can

1 (16-ounce) can stewed tomatoes with peppers and juice, chopped	1 tablespoon white vinegar
	3 tablespoons mayonnaise
	1 tablespoon horseradish
1 (3-ounce) box lemon gelatin	

Bring stewed tomatoes and juices to a boil in a pan. Add gelatin and vinegar. Stir until dissolved. Pour mixture into clean tomato can. Cover with foil; chill until firm. Using can opener, remove can bottom and slide aspic out. To serve, slice as desired. Top with a mixture of mayonnaise and horseradish.

Yield: 4-6 servings   Pat Weber

♣ Robert's Country Kitchen Vegetable Salad

1 (14½-ounce) can baby lima beans, drained	2 (11-ounce) cans white shoe-peg corn, drained
1 (15-ounce) can tiny green peas, drained	1 cup chopped celery
	1 cup chopped onion
1 (14½-ounce) can ½-inch slant cut green beans, drained	1 cup sugar
	½ cup oil
	¾ cup vinegar

Pour beans, peas and corn into a 2 1/2-3-quart bowl. Add celery and onions. Pour mixture of sugar, oil and vinegar over vegetables and marinate in refrigerator for 24 hours before serving.

Yield: 12-16 servings   Mary Ellen Bailey

Marinated Cucumber & Carrot Salad

2 medium cucumbers, sliced thin	1 teaspoon salt
	1 cup vinegar
1 medium onion, cut into rings	¼ cup vegetable oil
2 cups carrots, sliced thin	¾ cup sugar
½ cup celery, sliced	¼ teaspoon pepper
1 teaspoon celery seed	Lettuce leaves

Combine cucumber, onion, carrots and celery in a 9x12-inch shallow dish. Set aside. To make marinade, combine celery seed, salt, vinegar, oil, sugar and pepper; mix well. Pour marinade over vegetables; toss lightly. Cover and chill 8-10 hours. Drain. To serve salad, line a salad bowl with lettuce leaves and fill with drained vegetables.

Yield: 6-8 servings   Peggy Maness

♥ Cucumber Salad

1	(3-ounce) package lime gelatin	2½	tablespoons vinegar
1½	cups boiling water	½	teaspoon salt
½	cup sugar	1	large, unpeeled cucumber, grated

Dissolve gelatin in hot water. Add sugar, vinegar and salt. Stir until dissolved. Place in refrigerator. Chill until partially set. Grate cucumber and fold into gelatin mixture. Place in 8x8-inch glass dish and refrigerate until firm and ready to serve.

Yield: 6 servings   Pam Doherty

Artichoke Rice Salad

1	(5-ounce) package chicken flavored rice	12	pimento stuffed olives, sliced
4	spring onions, including green tops, sliced	2	(6-ounce) jars marinated artichoke hearts, drained, reserve marinade
½	green pepper, seeded and chopped	⅓	cup mayonnaise
		¾	teaspoon curry

Cook rice according to package directions, omitting butter. Cool in large bowl. Mix onions, peppers and olives. Cut artichokes in half. Combine rice and above ingredients. Mix mayonnaise, curry and reserved artichoke marinade. Toss the mixtures together and chill before serving.

Yield: 6-8 servings   Suzanne Wallace Casey
                                           Mrs. Virginia Wallace

♣ Copper Pennies

2	(16-ounce) cans sliced carrots, drained	⅓	cup vegetable oil
1	medium onion, sliced	1	tablespoon vinegar
1	(10¾-ounce) can tomato soup	1	teaspoon prepared mustard
½	cup sugar	1	teaspoon Worcestershire sauce
			Salt and pepper

Place carrots and onion in a bowl; set aside. To make dressing, mix soup, sugar, oil, vinegar, mustard and Worcestershire; add salt and pepper to taste. Pour dressing over carrots and marinate 12 hours. Flavor improves with age. Drain off some of liquid before serving. May be served hot or cold.

Yield: 10-12 servings   Wilburn Taylor

🔔 Crunchy Cracker Salad or Dessert
Baked meringue crust filled and chilled

3	egg whites	1	(3-ounce) package cream
½	teaspoon baking powder		cheese, softened
½	cup sugar	1	(16-ounce) can fruit cocktail,
40	Ritz crackers, crushed		drained
2	(1.3-ounce) envelopes whipped	1	(15.4-ounce) can crushed
	topping mix, prepared		pineapple, drained
	according to package directions	1	cup chopped nuts

Beat egg whites and baking powder together. Add sugar slowly to egg whites. Fold in crackers. Line 10x14-inch pan with mixture and bake at 250° for 12-15 minutes. Mix together the prepared topping mix, cream cheese, fruit cocktail, pineapple and nuts. Pour into crust and chill until ready to serve.

Yield: 12 servings   Mildred Simerson

Sweet Potato Waldorf Salad

3	large sweet potatoes or yams	1	cup diced celery
1	Granny Smith apple, cored	½	cup chopped walnuts or
	and diced		pecans, lightly toasted
1	tablespoon fresh lemon juice	1	cup pineapple tidbits, drained
2	tablespoons orange juice	½	cup miniature marshmallows
½	cup mayonnaise	½	cup raisins or dates
2-3	tablespoons honey or sugar		Lettuce leaves
½	teaspoon salt		

In a large pot, cover potatoes with water. Boil potatoes in skins for 25-30 minutes, just until tender. Drain, rinse and cool. Peel potatoes; cut into chunks or cubes. In a large bowl toss apples with 1 tablespoon lemon juice. Add mayonnaise, honey, salt, celery, walnuts, pineapple, raisins, marshmallows and orange juice. Toss ingredients to coat. Gently fold in potatoes. Cover; refrigerate. Serve on lettuce leaves with ham or turkey.

Yield: 8 servings

Fat Free Salsa Dressing

2	cups mild salsa	4	tablespoons fresh lime juice
2	teaspoons cumin	4	tablespoons water

Combine ingredients; mix well. Chill. Serve with Southwestern salads or tacos.

Yield: 2 cups

🖤 Mother's Tomato Cheese Salad

1	(10¾-ounce) can tomato soup, undiluted		Salt
			Dash of Tabasco
2	(¼-ounce) envelopes unflavored gelatin	1	cup diced celery
		½	cup chopped onion
1	(8-ounce) package cream cheese	¼-½	cup water (optional)
			Sliced olives (optional)
1	cup mayonnaise		

In a small saucepan, heat soup. Add gelatin and dissolve. Cream cheese with mayonnaise, salt and Tabasco to taste. Add celery and onions. Stir mixture until smooth and no longer lumpy. Thin with 1/4-1/2 cup water if mixture is too thick. Place mixture in a 1-quart casserole dish. Refrigerate until firm. Serve cold.

NOTE: *Sliced olives may be added to mixture before congealing. Lowfat mayonnaise and lowfat cream cheese may be substituted.*

Yield: 6-8 servings   Betty Lomax

🔔 🖤 Cold Spaghetti Salad

1	pound spaghetti	1	(8-ounce) bottle Italian dressing
1	tomato, chopped		
1	cucumber, chopped	5	tablespoons McCormick Salad Supreme Seasoning

Cook spaghetti according to package directions and drain. Add tomatoes and cucumbers to cooled spaghetti. Toss with dressing and seasonings. Refrigerate at least 24 hours before serving. Keeps well for 1 week.

NOTE: *May use fat free dressing.*

Yield: 10-12 servings   Maxine Bowman

🔔 Potato Salad

6	large potatoes, cooked, cooled and cubed	1½	teaspoon salt
		¼	teaspoon pepper
3	hard boiled eggs, diced	1	cup mayonnaise
1	cup diced celery	3	dozen whole seedless grapes
1	medium sweet onion, diced		

Combine potatoes, eggs, celery, onion, salt and pepper. Stir in mayonnaise. Add grapes. Chill until served.

Yield: 12 servings   Marie Blount

Sour Cream Horseradish Potato Salad

2	cups sour cream	¾	cup green onions, finely
2	cups mayonnaise		chopped
3-4	tablespoons prepared	½-¾	cup fresh parsley, chopped
	bottled horseradish	10-12	medium to large red
2	teaspoons celery seed		potatoes, boiled, unpeeled
½	teaspoon salt		and sliced

In a mixing bowl, combine sour cream, mayonnaise, horseradish, celery seed and salt. In a separate bowl, mix onions and parsley. In a large serving dish, arrange a single layer of potato slices and cover with a layer of mayonnaise mixture. Sprinkle with part of the mixture of onions and parsley. Continue layering potatoes, mayonnaise mixture and onions and parsley until all ingredients are used, ending with onions and parsley on top. Cover and refrigerate 8-10 hours before serving.

NOTE: *A favorite recipe from my brother. May substitute cream style horseradish sauce.*

Yield: 8-10 servings   Cheryl S. Lentz

Greek Potato Salad

1	tablespoon margarine	1	(8-ounce) package feta
½	cup slivered almonds		cheese, crumbled
½	teaspoon oregano	½	cup black olives, sliced
1½	pounds new potatoes, boiled,	7	radishes, sliced
	cooled and cubed	2	cucumbers, peeled and
			quartered

Melt margarine. Add almonds and oregano and stir until lightly browned. Cool. Combine almond mixture, potatoes, cheese, olives, radishes and cucumbers.

DRESSING:

¼	cup olive oil	¼	teaspoon Worcestershire
½	cup vinegar		sauce
1	tablespoon mustard	½	teaspoon black pepper
1	teaspoon salt		

Mix oil, vinegar, mustard, salt, Worcestershire sauce and pepper. Add to salad, tossing lightly, and chill until served.

NOTE: *Cheddar or Colby cheese may be substituted for feta cheese.*

Yield: 6 servings   Amy Harrell Pullen

Greek Pasta Salad

DRESSING:

2   tablespoons lemon juice
½   cup olive oil
½   teaspoon salt

¼   teaspoon pepper
¼   teaspoon dried oregano
1   clove garlic, crushed

To make dressing, combine lemon juice, oil, salt, pepper, oregano and garlic in blender until thick and creamy. Chill.

SALAD:

3   cups rotini pasta, cooked, drained and cooled
1   cucumber, peeled and thinly sliced

8   radishes, thinly sliced
1   cup kalamata olives
1½   cups feta cheese, crumbled

Combine pasta, vegetables and cheese. Pour dressing over salad and toss to coat. Chill well. Serve cold.

NOTE: *Kalamata (or calamata) olives are almond shaped Greek ripe olives which are eggplant in color.*

Yield: 6-8 servings

Eric E. Nianouris

Congealed Beet Salad

1   (15½-ounce) can beets, drained, reserving juice Water
2   (3-ounce) packages lemon gelatin
1½   tablespoons apple cider vinegar

1   teaspoon salt (optional)
1½   tablespoons grated onion
2   tablespoons horseradish
1½   cups chopped celery
6   lettuce leaves
  Mayonnaise for garnish

Cut beets in very thin strips (julienne). Add enough water to reserved beet juice to equal 2 cups liquid. Heat one cup of the beet juice and water mixture in a saucepan to boiling. Add gelatin, stirring until dissolved. Add remainder of beet-water mixture, vinegar and salt. Stir. Chill until partially set. Stir in beets, onion, horseradish and celery; chill until firm. Serve on lettuce with mayonnaise garnish.

Yield: 4-6 servings

Sue Bacon

B
L
E
S
S
I
N
G
S

♣ Apricot Salad

1	(20-ounce) can crushed pineapple, undrained
½	cup sugar
2	(3-ounce) boxes apricot gelatin

1	(8-ounce) package cream cheese, softened
1	cup diced celery
1	cup chopped pecans
1	(12-ounce) can evaporated milk, chilled

Place crushed pineapple in medium saucepan and add sugar. Bring slowly to a boil. Add gelatin, cream cheese, celery and pecans. Mix well. Pour evaporated milk into a large bowl and whip with electric beater for 5-6 minutes. Fold pineapple mixture into the whipped milk. Pour into large rectangular glass dish and refrigerate until congealed. Serve cold.

Yield: 12-15 servings

Marti Hoogendonk

♥ Golden Glow Salad

1	(3-ounce) package lemon gelatin
1	cup boiling water
1	(16-ounce) can crushed pineapple, drained, reserving juice

½	teaspoon salt
1	cup raw grated carrots
½	cup chopped pecans

Dissolve gelatin in water. Add juice and salt. Chill. Just before gelatin sets, add pineapple, carrots and pecans; pour into molds. Chill until firm. Serve cold.

NOTE: *This is an old recipe I have used for over 30 years.*

Yield: 8 servings

Helen Whicker

Four Cup Salad
Yummy!

1	(3-ounce) package orange gelatin
½	cup hot water
1	cup grated sharp cheddar cheese

1	cup crushed pineapple, slightly drained
1	cup mayonnaise
½	cup evaporated milk

Dissolve gelatin in 1/2 cup water. Add remaining ingredients; blend well. Pour into a 1 1/2-quart mold or dish. Chill until firm. Good served with ham or chicken.

Yield: 6 servings

Mrs. R. O. Everett II
Mrs. Ralph Hamner

Cranberry Mousse

A great Christmas salad

1	(20-ounce) can crushed pineapple, drained, juice reserved
1	(6-ounce) package strawberry gelatin
1	cup water
1	(16-ounce) can whole berry cranberry sauce
3	tablespoons fresh lemon juice
1	teaspoon grated lemon zest
¼	teaspoon ground nutmeg
2	cups sour cream
½	cup chopped pecans

Add pineapple juice to gelatin in a 1-quart saucepan. Stir in water. Heat to boiling, stirring to dissolve gelatin. Remove from heat. Blend in cranberry sauce. Add lemon juice, zest and nutmeg. Chill until slightly thickened. Blend sour cream into gelatin mixture. Fold in pineapple and pecans. Pour into a 2-quart mold and chill until firm. Unmold onto a serving plate.

NOTE: *This is a family tradition in our home on Christmas day.*

Yield: 8 servings   Teresa Williams

 Cola Salad

Sweet and tangy

	Water
1	(10-ounce) jar maraschino cherries, drained, reserving juice
1	(20-ounce) can crushed pineapple, drained, reserving juice
1	(3-ounce) package cherry gelatin
1	(3-ounce) package strawberry gelatin
1	(8-ounce) package cream cheese, softened
1	cup chopped pecans
1	(12-ounce) bottle carbonated cola beverage

In a saucepan, add water to juices to make 2 cups of liquid; heat to boiling. Place dry gelatins in large bowl and add hot juice mixture, stirring until gelatin is dissolved. Add cream cheese, cherries, pineapple and pecans. Mix well, then add cola. Pour into 9x13-inch glass dish or mold and refrigerate until set. Serve cold.

NOTE: *This can be fat-free and lower in calories by substituting fat-free cream cheese and diet cola.*

Yield: 15-20 servings   Sybil P. Baker

Cherry Pineapple Salad

1 **(14.5-ounce) can tart pitted cherries in water, undrained**	1 **(8-ounce) can crushed pineapple, undrained**
⅔ **cup sugar**	1 **banana, sliced**
1 **(3-ounce) package cherry gelatin**	½ **cup chopped pecans**

On low heat, mix cherries, sugar and gelatin in a saucepan. Simmer until gelatin has dissolved. Add pineapple, banana and pecans. Pour into 9x9-inch glass dish. Cover and refrigerate until set. Serve cold. Recipe may be doubled.
NOTE: *This is one of my children's favorites! I always serve this at Christmas.*

Yield: 9 servings   Ruby Craig Long

Blueberry Salad

1 **(8-ounce) can crushed pineapple, drained, reserving juice, plus water added to equal 2 cups**	1 **(6-ounce) box blackberry gelatin**
1 **(15-ounce) can blueberries, drained**	1 **(8-ounce) package cream cheese**
1½ **cups cold water, plus water to add to pineapple juice**	½ **pint sour cream**
	½ **cup sugar**
	1 **cup chopped pecans**

Combine drained pineapple and blueberries. Add water to reserved pineapple juice to make 2 cups and bring to boil. Add gelatin and 1 1/2 cups cold water. Add blueberries and pineapple. Place in a 9x13-inch dish; refrigerate overnight to congeal. Before serving, cream the cream cheese, sour cream, sugar and pecans. Spread on top of congealed salad.

Yield: 8 servings   Carr Garner

Frozen Fruit Cupcakes

1 **(16-ounce) container sour cream**	1 **(8-ounce) can crushed pineapple, drained**
¾ **cup sugar**	¼ **cup chopped nuts**
⅛ **teaspoon salt**	¼ **cup maraschino cherries, chopped**
2 **bananas, mashed**	
2 **tablespoons lemon juice**	

Blend sour cream, sugar and salt. Sprinkle bananas with lemon juice. Stir fruit and nuts into sour cream mixture, just until coated. Spoon into muffin tins lined with cupcake papers. Freeze. Serve frozen.

Yield: 8-10 servings   Evelyeen W. Smith

♥ Molded Cranberry Salad

2	(3-ounce) boxes raspberry gelatin	2-4	heaping tablespoons frozen orange juice concentrate
2	cups hot water	1	(15¼-ounce) can crushed pineapple with juice
1	tablespoon unflavored gelatin		Chopped nuts (optional)
¼	cup cold water	⅛	teaspoon salt
1	(16-ounce) can cranberry sauce		

Dissolve raspberry gelatin in hot water. Soak unflavored gelatin in 1/4 cup cold water and add to raspberry mixture. In a bowl, mash cranberry sauce until smooth. Add raspberry gelatin mixture, orange juice concentrate, pineapple, nuts and salt. Pour into a 1 1/2-quart mold or glass dish. Refrigerate until firm and ready to serve.

NOTE: *This recipe was given to me by my grandmother, Mrs. C. T. Dowell.*

Yield: 8-10 servings   Ann Scarborough

♠ Walnut Buttermilk Salad

1	(6-ounce) package peach gelatin	2	cups buttermilk
1	(8-ounce) can crushed pineapple, undrained	1	(12-ounce) container frozen whipped topping, thawed
		1	cup chopped walnuts

Heat gelatin and pineapple with juice to boiling. Cool; add buttermilk. Fold in whipped topping and walnuts until smooth. Pour into 9 1/2x11-inch glass dish. Chill several hours until firm. Cut into individual squares to serve.

NOTE: *Good as salad or dessert. Other fruits may also be added.*

Yield: 12-16 servings   Jo Walcher

Grapefruit Ring

2	(3-ounce) packages lemon gelatin	2	grapefruits, peeled, seeded and sectioned
1½	cups boiling water	1	cup grapes, halved and seeded
1¾	cup cold water	½	cup slivered almonds
½	cup frozen lemonade concentrate		

Dissolve gelatin in boiling water. Stir in cold water and lemonade. Chill until mixture is partially set. Fold in grapefruit sections, grapes and almonds. Spoon into a 1 1/2-quart mold or 8 large single molds. Chill. When set; serve.

Yield: 8-10 servings   Jean Miller Wurster

♣ Orange Soufflé Salad

2	(3-ounce) packages orange gelatin	1	pint orange sherbet
2	(11-ounce) cans mandarin oranges, drained, reserving ½ cup juice from each can	1	tablespoon currant or apple jelly
1	cup orange juice	1	tablespoon mayonnaise
		3	tablespoons whipped topping

Dissolve gelatin in 2 cups of hot liquid made by combining mandarin orange juice plus orange juice added to make 2 cups. Add sherbet to mixture, then oranges. Refrigerate until set. To make dressing, combine jelly, mayonnaise and topping. Serve on salad.

NOTE: *This recipe was given to me by Ginny Williamson. My family and friends have enjoyed it on many occasions*

Yield: 10-12 servings   Lawana Ford

● Kid's Salad

Easy to make. Fun for adults, too!

1	(8-ounce) carton cottage cheese	1	(3-ounce) box flavored gelatin, green or orange
1	(20-ounce) can crushed pineapple, drained	1	(11-ounce) can mandarin oranges (optional)
1	(8-ounce) carton frozen whipped topping, thawed		

Mix cottage cheese and pineapple; fold in topping and gelatin. Spoon into decorative bowl; chill until firm. Garnish with orange sections; serve.

Yield: Serves 6-8   Carolyn Haggerty

Crunchy Pea Salad

1	head iceberg lettuce, shredded	½	cup mayonnaise
1	cup chopped celery	½	cup sour cream
½	cup chopped green pepper	1½-3	tablespoons sugar
½	cup chopped green onion	¼-½	cup Parmesan cheese
2	cups frozen green peas, thawed; or canned	1-1½	cups shredded sharp Cheddar cheese
		¼-½	cup cooked, crumbled bacon

Layer all vegetables in sequence in casserole dish. In bowl, combine mayonnaise, sour cream and sugar to taste; spoon mixture over salad. Sprinkle with cheeses. Top with bacon. Refrigerate 2-4 hours, or overnight.

Yield: 8-10 servings   Sandy Elias

🔔 Hawaiian Salad

Great for a spring or summer luncheon

1	(3-ounce) package lemon gelatin, or flavor of choice	1	(8-ounce) package cream cheese, softened
1	(20-ounce) can crushed pineapple, reserve juice	1	(12-ounce) container cottage cheese
2	tablespoons cherry juice	1	cup grated cheddar cheese
1	(10-ounce) jar maraschino cherries, reserve juice	¾	cup diced celery
		1	cup chopped nuts

Combine pineapple juice, 2 tablespoons of the cherry juice, and enough water to equal 1 cup. Dissolve gelatin with this 1 cup liquid and set aside. Cream cheeses and stir in celery, and 3/4 cup of cherries and nuts. Mix gelatin mixture with cheese mixture. Refrigerate until firm and ready to serve.

Yield: Serves 8-12   Dellene Lyerly Gudger

Cranberry Salad with Apples & Pecans

1	(3-ounce) package cherry gelatin	½	cup diced apple
¾	cup boiling water	½	cup chopped pecans
1	(16-ounce) can whole berry cranberry sauce	2	tablespoons sour cream
1	orange, peeled, sectioned, seeded, chopped and drained	2	tablespoons mayonnaise or salad dressing
			Lettuce leaves

Combine gelatin and water; stir until gelatin dissolves. Add cranberry sauce, stirring until blended. Chill mixture to the consistency of unbeaten egg white. Fold in oranges, apples and pecans. Spoon mixture into 6 oiled individual molds or one 5-cup mold. Cover; chill until firm. To serve, unmold salad onto lettuce leaves. Mix sour cream and mayonnaise; top salads with spoonfuls of the mixture.

Yield: 6 servings   Joan Harris

Creamy Honey Dressing

1	cup sour cream or cream cheese	2	tablespoons orange juice concentrate
2	tablespoons honey		Milk (optional)

Whisk ingredients in bowl; thinning with milk if needed. Chill. Spoon dressing over fresh fruit salad.

Yield: 1 cup

♥ Basic Vinaigrette
Easy and elegant

1 tablespoon Dijon mustard	½ teaspoon fresh ground
4 tablespoons red wine vinegar	pepper
1 teaspoon sugar	½ cup olive oil
½ teaspoon salt	Fresh minced parsley or
	chives (optional)

Stir together mustard, vinegar, sugar, salt and pepper. In a small stream, slowly add in olive oil while whisking mixture. If desired, add parsley or chives. Toss vinaigrette with fresh salad greens.

Yield: 3/4 cup

Elizabeth Kaufmann

Dutch Cupboard Salad Dressing
Great on Spinach Salad

4 slices bacon	¼ cup apple cider vinegar
½ cup sugar	1 cup cold water
½ teaspoon salt	¼ teaspoon celery seed
1 tablespoon cornstarch	(optional)
1 egg, well beaten	

Fry bacon in skillet until brown and crisp. Drain and crumble bacon, leaving 2 teaspoons fat in the skillet. Mix sugar, salt and cornstarch in a small bowl. Add beaten egg, vinegar and water; mix well. Return bacon to skillet and stir in egg mixture. Cook over low heat stirring or whisking until bubbly and desired thickness. Add more water if a thinner consistency is desired. Refrigerate until ready to use.

NOTE: *Egg substitute may be used. Also good on cooked vegetables.*

Yield: 1 1/4 cups

Tomato Salad Dressing

1 cup salad oil	¼ cup ketchup
½ cup vinegar	Juice of 1 lemon
½ cup sugar	1 onion, grated fine
⅛ teaspoon salt	

Combine all ingredients and mix well. Refrigerate in a large jar covered with lid. Shake jar to mix well, each time the dressing is used.

Yield: 2 cups

Lois Loeblein

🔔 Japanese Ginger Salad Dressing
Delicious!

1½-2	teaspoons grated fresh ginger	2½	tablespoons honey
6-8	pieces crystallized ginger	2	tablespoons tomato paste
⅓	cup chopped Bermuda onion		Juice and grated zest of 1 lemon
¾	cup canola oil	¼-½	cup water
½	cup raspberry vinegar	1	tablespoon toasted sesame seeds (optional)
½-¾	cup dark soy sauce		

Put all ingredients in a blender container. Process until well combined. Refrigerate. Great dressing for salads or as a meat marinade.

NOTE: *My version of a dressing served at the Japanese restaurant at Epcot Center in Florida. May use to marinate BEEF KABOBS (see Page 167).*

Yield: 3 cups   Libby Gish

Town Steak House Roquefort Cheese Dressing

1	(3-ounce) package Roquefort cheese	1	teaspoon ketchup
1	(3-ounce) package cream cheese		Drop Tabasco
2	tablespoons milk	⅓	clove garlic
3	tablespoons mayonnaise	½	teaspoon Worcestershire sauce

Cream the cheeses, then add milk and mayonnaise. Add ketchup, Tabasco, garlic and Worcestershire; mix well. Use this as a dip or salad dressing.

NOTE: *The Town Steak House, now closed, was a long time favorite restaurant in Winston-Salem, NC.*

Yield: 1 cup   Genny Perdue

❤ Honey Dijon Dressing

1	cup lowfat or fat-free mayonnaise	2	tablespoons oil
¼	cup honey Dijon mustard	¾	teaspoon apple cider vinegar
¼	cup honey	¼	teaspoon onion salt
		¼	teaspoon red pepper

Put all ingredients in a blender container. Mix well and chill before using.

Yield: 1 1/2 cups   Marcia Parrott

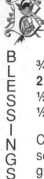

🔔 Poppy Seed Dressing

¾	cup sugar	1	cup vegetable oil
2	teaspoons dry mustard	¼	onion
½	teaspoon salt	2	tablespoons poppy seeds
½	cup cider vinegar		

Combine all ingredients in a blender container and process on high for 15-30 seconds. May be used as a vegetable marinade or dressing on fresh salad greens or fruit.

Yield: 2 cups   Ruth Philpott

🔔 Raspberry Vinegar Poppy Seed Dressing

2	tablespoons fresh onion juice	1	teaspoon salt
1½	cups sugar	2	cups vegetable oil
⅔	cup raspberry vinegar	2	tablespoons poppy seeds
1	teaspoon English or Dijon mustard		

To make onion juice, puree 1/2 peeled onion in blender container; add sugar, vinegar, mustard and salt. Blend. Empty into a bowl. With a whisk, slowly add oil and blend in poppy seeds. Serve with green salads or fruit.

NOTE: *This recipe is from a favorite resort in Hot Spring, VA.*

Yield: 3½-4 cups   Donna Goodman

Crunchy Sourdough Herb Croutons

10	slices light sourdough bread	½	(0.4-ounce) package ranch salad dressing mix (or gourmet Caesar or Parmesan Italian salad dressing mix)
8-10	tablespoons unsalted margarine, melted		

Cube bread slices into eighths. In a 9x12-inch baking dish, toss the cubes with melted margarine, using a wooden spoon. Empty half of salad dressing packet into a ziplock bag. Add bread cubes. Toss to coat. Return bread cubes to baking dish. Cook in microwave for 4 1/2-5 minutes, stirring once after 2 1/2 minutes. Remove from oven, cool. Store in airtight plastic bag. When ready to use, sprinkle desired amount on salads.

NOTE: *You may slow cook croutons in 225° oven for 2 hours or place in 350° oven, turn oven off, and leave in oven overnight until crisp.*

Yield: 80 croutons

Favorite Fruits

Bananas and Melons,
Citrus Sweets, Apples, Pears
& Orchard Treats

Butterscotch Candied Apples

1	cup butterscotch baking morsels		Wooden tongue depressors or popsicle sticks
⅛-¼	cup red cinnamon candy hearts	4-5	whole Red Delicious apples, stemmed, washed and dried
1-1½	tablespoons water		Mini-chocolate chips,
1	(12.25-ounce) bottle fat-free caramel ice cream topping		crunchy cereal or cake sprinkles for decoration

Soften butterscotch chips in Pyrex bowl in microwave for 1-2 minutes, stirring often. Microwave candy hearts and water in another Pyrex bowl for 1-2 minutes until melted, stirring often. Add caramel topping to softened chips. Stir in cinnamon mixture, blending well. Insert sticks into apple stem ends. Dip each apple into warm mixture to coat. Place apples on buttered wax paper. Cool. For thicker coating, dip apple again. Sprinkle on desired decoration. Refrigerate to harden coating.

NOTE: *For APPLE CHUNKS WITH CINNAMON SAUCE, use the warm caramel-cinnamon coating mixture as a dip or topping for raw apple chunks. For CHOCOLATE PEANUT BUTTER APPLES, dip fresh apples in a melted mixture of 1 cup chocolate chips, 1 cup peanut butter chips and 1 tablespoon vegetable oil.*

Yield: 4-5 apples

Stuffed Apples

Pineapple juice	Peanut butter
Whole apples, cored and top sliced off; or cut into halves	Mini-chocolate chips or raisins (optional)
Honey nut cream cheese	

Brush apples with juice to prevent browning. Fill centers with mixture of equal parts of cream cheese and peanut butter and stir in chips or raisins if desired. Serve on a wooden stick or cut into wedges.

Yield: 1 apple

Caramel Apple Dip

4-6	tablespoons margarine, melted	1	cup light brown sugar
		1	cup sour cream

Combine margarine and sugar. Cool. Stir in sour cream. Stir; blend until smooth. Chill for several hours. Serve with sliced apples or other fresh fruit.

Yield: 1 1/2 cups

Apple Dumplings
Simple and delicious

4	medium Granny Smith apples, peeled, cored and cut into 8 pieces each	1	cup water
1	(12-ounce) can Hungry Jack biscuits, separated into 30 layers	1	cup sugar
		½	cup margarine
		¼-½	cup brown sugar
		½	teaspoon cinnamon

Wrap each apple piece with 1 layer of biscuit. Arrange in 3 rows in a greased 9x13-inch pan. In a small pan, heat water, sugars and margarine to a boil. Pour syrup over dumplings. Sprinkle tops with a mixture of brown sugar and cinnamon. Bake at 350° for 30 minutes or until brown and bubbly. Cool to serve. Freezes well.

Yield: 30 dumplings   Sharon Skowronek

Baked Apples

1	cup sugar	1	stack of 34 Ritz crackers, crushed
6	tablespoons flour	1	stick butter, cut into small pieces
2	(20-ounce) cans sliced apples, with juice		
2	cups shredded sharp cheddar cheese		

Mix sugar and flour. Add apples with juice. Add cheese and mix well. Place in 9x13-inch casserole dish. Sprinkle crushed crackers on top of mixture. Dot cracker crumbs with butter. Bake at 350° for 35 minutes or until bubbly. Serve hot.

Yield: 10-12 servings   Collin Grubb

Apple Raspberry Surprise

6-8	apples, quartered and cored	1	cup flour
1	(3-ounce) box raspberry gelatin	1	cup sugar
1	stick margarine, melted	½	cup pecan pieces

Slice apples into a 9x11-inch casserole dish. Sprinkle gelatin over apples; set aside. Mix margarine, flour, sugar and nuts in a bowl until consistency is crumbly. Sprinkle mixture over apples. Bake at 350° for 45 minutes or until apples are done. Serve hot.

Yield: 8-10 servings   Carolyn McDonald

Betty's Baked Apples

3	teaspoons cinnamon	2	tablespoons butter
6	tablespoons sugar	½	cup water, very hot
6	large red baking apples, cored and quartered	½	cup corn syrup

Mix together cinnamon and sugar. Place apples in a flat baking dish. In the center of each piece of apple put 1/2 teaspoon butter and 1 tablespoon of the cinnamon-sugar mixture. Combine water and syrup; pour over apples. Bake at 350° for about 1 hour, basting occasionally to glaze. Serve hot.

NOTE: *These are great made the day before and reheated. One of my grandchildren's favorites.*

Yield: 6 servings   Betty S. Carli

Cinnamon Stewed Apples

4-6	cooking apples, peeled, cored and cut into ½-inch wedges	5	tablespoons sugar
		1	teaspoon cinnamon
1½	cups water	2	tablespoons butter

Place apples and water in a medium sized saucepan. Cook, covered, over low heat until the apples are tender, about 10 minutes. Add the sugar; simmer uncovered for 5 minutes. Mix in the cinnamon and butter, stir until the butter melts. Cool and serve.

Yield: Serves 4   Monica M. Alfonsi

Cranberry Apple Bake

3-4	cups chopped apples	½	cup brown sugar
	Few drops lemon juice	⅓	cup flour
2	cups whole, raw cranberries	½	cup butter, melted
1	cup sugar	⅓	cup chopped pecans
1½	cups uncooked quick oats		

In a bowl, sprinkle apples with lemon juice to prevent browning. Add cranberries and sugar; mix well. Place in a 2-quart casserole dish. Combine oats, brown sugar, flour, butter and pecans. Spread the oat mixture over top of apple-cranberry mixture. Bake at 300° for 1 hour. Serve hot.

Yield: 8 servings   Shully Storey

Baked Apricots

1 (1-pound) box light brown sugar
4 (16-ounce) cans apricots, drained, reserve half of liquid

½ cup butter
1 stack of 34 Ritz crackers, crushed

Mix brown sugar, apricots and reserved liquid; soak in refrigerator overnight. Brown Ritz cracker crumbs in butter. Put apricot mixture in a 9x13-inch pan and top with crumbs. Bake uncovered at 350° for 30 minutes. Serve hot.

Yield: 6-8 servings   Suzanne Wallace Casey

Raspberry and Cranberry Compote

1 (10½-ounce) package frozen raspberries, thawed
2 cups (½-pound) cranberries, fresh or frozen, thawed

½ cup sugar
3 tablespoons port or sweet sherry wine

Drain raspberries and combine with cranberries in a saucepan; cover and simmer on low heat for 5 minutes. Add sugar; stir gently and allow to cool. Add port or sherry and chill.

YOGURT CREME:
½ cup heavy cream
1 cup vanilla yogurt

Whip cream until it holds soft peaks. Stir yogurt to soften it slightly and fold into whipped cream. Chill. Serve in parfait glasses, alternating layers of berries and cream.

Yield: 6-8 servings   Dorothy Collin Grubb Horne

♥ Almond Pineapple Fruit Dip

1 (8-ounce) package light cream cheese
¾ cup crushed pineapple, drained

1 tablespoon brown sugar
1 teaspoon almond extract

Combine all ingredients and process in a food processor. Chill. Serve with your favorite fruit.

Yield: 1 1/2 cups   Sandee Carrigan

🔔 Mother's Hot Fruit
Great with any meal!

2	(16-ounce) cans peach halves
2	(16-ounce) cans pear halves
1	(16-ounce) can apricots
1	(16-ounce) can seedless black Bing cherries

12	soft coconut macaroon cookies
½	cup brown sugar
1	cup brandy, any flavor

Drain fruits thoroughly. Crumble macaroons and mix with sugar. In a 9x13-inch pan, alternate layers of fruit with macaroon mixture, reserving some crumbs for top. Pour 3/4 cup of the brandy over fruit and let set for 2 hours. Add remaining brandy and bake at 350° for 1 hour. Serve hot or warm.

Yield: 18 servings   Norma Goldman

🔔 Ambrosia
A family holiday tradition

10	large sweet oranges, peeled and sectioned
5	large sweet apples, peeled, cored and chopped
2	large bananas, peeled, quartered, sliced thin

2	(20-ounce) cans crushed pineapple, with syrup Sugar
1	(3.5-ounce) can shredded coconut
1	cup pecan halves, chopped if desired

In a medium glass bowl, gently toss all ingredients, adding sugar to taste. Refrigerate. Serve cold in sherbet glasses.

Yield: 12 servings   Max and Sara Ann Spear

Pineapple Casserole

2	(20-ounce) cans crushed pineapple, drained
2	cups grated sharp cheddar cheese
1	cup brown sugar

6	tablespoons flour
1	stack of 34 Ritz crackers, crushed
2	sticks butter, melted

Place pineapple in an 8x10-inch casserole dish. Mix cheese, sugar and flour; spread over pineapple. Sprinkle with cracker crumbs. Pour butter over the top. Bake at 350° for 35 minutes or until brown. Serve hot.

Yield: 6 servings   Grace Dupin

Cranberry Casserole
Good side dish for Thanksgiving and Christmas!

	cup uncooked quick oats	1½	cups fresh cranberries
	tablespoons flour	3	medium apples, diced
½	cup sugar	1	cup chopped pecans or
½	cup brown sugar		English walnuts
	teaspoon cinnamon	½	cup margarine

Combine oatmeal, flour, sugars and cinnamon. Add cranberries, apples and nuts. Spread in a lightly greased 9-inch square glass baking dish. Top with slices of margarine. Bake at 350° for 30 minutes. Serve warm.

NOTE: *My husband, A.J. and sons, Drew and Bowen, enjoyed this as a dessert.*

Yield: Serves 9   Stella Gillespie

Rainbow Trifle Fruit Salad

2	cups fresh blueberries, rinsed and stemmed	1-1½	cups fresh pineapple chunks
2	cups fresh strawberries, hulled, washed and sliced	1-1½	cups melon balls (honeydew, cantaloupe or
1½	cups seedless green grapes, washed and stemmed		watermelon or a combination)
1½	cups seedless red grapes, washed and stemmed		Frozen orange or pineapple juice concentrate

Place each fruit in a separate bowl and toss with juice to coat. Drain and set aside.

BANANA CREAM TOPPING:

2½	cups milk	2	(8-ounce) cans crushed
1	cup sour cream		pineapple, undrained
2	(3¾-ounce) package instant banana cream or coconut pudding mix	1	kiwi peeled and sliced, for garnish

Combine milk, sour cream, pudding mix and pineapple in a bowl; set aside. Layer fruits in a 4-quart glass or trifle bowl. Spoon topping over fruit covering to edge of bowl. Cover; refrigerate several hours or overnight. Before serving, garnish with kiwi.

NOTE: *For INDIVIDUAL FRUIT TRIFLES, layer fruits in dessert dishes and top with pudding mixture. For a CREAMY BANANA FRUIT DIP, combine topping ingredients, reducing milk to 1 1/2 cups.*

Yield: 15-20 servings

Pears Esprit

Rave reviews!

1	cup burgundy	2	teaspoons cinnamon
1	cup sugar	6	firm pears (Bosc variety
½	cup water		preferred), peeled

Combine burgundy, sugar, water and cinnamon in a saucepan. Bring to a boil; add pears and simmer 20 minutes, basting pears often. Remove from heat. Cool pears in syrup for 15 minutes to absorb flavor. Chill.

CUSTARD:

2¼	cups half-and-half	3	tablespoons cornstarch
3	egg yolks	½	cup sugar
1	teaspoon vanilla		

Bring 2 cups of the half-and-half to a simmer. Beat egg yolks, remaining 1/4 cup cold half-and-half and vanilla in a bowl. Stir cornstarch and sugar together; add yolk mixture. Slowly add heated half-and-half, mixing with a whisk. Cook over low heat, stirring constantly until mixture thickens enough to coat spoon. Set aside.

BITTERSWEET CHOCOLATE SAUCE:

4	ounces bittersweet	2	tablespoons brandy
	chocolate bits	2	tablespoons whipping cream

Heat chocolate, brandy and cream in top of double boiler. Whisk until smooth. To serve, place warm custard and a chilled pear in each of 6 goblets. Top with warm sauce and serve immediately.

NOTE: *Takes time and some last minute preparation, but is worth the effort.*

Yield: 6 servings

Marie Fork

Fluffy Fruit Dip

1	(7-ounce) bottle marshmallow creme	⅓	cup powdered sugar
1	(8-ounce) package cream cheese	⅓	cup sour cream
		¾	teaspoon almond extract

Combine ingredients in bowl. Process or blend until smooth. Chill. Serve with fresh fruit or berries.

Yield: 1 1/2 cups

Blueberry - Pineapple Crunch

1	(15¼-ounce) can crushed pineapple	1	(18.25-ounce) box yellow cake mix
2½	cups fresh blueberries	6	tablespoons butter or margarine, melted
1	cup sugar	1	cup chopped pecans

Lightly grease 9x13-inch pan. Spread undrained pineapple on bottom of pan. Add blueberries and sprinkle with 3/4 cup sugar. Spread dry cake mix evenly over fruit. Drizzle melted butter over all. Bake at 350° for 25 minutes. Remove from oven. Cut slits to bottom of pan for juice to rise. Sprinkle top with pecans and remaining 1/4 cup sugar. Bake an additional 15 minutes. Serve warm or cold.

NOTE: *This recipe was shared by a customer at my berry farm in Lenoir County, NC.*

Yield: 10-12 servings   Peggy Maness

Jubilant Cherries and Raspberries

2	(17-ounce) cans pitted dark sweet cherries in heavy syrup, drained, reserve syrup in refrigerator	2	teaspoons cinnamon-sugar Pinch of ground cloves
½-¾	cup black raspberry liqueur	3-4	tablespoons cornstarch
1	(10-ounce) bottle seedless red raspberry jam	2	pints vanilla ice cream Toasted, sliced almonds (optional)

In a bowl, soak cherries in liqueur overnight in refrigerator. To make sauce, remove cherries from marinade with a slotted spoon. Cook reserved cherry syrup, marinade liquid, jam, cinnamon-sugar and cloves, gradually adding cornstarch and blending with a whisk until thickened. Add cherries and simmer for 15 minutes. Serve hot over ice cream or refrigerate cherry mixture until needed. Garnish with almonds.

NOTE: *For CHERRIES and RASPBERRY ROMANOFF, serve chilled Jubilant Cherries and Raspberries mixture in bowls. Top each serving with a mixture of 2 tablespoons each of sour cream and whipped dessert topping (omitting ice cream). Sprinkle or sift cinnamon-sugar or brown sugar on top.*

Yield: 8 servings

Dessert Fruit & Frosting Fondue
A tabletop of fun and frosted sweets

FONDUE:
3   (16-ounce) plastic cans of ready-to-spread frosting (1 each of
    chocolate, vanilla and strawberry)

DESSERT DIPPERS:
    Assorted pound cake or angel food cake cubes, ladyfingers,
    shortbread or sugar wafer cookies, doughnut holes, crunchy pretzel
    sticks or rods, animal crackers or tiny graham crackers.

FRUIT DIPPERS:
    Assorted fruits such as whole strawberries, cherries, pineapple
    chunks, banana chunks, grapes, kiwi slices, or apple and pear slices

Remove lids and foil covers from frosting. Microwave each can on high for 1-2 minutes to melt, or melt in a double boiler. Pour melted frosting into fondue pots or keep warm in bowls on a heated serving tray. Arrange your choice of dessert and fruit dippers in bowls around the fondue pots. Spear dippers and coat with melted frosting.

NOTE: *For SOUR CREAM FROSTING FONDUE, add 1/4 cup sour cream to each can of frosting before melting. For KAHLÚA FONDUE add 1 cup marshmallow crème and 1/4 cup Kahlúa to chocolate frosting.*

Yield: 6 cups fondue

Honeyed Grapefruit Halves

2   pink grapefruits, halved
4   teaspoons honey
4   teaspoons brown sugar
½   teaspoon cinnamon-sugar

4   maraschino cherries or fresh
    strawberries, whole, halves
    or sliced (optional)

Place grapefruit halves, cut side up, in a baking pan. With a knife, loosen and separate grapefruit sections. Drizzle with honey; sprinkle with brown sugar and cinnamon-sugar. Broil 5-inches from heat for 2-3 minutes or until bubbly. Garnish with a cherry or strawberry if desired. Serve warm.

NOTE: *For BROILED GRAPEFRUIT ROMANOFF, spoon a mixture of equal parts of sour cream and brown sugar on grapefruit halves. Broil 2-3 minutes until bubbly and lightly browned. Garnish as above.*

Yield: 4 servings

♥ Mint Melon Medley

1	cup 7-Up, chilled	6	teaspoons non-alcoholic
5	cups assorted cantaloupe,		crème de menthe syrup
	watermelon and honeydew		Fresh mint leaves, rinsed
	melon balls		(optional)
2	cups pineapple sherbet, softened		

Toss and soak melon balls in 7-Up for 1 hour in refrigerator. When ready to serve, place drained melon balls into 4 stemmed glasses. Combine and blend sherbet and syrup. Spoon sherbet mixture over melon balls. Garnish with mint if desired before serving.

Yield: 4 servings

Peach Crisp

1	quart sliced peaches, fresh	½	cup water
	or frozen	½	cup flour
1	teaspoon cinnamon	¾	cup sugar
½	teaspoon salt	⅓	cup butter or margarine

Put peaches in an 8x8-inch baking dish. Sprinkle with cinnamon and salt. Add water. Combine flour and sugar; cut in butter until mixture is crumbly. Sprinkle over peaches. Bake at 375° for 50 minutes or until peaches are tender. Serve hot or cold.

Yield: 6-8 servings   Peggy Whitaker

Friendship Brandied Fruit

1	cup bottled maraschino cherries, drained	1	(¼-ounce) package of dry yeast
1	cup canned pineapple tidbits or chunks, drained	1½	cups sugar
1	cup canned cling peach slices, drained	1	(2-quart) glass apothecary jar with a wide-mouth and a lid

Place all ingredients in jar; stir with plastic spoon. Put jar top on loosely; allow to ferment in a warm place on kitchen counter for 2 weeks (do not refrigerate). Stir mixture daily with plastic or wooden spoon for 7 days. Fruit is now ready to use in cakes or as topping for ice cream, puddings and pound cakes. Maintain at least 3 cups volume in jar; or fermentation will stop. Every 2 weeks, 1 cup of drained fruit and 1 cup of sugar may be added to mixture. Stir every 3 days. When mixture totals 6 cups, 3 cups of mixture may be shared with a friend.

Yield: 4 cups

Peach Surprises

4-5 coconut macaroon cookies, crumbled

4 tablespoons frozen orange juice concentrate, thawed

1 (10-ounce) bottle red plum jam or red currant jelly

1 (16-ounce) can peach halves, drained

Blend cookies with orange juice concentrate in a bowl. Mound mixture in center of each peach and place in a 1-quart baking dish. Melt jam in jar (with lid removed) on high in microwave for 3-4 minutes. Pour 1/2-3/4 cup jam over peaches. Bake at 350° for 15-20 minutes. Serve hot.

NOTE: *For FLAMING PEACHES, place a sugar cube saturated with almond or lemon extract in the center of each unstuffed peach half. Surround a holiday ham with peaches. Carefully ignite each sugar cube for a spectacular presentation. For BAKED CHUTNEY PEACHES, stuff each peach half with 1 tablespoon chutney. Sprinkle with a dash of curry and bake at 350° for 30 minutes.*

Yield: 4-6 servings

Frosted Fruits

Assorted fresh fruit (red, yellow or green apples, red, purple & green grapes, plums, pears, cherries, cranberries & strawberries)

Light corn syrup
Super-fine or extra-fine sugar

Brush syrup on dry fruit with a pastry brush. Sift or sprinkle sugar over fruit or roll large fruits in sugar to evenly coat. Set fruits aside on a non-stick surface to dry or until fruit forms a "frosty crust". Arrange fruits in a crystal bowl for a table centerpiece or use fruits to garnish dessert or cheese trays.

Yield: As desired

Fruit Candy

Seedless grapes or strawberries, stemmed, rinsed and dried
Sliced banana rounds
Dried apricots, peaches or pineapple

1 (7.25-ounce) bottle of Magic Shell chocolate or peanut butter ice cream topping, shaken well

Place choice of fruits on a parchment lined cookie sheet. Drizzle on "Magic Shell," coating fruit. Carefully transfer to disposable pie tins. Freeze 10 minutes, until coating is firm. Remove from pie tin, coat again. Replace on pie tin; freeze again until coating is firm. Gently remove; serve chilled on platter as a quick snack or dessert garnish.

Yield: As desired

Honey Roasted Bananas

| 4 | teaspoons sweet butter | ¼-½ | teaspoon cinnamon-sugar |
| 2 | bananas, peeled and sliced lengthwise | 1½ | tablespoon honey |

Preheat oven to 350°. Grease a small baking dish with 1 teaspoon butter; place bananas on bottom of dish. Evenly sprinkle with cinnamon-sugar mixture. Bake 8 minutes. Remove from oven. Drizzle honey over bananas. Top with 3 teaspoons butter cut into small pieces. Bake 2 minutes more. Broil for 2 minutes or until honey and butter have caramelized and bananas are golden brown. Serve hot topped with pan juices.

Yield: 2 servings

Baked Bananas Foster
Easy version of a classic dessert!

½	cup butter, melted	6	large firm ripe bananas, peeled, cut in half crosswise, then cut lengthwise
½	cup brown sugar		
½	teaspoon cinnamon-sugar		
½	cup dark rum	1	pint vanilla, butter pecan or coffee ice cream or frozen yogurt
2	tablespoons banana liqueur (optional)		Whole or chopped pecans, toasted (optional)

Preheat oven to 375°. In a bowl, combine butter, brown sugar, cinnamon-sugar, rum and liqueur. Pour mixture over bananas arranged in a single layer in an ovenproof baking dish that has been sprayed with butter-flavored non-stick cooking spray. Bake on center oven rack for 15-20 minutes until bubbly. To serve, scoop ice cream into dessert dishes and spoon hot bananas and sauce on top. Garnish with pecans if desired. Serve immediately.

Yield: 6 servings

♥ Honey Apricot Fruit Dip

| 1 | (16-ounce) can light apricot halves, drained | 1 | teaspoon honey |
| | | ¼ | cup light sour cream |

Process all ingredients in food processor. Chill. Serve with fruit.

Yield: 1 cup   Sandee Carrigan

Double Dates

4	ounces honey nut or plain cream cheese	15-20	pitted dates, split lengthwise, leaving halves hinged
1	(2-ounce) package pecan pieces, chopped	5	bacon slices, each slice quartered into 2-inch pieces

In a bowl, blend cheese and pecans. Stuff dates with a small amount of mixture, press halves together and wrap each filled date with a piece of bacon. Place on cookie sheet. Bake at 375° for about 20 minutes or until bacon is crisp. Drain on paper towels. Serve warm.

NOTE: *For CRUNCHY PEANUT BUTTER DATES: Combine 3 tablespoons each of peanut butter and wheat germ. Blend in 1 teaspoon honey. Stuff dates with mixture. Press halves together and refrigerate until ready to serve.*

Yield: 15-20 dates

Instant Pear Sorbet
A refreshing treat! Easy and quick!

2	(15¼-ounce) cans pear halves with syrup	2	tablespoons cream cheese (optional)
2	tablespoons mint jelly (optional)		Fresh mint leaves, rinsed (optional)
1	teaspoon cinnamon sugar (optional)		

Freeze unopened cans of pears for 24 hours until firm. Submerge frozen can in hot tap water briefly to loosen contents. Open both ends of can, remove frozen pears, cut into 4-8 slices and place in food processor. Add jelly, sugar and cream cheese if desired. Process until smooth, stirring often. Serve icy cold in glass dishes. Garnish with mint if desired. May be frozen.

NOTE: *For RAINBOW SORBET: Substitute other canned fruits in syrup, such as apricots, blueberries, peaches, mandarin oranges or crushed pineapple, for pears. Process the fruit as above and simply blend in 2 tablespoons of your choice of flavorings such as pear liqueur, apricot brandy, Grand Marnier, rum, bourbon, peach schnapps or crème de cassis before serving.*

Yield: 4 servings

Salisbury
Strawberries

Ripened on the Curly Vine,
Juicy Red & So Sublime

🔔 🍓 Strawberry Blintz for Brunch

BATTER:

1½ cups powdered sugar
6 eggs
3 cups flour
3 tablespoons baking powder
¼ teaspoon salt

¾ cup half-and-half or milk
2-3 teaspoons almond extract
1½ cups butter or margarine, melted and cooled

In a bowl, mix all ingredients with electric mixer. Spread 2 1/2 cups of the batter in bottom of a 3 1/2-quart casserole dish. Set aside remaining batter.

FILLING AND TOPPINGS:

1 (12-ounce) carton cottage cheese
3 (8-ounce) tubs strawberry cream cheese, softened
2 eggs
½ cup powdered sugar
Juice of 1 lemon
2-3 teaspoons almond extract

⅛ teaspoon salt
2 (10-ounce) packages frozen strawberry halves, thawed and drained
Pourable strawberry fruit
Sour cream
Fresh strawberries, sliced (optional)

In a bowl, using electric beater, blend cheeses, eggs, sugar, lemon juice, almond extract and salt, 5 minutes until creamy and smooth. Spoon filling mixture over batter in casserole dish. Sprinkle berry halves over filling. Spread on remaining 2 1/2 cups of batter, covering berries. Bake at 300°-325° for 1 hour and 20-30 minutes, or until center is set and blintz is golden. Cool slightly. Cut into squares. Serve with pourable strawberry fruit or dollops of sour cream and fresh berries.

Yield: 12-15 servings

🍓 Strawberry Bread

3 cups flour
2 cups sugar
1 teaspoon salt
1 teaspoon baking soda
3 teaspoons cinnamon
½ teaspoon nutmeg
½ teaspoon ginger

4 eggs, beaten
1 cup oil
2 (10-ounce) packages frozen sliced strawberries, thawed, undrained
1¼ cups pecans, chopped

Combine dry ingredients. Add eggs, oil and strawberries. Fold in nuts. Put in two 1 1/2-quart greased 8 1/4x4 1/2-inch glass loaf dishes. Bake at 350° for 60-70 minutes. Cool bread in loaf pans 5 minutes before removing. Slice to serve.

NOTE: *Freezes well. Fresh chopped strawberries may be substituted.*

Yield: 2 loaves   Jo Ann Smith

🍓 A Berry Special Salad

SALAD:

1	(1-pound) bag fresh spinach, large stems removed, well washed and patted dry, chilled
1	(16-ounce) can bean sprouts, chilled, rinsed and drained
1	(8-ounce) can sliced water chestnuts, chilled, drained
6	strips bacon, cooked, drained and crumbled
3	eggs, hard boiled, sliced
1	cup sliced fresh mushrooms
1½	cups fresh strawberries, sliced and stemmed

Combine spinach, bean sprouts, water chestnuts, bacon, eggs, mushrooms and berries in a large salad bowl.

STRAWBERRY DRESSING:

1	cup vegetable salad oil or mayonnaise
1	medium Bermuda or sweet onion, peeled and cut into chunks
¼	cup cider vinegar
¾	cup sugar
1	tablespoon Worcestershire sauce
1	(10-ounce) package frozen strawberries, with syrup
	Salt and pepper

In a blender, process oil, onions, vinegar, sugar, Worcestershire, berries and salt and pepper to taste, stopping to stir often with a rubber spatula. Just before serving, pour dressing over individual salads served on plates or toss dressing with salad and serve on buffet table in a large salad bowl.

NOTE: *Salad greens may be prepared a couple of hours ahead and stored in refrigerator in a plastic bag with dampened paper towel to keep crisp.*

Yield: 8 servings

🍓 Strawberry Summer Salad

1	pint strawberries, stemmed and halved
1	teaspoon finely chopped fresh mint or ½ teaspoon dried mint
½	teaspoon honey
½	cup light sour cream
2	cups seasonal fresh fruits (blueberries, sliced peaches, plums, kiwi fruit or oranges)
4	lettuce leaves

To make *CREAMY STRAWBERRY DRESSING,* in electric blender container blend about 1/2 cup strawberries to make 1/4 cup puree; reserve remaining strawberries. In bowl, stir puree, mint, honey and sour cream to blend. To assemble salad, line individual salad plates with lettuce leaves. Arrange reserved strawberries and other fruits on lettuce. Top with *DRESSING.*

Yield: 4 servings   Michelle Patterson, Patterson's Farms, Inc.

🍓 Strawberry Soup

A luscious soup or dessert treat!

2	(10-ounce) packages frozen strawberries with syrup	1	envelope unflavored gelatin
1¼	cups sour cream	2	tablespoons fresh lemon juice
¾	cup powdered sugar	1½	teaspoons cinnamon-sugar
½	cup frozen orange juice concentrate, thawed	10	fresh strawberries, washed, stemmed, sliced for garnish
½-1	cup black raspberry liqueur or raspberry blend frozen juice concentrate, thawed		Fresh mint leaves, rinsed, for garnish

Place frozen berries, sour cream and powdered sugar in a blender; process and stir until smooth. In a microwavable bowl, blend orange juice and gelatin; cook mixture on high in microwave 3 minutes or until foamy and gelatin has dissolved. Stir well; set aside briefly. To blender, add desired amount of liqueur. Add lemon juice, cinnamon-sugar and gelatin mixture. Blend to mix well. At this point, covered blender container may be refrigerated. When ready to serve, pour into small bowls. Garnish with berries and mint. Serve cold.

NOTE: *For FROSTY STRAWBERRY SORBET, freeze soup mixture in covered plastic container. Use ice cream scoop to serve. For BERRY DELICIOUS MOUSSE increase amount of gelatin in soup mixture to 3 3/4 teaspoons. Add 1/2 (3-ounce) package cream cheese when blending, if desired, and prepare as for STRAWBERRY SOUP. When serving sorbet or mousse as dessert, you may use toasted pound cake croutons as garnish. To make TOASTED POUND CAKE DESSERT CROUTONS, place 1 cup pound cake pieces (1/2-3/4-inch cubes or canapé cutter shapes) on a 10x13-inch cookie sheet and broil for 6 minutes until golden. Cool.*

Yield: 5 cups   Libby Gish

🔔 🍓 Strawberry Frozen Fruit Salad

1	(8-ounce) package cream cheese, softened	1	(8-ounce) can crushed pineapple, drained
¾	cup sugar	1	(10-ounce) package frozen strawberries
1	(8-ounce) carton frozen whipped dessert topping, thawed	½	cup chopped nuts
		2-4	bananas, sliced

Combine cream cheese, sugar, whipped topping, pineapple, strawberries and nuts. Fold in bananas. Place mixture into a 9x13-inch glass dish and freeze. Thaw slightly before serving.

Yield: 10-12 servings   Shirley Lewis

🔔 🍓 A Different Strawberry Salad

FIRST LAYER:

1 cup crushed pretzels	1 tablespoon sugar
1/2 stick margarine, melted	

Mix pretzels, margarine and sugar. Press into greased 9x13-inch pan. Bake at 400° for 7 minutes. Cool.

SECOND LAYER:

1 (8-ounce) package cream cheese	2 cups frozen whipped dessert topping, thawed
1 cup sugar	

Combine cream cheese, sugar and topping; blend until smooth. Spread on pretzel layer.

THIRD LAYER:

1 (6-ounce) package strawberry gelatin	2 (10-ounce) packages frozen strawberries, thawed
2 cups boiling water	

Dissolve gelatin in water and stir in strawberries. Pour gelatin and strawberry mixture on top of cream cheese layer. Refrigerate until congealed. Serve cold.

Yield: Serves 10-12   Martha Lassiter

🍓 Strawberry Brûlée Supreme

1 quart fresh strawberries, washed, hulled	1 (8-ounce) tub strawberry flavored cream cheese or regular cream cheese
3 tablespoons granulated sugar	1 1/2 cups sour cream
4-6 tablespoons raspberry liqueur	1/3 cup powdered sugar
	1 cup light brown sugar

In a bowl, toss berries with granulated sugar. Add raspberry liqueur; toss and let stand for about 1 hour, stirring often. Arrange berries in an oven-proof dish or divide equally into individual oven-proof ramekins. In a small bowl, combine cream cheese, sour cream and powdered sugar. Beat with electric mixer on medium speed until fluffy and light. Spread cream cheese mixture evenly over strawberries. Sift brown sugar on top. Place dishes under a preheated broiler for 2-4 minutes until sugar caramelizes. Serve hot or cold. Mixture will get firm when chilled.

Yield: 8-10 servings

Strawberry - Banana Refrigerator Cake
A colorful and moist cake

1 (18.25-ounce) package strawberry cake mix, prepared according to package directions	1 (4-ounce) package instant banana cream pudding mix
2 (10-ounce) packages sweetened, sliced frozen strawberries and juice, thawed	1 cup half-and-half 2 cups frozen whipped dessert topping, thawed Fresh strawberries and blueberries for garnish

Preheat oven to 350°. Grease and flour a 9x13-inch pan. Following directions on cake mix for basic recipe, prepare, bake and cool cake. Poke holes 1-inch apart on top of cake using the tip of a wooden spoon handle. Puree strawberries and syrup in blender and spoon evenly over cake, allowing mixture to soak into holes. Make topping by preparing pudding according to package directions substituting half-and-half for milk. Fold whipped topping into pudding mixture and spread over cake. Garnish with berries. Refrigerate at least 4 hours before serving. Keep refrigerated.

NOTE: *The patriotic colors make it a great choice for a Fourth of July dessert.*

Yield: 10-12 servings

♪ 🍓 Strawberry Cake

1 (3-ounce) package strawberry gelatin	1 tablespoon vegetable oil
1 (18.25-ounce) package white cake mix	¹/₂ cup water ¹/₂ cup fresh strawberries 4 eggs

With mixer, beat gelatin, cake mix, oil, water and berries. Add eggs one at a time beating well after each addition. Pour cake batter into a 9x13-inch cake pan. Bake at 350° for 35 minutes. Cool.

ICING:

1 (4-ounce) stick melted margarine	¹/₂ cup fresh strawberries, mashed
1 (1-pound) box powdered sugar	

Mix margarine, sugar and mashed berries. Top cake with icing. Slice to serve.

NOTE: *May substitute 1 (10-ounce) package frozen strawberries, thawed and drained, in cake batter.*

Yield: 10-12 servings   Sarah Baker

🔔 🍓 Strawberry Cheesecake

GRAHAM CRACKER NUT CRUST:

³/₄ cup ground nuts	3 tablespoons melted butter or
³/₄ cup graham cracker crumbs	margarine

Combine nuts, cracker crumbs and butter. Press firmly in bottom of a 9-inch or 10-inch springform pan.

FILLING:

4 (8-ounce) packages	4 eggs
cream cheese	1 tablespoons lemon juice
1¹/₂ cups sugar	2 teaspoons vanilla

Beat cream cheese with electric mixer until light and fluffy. Add sugar. Beat until smooth. Add eggs one at a time. Add lemon juice and vanilla; beat well. Spoon filling into crust. Set springform pan on cookie sheet and bake for 40-50 minutes (or 50-55 minutes if using 9-inch pan). Remove from oven and cool for 15 minutes before spreading with topping.

TOPPING:

2 cups sour cream	1 teaspoon vanilla
¹/₄ cup sugar	

Combine sour cream, sugar and vanilla and blend well. Spoon topping over filling and spread to within 1/2-inch of pan edge. Return to 350° oven and bake for 5 minutes. Cool completely, then refrigerate for 24 hours.

GLAZE:

1 (12-ounce) jar strawberry jam	¹/₄ cup water
1 tablespoon cornstarch	1 pint strawberries

Combine jam with cornstarch in saucepan; mix well. Add water; cook over medium heat about 5 minutes, stirring until sauce is thick and clear. Cool. Arrange berries on top of cheesecake. Spoon glaze over berries. Refrigerate again before slicing to serve.

Yield: 8-12 servings   Carolyn McDonald

🍓 Strawberry Smoothie

4 scoops strawberry ice cream	4 ice cubes
1 cup fresh strawberries,	¹/₂ cup powdered sugar
rinsed, stemmed and sliced	1¹/₂ cups milk

Blend all ingredients on high in blender until creamy. Serve immediately.

Yield: 4 servings

Lindy's Strawberry Pie

CRUST:

1/2 **cup butter**	1/4 **cup pecans**
1 **cup flour**	1/4 **cup powdered sugar**

Mix butter, flour, pecans and sugar. Press into 9-inch pie pan. Bake 10 minutes at 350°. Cool.

FILLING:

1 **quart strawberries,**	3 **tablespoons cornstarch**
stemmed, sliced	1 **(8-ounce) tub frozen whipped**
1 **cup sugar**	**dessert topping, thawed**

Combine in a small saucepan 1/2 of the strawberries, sugar and cornstarch; simmer until slightly thick. Cool slightly. Line pie shell with remaining strawberries. Pour cornstarch mixture over strawberries. Chill. Serve with topping.

NOTE: *This recipe is from Larry Hendrix's grandmother, Mrs. Maggie Hargis, from Lynchburg, VA.*

Yield: 6 servings   Barbara Hendrix

Strawberry Pie

1 **(8-inch) unbaked pie crust**	1/2 **cup sifted powdered sugar**
4 **cups fresh whole**	1 **cup water**
strawberries, washed and	11/2 **tablespoons cornstarch**
hulled	1/2 **cup granulated sugar**

Bake pie shell according to package directions. Cool. Combine powdered sugar with 3 cups strawberries. Let stand 1 hour. Crush remaining cup of strawberries in a saucepan with 1 cup water for 2 minutes. Mix the cornstarch and granulated sugar; stir into the cooked berries. Cook 20 minutes until sauce is clear, stirring constantly. Fill the baked pie shell with whole sugared strawberries. Pour the hot strawberry sauce over berries. Cool before serving.

Yield: 6 servings   Mary Eichelberger

Berry Freeze

Fresh whole strawberries, stemmed, rinsed, patted dry

Place loose berries on a parchment lined cookie sheet. Place tray in freezer. When frozen firm, place berries in covered plastic container or ziplock bag. Store in freezer. To freeze berries in syrup; slice, sprinkle with sugar to coat, and seal in plastic bags. Freeze. Thaw when needed.

Yield: As desired

🍓 Easy Strawberry Pie

1	(10-ounce) package frozen strawberries, thawed	2	egg whites
1	tablespoon lemon juice	1	teaspoon vanilla
1/8	teaspoon salt	1/2	pint whipping cream
1	cup sugar	1	(9-inch) crumb crust or baked pie shell

Place berries, lemon juice, salt, sugar, egg whites and vanilla in large bowl. Beat until stiff, like a meringue, for 20 minutes or more. Whip cream and fold into strawberry mixture. Pour into pie shell. Freeze for several hours until firm. Serve frozen. Will keep in freezer for weeks.

Yield: 8 servings   Mary Keith Perry

🍓 Old Fashioned Strawberry Custard Pie

3	cups chopped fresh strawberries	1 1/2	cups sugar
1	(9-inch) unbaked pie shell	3	tablespoons flour
1	tablespoon butter, softened	2	eggs, beaten

Place strawberries in pie shell. In a bowl, blend butter, sugar, flour and eggs, beating and mixing well. Pour mixture over strawberries. Bake at 450° for 10 minutes, reduce heat to 350°. Bake an additional 30 minutes. Serve warm.

NOTE: *When served warm, second helpings are usually requested.*

Yield: 8 servings   Meetta Lampert

🍓 Mom's Great Strawberry - Rhubarb Pie

1 1/3	cups sugar	2	tablespoons butter or margarine
1/3	cup plus 2 tablespoons flour		Pastry for a double crust 9-inch pie
2	cups fresh rhubarb, peeled and cut into 1/2-inch pieces		
2	cups sliced fresh strawberries		

Stir together sugar and flour. Mix rhubarb and strawberries together. Place 1/2 the rhubarb-strawberry mixture into pastry lined pie shell. Sprinkle with 1/2 the sugar-flour mixture. Repeat with remaining rhubarb-strawberry and sugar-flour mixture. Dot with butter. Cover with top crust. Cut slits in pastry top. Seal and flute edges and sprinkle pie top with sugar. Cover edges with a strip of foil to prevent excess browning. Remove foil during the last 15 minutes of baking. Bake at 425° for 40-50 minutes. Serve warm.

Yield: 6-8 servings   Martha Owens

🍓 Strawberry Cookie Mousse

1 quart natural strawberry ice cream, softened	15-20 S'mores (fudge covered graham cookies, with marshmallow filling), or creme-filled chocolate sandwich cookies, coarsely chopped
1 (8-ounce) carton frozen extra creamy whipped dessert topping, thawed	

In a large mixing bowl, blend ice cream, whipped topping and cookies. Freeze in a 2-quart container. Remove from freezer about 15 minutes before serving to soften slightly. Serve in dessert dishes.

Yield: 8-10 servings

🍓 Strawberry Pudding
A family favorite

1 cup sugar	1 (11-ounce) box vanilla wafers
1/2 tablespoon flour	1 pint fresh strawberries, stemmed, sliced
1 cup water	
1 egg yolk, beaten	1 (8-ounce) tub frozen whipped dessert topping, thawed
1 teaspoon vanilla	

In a saucepan combine sugar, flour and water. Cook slowly, stirring constantly until mixture is clear. Cool; add egg yolk and vanilla; stir well. Line the bottom of a 9x13-inch pan with wafers. Top with strawberries and cover with custard mixture. Continue layering wafers, strawberries and custard until all ingredients are used. Serve with desired amount of whipped topping.

NOTE: *Four sliced bananas may be substituted for strawberries. This was my mother's (Mrs. J. D. Smith) recipe.*

Yield: 6 servings   Martha S. Adams

🍓 💜 Strawberry - Yogurt Freeze

2 (8-ounce) containers pre-mixed lowfat strawberry yogurt	1 pint fresh strawberries, stemmed
	1 teaspoon grated orange zest

Spoon yogurt into partitioned ice cube tray. Freeze 3-4 hours until firm. Place cubes in food processor bowl. Process until finely chopped. Add strawberries and orange zest. Process until smooth. Serve immediately or freeze for 1-2 hours, stirring often until firm. Scoop portions to serve.

Yield: 6 servings   Michelle Patterson
                    Patterson's Farms, Inc.

🔔 🍓 Strawberry - Raspberry
Brownie Truffles
They melt in your mouth!

1	(22.4-ounce) box raspberry fudge brownie mix, prepared and baked according to package directions, cooled and coarsely crumbled
3	tablespoons raspberry liqueur (or frozen cherry juice concentrate)

2-3	tablespoons cream cheese
1/2	cup finely chopped or ground pecans or almonds
1	(16-once) box strawberry flavored powdered sugar or regular powdered sugar

In a medium bowl, combine brownie crumbs, liqueur, cream cheese and nuts with a fork or mixer until thoroughly blended. Chill mixture in refrigerator for 30 minutes. Shape rounded teaspoonfuls of brownie dough mixture into small (3/4-1-inch) balls. Roll truffles in powdered sugar. Keep refrigerated until ready to serve.

NOTE: *If raspberry brownie mix is unavailable, you may substitute regular brownie mix and swirl 2 tablespoons raspberry jam through batter before baking.*

Yield: 40-50 truffles

🔔 🍓 ♥ Strawberry Trifle
Dieter's delight!

2	(1-pound) angel food cakes
2	(3-ounce) boxes sugar-free strawberry gelatin, mixed according to package directions
2	bananas, mashed

1	(3-ounce) box sugar-free, fat-free instant vanilla pudding mix, mixed according to package directions
1	(8-ounce) container frozen light whipped dessert topping, thawed

Tear cake into chunks and layer 1/3 of cake chunks in bottom of trifle bowl. Stir bananas into liquid (not congealed) gelatin mixture. Pour 1/3 of gelatin mixture over cake layer. Layer 1/3 of pudding on top of gelatin and cake. Spread 1/3 of whipped topping over pudding. Repeat this process to create 3 layers and use all ingredients. Refrigerate several hours before serving.

NOTE: *Great for dieters and diabetics*

Yield: 12 servings   Rochelle Redcay

🔔 🍓 ♥ Strawberry Banana Slush

3¼ cups sugar
2 (10-ounce) packages frozen
strawberries with syrup,
thawed and pureed
4 bananas, peeled and mashed
1 (6-ounce) can frozen orange
juice, berry or tropical fruit
concentrate, thawed

1 (6-ounce) can frozen pink
lemonade concentrate,
thawed
2 (0.14-ounce) packages
strawberry flavored
powdered drink mix
2 quarts 7-Up, well chilled
1 quart water
FLOATING ICE RING molded
with strawberries (see index)

In a 6-quart container, mix sugar, pureed berries, bananas, orange juice, lemonade and flavored drink mix. Cover and freeze mixture until firm. Remove from freezer about 3 hours before serving to partially thaw. To serve, break into chunks and dilute mixture by adding 7-Up and water. Stir until mixture is slushy; serve immediately. If serving in punch bowl, stir often to keep mixture well blended.

Yield: 4 quarts or 28 (6-ounce) servings

🍓 ♥ Strawberry Sparkling Lemonade

6 (10-ounce) packages frozen
strawberries with syrup
⅔ cup sugar
1½ cups fresh lemon juice
7 cups 7-Up or diet 7-Up

Fresh whole or sliced
strawberries
Fresh lemon slices
Fresh mint sprigs
2 ice cube trays

To make STRAWBERRY ICE CUBES, puree 2 packages of berries in a blender container. Pour puree into 2 ice cube tray compartments (20 cubes each) and freeze until firm. Puree remaining 4 packages of berries in blender. Dissolve sugar with lemon juice in a bowl; add pureed berries and stir well. When ready to serve, place frozen strawberry ice cubes in individual glasses. Add 7-Up to lemonade mixture in a pitcher and immediately pour over strawberry ice cubes. Garnish with strawberries, lemon or mint.

Yield: 4 quarts lemonade, 40 ice cubes

Strawberry Banana Colada

A non-alcoholic cocktail!

1	(10-once) package frozen strawberries with syrup	2	bananas, peeled, cut in half
1	(8-ounce) can crushed pineapple, undrained	2-3	tablespoons cream of coconut
		12	ice cubes

Combine all ingredients in a blender and process until smooth. Serve immediately in glasses.

Yield: 3 cups

Strawberry Cheesecake Shake

1	(10-ounce) package frozen sliced strawberries in syrup, thawed	1	pint vanilla ice cream
1/3	cup cream cheese, softened	1/2	cup milk Fresh whole strawberries (optional)

Place all ingredients in blender container and process until smooth. Stop blending to scrape sides of blender container once during process. Garnish with strawberries. Serve cold, immediately.

NOTE: *Light cream cheese, lowfat ice cream and skim milk may be substituted.*

Yield: 4 (1-cup) servings

Strawberry Syrup

2	(10-ounce) packages frozen strawberries	4	tablespoons pectin
		1 1/2	cups sugar

Process strawberries in blender container to puree. Place strawberry puree in a 3-quart saucepan. Mix pectin and sugar; add to berries. Bring to a boil and boil for 1 minute. Cool. Store in covered plastic container in refrigerator. Heat syrup and serve over French toast, waffles, pancakes, toast or biscuits.

Yield: 2 cups

🍓 Strawberry Butter

4 **tablespoons strawberry preserves**	1 **cup butter or margarine, softened**

In a small bowl, blend butter and preserves together. Spoon into plastic container with a lid or press into decorative molds. Freeze until firm. Store in refrigerator until needed or serve at room temperature.

Yield: 1 cup

🍓 Strawberries & Cream Bagel

2 **bagels, split horizontally**	1/2 **teaspoon almond or vanilla extract**
1 **teaspoon butter**	2 **tablespoons powdered sugar**
1/2 **(8-ounce) tub strawberry flavored or plain cream cheese**	4 **strawberries, washed, stemmed, sliced, for topping**
1/2 **cup mashed strawberries**	

Spread bagels evenly with butter and toast lightly. In a small bowl, blend together cream cheese, mashed berries, almond extract and sugar. Spread mixture over warm bagels. Garnish the top of each bagel with sliced berries.

Yield: 4 servings

🍓 My Mom's Strawberry Freezer Jam

2 **quarts fresh strawberries, stems removed**	2 **(1.7-ounce) boxes fruit pectin**
8 **cups sugar**	1 1/4 **cups water**
	10 **sterilized glass jars**

Prepare fruit and crush to 4 cups. Place berries in a large bowl with sugar. Stir and set aside for 10 minutes. Heat water and fruit pectin in small pan. Bring to boiling, stirring constantly. Boil and stir for 2 minutes. Pour liquid over fruit and sugar mixture. Stir about 4 minutes until sugar has completely dissolved and no grains remain. Pour into jars. Cover with lids and let stand at room temperature for 24 hours to set before using. Store in freezer.

NOTE: *For RASPBERRY JAM or BLACKBERRY JAM, use 6 pints of whole berries and 10 cups sugar. This is my mother, Marge Carmichael's special jam.*

Yield: 10 cups jam   Jo Franklin

🍓 Strawberry Fruit Dip

1	(8-ounce) jar strawberry preserves
1	(8-ounce) tub strawberry cream cheese, softened

1	(8-ounce) tub frozen whipped dessert topping, thawed

Mix preserves and cream cheese. With a rubber spatula, fold in whipped topping. Chill 6 hours before serving with fruit slices for dipping.

Yield: 3 cups

🔔 🍓 Strawberry Almond Candies
Berry delicious

2	(3-ounce) packages strawberry-banana gelatin
2	(3-ounce) packages strawberry gelatin
1	(14-ounce) can sweetened condensed milk

1	(6-ounce) bag shredded or flaked coconut
1	(8-ounce) can almond paste
15-20	drops red food coloring
2	(4.25-ounce) tubes green cake decorating icing with plastic decorator tips

In a bowl, mix packages of strawberry-banana gelatin with milk. With a fork or pastry blender, add in coconut, almond paste and food coloring until thoroughly combined. Cover and chill mixture overnight. To make candies, roll teaspoonfuls of candy dough into a ball. Form into 1x1 1/2-inch cone-shaped strawberries and roll in packages of dry strawberry gelatin. Place candies on foil. Using decorative tip, squeeze icing onto crown ends of berries to form a star pattern or leaf cap. Chill until ready to serve.

NOTE: *For variation, roll out candy dough and cut out tiny heart shapes before sprinkling with gelatin to make ALMOND HEART CANDIES. To make MARZIPAN PUMPKIN CANDY substitute orange gelatin and orange food coloring; shape, cut, or form into pumpkins.*

Yield: 40 candies

🍓 Berry Cookie Tarts

1/2	cup soft cream cheese with strawberries
1/3	cup powdered sugar

4	(4-inch) round sugar cookies
3/4-1	cup sliced fresh strawberries

Spread 2 tablespoons of a mixture of cream cheese and sugar on each cookie. Arrange berries on top. Refrigerate until served.

Yield: 4 tarts

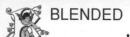 

🔔 🍓 Strawberry Tulips

24	large strawberries, leaves and stems removed, rinsed		sugar
		1/4-1/2	teaspoon almond extract
1	(8-ounce) package cream cheese	2 1/2	tablespoons sour cream
5	tablespoons powdered		Fresh mint leaves (optional)

Place berries on flat end, pointed side up on a cutting board. With a knife, carefully slice berry through center cutting to within 1/4-inch of berry base, cutting almost in half vertically. Make 2 more cuts to form 6 equal "petals", leaving base of berry solid. Carefully pull strawberry petals apart. In a small bowl, beat cream cheese, sugar, almond and sour cream until fluffy. Place mixture in a pastry bag with star tip attached. Fill each berry center with creamy mixture. Garnish with mint leaves if desired. Serve as tiny desserts.

Yield: 24 servings

🍓 Long Island Strawberry Tart

CRUST:

5	ounces finely ground blanched almonds	4	tablespoons sugar
		1 1/2	cups flour
1	(4-ounce) stick unsalted butter, room temperature	1	egg, beaten
		1/2	teaspoon vanilla

Mix almonds, butter, sugar, flour, egg and vanilla until well blended. Press evenly into bottom of a 9-inch springform pan. Chill 30 minutes. Preheat oven to 350°. Bake 15-20 minutes until light gold in color. Cool before filling.

FILLING AND GLAZE:

3	pints fresh strawberries	1	tablespoon unflavored gelatin
1	(6-ounce) jar red currant jelly		
		1/4	cup Grand Marnier

Wash and hull strawberries. Arrange berries, tips up, in tart shell. To make glaze, melt jelly, gelatin and Grand Marnier in a small saucepan. Stir over low heat until mixture is clear. Spoon over berries. Chill at least 2 hours. Remove springform pan collar before serving tart.

Yield: 8 servings

Joyce Caddell

Divine Desserts
& Favorite Finales

Baked Cobblers, Pies & Pastries,
Frosted Cakes to Tempt the Eyes.
Chilly Puddings, Trifles, Mousses,
Ice-Creams & Frosty Fluffy Pies

♥ Fat Free
Carrot Cake Extraordinaire

2	cups flour	2	teaspoons vanilla
2	teaspoons baking soda	1	(8-ounce) can crushed
1/4	teaspoon salt		pineapple
2	teaspoons cinnamon	2	cups grated carrots
4	egg whites, beaten well	4	ounces grated, frozen
3/4	cup apple sauce		coconut
3/4	cup buttermilk	1	cup walnuts, grated
2	cups sugar		

Combine flour, soda, salt and cinnamon; set aside. In a large bowl, combine egg whites, applesauce, buttermilk, sugar and vanilla. Mix in flour mixture, pineapple, carrots, coconut and walnuts. Bake in a 9x12-inch baking pan at 350° for 30-40 minutes, until toothpick inserted in center of cake comes out clean. Cool.

GLAZE:

1	cup powdered sugar	1	tablespoon frozen orange juice concentrate, thawed

Combine glaze ingredients, adding more juice if necessary until mixture is spreadable. Spread over cake; slice to serve.

NOTE: *Lowfat and delicious, but not calorie free!*

Yield: 16 servings   Bert Burnham

Cranberry Cake

1	cup sugar	1/4	teaspoon salt
3	tablespoons butter	1	cup milk
2	cups flour	2	cups raw cranberries
2	teaspoons baking powder		

Cream sugar and butter. Stir together flour, baking powder and salt. Add to butter mixture alternately with milk. Fold in cranberries. Pour into a greased 9x13-inch pan. Bake at 350° for 30 minutes.

SAUCE:

1/2	cup butter	1/2	cup evaporated milk
1	cup sugar	1	teaspoon vanilla

In a saucepan, slowly bring butter, sugar and milk to a boil. Add vanilla. To serve, cut cake and pour warm sauce over cake.

Yield: 16 servings   Sara Cook

Fruit Cocktail Cake

Delicious and easy!

1¹/₂	cups sugar	¹/₂	cup oil
1¹/₂	teaspoons baking soda	2	eggs, beaten
¹/₂	teaspoon salt	1	(16-ounce) can fruit cocktail,
2	cups flour		with juice

Sift together sugar, baking soda, salt and flour. Add oil, eggs and fruit cocktail. Pour into greased 9x13-inch cake pan. Bake at 350° for 35-45 minutes.

TOPPING:

¹/₂	cup evaporated milk	1	teaspoon vanilla
³/₄	cup sugar	¹/₂	cup chopped nuts
¹/₂	cup (1 stick) margarine	¹/₂	cup coconut

Mix topping ingredients and cook over medium heat until thick, stirring constantly. To serve, pour topping over hot cake.

NOTE: *Everyone loves this cake and it stays moist!*

Yield: 16 servings

Jane Dutton,
Robin Perry

Pineapple Cake

2	cups flour	1	(20-ounce) can crushed
2	cups sugar		pineapple, undrained
2	teaspoons baking soda	¹/₂	cup chopped nuts
2	eggs, beaten	1	teaspoon vanilla
		1	teaspoon almond extract

Mix all ingredients together. Pour into a greased 9x13-inch baking dish. Bake at 350° for 30 minutes. Frost while hot.

FROSTING:

1	(8-ounce) package	2	cups powdered sugar
	cream cheese	2	teaspoons almond extract
¹/₄	cup margarine		

Beat cream cheese and margarine until creamy and smooth. Add sugar and almond extract; mix well. Spread frosting on top of hot cake. Cool completely before cutting to serve. Refrigerate. Freezes well.

Yield: 10-12 servings

Doris Brownlee

Earthquake Cake

1½ cup chopped pecans
1 (6-ounce) package fresh frozen coconut, thawed
1 (18.25-once) package German chocolate cake mix, prepared according to package directions

1 stick butter
1 (8-ounce) package cream cheese
1 (16-ounce) box powdered sugar

Grease a 9x13-inch pan. Sprinkle pecans and coconut on bottom of pan. Pour cake batter over nuts and coconut. Melt butter and cream cheese together. Add powdered sugar and mix well. Pour over cake batter. Bake at 350° for 45 minutes. Remove from oven and cool. Cut into squares to serve.

NOTE: *You may substitute a variety of cake mixes such as banana, white, yellow or chocolate. Try caramel or spice cake for the fall season.*

Yield: 24 servings

Chocolate Delight Cake

1 (4-ounce) bar German chocolate
¼ cup water
1 (8-ounce) package cream cheese, softened
2 sticks margarine
2 (16-ounce) boxes powdered sugar

¼ cup shortening
3 eggs
2¼ cups flour
1 teaspoon baking soda
1 teaspoon salt
1 cup buttermilk
1 teaspoon vanilla

Preheat oven to 325°. Grease and flour a tube pan or three 9-inch layer pans. Melt chocolate bar in a saucepan with water. Combine melted chocolate, cream cheese, margarine and powdered sugar in a bowl. Beat with electric mixer until smooth and creamy. Set aside 3 cups of mixture to be used as frosting. Add shortening and eggs to remaining chocolate mixture and beat well. Add flour, soda and salt; mix well. Add buttermilk and vanilla; thoroughly mix. Bake 45 minutes if using layer pans; bake up to 60 minutes for tube pan or until a toothpick inserted in the center comes out clean. Cool, and frost with reserved frosting. Slice to serve.

NOTE: *My mother gave me this recipe at least 25 years ago. It has been a family favorite, especially of our youngest son.*

Yield: 12-16 servings   Joyce M. Plyler

Banana Cake

1/2	pound sweet butter or margarine	1/2	teaspoon salt
3/4	cup sugar	2/3	teaspoon baking soda
2	eggs	5	tablespoons buttermilk
1	cup ripe bananas, mashed	1	teaspoon vanilla
1 3/4	cups flour	1 1/2-2	medium ripe bananas, sliced

Preheat oven to 350°. Grease and flour two 9-inch layer cake pans or Bundt pan. Cream butter and sugar together until light and fluffy. Add eggs, 1 at a time, beating well after each addition. Add mashed bananas, mixing thoroughly. Sift dry ingredients; add to butter and egg mixture. Stir until flour has been incorporated completely. Add buttermilk and vanilla. Mix for 1 minute. Pour batter into prepared pans. Set on middle rack and bake 25-30 minutes. Cool on rack for 10 minutes. Unmold and cool on rack 2 more hours.

FROSTING:

1	(8-ounce) package low fat cream cheese, room temperature	2-3	cups powdered sugar, plus sugar for topping
4	tablespoons sweet butter or margarine, room temperature	1	teaspoon vanilla
			Juice of 1/2 lemon
		1 1/2	cups chopped walnuts (optional)

Cream together cheese and butter. Slowly sift in powdered sugar and combine, beating until fully blended and free of lumps. Stir in vanilla and lemon juice. Frost one layer. Arrange slices of banana over frosting. Cover with second cake layer and frost the top and sides of cake. Cover sides of cake with chopped nuts and cover top with sliced bananas. Dust top of cake with powdered sugar. Slice to serve.

Yield: 12-15 servings

Claire Mitchell Allen

Kahlúa Cake

1	(18.25-ounce) box chocolate cake mix	3/4	cup oil
1	(3.4-ounce) box instant chocolate pudding mix	1	(16-ounce) carton sour cream
		1/2	cup Kahlúa or coffee liqueur
4	eggs	1	(12-ounce) package chocolate chips

Preheat oven to 350°. Mix all ingredients together with electric mixer at medium speed. Pour into a well greased Bundt pan. Bake for 1 hour. Slice to serve.

Yield: 12-16 servings

Jennifer Flynn

Jane's Apple Cake

2	cups sugar	3	cups sifted flour
1¼	cups oil	2	teaspoons baking soda
2	eggs, beaten slightly	1	teaspoon salt
4	cups apples, peeled and	2	teaspoons cinnamon
	chopped	1	cup raisins
2	teaspoons vanilla		

Mix together in a large bowl sugar, oil and eggs. Add apples and vanilla. In a separate bowl combine flour, baking soda, salt and cinnamon. Combine both wet and dry mixtures; then add raisins. Pour into greased 9x13-inch cake pan and bake at 325° for 1 hour, or pour into two 9x5-inch loaf pans and bake at 350° for 1-1 1/2 hours. Cake freezes well. Slice to serve.

Yield: 1 sheet cake or 2 loaves

Art Gourmet
Marilyn & Bob Smitherman

Simple Chocolate Sheet Cake

2	cups flour	3	tablespoons cocoa
2	cups sugar	½	cup buttermilk
1	cup water	2	eggs, beaten
½	cup vegetable oil	1	teaspoon soda
1	stick margarine	⅛	teaspoon salt

Preheat oven to 350°. Grease and flour a 10x15-inch sheet pan. Mix flour and sugar together in a large bowl; set aside. In a saucepan, mix together water, oil, margarine and vanilla. Add buttermilk, eggs, soda and salt. Stirring constantly, bring mixture to a boil for 1 minute. Pour over flour mixture and mix. Pour batter into sheet pan. Bake 40 minutes.

FROSTING:

4	tablespoons milk	1	teaspoon vanilla
3	tablespoons cocoa	1	(16-ounce) box
1	stick margarine		powdered sugar

In a saucepan, mix together milk, cocoa, margarine and vanilla. Bring to a boil. Remove from heat and cool slightly. Add powdered sugar; mix well. Add more milk to frosting if necessary. Spread over hot cake. Slice to serve.

Yield: 8-12 servings

Melissa Lassiter

Banana Blueberry Cake

Quick and easy cake

3 cups flour	1/2 cup buttermilk
2 1/2 cups sugar	1 1/2 teaspoons vanilla
1 teaspoon baking soda	2 cups mashed, ripe banana
1/4 teaspoon salt	1 cup chopped pecans
3 eggs, beaten	1 cup canned blueberries,
1 cup vegetable oil	drained

Combine flour, sugar, soda and salt in a large bowl. Combine eggs, oil and buttermilk in a small bowl; add to dry ingredients, stirring until they are moistened. Do not beat. Add vanilla, banana and pecans; stir well. Gently stir in blueberries. Spoon batter into a greased and floured 10-inch tube pan. Bake at 350° for 1 1/2 hours or until a toothpick inserted in center comes out clean. Cool in pan 10 minutes; remove from pan; cool completely. Slice to serve.

Yield: Serves 8-10   Laura Murph

Red Blush Cake

1 stick butter	1 teaspoon salt
1 1/2 cups sugar	1 teaspoon vinegar
2 eggs	1 cup buttermilk
1 teaspoon soda	2 1/2 cups flour
1 teaspoon vanilla	2 ounces red food coloring
2 tablespoons cocoa	

Cream butter and sugar; add eggs, beating well. Add soda, vanilla, cocoa, salt and vinegar. Mix well; add buttermilk and flour alternately. Blend in food coloring. Grease and flour two 9-inch layer pans. Pour in batter. Bake at 350° for 15-20 minutes or until tested done. Cool layers 10 minutes, remove from pans to frost.

FROSTING:

2 teaspoons flour	2 sticks margarine, softened
1 cup milk	1 teaspoon vanilla
1 cup sugar	

Mix flour and milk in a saucepan. Cook, stirring constantly until smooth. Set aside to cool. Cream sugar, margarine and vanilla. Add the cooled, cooked milk mixture and beat until light and fluffy. Frost one cake layer. Top with second cake layer. Frost the top and sides of assembled cake. Slice to serve.

NOTE: *This was my mother, Grace Stiller's recipe.*

Yield: 12-15 servings   Fran Lawson

Caramel Chocolate Cake

1 cup butter, softened	3 tablespoons cocoa
2 cups sugar	1/2 cup warm water
3 eggs	1 teaspoon baking soda
3 cups flour	1 teaspoon vanilla
1 cup buttermilk	

Preheat oven to 350°. Cream butter and sugar until light and fluffy. Add eggs one at a time, mix well. Add flour alternately with buttermilk, beginning and ending with flour. Mix cocoa, water and soda; stir well. Add to flour mixture, beating well. Stir in vanilla. Pour batter into 2 greased and floured 9-inch pans. Bake for 35-40 minutes. Cool in pans 10 minutes; remove from pans and cool completely on wire racks.

FROSTING:

1 cup butter (no substitution)	1 cup evaporated milk
2 cups sugar	1 teaspoon vanilla

Melt butter in heavy saucepan over medium heat. Add sugar and milk. Cook mixture over medium heat, stirring constantly until candy thermometer reaches 234° (soft ball stage). Remove from heat and add vanilla. Do not stir. Cool 10 minutes; then beat on medium speed until thick enough to spread. Work quickly to spread frosting over cooled layers. Slice to serve.

NOTE: *When the occasion calls for a cake, just "bite the dust" and serve a winner! You'll be making it again and again.*

Yield: Serves 16

Nell Bullard

Key Lime Cake

1 (18.25-ounce) package lemon supreme cake mix	4 eggs
	1/2 cup water
1 (3.4-ounce) package instant lemon pudding mix	1/2 cup key lime juice
	1/2 cup vegetable oil

Preheat oven to 350°. Grease and flour a 9x13-inch pan. Combine all ingredients in a large bowl; beat 2 minutes at medium speed with an electric mixer. Pour into prepared pan. Bake 35 minutes or until a toothpick inserted in the center comes out clean. Cool cake in pan on a wire rack.

GLAZE:

2 cups powdered sugar, sifted	1/4 cup key lime juice

Combine sugar and juice; drizzle over cake and cut into squares to serve.

Yield: 15-18 servings

Italian Cream Cake

1¹/₂	cups buttermilk	5	eggs, separated
1	teaspoon soda	2	cups flour
¹/₂	cup solid vegetable	1	teaspoon baking powder
	shortening	1	teaspoon vanilla
2	cups sugar	1	cup pecans
1	stick margarine	1	(3.5-ounce) can coconut

Grease and flour three 8- or 9-inch layer pans. Preheat oven to 350°. Combine buttermilk and soda, let stand for 5 minutes. Combine shortening, sugar and margarine in another bowl; cream well. Add beaten egg yolks and mix well. Add flour, baking powder, buttermilk-soda mixture and vanilla; mix thoroughly. Fold in beaten egg whites, nuts and coconut. Pour batter into prepared pans. Bake for 25 minutes. Cool layers on wire racks.

FROSTING:

1	(8-ounce) package cream	1	(16-ounce) box
	cheese, softened		powdered sugar
¹/₂	stick margarine	1	teaspoon vanilla

Combine cream cheese and margarine; beat well. Add sugar and vanilla; continue beating until blended. Assemble cake by spreading frosting between all layers and on the top and sides of cake. Slice to serve.

Yield: 12 servings   Shirley Lewis

Rum Cake

³/₄	cup chopped pecans	¹/₂	cup oil
1	(18.25-ounce) box yellow	¹/₂	cup light rum
	cake mix with pudding	4	eggs
¹/₂	cup water		

Preheat oven to 325°. Grease and flour Bundt or tube pan. Put nuts in bottom. Combine cake mix, water, oil, rum and eggs in a bowl. Beat with electric mixer at medium speed for 2 minutes. Pour batter into pan and bake 50-60 minutes.

TOPPING:

| 1 | cup sugar | ¹/₄ | cup light rum |
| 1 | stick butter or margarine | ¹/₄ | cup water |

When cake is almost done, prepare topping. Combine all ingredients and boil for 2-3 minutes. Pour topping over cake while cake is still hot. Slice, when ready to serve.

Yield: 12-15 slices   Nan Fisher

1 - 2 - 3 - 4 Counting Cake
Delicious and versatile!

1 cup butter or solid vegetable shortening	1½ teaspoons almond or vanilla extract
2 cups powdered sugar	3 teaspoons baking powder
3 cups sifted cake flour	½ teaspoon salt
4 eggs, well beaten	1 cup milk

Preheat oven to 350°. Grease and flour a 9x12-inch cake pan. Cream butter and sugar in a large bowl. Sift flour, baking powder and salt together. Add eggs and extract. Beat well until smooth and creamy. Add milk and the flour mixture alternately to butter mixture. Beat until smooth. Spoon batter into prepared pan. Bake until toothpick inserted in center comes out clean, or about 25-35 minutes.

GLAZE:

¼ cup lemon, orange or pineapple juice	2 tablespoons butter
1½ teaspoon grated orange or lemon zest	2½ cups powdered sugar, sifted

In small saucepan, heat juice, orange or lemon zest and butter. Add sugar and mix well. To glaze, spread warm mixture over cake. Cut in squares to serve.

NOTE: *The 1-2-3-4 title refers to the universal numerical way cooks remembered and counted cake ingredients. This version of an old favorite may be made as two round cake layers, a Bundt cake, two 9x5x3 loaves or 1-2-3-4 CUPCAKES. To make tiny PETITS 1-2-3-FOURS, bake cake in an 11x15-inch air-bake jelly roll pan. Glaze. Cool and cut into 1 1/2-inch squares. Serve in small paper baking cups. Adjust cooking times according to size of baking pans used.*

Yield: 24 servings

Chocolate Chip Cake

1 (18.25-ounce) package yellow butter cake mix	1 (8-ounce) carton sour cream
4 eggs	1 (6-ounce) package chocolate chips
½ cup vegetable oil	½ cup chopped nuts
1 (3.4-ounce) package instant vanilla pudding mix	

Preheat oven to 350°. Grease and flour 10-inch tube pan. Combine all ingredients, except chips and nuts, in a large bowl. Mix thoroughly and fold in chips (add more if desired) and nuts. Spoon batter into tube pan and bake 1 hour. Cool in pan. Slice, when ready to serve.

Yield: 12-16 servings   Sharon H. Hampton

Chocolate Zucchini Cake

2¹/₂ cups flour
¹/₂ cup cocoa
2¹/₂ teaspoon baking powder
1¹/₂ teaspoon soda
1 teaspoon salt
1 teaspoon cinnamon
³/₄ cup soft butter
2 cups sugar
3 eggs

2 teaspoons vanilla
2 teaspoons grated lemon peel
2 cups coarsely shredded zucchini
²/₃ cup milk
1 cup chopped pecans or walnuts
Powdered sugar

Combine flour, cocoa, baking powder, soda, salt and cinnamon. In a separate bowl, beat together butter and sugar. Add and beat in eggs, one at a time. Stir in vanilla, lemon peel and zucchini. Alternately add the mixture of dry ingredients and the milk, to the zucchini mixture. Mix in nuts. Pour batter into a greased and flour-dusted 10-inch tube or Bundt pan. Bake at 350° for 1 hour. Cool in pan for 15 minutes. Invert on wire rack; remove pan. After cake is completely cool, sift powdered sugar over cake. Slice to serve.

Yield: 12-16 servings

Moffit Swaim Churn

Amaretto Nut Cake

1 cup chopped nuts
1 (18.25-ounce) box yellow cake mix, without pudding
1 (3.4-ounce) box instant vanilla pudding mix

¹/₂ cup water
¹/₂ cup oil
¹/₂ cup amaretto
4 eggs

Grease and flour Bundt pan. Sprinkle 1/4 cup of chopped nuts on bottom of pan. Mix cake mix, pudding mix, water, oil, amaretto and eggs. Beat until creamy. Add remaining 3/4 cup nuts; pour into pan. Bake at 325° for 1 hour. Glaze cake in pan, while warm.

GLAZE:

1 stick margarine
1 cup sugar

¹/₄ cup water
¹/₄ cup amaretto

Mix all ingredients and boil 2 minutes. Pour hot glaze mixture around sides of pan. Let warm cake stand 45 minutes to absorb glaze, then remove cake from pan. Slice to serve.

Yield: 12-16 servings

Joan Whitacre

Lemon Apricot Cake

1	(18.25-ounce) package lemon flavored cake mix	4	eggs
1/2	cup sugar		Juice of 1 lemon
1	cup apricot nectar		Grated lemon rind
3/4	cup vegetable oil	1	cup powdered sugar

Blend together cake mix, sugar, nectar and oil. Add eggs, 1 at a time. Beat well after each addition. Pour into a greased tube pan. Bake at 340° for 1 hour or until golden brown. Cool in pan for 15 minutes; invert onto plate. Prick top and sides with toothpick. Mix lemon juice, rind and powdered sugar; and drizzle on warm cake. Freezes well. Slice to serve.

Yield: 12 servings   Peggy Maness

Beulah's Poppy Seed Cake

1/4	cup poppy seeds	1	(3.4-ounce) instant vanilla pudding mix
1	cup unsweetened pineapple juice	5	eggs, slightly beaten
1	(18.25-ounce) box yellow cake mix	1/2	cup vegetable oil
		1	tablespoon margarine
		3	tablespoons sugar

Soak poppy seeds in pineapple juice for 1 hour. Combine with cake mix, pudding mix, eggs and oil. Mix well only until all ingredients are combined. Grease a tube pan with margarine and sprinkle with sugar. Pour in batter and bake at 350° for 45 minutes to 1 hour. Freezes well. Slice to serve.

Serves: 14 servings   Beverly Gobble

Pistachio Marble Cake

1	(18.25-ounce) package yellow cake mix, without pudding	1	cup water
1	(3.5-ounce) box instant pistachio pudding	1/2	cup oil
		1	teaspoon almond extract
4	eggs	1/4	cup chocolate syrup

Grease and flour 10-inch tube pan or Bundt pan. Combine cake mix, pudding mix, eggs, water, oil and extract in large bowl; blend. Beat at medium speed with electric mixer for 2 minutes. Pour 1/3 of batter into separate bowl; stir in chocolate syrup. Spoon batters alternately into prepared pan. Swirl spatula through batter to marbleize. Bake at 350° for 40-50 minutes. Cool 15 minutes before removing from pan. Freezes well. Slice to serve.

Yield: 12-16 slices   Carolyn Glasgow

Snappy Turtle Cake

1	(18.25-ounce) package chocolate mocha flavored or German chocolate cake mix
3/4	cup butter or margarine, softened

7-8	ounces (about 24) miniature Milky Way or caramel candies
1/2	cup evaporated milk
1	cup mini chocolate or peanut butter baking chips
1/2-3/4	cup chopped pecans

Preheat oven to 350°. Prepare cake mix according to package directions. Add butter; mix well. Pour half of batter into 9 1/4x11 3/4-inch foil pan. Bake 15 minutes. While cake is baking, melt candies and milk in saucepan, stirring constantly until blended and smooth. Pour candy mixture over hot cake. Top with chips and nuts. Pour remaining batter over nuts. Return to oven; bake 15 minutes. Reduce oven temperature to 325°. Bake 15-20 minutes.

MOCHA FROSTING:

1	(1-pound) box chocolate flavored powdered sugar or powdered sugar mixed with 4 tablespoons cocoa
1	stick butter or margarine
1	teaspoon vanilla

1/8	teaspoon salt
1/2	cup milk or evaporated milk
1 1/2	teaspoons instant coffee granules
1	cup pecan pieces

In a saucepan, combine all ingredients. Bring mixture to a boil for 1 minute, stirring constantly until blended and smooth. Pour hot frosting mixture over warm cake. Cool before cutting into squares to serve.

Yield: 12 servings

Easy Crumb Pie Crust

1 1/2	cups graham cracker crumbs (about 20 crackers)
1/4	cup powdered, granulated or light brown sugar

1/2	cup butter or margarine, melted
1/4	cup chopped pecans (optional)

In a mixing bowl, combine crumbs with sugar. Pour in butter and blend until all crumbs are moistened. Press and pat mixture onto the bottom and sides of a 9-inch glass pie plate. (Hint: Place a second glass pie plate on top of crumb crust and press firmly to evenly mold and shape crust.) Bake in a 375° oven for 8-10 minutes. Cool before filling crust as desired.

NOTE: *May use cinnamon or honey graham, vanilla wafer, chocolate, gingersnap, or other cookie crumbs. If using creme-filled cookies, omit sugar.*

Yield: 1 (9-inch) pie shell

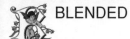

Cream Puff Swans

1	cup water	1	cup flour
1	stick butter	4	eggs
1/8	teaspoon salt		

Preheat oven to 400°. Combine water, butter and salt in a saucepan and bring to a boil. Add flour all at once and beat with a wooden spoon until mixture leaves edges of pan. Remove from heat and let cool briefly. Place dough in a food processor; add eggs, one at a time and process, or in a bowl, beat mixture well with a wooden spoon after the addition of each egg.

TO MAKE THE BODY OF SWAN: place 3/4 of dough in a pastry bag, using a #9B serrated edge tip. Squeeze 8 dollops that are about golf ball size 2-inches apart on a floured cookie sheet. Bake for 10 minutes. Reduce heat to 350° and bake for 10 more minutes. Turn oven off and let puffs remain until dry, about 20 minutes.

TO MAKE THE NECK OF SWAN: Place remaining 1/4 of cream puff dough into smaller pastry bag with a #3 tip. Squeeze dough into 8 "S" shapes onto a cookie sheet to represent head and neck of swan. Necks cook faster. Bake at 400° for 7 minutes. Reduce heat to 350° and bake 7 minutes more. Turn oven off and let puffs remain until dry, about 20 minutes.

PRALINE FILLING:

		1/2	cup water
1	cup hazelnuts or filberts	8	ounces whipping cream,
1	cup sugar		whipped

Preheat oven to 350°. Bake nuts on cookie sheet for 10 minutes. Remove skins by rubbing cooled nuts between paper towels. In a saucepan, cover sugar with water; bring to boil over high heat. Do not stir. Cook until light caramel in color. Add the nuts; pour mixture onto an oiled cookie sheet. When cold and hard, break into pieces and grind in food processor. Fold whipped cream into praline mixture. Refrigerate until ready to fill body of swan with praline mixture.

SAUCE AND GARNISH:

12 ounces prepared chocolate sauce, or pureed strawberries or raspberries	Fresh mint leaves Fresh raspberries

TO ASSEMBLE EACH SWAN: In the center of a dessert plate, spoon 1 1/2-ounces of preferred sauce. Slice off top 1/3 of cream puff. Divide top slice in half vertically to make 2 wings. With fingers, remove small amount of dough to create a hollow in center of remaining 2/3 of cream puff (the body of the swan). Place body in center of sauce. Spoon 2-3 heaping tablespoons of praline filling into body of swan. Place wings along sides of top of body. Press wings slightly into filling to attach to body. Insert neck into filling at front of body. Add more praline mixture to cover base of neck and give "fluff" to swan. To serve, garnish plate with a tiny fresh mint leaf tip and a raspberry or strawberry to represent a rose bush.

Yield: Serves 8   Cynthia Capps Pitt

Cream Puffs

PUFFS:

$1/2$	**cup butter or margarine**
1	**cup boiling water**
1	**cup sifted flour**

$1/4$	**teaspoon salt**
4	**eggs**

Melt butter in water. Add flour and salt all at once; stir vigorously. Cook; stir until mixture forms a ball that doesn't separate. Remove from heat; cool slightly. Add eggs one at a time, beating until smooth after each egg. Drop by heaping tablespoons 3 inches apart onto greased cookie sheet. Bake at 450° for 15 minutes, then at 325° for 25 minutes; remove from oven and split. Turn oven off; put cream puffs back in oven to dry, about 20 minutes. Cool on rack.

FILLING:

$3/4$	**cup sugar**
$1/3$	**cup flour or**
	3 tablespoons cornstarch
$1/4$	**teaspoon salt**

2	**cups milk**
3	**egg yolks, beaten slightly**
2	**tablespoons butter**
1	**teaspoon vanilla**

In saucepan, combine sugar, flour and salt; gradually stir in milk. Cook and stir over medium heat until bubbly. Cook and stir 2 minutes longer; remove from heat. Stir small amount of hot mixture into yolks, immediately return to hot mixture. Cook 2 minutes stirring constantly. Remove from heat. Add butter and vanilla. Chill mixture. When ready to serve, spoon 2-3 tablespoons of filling into each cream puff.

ICING:

1	**cup powdered sugar**
2-3	**tablespoons cocoa**
1	**tablespoon prepared coffee**

1	**tablespoon melted butter**
	Hot water

Mix icing ingredients adding enough hot water to obtain desired consistency. Drizzle icing on top of each filled cream puff. Refrigerate leftover cream puffs.

Yield: 10 cream puffs   Mary Goodman

Fruit Sonker
"Super Easy"

1	**stick butter, melted**
1	**cup self-rising flour**
1	**cup sugar**

1	**cup milk**
2	**(20-ounce) cans of pie filling**
	or 1 quart undrained fruit

Heat; sweeten fruit to taste. Pour butter into a 2 quart baking dish. In bowl combine sugar and flour; add milk; stir or blend until smooth. Pour batter into butter in dish. Do not stir. Add fruit. Do not stir. Bake at 350° for 1 hour. Great with ice cream.

Yield: 8 servings   Kay Paul

Grand Marnier Soufflé

8	eggs, separated	2	tablespoons flour
1/4	cup plus 3 tablespoons butter, softened	1/8	cup milk
1/4	cup plus 3 tablespoons sugar	4	tablespoons Grand Marnier liqueur

Preheat oven to 300°. Beat 8 egg whites until stiff; set aside. Coat inside of a 6-8-inch ovenproof soufflé dish with 3 tablespoons butter. Add 3 tablespoons sugar, turning dish to coat bottom and sides; pour out excess. Over medium heat, melt remaining butter; whisk in flour. Gradually add milk, then liqueur, remaining sugar and 6 egg yolks. Blend together. When ingredients form a smooth paste, remove from heat, let cool for a moment. Carefully fold in egg whites; do not over-mix. Loosely combine ingredients; pour into prepared dish and bake 20 minutes.

WHIPPED CREAM:

1	cup whipping cream	1	teaspoon vanilla
4	tablespoons sugar		

Combine ingredients in a bowl and whisk with wire whisk about 5 minutes until firm. Spoon sweetened cream over warm soufflé when served, if desired.

Yield: 4 servings

Anthony Vitellozzi
General Manager, La Cava Restaurant

Mystery Mocha Cake
Yummy dessert!

3/4	cup sugar	1	teaspoon vanilla
1	cup sifted flour	1/2	cup brown sugar
2	teaspoons baking powder	1/2	cup sugar
1/8	teaspoon salt	4	tablespoons cocoa
1	(1-ounce) square unsweetened chocolate	1	cup cold, double-strength coffee
2	tablespoons butter or margarine		Frozen whipped dessert topping, thawed
1/2	cup milk		

Sift sugar, flour, baking powder and salt into a large bowl. Melt chocolate and butter over hot water in a double boiler. Add to flour mixture; blend well. Combine milk and vanilla; mix well with chocolate mixture. Pour into greased 8x8-inch pan. Combine sugars and cocoa. Sprinkle evenly over batter. Pour coffee over the top. Bake at 350° for 40 minutes. Partially cool; cut into squares. Turn each piece upside down onto serving plate; spoon sauce from pan onto each piece. Top with whipped topping.

Yield: 9 servings

Doris Brownlee

♥ Chocolate Toffee Meringue Clouds

A heavenly dessert, tried and true.

MERINGUE:

6	egg whites	1/8	teaspoon salt
1/2	teaspoon cream of tartar	2	cups powdered sugar

Preheat oven to 275°. In a medium bowl, combine egg whites, cream of tartar and salt. Beat with electric mixer until foamy. Gradually add sugar, beating until stiff and glossy. Spoon 6 dollops of meringue onto each of two 14x17 1/2-inch air-bake cookie sheets. Bake for 50-60 minutes or until a very light golden brown around the edge. Turn oven off. Allow meringue to cool in closed oven for 2 hours or overnight before removing.

TOFFEE FILLING AND TOPPING:

2	cups heavy whipping cream, chilled or frozen lowfat whipped topping, thawed	1/2	cup coarsely chopped chocolate coated toffee candy bars
1/2	cup powdered sugar		(reserve 3 tablespoons)
1/3	cup cocoa		Chocolate syrup (optional)

In a medium bowl, combine cream, sugar and cocoa. Beat on high until mixture forms a stiff peak. Fold in crushed candy. Chill until ready to serve. To serve, place 1 "cloud" on each of 12 plates. Spoon topping on each meringue. Sprinkle with reserved chopped candy pieces and drizzle lightly with chocolate syrup, if desired. May be refrigerated.

NOTE: *To make CHOCOLATE TOFFEE CLOUD TORTE, spread meringue into two 8-inch circles before baking. When cool, spread filling on meringue layer, top with second meringue and top with remaining filling. The powdered sugar creates a very airy, light meringue.*

Yield: 12 or more servings   Libby Gish

Sour Cream Pound Cake

1/2	pound butter, softened	3	cups unsifted flour
3	cups sugar	1/4	teaspoon baking soda
1/2	pint sour cream	1	teaspoon vanilla
6	eggs	1	teaspoon almond extract

Preheat oven to 300°. Grease and flour a 10-inch tube pan. Cream butter, sugar and sour cream in mixing bowl. Add eggs, one at a time and mix well. Add remaining ingredients and thoroughly mix. Pour batter into pan and bake for 1 hour, 25 minutes. Cool. Slice and serve.

Yield: 24 servings   Lina Drinkard

Banana Pineapple Pound Cake
A real favorite!

3   cups flour
2   cups sugar
1   teaspoon baking soda
1   teaspoon cinnamon
1   teaspoon salt
1¹/₂ teaspoons vanilla

2   cups mashed bananas
    (2-3 very ripe bananas)
1   (8-ounce) can crushed
    pineapple; undrained
3   eggs
1¹/₂ cups oil
¹/₂ cups pecans, finely chopped

Preheat oven to 325°. Grease and flour a Bundt or tube pan. In a large bowl, mix all ingredients well with a spoon. Pour into pan and bake about 1 1/2 hours. Cool in pan. Remove from pan; place on cake plate and frost if desired.

FROSTING:

1   stick margarine
1   (8-ounce) package
    cream cheese

1   (16-ounce) box
    powdered sugar
1   teaspoon lemon extract

Cream margarine and cheese. Add sugar and vanilla; beat until creamy. Spread frosting on cake. Slice, when ready to serve.

NOTE: *Moist, travels well. Just as good without frosting.*

Yield: 12-16 servings   Kay Wilson

Chocolate Sour Cream Pound Cake

1   cup margarine, softened
2   cups sugar
1   cup brown sugar
6   large eggs
2¹/₂ cups flour

¹/₄ teaspoon baking soda
¹/₂ cup cocoa
1   (8-ounce) carton sour cream
2   teaspoons vanilla

Preheat oven to 325°. Grease and flour a 10-inch tube pan. Beat margarine at medium speed for 2 minutes until soft and creamy. Gradually add sugars, beating 5-7 minutes. Add eggs, one at a time, beating just until pale and yellow color disappears. Combine flour, soda and cocoa. Add flour mixture to creamed mixture alternately with sour cream, beginning and ending with flour mixture, mixing at lowest speed just until blended after each addition. Stir in vanilla. Pour batter into tube pan. Bake 1 hour, 20 minutes. Cool in pan on wire rack for 10-15 minutes. Remove from pan; cool completely. Slice; serve.

Yield: 18-20 slices   Virginia Clawson

Orange Pound Cake

1¹/₂	cup butter or margarine, softened	³/₄	cup whole or skim milk
3	cups sugar	3	cups flour
6	eggs	¹/₂	teaspoon baking powder
3	tablespoons fresh orange juice	¹/₂	tablespoon vanilla
1	tablespoon lemon juice	1	teaspoon orange extract
		¹/₄	teaspoon almond extract
			Zest of 2 oranges

Preheat oven to 325°. Grease and flour Bundt pan. Cream butter on medium speed; gradually add sugar. Add eggs, one at a time, beating well after each. Combine orange, lemon juice and milk. Gradually mix liquid and creamed mixtures on low speed; gradually add flour one cup at a time and add baking powder. When just blended, add extracts. Stir in half of orange zest. Pour into prepared pan and bake 1 hour, 25 minutes. Cool in pan 15 minutes. Invert cake onto a cooling rack and remove pan. When cool enough to handle, transfer to serving dish. Glaze cake while still warm.

GLAZE:

2	cups powdered sugar	¹/₂	teaspoon orange extract
4	tablespoons fresh orange juice		Remainder of orange zest

Combine sugar, juice and extract; mix until smooth. Add orange zest and blend. Spoon glaze over warm cake.

NOTE: *Best if prepared one day ahead.*

Yield: 24 slices

Susan Hobbs

Banana Split Cake

3	sticks margarine, softened	1	(13-ounce) container frozen whipped topping, thawed
2	cups graham cracker crumbs		
2	cups powdered sugar	1	(6-ounce) jar maraschino cherries
3	eggs		
4-6	ripe bananas		Chopped nuts
1	(15-ounce) can crushed pineapple, drained		

Melt 1 stick of the margarine in saucepan; combine with crumbs and press into 9x12-inch pan. Beat remaining 2 sticks margarine with sugar. Add eggs and beat 15 minutes. Mixture should be consistency of whipped butter. Spoon mixture over graham cracker crumbs. Slice bananas over this and top with pineapple and whipped dessert topping. Dot with cherries and sprinkle with nuts. Refrigerate until ready to serve.

Yield: 10-12 servings

Tina Hartsell

Orange Soda Pound Cake

2³/₄	cups sugar	3	cups cake flour
1	cup shortening	1	cup Orange Crush
¹/₄	cup butter		carbonated beverage
5	eggs	1	teaspoon vanilla
¹/₂	teaspoon salt	1	teaspoon orange flavoring

Preheat oven to 325°. Cream together sugar, shortening and butter. Add eggs, one at a time, beating well after each. Cream until light and fluffy. Sift dry ingredients together. Add alternately with orange soda. Add flavorings. Pour into greased and floured tube pan. Bake for 1 hour, 10 minutes. Remove from pan and spread with topping while warm.

TOPPING:

1	cup powdered sugar	¹/₂	teaspoon orange flavoring
1	(3-ounce) package	1	teaspoon Orange Crush
	cream cheese, softened		carbonated beverage
¹/₂	teaspoon vanilla		

Cream together all ingredients and spread topping on warm cake. Slice; serve.

Yield: 12-16 slices   Lisa M. Black

Sherry Pound Cake

¹/₂	cup chopped pecans	³/₄	cup vegetable oil
1	(17.5-ounce) box Duncan	4	eggs
	Hines yellow cake mix	¹/₄	cup brown sugar
1	(3-ounce) box instant vanilla	¹/₄	cup sugar
	pudding	2	tablespoons ground
¹/₂	cup water		cinnamon
¹/₂	cup golden sherry		

Preheat oven to 350°. Sprinkle nuts in bottom of a greased and floured Bundt pan. In a large bowl, mix the remaining ingredients well. Pour batter into pan. Bake for 50-60 minutes.

GLAZE:

³/₄	cup butter	¹/₄	cup chopped pecans
1	cup sugar	¹/₄	cup golden sherry
¹/₄	cup water		

While cake is baking, make a glaze by boiling the butter, sugar, water and pecans for 2 minutes. Stir in the sherry. While cake is still warm in the pan, pour over 1/2 the glaze mixture. Cool cake in pan for 10 minutes. Invert cake onto cake plate. Pour remaining glaze over cake. Slice to serve.

Yield: 12 servings

Brown Sugar Pound Cake
with Caramel Icing

¹/₂	cup butter	2	cups flour
1	cup solid vegetable shortening	¹/₂	teaspoon salt
		¹/₂	teaspoon baking powder
1	(16-ounce) box light brown sugar	1	cup milk
		1	cup chopped pecans
¹/₂	cup sugar	1	tablespoon vanilla
5	eggs	1	teaspoon maple flavoring

Preheat oven to 325°. Cream butter and shortening in a mixing bowl. Gradually add sugars; blend well. Add eggs one at a time, beating well after each. Sift together flour, salt and baking powder. Gradually add flour mixture alternately with milk, starting and ending with flour. Add nuts and flavorings. Bake in a greased and floured tube pan for 1 hour, 15 minutes.

CARAMEL ICING:

4	ounces butter	¹/₄	cup milk
1	cup brown sugar	2	cups powdered sugar, sifted

Melt butter in a saucepan; add brown sugar. Boil over low heat for 2 minutes, stirring constantly. Stir in milk and bring to a boil. Cool to lukewarm; add sugar. Ice cake when mixture has thickened and cake is still warm. Slice; serve.

NOTE: *Keeps well and stays moist. A favorite of many!*

Yield: 12-15 servings   Helen "Pete" Dare

Bryce Bread Pudding

1	(15-16-ounce) loaf French bread	2	eggs, beaten
		2	cups sugar
5	cups milk	¹/₂	cup raisins (optional)

Grease a 9x12-inch pan. Break French bread into pieces and place in pan. In a bowl, mix milk, eggs and sugar. Add raisins. Pour mixture over bread. Bake at 325° for 1 hour.

TOPPING:

1	(4-ounce) stick butter	¹/₄	cup bourbon
1	cup sugar		

Blend butter, sugar and bourbon in a saucepan over medium heat. Stir constantly until heated through. Pour over baked pudding and let stand at least 10 minutes or more before serving.

Yield: 8-9 servings   Claudia Swicegood

Bread Pudding with Whiskey Sauce

1	pound loaf French bread, sliced	1	cup sugar
4	cups milk	1	cup golden raisins
3	eggs, slightly beaten	2	tablespoons vanilla
		3	tablespoons butter, melted

Break bread into small chunks and place in bowl. Add milk and let stand 10 minutes, then crush and mix with hands until well blended. Add sugar, raisins and vanilla; mix with spoon. Pour batter into 9x13-inch baking pan. Bake at 325° for 1 hour. Cool.

SAUCE:

1/2	cup butter	1/2	cup half-and-half
1	cup sugar	2	tablespoons whiskey

Cook butter, sugar and half-and-half until sugar dissolves. Bring to boil; reduce heat and simmer 5 minutes. Cool and add whiskey. When sauce has returned to room temperature, top pudding with sauce and serve.

NOTE: *This recipe is originally from Margaret Lewis, the mother of a dear friend.*

Yield: 16 servings   Ruth L. Meade

Date Pudding
Fruit for the Gods

FILLING:

1	(8-ounce) box non-sugared, pitted dates	1	cup sugar
1	cup water	1	teaspoon vanilla

In a saucepan, cook dates, water and sugar until smooth. Add vanilla. Cool and set aside.

CRUMBS:

1½	cups flour	2	cups regular oatmeal
1/2	teaspoon baking soda	1	cup melted butter
1/2	teaspoon salt	1	cup chopped pecans
1½	cups brown sugar		Whipped topping

Mix flour, soda, salt, sugar, oatmeal, butter and nuts until crumbly. Put half the crumbs in an 8x12-inch baking pan. To complete the pudding, spread filling over the crumbs. Top with remaining crumbs and pat down smoothly. Bake at 350° for 30 minutes. Best when served warm with whipped topping.

NOTE: *My Aunt Bonnie's recipe and my childhood favorite!*

Yield: 10-12 servings   Beverly Mitchell

Cherry Pudding

1 (14.5-ounce) can tart, red pitted pie cherries, drained, reserving liquid	1/2 cup milk
	1 cup flour
	1 teaspoon baking powder
1 1/2 cups sugar	1/8 teaspoon salt
1/4 cup butter or margarine	

Butter a 1 1/2-quart casserole dish; add cherries. Combine cherry juice and 1/2 cup of sugar and heat to boiling. In a separate bowl, combine remaining sugar, margarine, milk, flour, baking powder and salt. Pour this mixture over the cherries and then pour hot juice over the top. Bake at 375° until brown, about 30-40 minutes.

NOTE: *This was my grandmother's recipe. She was an excellent cook.*

Yield: Serves 6-8   Doris Turner Alexander

Bully Pudding
Christmas Dinner Dessert

1/2 cup butter	1 teaspoon salt
1 cup sugar	1 cup chopped dates
2 eggs	1 cup whole pecans
1 cup milk	Heavy whipping cream, whipped
1 tablespoon flour	
1/2 teaspoon baking powder	

Thoroughly mix butter, sugar, eggs, milk, flour, baking powder, salt, dates and nuts. Pour into a 2-quart buttered baking bowl. Bake at 350° for 45 minutes. Cool and serve with whipped cream.

NOTE: *An old English recipe that we always serve at Christmas.*

Yield: 6-8 servings   Ellen Reamer

Rice Pudding

1 cup rice, cooked according to package directions	1/2 teaspoon salt
	1/2 cup sugar
2 eggs, separated	1 teaspoon vanilla
2 1/4 cups milk	Cinnamon

Cook rice and set aside. Combine egg yolks, milk, salt and sugar. Mix well; add rice and vanilla. Beat egg whites until stiff. Fold into rice mixture. Pour into a 9x11-inch baking pan; sprinkle with cinnamon to taste. Bake at 350° for 30 minutes. Spoon into dessert dishes; serve.

Yield: 4 servings   Betty Carli

Indian Pudding

1/4 **cup corn meal**	1 **tablespoon butter or**
1 **cup water**	**margarine**
1 **teaspoon salt**	1 **teaspoon ground cinnamon**
2³/4 **cups buttermilk**	1/2 **teaspoon ginger**
2 **eggs, well beaten**	1/4 **teaspoon cardamom**
1/4 **cup light brown sugar**	1/4 **teaspoon nutmeg**
1/2 **cup light molasses**	

Heat corn meal, water, salt and 2 cups of buttermilk for 10 minutes on low boil. Combine eggs, sugar, molasses, butter and spices; add to buttermilk mixture. Pour into a 1 1/2-2 quart greased baking dish and bake at 325° for 30 minutes. Stir in the remaining 3/4 cups buttermilk and bake an additional 1 1/2 hours.

Yield: 8-10 servings   The Reverend William J. Cowfer

Lemon Pudding
Bon appetit!

1 **tablespoon butter**	**Juice and lightly grated rind**
³/4 **cup sugar**	**of 1 lemon**
2 **tablespoons flour**	2 **eggs, separated**
	1 **cup milk**

Lightly grease a 1 1/2-2-quart soufflé or baking dish. Place a pan of hot water (large enough to accommodate the baking dish) into the oven and set oven temperature to 350°. Cream butter and sugar until light in texture and a pale cream color (about 6-10 minutes). Add flour, lemon juice and rind. Add egg yolks that have been beaten; then add milk. Beat well. Fold in egg whites that have been beaten (not too stiffly). Pour into prepared baking dish and place dish in the pan of water in oven. Bake about 45 minutes. Test center for doneness with a cake straw or toothpick. Serve warm or chilled.

NOTE: *May use a little less sugar according to taste.*

Yield: 5 servings   Mrs. John G. Riley (Jane)

Chocolate Mint Sundae Topping

12 **(1¹/2-inch) chocolate covered**	2 **tablespoons milk or cream**
mint patties	

Microwave mint patties and milk in a small microwave-safe bowl, covered with plastic wrap for 30-45 seconds or until patties are melted. Stir; serve sauce over ice cream.

Yield: 4 servings

Mary Hanford's Persimmon Pudding

2	cups persimmon pulp	1	teaspoon salt
3	eggs	2	teaspoons cinnamon
1¹/₄	cups sugar	1	teaspoon ginger
1¹/₂	cups flour	¹/₂	teaspoon nutmeg
1	tablespoon baking powder	2¹/₂	cups milk
1	teaspoon baking soda	¹/₂	cup butter, melted

Wash, seed and mash persimmon. (It can be frozen at this point.) Beat eggs with sugar and add to pulp. Mix flour, baking powder, baking soda, salt and spices. Add dry ingredients to persimmon mixture, alternately with the milk. Stir in butter. Pour into a greased 9x13-inch baking dish. Bake at 325° for 1 hour.

Yield: 6-8 servings   Eleanor Hoey Bradshaw

Baked Truffle Pudding

2	eggs	3	tablespoons flour
1	cup sugar	1	cup chopped pecans
1	teaspoon vanilla	1	(8-ounce) container frozen
¹/₂	cup butter, melted		whipped topping, thawed
1	heaping tablespoon cocoa		

In an ovenproof 1-quart bowl, beat eggs; add sugar, vanilla and butter. Mix well. Sift together cocoa and flour; add nuts. Combine egg and flour mixtures. Set bowl in pan of hot water, covering half the depth of bowl. Bake at 350° for 45 minutes. Pudding will be syrupy on bottom. To serve, spoon syrup over warm (or room temperature) pudding. Top with whipped topping.

Yield: 6-8 servings   June Eshelman

♥ Hot Banana Split

2	firm, ripe bananas, peeled and halved lengthwise	4	tablespoons miniature marshmallows
4	tablespoons creamy peanut butter	2	scoops vanilla ice cream
4	tablespoons mini-chocolate chips		Chopped pecans Maraschino cherries for garnish

Place cut sides of bananas in 2 shallow microwave serving dishes; spread surface with peanut butter and gently press chocolate pieces and marshmallows into peanut butter. Microwave on high until chocolate and marshmallows begin to melt. Top with ice cream, chopped pecans and cherries. Serve.

Yield: Serves 2-4

Apple Pear Winter Tart

6-7	Granny Smith apples, peeled, cored, sliced lengthwise	1/2	cup sugar
3-4	Bartlett or William pears, peeled, cored, sliced lengthwise	1/2	cup brown sugar
		1/4	cup white corn syrup
		1/2	teaspoon nutmeg
1/4	teaspoon salt	1/4	teaspoon cloves
1/4	teaspoon white vinegar	2	teaspoons cinnamon
4	cups cold water	1/4	teaspoon vanilla

Preheat oven to 350°. Place apple and pear slices in separate containers. Mix salt, vinegar and water. Pour half of liquid over each fruit to prevent discoloration; set aside. Drain fruit just before cooking. In medium heavy-bottom saucepan, add both sugars, corn syrup and 2/3 of apple slices. Cook over medium heat, stirring occasionally until apples are soft. Add nutmeg, cloves, cinnamon and vanilla; place in food processor. Pulse 2-3 times or until apples are pureed but slightly chunky. Cool.

GRAHAM CRACKER CRUST:

3	cups graham cracker crumbs	1 1/2	teaspoons cinnamon
1	cup powdered sugar	9	tablespoons melted butter

Place all dry ingredients in medium bowl. Mix by hand. Add butter by drizzling onto dry mixture; blend until completely moist. Spray 11x1 1/2-inch round tart pan with vegetable spray. Press crumb mixture into pan, completely covering bottom and sides, about 1/8-inch thick. Bake crust for 8-10 minutes. Remove from oven and cool.

TO COMPLETE TART:

Fill cooled crust with the apple puree. Smooth surface with wet spatula. Starting with remaining apples, overlap apples around the outer edge of tart. In the opposite direction, overlap pears. Continue alternating between apples and pears until completely covered.

TOPPING:

1/4	cup brown sugar	4	tablespoons melted butter
1/4	cup sugar		

Sprinkle sugars over fruit topping, drizzle with butter. Place tart in oven preheated to 350°. Bake 45-60 minutes. Remove when nicely browned. Cool to room temperature. Refrigerate for 45 minutes before serving.

Yield: Serves 12-16

James Pierson
Executive Chef
Country Club of Salisbury

Crumb - Topped Apple Pie

4-6 apples, peeled, cored, and sliced	1 (9-inch) unbaked pie crust
1 cup sugar	1/3 cup butter or margarine
1 teaspoon cinnamon	3/4 cup flour

Mix apples, 1/2 cup of sugar and cinnamon together. Spoon into pie crust. Mix remaining 1/2 cup sugar, butter and flour until crumbly; sprinkle over apple mixture. Pie may be baked at 350° for 30 minutes or frozen and later baked at 350° for 1 hour or until golden brown and bubbly. Serve warm.

NOTE: *Pies stack and freeze well. They are great served with ice cream!*

Yield: 6 servings   Adair Doran

Creamy Dutch Apple Dessert

1/4 cup butter or margarine	1/4 cup lemon juice
1 1/2 cups graham cracker crumbs	1 (20-ounce) can apple pie filling
1 (14-ounce) can sweetened condensed milk	1/4 cup chopped walnuts
	1/2 teaspoon cinnamon
1 (8-ounce) container sour cream	Ice cream

Preheat oven to 350°. Melt butter in a shallow 1 1/2-quart (10x6-inch) baking dish. Sprinkle in crumbs and stir; press in bottom of dish. In a medium bowl, mix together milk, sour cream, and lemon juice. Spread evenly over crumbs. Spoon pie filling evenly over creamy layer. Bake for 25-30 minutes or until set. Cool slightly. Mix together nuts and cinnamon. Sprinkle over pie filling. May be served warm or cold. Delicious with ice cream. Refrigerate leftovers.

Yield: Serves 10-12   Myrna Crocker

Apple Pecan Cobbler

2 1/2 pounds apples, peeled and sliced	1/2 teaspoon cinnamon
	1/4 cup butter, softened
1 (12-ounce) package butterscotch chips	1 cup chopped pecans
	3/4 cup oatmeal
1/2 cup brown sugar	Ice cream (optional)
3/4 cup flour	

Preheat oven to 375°. Place apples in 9x13-inch pan. Sprinkle chips, 1/4 cup brown sugar, 1/4 cup flour and cinnamon on top of apples. Bake for 20 minutes. Blend remaining 1/2 cup flour, butter, pecans, oatmeal and remaining 1/4 cup sugar and sprinkle over apples. Bake an additional 30-40 minutes. Cool and serve plain; or with ice cream.

Yield: 10-12 servings   Joyce Plyler

Easy Blueberry & Peach Cobbler

1/2	cup margarine	2	cups fresh, sliced peaches
1	cup flour	2	cups fresh blueberries
1 1/4	cup sugar		Vanilla ice cream (optional)
2	teaspoons baking powder		Whipped dessert topping
1/4	teaspoon cinnamon		(optional)
3/4	cup milk		

Melt margarine in 2 1/2-quart baking dish. Combine flour, 3/4 cup sugar, baking powder and cinnamon. Add milk, stir until smooth. Pour into baking dish. Combine fruit and remaining sugar; spoon over batter. Bake at 350° for 45-50 minutes. Serve warm with or without ice cream or topping.

Yield: Serves 6   Peggy Maness

Summer Cobbler

1/4	cup brown sugar	1	cup flour
3/4	cup plus 2 tablespoons sugar	1 1/2	teaspoons baking powder
1	tablespoon cornstarch	1/2	teaspoon salt
1/2	cup water	1/2	cup milk
1	tablespoon lemon juice	1/4	cup butter, melted
2	cups sliced peaches	1/4	teaspoon nutmeg
1	cup blueberries		Vanilla no-fat ice cream

Combine brown sugar, 1/4 cup sugar, cornstarch and water. Cook until thick on medium heat, stir constantly. Remove from heat; stir in lemon juice and fruit. Pour into lightly greased 8-inch square pan. Combine flour, 1/2 cup sugar, baking powder and salt. Combine milk and butter; add to flour mixture. Beat until smooth; spread over fruit. Combine remaining sugar and nutmeg; sprinkle over batter. Bake at 375° for 40 minutes until golden brown. Delicious with ice cream.

Yield: 6-8 servings   Joan Green

🔔 Cinnamon Apple Crisp

1	tablespoon red cinnamon candies dissolved in 1 cup boiling apple juice	1	(18.25-ounce) box white cake mix
6	apples peeled, cored, sliced thin	1	cup packed light brown sugar
		1/2	cup butter, melted
			Cinnamon sugar

Arrange apples in ungreased 13x9x2-inch pan. Pour liquid and 1 tablespoon cinnamon sugar over top. Combine cake mix, sugar and butter; blend until crumbly. Sprinkle over apples. Sprinkle on cinnamon sugar. Bake at 350° 50-55 minutes.

Yield: 12-16 servings

Frosted Pumpkin Crisp Delight
Great for a Thanksgiving crowd

1 (30-ounce) can Libby's pumpkin pie mix (do not substitute canned solid pumpkin)	1/2 teaspoon cinnamon
	1/8 teaspoon ground nutmeg
	1/8 teaspoon ground ginger
1 (14-ounce) can sweetened condensed milk	1 (18.25-ounce) package spice cake mix
3 eggs	2 cups chopped pecans
1 cup powdered sugar	1 cup melted butter or margarine, cooled

Preheat oven to 350°. Prepare a 10 1/2x15 1/2-inch jelly roll pan by spraying with non-stick cooking spray and lining with wax paper. Spray waxed paper with cooking spray. In a mixing bowl, combine pumpkin, milk, eggs, sugar, cinnamon, nutmeg and ginger. Mix well with electric mixer. Pour mixture into prepared pan. Sprinkle dry cake mix over batter. Sprinkle on pecans. Drizzle margarine over pecans. Bake at least 60-80 minutes or until middle of cake is done and a toothpick inserted into cake center comes out clean. Invert onto serving tray. Remove wax paper and let stand to cool.

FROSTING:

1 (8-ounce) carton frozen whipped topping, thawed	1 1/2 cups powdered sugar
	1 1/2 teaspoons vanilla
1 (8-ounce) package cream cheese, softened	

Combine whipped topping, cream cheese, powdered sugar and vanilla. Mix and blend until spreadable consistency. With a spatula, spread frosting on top of cooled cake. Chill. When ready to serve, cut into squares. Keep refrigerated.

NOTE: *This is a family favorite that I created as an easy alternative to the traditional pumpkin roll.*

Yield: 24 servings   Libby Gish

Blueberry Pie

4 cups blueberries	1/2 teaspoon cinnamon
1 cup sugar	1/8 teaspoon salt
3 tablespoons flour	1 teaspoon lemon juice
1/2 teaspoon grated lemon peel	2 (9-inch) unbaked pie crusts

Preheat oven to 400°. Combine berries, sugar, flour, peel, cinnamon, salt and lemon juice. Place 1 crust in pie pan. Pour in filling. Top with remaining crust, sealing edges well. Cut vents in top of crust. Bake 35-40 minutes. Serve warm.

NOTE: *My son and grandson's favorite!*

Yield: 6-8 servings   Pam Doherty

Michigan Blueberry Pie

4	cups fresh blueberries	1/2	teaspoon nutmeg
1/2	cup dark brown sugar	1/4	teaspoon salt
1/2	cup sugar	1	baked pastry or graham
3 1/2	tablespoons flour		cracker pie shell
1	tablespoon margarine		Whipped topping
1	tablespoon lemon juice		

Combine 2 cups of the blueberries with sugars, flour, margarine, lemon juice, nutmeg and salt. Bring mixture to a boil and cook until juices thicken. Allow to cool. Add remaining 2 cups blueberries to cooked mixture. When cool, pour into pie shell and chill until time to serve. Top with whipped topping.

Yield: 6-8 servings　　　　　　　　　　　　　　　　Molly Campbell Clark

East Tennessee Buttermilk Pie

1/2	stick margarine, melted and cooled	1	teaspoon vanilla
		1	cup sugar
1/4	cup buttermilk	1	(9-inch) unbaked pie shell
2	eggs, slightly beaten		Whipping cream, whipped
2	tablespoons flour		

Mix margarine, buttermilk, eggs, flour, vanilla and sugar. Pour into pie shell. Bake at 350° for 30 minutes. Delicious served with whipped cream.

Yield: 6 servings　　　　　　　　　　　　　　　　　　Lisa Ganem

Chocolate Pie

1/4	cup cornstarch	2	cups milk, scalded
1	cup plus 6 tablespoons sugar	3	eggs, separated
1/8	teaspoon salt	1	teaspoon vanilla
3	tablespoons cocoa	1	(9-inch) baked pie shell,
1/4	cup water		cooled

Preheat oven to 300°. Combine cornstarch, 1 cup sugar and salt. Dissolve cocoa in water. Add dry mixture and cocoa mixture to milk. Cook in double boiler about 5 minutes until thickened. To prevent eggs from "scrambling", add small amount of hot mixture to beaten egg yolks; pour into cocoa mixture in double boiler and cook slightly. Add vanilla. Remove from heat. Pour into pie shell. Beat egg whites until foamy, add 6 tablespoons sugar, 1 tablespoon at a time. Beat until stiff peaks form. Spread meringue over filling; bake 5 minutes or until golden brown.

Yield: 6-8 servings　　　　　　　　　　　　　　　　Zandra Spencer

Mock German Chocolate Pie

1½	cups sugar	⅛	teaspoon salt
3	tablespoons flour	1	teaspoon vanilla
4	tablespoons cocoa	1	cup pecan pieces
2	eggs beaten	1	cup canned coconut
½	cup margarine, melted	2	(9-inch) unbaked pie shells
1	(12-ounce) can evaporated milk		

Preheat oven to 350°. Sift together sugar, flour and cocoa. Add eggs, margarine, milk, salt and vanilla to dry ingredients. Mix well. Sprinkle 1/2 cup pecans and 1/2 cup coconut in bottom of each pie shell and then pour in custard mixture. Bake for 45 minutes.

Yield: 2 pies, 12 servings   Anne S. Carlton

Mother's Brown Sugar Pie

4	eggs beaten	½	cup butter, melted
1	(16-ounce) box light brown sugar	1	cup milk
3	tablespoons flour	½	cup crushed pecans
		1	(10-inch) unbaked pie shell

Preheat oven to 400°. Combine eggs, sugar, flour, butter and milk. Fold in pecans and pour into pie shell. Bake for 15 minutes at 400°. Reduce heat to 350° and bake 30 minutes or until set.

NOTE: *My mother made this pie quite often when I was growing up.*

Yield: 8-10 servings   Carolyn C. Wilkerson

Chocolate Chess Pie

3	cups sugar	1	teaspoon vanilla
6	tablespoons cocoa	1	stick margarine, melted
4	eggs	2	(9-inch) unbaked pie shells
1	(12-ounce) can evaporated milk		

Preheat oven to 350°. In a mixing bowl, combine sugar and cocoa; add eggs. Combine milk and vanilla; add to mixture. Add margarine. Beat until thoroughly blended. Pour mixture into pie shells. Bake for 30 minutes. Cool before slicing.

Yield: 12 servings   Nadine Potts

Chess Pie or Chess Tarts

Great for picnics or tailgates!

3 eggs	1/2 tablespoon vanilla
1 1/2 cups sugar	1 (9-inch) unbaked pie shell or
1/2 cup margarine, melted	11 individual tart shells
1 tablespoon vinegar	

Preheat oven to 300°. Beat eggs and sugar with electric mixer or blender. Add margarine, vinegar and vanilla. Pour into pie shell or tart shells. Bake for 10 minutes. Increase heat to 350° and bake 35 minutes longer. Cool.

Yield: 1 pie or 11 tarts   Mimi Carlton

Southern Chess Pie

Sinfully rich!

1 (9-10-inch) unbaked pie shell	1/2 cup butter or margarine, melted
1 1/2 cups sugar, white or brown	
1 1/2 tablespoons cornmeal	1 tablespoon vinegar
1 1/2 tablespoons flour	1 teaspoon vanilla
1/4 teaspoon salt	1/4 teaspoon lemon extract (optional)
3-4 eggs, beaten	
1/4 cup milk or half-and-half	Whipped topping or ice cream

Preheat oven to 425°. Bake pie shell for 5 minutes and set aside. Combine sugar, cornmeal, flour and salt in large bowl. Add eggs, milk, butter, vinegar, vanilla and lemon extract. Mix well; pour into shell. Bake at 425° for 15 minutes. Reduce heat to 375° and bake 50 minutes longer. Cool on rack. Serve at room temperature. Refrigerate leftovers. Delicious served with whipped topping or ice cream.

Yield: 6-8 servings   Melda M. Killion

Chocolate Bourbon Walnut Pie

1 1/2 cups sugar	1 1/2 cups chopped walnuts
6 teaspoons flour	1 1/2 cups chocolate chips
3 eggs, beaten	1 1/2 ounces bourbon
3/4 cup butter, melted	1 (10-inch) unbaked pie shell

Preheat oven to 350°. Combine sugar and flour; add eggs. Slowly add butter to mixture. Stir in walnuts, chocolate chips and bourbon. Pour into pie shell. Bake for 50 minutes until golden brown.

Yield: 8-10 servings   Janie Golden

Cushaw Pie

3-4 pounds fresh cushaw, cut
into small pieces, peeled
2/3 (16-ounce) carton half-and-
half, or equal amount
evaporated milk
2 eggs beaten
1 1/2 cups sugar

1/8 teaspoon salt
1 teaspoon vanilla
2 (9-inch) unbaked pie shells
Nutmeg
Whipped topping
Fresh fruit

Preheat oven to 400°. Cook squash in a small amount of water until soft. Drain. Combine 3 cups of the pulp, milk, eggs, sugar, salt and vanilla; blend well. Pour into pie shells. Sprinkle with nutmeg. Bake for 15 minutes, then reduce heat to 300° and bake 35 more minutes. Allow to cool. May serve with whipped topping and fresh fruit.

NOTE: *Cushaws are large, long-necked squash which resemble a striped watermelon in color. They are difficult to cut. My husband, George Raynor, grew this squash in his garden every year and wrote several columns about them in the local newspaper. This was his favorite pie.*

Yield: 6-8 servings

Nancy Raynor

French Silk Pie

2 sticks butter (not margarine)
1 1/2 cups sugar
4 (1-ounce) squares
unsweetened chocolate
4 eggs
2 teaspoons vanilla

1 (8-ounce) carton frozen
whipped topping, thawed but
chilled, plus 8 tablespoons
for topping
1 (9-inch) pie crust, baked and
cooled

Cream butter and sugar together with electric mixer until mixture is light and fluffy. Melt chocolate by placing in a metal container sitting in a pan of hot water over low heat (double boiler style). When chocolate has melted, cool and add to creamed butter and sugar mixture. Add 4 eggs, one at a time, beating for 5 minutes after each addition. Add vanilla and blend well. Fold in the 8-ounce carton of whipped topping. Pour into pie shell and refrigerate overnight. When ready to serve, top each of 8 pieces of pie with a dollop of whipped topping.

NOTE: *Prepare this pie the day before you plan to serve it.*

Yield: 8 servings

Juanita Williams

Fudge Pie

3	tablespoons cocoa	1	teaspoon vanilla
1	cup sugar	3	eggs, beaten
1/4	cup sifted flour	1/4	cup butter or margarine
1/4	teaspoon salt		

Preheat oven to 350°. Mix cocoa, sugar, flour and salt. Add vanilla to eggs and stir in dry mixture. Add butter to pie filling mixture, or melt butter in a 9-inch glass pie pan. Pour in filling and bake 20 minutes or until set. Cool.

NOTE: *My children's (Jan, Jim & John's) favorite pie.*

Yield: 8 servings   Virginia Broaddus

Lemon Meringue Pie

5	eggs, separated	1	teaspoon grated lemon rind
1	cup sugar	1/8	teaspoon salt
1/4	cup lemon juice	1	(9-inch) baked pie shell

Preheat oven to 325°. Beat egg yolks for 1/2 minute at medium speed. Add 1/2 cup sugar, lemon juice and rind. Stir and cook in top of double boiler until thick. Remove from heat. Beat egg whites and salt for 2 minutes at high speed. Continue beating, gradually adding remaining 1/2 cup sugar. Reserve half of meringue for topping; carefully fold the remainder into lemon mixture. Pour lemon custard into pie shell. Spread remaining meringue on top. Bake for 10-15 minutes or until golden.

Yield: 6-8 servings   Marilyn M. Overton

Mother's Lemon Meringue Pie

1 1/3	cups sugar		Grated zest of 1 lemon
1/4	cup cornstarch	1/4	cup lemon juice
1 1/2	cups cold water	1	tablespoon margarine
3	eggs, separated	1	(9-inch) baked pie crust

Combine 1 cup sugar and cornstarch in medium saucepan. Stir in water until smooth. Add slightly beaten egg yolks. Boil mixture, stirring constantly, over medium heat for 1 minute. Remove from heat. Add zest, juice and margarine. Pour pie filling into crust. To make meringue, beat egg whites with electric mixer until foamy and stiff peaks form. Gradually add remaining 1/3 cup sugar. Spread meringue on filling around the edges of crust, then swirl meringue to fill the center of pie. Bake at 350° for 15 minutes or until golden brown.

NOTE: *This was my mother, Carrie B. Hix's, recipe. Still a family favorite!*

Yield: 6 servings   Gena Hix Elias

Brandy Pecan Pie

3	eggs	1/2	cup whipping cream
1	cup sugar	1/4	cup brandy
1/2	teaspoon salt	1	teaspoon vanilla
2	tablespoons butter, melted	1	cup pecans
1/2	cup dark corn syrup	1	(9-inch) unbaked pie crust

Preheat oven to 375°. Beat eggs, sugar, salt, butter, corn syrup and cream. Stir in brandy, vanilla and pecans. Pour into pie crust. Bake 40-50 minutes until set. Cool.

NOTE: *A very rich pie and a family favorite since 1970.*

Yield: 8-12 servings   Cleo Catherine Dick

Robert's Favorite Pecan Pie

1/4	cup melted butter	3	eggs, beaten
1/2	cup brown sugar	1	cup chopped pecans
1/8	teaspoon salt	1/2	cup chocolate chips
1	teaspoon vanilla	1	(9-inch) unbaked pie crust
1	cup light corn syrup		

Preheat oven to 350°. Mix butter, sugar, salt, vanilla and corn syrup. Add to the eggs. Sprinkle pecans and chips over bottom of crust; pour in custard mixture. Bake 50 minutes.

NOTE: *May substitute coconut for half or for all of the chips.*

Yield: 8 servings   Bertie Broaddus

Coconut Pineapple Pie

1/4	cup butter or margarine, softened	1	(8 1/4-ounce) can crushed pineapple
1 1/2	cups sugar	1	(3 1/2-ounce) can flaked coconut
1	tablespoon cornmeal	1	(9-10-inch) unbaked pie crust
4	eggs		

Preheat oven to 450°. Mix butter, sugar and cornmeal. Add eggs, one at a time, mixing well after each addition. Add pineapple and coconut and mix well. Spoon into pie crust. Bake for 10 minutes. Reduce heat to 325° and bake 30-40 minutes more, until center is firm.

NOTE: *A favorite of my family.*

Yield: 8 servings   Frieda Vick

Pumpkin Chiffon Praline Pie

PRALINE CRUST:

¹/₃ **cup butter or margarine**	¹/₃ **cup chopped nuts**
¹/₃ **cup brown sugar**	1 **(9-inch) unbaked pie crust**

Cream butter and sugar; add nuts. Bake crust at 350° 10-12 minutes. Remove crust from oven; spread creamed mixture on crust. Bake 5 more minutes. Cool.

FILLING:

2 **eggs, beaten**	¹/₂ **teaspoon nutmeg**
¹/₂ **cup milk**	¹/₄ **teaspoon ground cloves**
1 **cup canned pumpkin**	¹/₄ **teaspoon ground cinnamon**
1 **(¹/₄-ounce) envelope**	1 **(8-ounce) carton frozen**
unflavored gelatin	**whipped topping, thawed**
¹/₂ **cup brown sugar**	**Whipped cream (optional)**
¹/₂ **teaspoon salt**	**Pecan halves (optional)**

In saucepan, combine eggs, milk, pumpkin, gelatin, sugar, salt and spices. Stir constantly, boil on medium heat 1 minute, until thick. Cool. Fold in topping; pour into crust. Chill. To serve, garnish with whipped cream and pecans.

Yield: 6-8 servings   Carol Freed

Swedish Rhubarb Pie

4-6 **rhubarb stalks, peeled and**	1¹/₂ **cups flour**
cut into 2-inch slices	4 **tablespoons butter**
³/₄ **cup plus 2 tablespoons sugar**	**Vanilla ice cream**
1 **tablespoon cornstarch**	

Place rhubarb in buttered pie pan. Sprinkle with 3/4 cup sugar. In bowl, mix cornstarch, flour, remaining sugar; cut in butter until crumbly. Sprinkle mixture over rhubarb. Bake at 375° for 20-25 minutes. Serve with ice cream.

NOTE: *Very popular in Sweden where homes have rhubarb in their garden.*

Yield: 6-8 servings   Jayne White (Mrs. Calvin J., Jr.)

Divine Raspberry Sauce

2 **(10-ounce) boxes frozen,**	²/₃ **cup red currant jelly or light**
sweetened raspberries, thawed	**corn syrup**

In blender, process berries and jelly; chill. Serve on ice cream, pies or cakes.

Yield: 2 1/2 cups

Zesty Raspberry Sauce

Great topping for ice cream, cheesecake. or pound cake

2/3 **cup sugar**
2 **tablespoons cornstarch**
1/4 **teaspoon salt**
1 1/2 **cups water**
1 **cup individually quick frozen raspberries**

1/8 **cup margarine, melted**
1/8 **cup lemon juice**
1 **ounce Grand Marnier**
1 **cup frozen strawberries, thawed, drained**

Combine sugar, cornstarch and salt in stock pot; mix well. Add remaining ingredients (except strawberries); bring to low boil. Cook until sauce has thickened; remove from heat and blend with mixer. Strain mixture through a very fine strainer to remove seeds; stir in strawberries. Place mixture in container; refrigerate 4-6 hours before serving over desserts.

Tony and Mary Ellen Kennedy
The Wrenn House

Coconut Crunch Pumpkin Pie

A Thanksgiving favorite!

2 **cups Libby's pumpkin pie mix**
1 **(13-ounce) can sweetened condensed milk**
2 **eggs**
2 **tablespoons brown sugar**
1 **teaspoon cinnamon**

1/2 **teaspoon ginger**
1/2 **teaspoon nutmeg**
1/2 **teaspoon salt**
1 **teaspoon vanilla**
1 **unbaked (9-inch) deep dish pie shell**

Combine ingredients in a bowl and mix well. Pour mixture into pie shell. Bake at 375° for 45 minutes or until center is set.

COCONUT CRUNCH TOPPING: (optional)
3 **tablespoons butter, softened**
1/4 **cup sugar**
2 **tablespoons brown sugar**
1/2 **teaspoon vanilla**

2 **tablespoons cream**
1/2 **cup flake coconut**
1/2 **cup nuts, chopped**

Cream butter, sugars and vanilla. Add cream, coconut and nuts; mix well. Sprinkle mixture with fingers over the hot pie. Place pie on rack 8-9 inches away from broiler unit. Broil for 3 minutes until bubbly. Cool. Slice to serve.

NOTE: *For PUMPKIN CUSTARD, omit crust; bake in a buttered custard dish.*

Yield: 6-8 servings

Magnificent Meringues

BASIC MERINGUE:

2   egg whites, room
     temperature
     Pinch of salt
1/4 teaspoon cream of tartar

2/3   cup powdered sugar
1/2-1 teaspoon vanilla, almond, or
       mint extract, or flavored
       liqueurs

Preheat oven to 350°. Using clean dry, grease-free electric beaters and metal or glass mixing bowl, beat egg whites, salt and cream of tartar until stiff peaks form. Gradually add sugar and choice of flavorings; beat until mixture is stiff and glossy. Spoon or spread *BASIC MERINGUE* into desired shape and size onto parchment lined air-bake cookie sheets for *MERINGUE COOKIES;* or into a 9-inch glass pie plate coated with non-stick spray for *MERINGUE PIE SHELLS, MERINGUE TORTES* or *MERINGUE BERRY CUPS.* Place in oven. Immediately turn oven off, leaving meringues in oven at least 8 hours or overnight until cool, dry, airy and crisp.

ANGEL COOKIES:

CAPPUCCINO ANGEL COOKIES: Add 1 teaspoon instant coffee granules or espresso powder.

CHOCOLATE ANGEL COOKIES: Add 2 tablespoons powdered cocoa.

BERRY ANGEL COOKIES: Add 2 tablespoons berry preserves.

CONFETTI ANGEL COOKIES: Add 1/2 cup chopped nuts plus 1/2- cup chocolate, mint chocolate, butterscotch or mini M&M baking bits.

SURPRISE ANGEL COOKIES: Envelope chocolate candy kisses or gumdrops with dollops of basic meringue, or press candies into center of cookies before baking.

To make *ANGEL COOKIES,* add desired ingredients to *BASIC MERINGUE* recipe. Spoon rounded teaspoonfuls of mixture onto prepared cookie sheets. Bake and cool as directed for *BASIC MERINGUE.* Store cookies in air-tight container.

Yield: 2 dozen cookies

Pineapple Sauce for Vanilla Ice Cream

1   cup crushed pineapple, with
     juices
1   cup sugar
3   teaspoons green crème de
     menthe

     Vanilla ice cream
1   (6-ounce) jar maraschino
     cherries for garnish

To make sauce, combine pineapple and sugar in a saucepan. Mix; blend over low heat until dissolved. Add crème de menthe to desired color and taste. In a parfait glass, layer sauce, then ice cream, until glass is filled, ending with sauce. Garnish with a cherry. Dessert may be frozen until used.

Yield: 2 cups sauce   Una Pursel

Million Dollar Pie

A great summer dessert!

2	(9-inch) unbaked pie shells	1	(8¼-ounce) can mandarin oranges, drained and cut up
1	(14-ounce) can sweetened condensed milk	1	tablespoon lemon juice
1	(20-ounce) can crushed pineapple, drained	½	cup chopped pecans
		1	(12-ounce) container frozen whipped topping, thawed

Bake and cool pie shells. Mix milk, fruits, juice, pecans and whipped topping in a bowl. Pour into 2 pie shells. Refrigerate overnight before serving.

NOTE: *May use graham cracker crusts, if desired.*

Yield: 2 pies, 12 servings   Anne Ramsay Saunders

Pineapple Pie

1½	cups pineapple juice	1	(3-ounce) package lime gelatin
1	cup sugar	1	(12-ounce) can evaporated milk, chilled
1	(8-ounce) can crushed pineapple, drained	2	(9-inch) vanilla wafer pie crusts
2	eggs, beaten		

In a saucepan, cook pineapple juice, sugar, crushed pineapple and beaten eggs until almost boiling. Stir in gelatin until dissolved. Cool. Whip milk until stiff and fold in gelatin mixture. Pour into pie crusts. Chill in refrigerator until set. Slice and serve.

Yield: 2 pies, 12 servings   Tomie Troxler

Passion Pie

1	(20-ounce) can unsweetened crushed pineapple, undrained	1	cup pecan pieces
1	cup sugar	2	(9-inch) pie crusts, lightly baked
6	tablespoons flour	6-8	bananas, sliced thin
1	cup coconut	1	(8-ounce) carton frozen whipped topping, thawed

In saucepan, mix pineapple with juice, sugar and flour. Heat until thick, stirring constantly. Cool. Add coconut and pecans. Pour into baked pie crusts that have been layered with bananas. Top with whipped topping. Refrigerate until ready to serve.

Yield: 8-12 servings   The Reverend Dr. Robert M. Lewis

Christmas Igloos
A beautiful winter dessert

1 (10-12 ounce) box butter cookies	1 pint whipping cream, whipped or 1 (12-ounce) tub frozen whipped topping, thawed
1 (16-ounce) can crushed pineapple, drained	
1 cup chopped nuts	1 (6-ounce) package frozen coconut
1 cup white raisins	
1 cup sugar	1 (6-ounce) jar maraschino cherries
1 stick margarine, melted	
1 teaspoon vanilla	

Stack 3 cookies in 16 groups. Mix pineapple, nuts, raisins, sugar, margarine and flavoring. Spread between and on top of cookies. Place on baking sheet in freezer until firm. Remove from freezer and ice each stack with whipped cream or topping to resemble igloos. Cover all over with coconut and top with cherries. May be frozen again and put in freezer bags. Allow flavors to blend while thawing in refrigerator before serving.

Yield: 16 servings

Jean Messer Williams

Blueberry Cream Cheese Pie

12 ounces cream cheese, softened	1¹/₂-2 bananas, sliced
¹/₂ cup sugar	1 (9-inch) deep dish pie shell, baked
¹/₂ pint whipping cream, whipped	

Mix cream cheese with sugar and fold in whipped cream. Slice bananas and place in bottom and around sides of cooked pie shell. Pour cheese mixture over bananas and prepare glaze.

GLAZE:

1 (12-ounce) package frozen blueberries	1 tablespoon cornstarch
	¹/₃ cup sugar

Combine frozen blueberries with cornstarch and sugar. Cook over low heat until thick. Do not break berries. Cool to room temperature. Spoon glaze over pie and chill several hours before serving.

Yield: 6 servings

Dottie Goodnight

B
L
E
S
S
I
N
G
S

Key Lime Pie

(3-ounce) package lime	2 drops green food coloring
gelatin	3 tablespoons lime juice
½ cup boiling water	1 (6-ounce) graham cracker
cup evaporated milk	crust
½ cup sugar	

In a small bowl dissolve gelatin in boiling water. Place in freezer until thick but not set. Pour milk into a large bowl in freezer for about 20 minutes until ice crystals form and it is well chilled. Remove from freezer and beat with mixer on high speed until stiff. Gradually beat in sugar, food coloring, gelatin and lime juice. Place in crust and refrigerate for 2 hours before serving.

Yield: 8 servings   Phyllis Gish

Mary Anne's Candy Bar Pie
Quick and delicious!

6 large marshmallows	1 (12-ounce) container light
(1.55-ounce) Hershey milk	whipped topping
chocolate candy bars	1 (6-ounce) graham cracker
⅓ cup milk	crust

Melt marshmallows, candy bars and milk in double boiler. Cool. Fold in 1/2 of whipped topping. Pour into crust. Top with remaining whipped topping. Chill. Slice; serve.

NOTE: *Our favorite! My son requests it often, and always at Christmas.*

Yield: 8 servings   Gayle D. Smerznak

Banana Split Pie

(8-ounce) package cream	2 bananas, thinly sliced
cheese	1 (8-ounce) can crushed
cup powdered sugar	pineapple, drained
2 tablespoons milk	1 (8-ounce) container whipped
graham cracker crust,	topping
prepared according to	½ cup chopped nuts
directions on box of graham	½ cup chopped maraschino
cracker crumbs	cherries

Combine cream cheese, powdered sugar and milk. Spread over crust. Add a layer of bananas. Spread pineapple over bananas. Top with whipped topping. Garnish with nuts and cherries. Refrigerate. Slice; serve.

Yield: 6 servings   Becky Lowery

Banana Split Refrigerator Cake

1	(18.25-ounce) package moist banana supreme cake mix	1	(6-ounce) jar maraschino cherries, drained and halved
1	(1.3-ounce) envelope whipped topping mix	2	ripe bananas, sliced
1	(3.4-ounce) package instant vanilla pudding mix	1	cup pineapple chunks
1½	cups milk	½	cup chopped pecans
1	teaspoon vanilla	1	(11.75-ounce) jar hot fudge ice cream topping, warmed
			Lemon juice, diluted with water

Preheat oven to 350°. Grease and flour 9x13-inch pan. Prepare, bake and cool cake following package directions. Combine topping mix, pudding mix, milk and vanilla in large bowl. Beat at medium speed with electric mixer until stiff. Spread over cooled cake. Place cherry halves, banana slices, pineapple pieces and chopped nuts randomly over pudding mixture; drizzle with fudge topping. Refrigerate until ready to use. Cut into 3-inch squares to serve.

NOTE: *To prevent banana slices from darkening, slice into a small amount of lemon juice diluted with water. Drain bananas before placing on cake.*

Yield: 12 or more servings

Angel Bavarian Cake

1	cup sugar	1	pint whipping cream, whipped, plus 1/2 pint whipping cream, whipped for icing
2	tablespoons flour		
1	teaspoon vanilla		
4	egg yolks, beaten		
1	pint half-and-half	1	large angel food cake, broken into chunks
1	(¼-ounce) package unflavored gelatin		
½	cup cold water	1½	cup fresh seasonal strawberries, peaches, blueberries or cherries; or maraschino cherries, drained
4	egg whites, beaten stiff		

To make custard, in a medium saucepan mix sugar and flour. Add vanilla and egg yolks, heating mixture over low to medium heat. Slowly add half-and-half and simmer. Cook until slightly thickened. Dissolve gelatin in the cold water; add to hot custard. Cool. Fold in 1 pint whipped cream and beaten egg whites. Line a large glass bowl with half the cake pieces. Pour in half the custard. Arrange a portion of the fruit decoratively on top. Repeat this process, ending with fruit. Refrigerate overnight. To ice cake, spread the remaining 1/2 pint of whipped cream over cake and top with remaining fruit. May not be frozen.

NOTE: *Arrange cake in 2-3 layers, depending on size and depth of bowl.*

Yield: 8-10 servings   Trudy Thompson (Mrs. W. R., Jr.)

♥ Easy Lemon Angel Delight
A wonderful light dessert

	angel food cake	1	(8-ounce) container frozen
	(3.4-ounce) packages instant		whipped topping, thawed
	lemon pudding mix	1/2	cup flaked coconut (optional)
	cups cold milk		

Break cake into small pieces. Mix pudding and milk in a bowl. Combine cake pieces and pudding mixture. Put in a 2-quart casserole dish and refrigerate until firm. Top with whipped topping. Sprinkle with coconut if desired. Prepare dessert the day before serving; keep refrigerated.

Yield: 10-12 servings   Shirley Terry

Orange Sherbet Cake

CAKE:

	(18.25-ounce) box orange	1/3	cup vegetable oil
	cake mix	2	eggs
	(3-ounce) box orange gelatin,	1	teaspoon vanilla
	dry	1	teaspoon orange flavoring
	cup water		

Preheat oven to 350°. Place all ingredients in a bowl and blend well with electric mixer for 2 minutes. Spoon batter into 3 greased and floured 9-inch cake pans. Bake for 20-25 minutes. Cake is done, when a toothpick inserted into center of cake comes out clean. Cool layers on rack.

FILLING:

1	(16-ounce) container	1/3	cup orange juice
	sour cream	1	teaspoon vanilla
2	cups sugar	1	teaspoon orange flavoring
12	ounces frozen coconut,		
	thawed		

Mix all ingredients until blended well. Set aside 1 cup of filling mixture to be used for icing: Place one cake layer on cake plate. Spread 1/2 of remaining filling on top. Repeat with second cake layer and second half of remaining filling. Place third layer on top.

ICING:

1	cup reserved filling	1	(16-ounce) container frozen
			whipped topping, thawed

Mix reserved filling and whipped topping. Cover the top and sides of cake with icing. Refrigerate cake up to a week. Gets better every day. Slice; serve.

Yield: 12 servings   Mildred Simerson

♥ Pumpkin Trifle
Luscious, layered dessert

1 (18.25-ounce) spice cake mix	4 (3.4-ounce) boxes instant
1 (16-ounce) can pumpkin	butterscotch pudding mix
1 teaspoon cinnamon	2½ cups cold milk
¼ teaspoon nutmeg	1 (12-ounce) container frozen
¼ teaspoon ginger	whipped topping, thawed
¼ teaspoon allspice	Maraschino cherries for
	garnish

Preheat oven to 350°. Prepare cake mix according to package directions and bake in 9x13-inch pan. Cool and crumble half of cake into pieces to yield 3 cups. Reserve 1/4 cup crumbs for garnish. Remaining half of cake may be frozen for later use. In a large bowl, combine pumpkin, spices, pudding mix and milk until smooth. In a glass trifle bowl layer: 1/4 of cake crumbs, 1/2 pumpkin mixture, 1/2 remaining cake crumbs and 1/2 of whipped topping. Repeat layers, ending with whipped topping. Garnish with reserved cake crumbs and cherries. Chill for 2 hours before serving.

NOTE: *May be made with lowfat or fat free ingredients.*

Yield: 10-12 servings

Ice Box Fruitcake

2 (12-ounce) boxes vanilla wafers, crushed	2 (6-ounce) jars maraschino cherries, drained, cut into small pieces
1 (15-ounce) box seedless raisins	2 (14-ounce) cans sweetened condensed milk
1 pound shredded coconut	1 (12-ounce) can evaporated milk
2 pounds finely chopped English walnuts	2 (10-ounce) bags large marshmallows
2 pounds finely chopped pecans	
2 pounds finely chopped Brazil nuts	

Combine wafer crumbs, raisins, coconut and all nuts in a large bowl, mix and add cherries. Stir in sweetened condensed milk. Place evaporated milk and marshmallows in a saucepan. Heat over low heat, stirring constantly until marshmallows melt. Add milk mixture to nut and fruit mixture; mix thoroughly. Pour into a greased 9x13-inch baking dish. Cover with foil and refrigerate 3 days before serving.

Yield: 12 servings

Mary Kay Zigmont

352

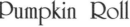
Pumpkin Roll

3	eggs	1	teaspoon baking powder
¾	cup flour	½	teaspoon nutmeg
1	cup sugar	½	teaspoon salt
⅔	cup canned solid pumpkin	1	cup chopped pecans
1	teaspoon cinnamon		Powdered sugar for dusting
½	teaspoon ginger		towel and cake
2	tablespoons lemon juice		

Preheat oven to 375°. Beat eggs 5 minutes. Add flour, sugar, pumpkin, cinnamon, ginger, juice, baking powder, nutmeg and salt. Beat well and pour into a well greased jelly roll pan. Sprinkle nuts evenly over batter. Bake 15 minutes or until center springs back. Loosen edges of cake with a knife. Invert onto clean damp towel dusted lightly with powdered sugar. Roll up cake in towel, starting with short end. Cool completely.

FILLING:

1	(8-ounce) package cream cheese, softened	1	cup powdered sugar, plus extra for dusting onto rolled cake
4	tablespoons margarine		
½	teaspoon vanilla		

Mix all ingredients in a bowl until blended and smooth. Unroll cake and spread with filling. Discard towel. Re-roll cake, dust with powdered sugar, and cover with plastic wrap. Refrigerate until ready to serve. Freezes well.

Yield: 10 servings   Sally Brodie

♥ Chocolate Eclair Cake

2	(3.4-ounce) boxes instant, sugar and fat free French vanilla pudding mix	1	(12-ounce) container frozen nonfat whipped topping, thawed
2	cups skim milk	1	(16-ounce) box graham crackers (reduced fat, if available)
1	cup nonfat French vanilla coffee creamer (found in dairy case)	1	(12-ounce) can light chocolate frosting

Mix pudding with milk and coffee creamer; fold in whipped topping. Divide mixture in half. Arrange layer of crackers to fit in a 9x13-inch baking dish. Add a layer of pudding. Repeat with a layer of crackers and a layer of pudding, ending with a layer of crackers. Spread frosting evenly on top of crackers; refrigerate until ready to serve.

Yield: 9-12 servings   Mary Kay Zigmont

Stained Glass Torte

1 (3-ounce) package lemon, orange or pineapple gelatin	1/2 cup sugar
1 (3-ounce) package lime gelatin	1 cup pineapple juice
	2 cups heavy cream, whipped
1 (3-ounce) package cherry, strawberry or raspberry gelatin	1 teaspoon vanilla extract
	1/4 teaspoon almond extract
4 1/2 cups boiling water	Graham cracker crumb crust (use your favorite recipe baked in a springform pan), reserving a few crumbs for garnish
1 (1/4-ounce) envelope unflavored gelatin	
1/4 cup cold water	

Dissolve each of the 3 packages of flavored gelatin in 1 1/2 cups boiling water in separate bowls. Stir until each is dissolved. Pour each gelatin mixture into separate shallow pans. Chill until firm. Cut into tiny cubes; refrigerate. Soften unflavored gelatin in cold water; add sugar. Heat pineapple juice to boiling in a saucepan. Add unflavored gelatin mixture and stir until dissolved. Cool thoroughly. Fold into whipped cream with flavorings added and gently add colored gelatin cubes. Pour into a 9 1/2 or 10-inch springform pan that has a graham cracker crust on the bottom. Sprinkle top with reserved crumbs. Chill until firm. Cut into wedges to serve.

Yield: 18-20 servings   Carolyn McDonald

Royal Trifle

2 (3-ounce) packages lady fingers	2 tablespoons cornstarch
Sherry or rum (optional)	1/8 teaspoon salt
	2 cups half-and-half
1 (10-ounce) jar raspberry preserves	4 egg yolks, well beaten
	2 tablespoons butter
1/4 cup blanched, slivered almonds	1 1/2 teaspoons vanilla
	1 cup heavy cream, whipped
3/4 cup sugar	

Sprinkle a few drops of sherry or rum on each lady finger and spread raspberry preserves on each. Line a very deep dish with the prepared lady fingers and sprinkle almonds over them. In a double boiler, mix sugar, cornstarch and salt. Gradually stir in half-and-half. Cook covered over hot water 8 minutes without stirring. Uncover and cook for about 10 minutes more. Add egg yolks and butter. Cook and stir these ingredients 2 minutes longer. Cool, stirring occasionally. Add vanilla and chill the mixture. Custard will have the consistency of heavy whipped cream. Pour custard over lady fingers; refrigerate. Spread whipped cream on top before serving.

Yield: 12-14 servings   Mrs. Ronald D. Smith

Custard Pie

4	eggs, beaten	1/2	teaspoon salt
2	tablespoons water	1/2	cup margarine, melted
2	tablespoons cornmeal	2	teaspoons vanilla
1	(16-ounce) box light brown sugar	2	cups chopped pecans
		2	(9-inch) unbaked pie shells

Preheat oven to 325°. Mix eggs, water, cornmeal, sugar and salt. Stir in margarine and vanilla. Fold in nuts and pour into shells. Bake 45 minutes. Slice to serve.

Yield: 2 pies, 12 servings

Jewel Ziprik

Chocolate Ice Box Pie

1	(8-ounce) package semi-sweet chocolate bits	3	tablespoons milk
2	tablespoons sugar	4	eggs, separated
		1	(9-inch) pie shell, baked

Melt chocolate bits, sugar and milk together in double boiler. Add 4 egg yolks, one at a time, beating well after each addition. Beat 4 egg whites until stiff and fold into chocolate mixture. Pour into baked pie shell and chill several hours before serving.

Yield: 6 servings

Ginny Williamson

Chocolate Meringue Pie

20	round crackers, crushed	6	(1.45-ounce) milk chocolate bars
1	cup sugar	1	(8-ounce) carton frozen whipped topping, thawed
1	cup chopped pecans		
3	egg whites, room temperature		

Preheat oven to 350°. Combine crumbs, 1/2 cup sugar and pecans; mix well. To make meringue, beat egg whites until soft peaks form. Gradually add 1/2 cup sugar. Beat until stiff. Fold in cracker crumb mixture. Lightly grease pie pan. Spread meringue mixture on bottom and sides of pan. Bake 30 minutes and cool. Melt chocolate over hot water in double boiler. Cool slightly. Fold into whipped topping and spoon into shell. Refrigerate. Pie keeps well refrigerated for 2 days. Slice to serve.

Yield: 6-8 servings

June Eshelman

Black Bottom Pie

1	cup sugar	1		(0.25-ounce) envelope
1	tablespoon cornstarch			unflavored gelatin
2	cups milk, scalded	1/4		cup cold water
4	beaten egg yolks	4		egg whites
1	teaspoon vanilla			Banana slices (optional)
1	(6-ounce) package semisweet			Chocolate shavings
	chocolate pieces			(optional)
1	(9-inch) pastry shell, baked			

Combine 1/2 cup sugar and cornstarch. Slowly add milk to beaten yolks; then add sugar mixture. Cook and stir in the top of a double boiler until custard coats the spoon. To 1 cup of the custard add the chocolate and stir until melted. Pour into the bottom of cooled pie shell; chill. Soften the gelatin in the cold water and add to the remaining hot custard. Stir until dissolved and chill until slightly thick. Beat the egg whites until soft peaks form. Gradually beat in the remaining 1/2 cup sugar and continue beating until thick. Fold in the custard-gelatin mixture and pile onto the chocolate layer; chill until set. Garnish with banana slices and chocolate shavings when serving.

Yield: 6-8 servings   Patty Mason

Grasshopper Pie

1	cup chocolate wafer crumbs	2	tablespoons white crème de
4	tablespoons (1/2 stick) butter		cacao
	or margarine, melted	2	tablespoons green crème de
2	tablespoons sugar		menthe
32	large marshmallows	11/2	cups whipping cream
1/2	cup milk		Chocolate curls for garnish

Blend wafer crumbs with butter or margarine and sugar. Press over bottom and side of a buttered 9-inch pie plate. Bake at 350° for 8 minutes. Cool completely in pie plate on a wire rack. Melt marshmallows in milk in the top of a double boiler over hot water; stir until blended. Cool completely. Stir in the crème de cacao and the crème de menthe. Beat cream until stiff; fold into the marshmallow mixture. Spoon into the cooled crust. Chill 3 hours or until firm. Garnish with chocolate curls when serving.

Yield: 6-8 servings   Patty Mason

Almond Ice Box Dessert

1½ cups vanilla wafer crumbs
½ gallon vanilla ice cream, softened
1½ stick margarine, softened

2 cups powdered sugar
1 egg
1½ teaspoon almond flavoring
Toasted, slivered almonds

Line 9x13-inch baking dish with 1 cup crumbs. Top with 1/2 of ice cream; return to freezer while next layer is prepared. Combine margarine, sugar, egg and almond extract; mix well. Remove dish from freezer and spread mixture over ice cream layer. Top with remaining ice cream. Sprinkle on the remaining 1/2 cup crumbs and toasted almonds. Return to freezer for 2 hours before serving.

NOTE: *This recipe was given to me by Ginny Williamson. My family and friends have enjoyed it on many occasions.*

Yield: 9-12 servings   Lawana Ford

Fruit Pizza

Great for luncheons! Colorful and delicious

1 (20-ounce) package refrigerated cookie dough
1 (8-ounce) package cream cheese, softened
¼ cup powdered sugar
1 (8-ounce) carton frozen whipped topping, thawed
2-3 kiwi fruit, peeled and thinly sliced
1-2 firm bananas, sliced

1 (11-ounce) can mandarin oranges, drained
½ cup red grapes halves
¼ cup sugar
¼ cup orange juice
2 tablespoons water
1 tablespoon lemon juice
1½ teaspoons cornstarch
⅛ teaspoon salt

Preheat oven to 375°. Pat cookie dough into an ungreased 14-inch pizza pan. Bake for 10-12 minutes; cool. In a mixing bowl, beat cream cheese and sugar until smooth. Fold in whipped topping. Spread over crust. Arrange sliced fruit in rows of contrasting colors on top. To make a glaze; combine sugar, orange juice, water, lemon juice, cornstarch and salt in a saucepan. Bring to a boil, stirring constantly for 2 minutes until thickened. Cool. Brush glaze over fruit. Chill in refrigerator. Slice into wedges to serve.

NOTE: *Use any kind of colorful fruit available in season. May also be made in a 9x13-inch casserole baking dish. The glaze prevents fruit from browning and adds a beautiful gloss. For a SHORTCUT FRUIT GLAZE, melt grape or currant jelly and brush on top of fruit.*

Yield: 16-20 servings   Dellene Lyerly Gudger

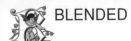
Blueberry Delight

CRUST:

1 (11.1-ounce) box cheesecake mix (package of filling and pie crust mix included)
1/2 cup chopped pecans

1/2 stick melted butter
1 tablespoon sugar
1/4 teaspoon cinnamon
Cooking oil spray

Combine contents of pie crust mix packet with pecans, butter, sugar and cinnamon. Press into 9x12-inch sprayed pan. Set aside.

FILLING:

Packet of filling mix from box of cheesecake mix
1 1/2 cups milk
1 (12-ounce) container frozen whipped topping, thawed

1 (21-ounce) can blueberry pie filling

In a bowl, blend filling mix and milk as directed on box. Place mixture and whipped topping in a blender container. Blend until smooth and light. Pour filling into crust. Spoon pie filling on top. Cover with plastic wrap and refrigerate for 1 hour before serving.

Yield: 12 servings

Bertie Broaddus

♥ Orange Mold Cake

Pretty, delicious and light

1 (1/4-ounce) envelope unflavored gelatin
1/2 cup water
Dash of salt
1 cup sugar
1 (12-ounce) can concentrated orange juice
1/4 cup lemon juice

3 (1.3-ounce) envelopes whipped topping mix
1 large angel food cake, broken into bite sized pieces
Nonstick cooking spray
Seedless grapes
Mandarin orange slices, halved

Combine gelatin, water, salt and sugar in a saucepan. Stir over low heat until gelatin dissolves; add juices. Chill mixture until it is the consistency of egg yolk. Mix whipped topping in a large bowl according to directions; omit vanilla. Fold chilled gelatin mixture into whipped topping. Spray a large mixing bowl with nonstick cooking oil. Cover bottom and sides of bowl with gelatin. Add a layer of cake pieces. Continue layering with gelatin and cake, ending with gelatin. Refrigerate overnight. To loosen cake; run water over outside of bowl and run a flat knife around edge of cake. To serve, unmold onto cake plate and garnish with grapes and orange halves.

Yield: 10-12 servings

Oliver Gilbert Scott

Frozen Lemon Dessert

3	eggs, separated	1/2	pint whipping cream, whipped
4	tablespoons lemon juice		
1/2	cup sugar	1	cup vanilla wafer crumbs

Beat egg yolks, lemon juice and sugar together in a saucepan; cook until thick. In a separate bowl, whip egg whites. Fold whipped cream and egg whites together; then fold in lemon mixture. Pour into buttered freezing tray or large loaf pan that has been lined with vanilla wafer crumbs. Freeze. Slice to serve.

Yield: 6-8 servings   Doris Turner Alexander

Lemon Soufflé

2	(1/4-ounce) envelopes unflavored gelatin	1/8	teaspoon salt
1/2	cup cold water	2	teaspoons grated lemon zest
5	eggs, separated	2	cups heavy cream, whipped
1 1/2	cups sugar		Strawberries or raspberries
1/2	cup lemon juice		Shaved chocolate

In a saucepan combine gelatin and water. Heat until dissolved, stirring frequently. Set aside to cool. Beat yolks and sugar until thick, like a mousse. Add lemon juice slowly, stirring constantly. Beat in cooled gelatin and set aside. In a bowl, beat egg whites with salt until just stiff. Fold into lemon mixture along with zest. Fold in whipped cream and pour into soufflé dish. Chill at least 4 hours. Before serving, garnish top with strawberries or raspberries and shaved chocolate.

Yield: 6-8 servings   Pat Fromen

Italian Cheesecake

1	pound cream cheese	3	tablespoons flour
1	pint sour cream	3	tablespoons cornstarch
1 1/2	pounds ricotta cheese	1 1/2	cups sugar
1	stick butter	1	teaspoon lemon juice
4	eggs	1	teaspoon vanilla

Mix all ingredients in a large bowl with electric mixer until blended. Pour into a buttered 9-inch springform pan. Bake 1 hour at 350°. Leave in oven for 1 hour with heat turned off and door ajar. Refrigerate before serving. Flavor is better if prepared a day or two in advance.

Yield: 10 servings   Dottie Abramowski

Delicious Cheesecake

CRUST:

1¼	cups graham cracker crumbs

¼	cup sugar
⅓	cup butter, softened

Preheat oven to 350°. Mix crumbs, sugar and butter until crumbly. Press into bottom of greased 9-inch springform pan. Bake 10 minutes and allow to cool.

FILLING:

3	(8-ounce) packages cream cheese, softened
¾	cup sugar
4	eggs
1	teaspoon vanilla

1	pint sour cream
¼-½	cup sugar
	Fresh fruit or fruit glaze (optional)

In a bowl beat cream cheese and sugar. Add eggs, one at a time, beating after each. Add vanilla. Pour mixture over cooled crust; bake at 350° for 30 minutes. While cake is baking, whip sour cream and sugar together. At end of baking time, remove cake from oven and spread sour cream mixture over top. Return to oven for an additional 10 minutes. Remove from oven and cool slightly. Refrigerate for at least 2 hours before serving. Tastes best if made 12-24 hours ahead of serving time. Garnish with fresh fruit or fruit glaze if desired.

Yield: 8-12 servings   Adair Doran

Jim's Cheesecake

CHEESECAKE:

1	(8-ounce) package cream cheese, room temperature
1	cup sugar
2	eggs, slightly beaten

½	teaspoon lemon juice
1	(8 or 9-inch) graham cracker crust

Preheat oven to 350°. Beat cream cheese until very fluffy. Gradually add sugar and beat well. Add eggs and lemon juice; mix thoroughly. Put into an 8 or 9-inch graham cracker crust. Bake for 30 minutes.

TOPPING:

1	(8-ounce) container sour cream

1	teaspoon vanilla
2	tablespoons sugar

Mix sour cream, vanilla and sugar. Spread on cheesecake as soon as it is removed from oven. Bake at 350° for 5 minutes to set topping. Cool before serving.

Yield: 6-8 servings   Betty Carli

♥ Chocolate Swirl Cheesecake

1/2	cup graham cracker crumbs	1 1/4	cups sugar
2	(8-ounce) packages fat free cream cheese, softened	1/3	cup lowfat sweetened condensed milk
1	(8-ounce) package light cream cheese, softened	1	egg
1	cup egg substitute	2 1/2	(1-ounce) squares semisweet chocolate, melted

Preheat oven to 325°. Coat a 9-inch springform pan with nonstick spray. Sprinkle bottom of pan with graham cracker crumbs. Using an electric mixer set at medium speed, beat all cream cheese in a mixing bowl until light and fluffy. Add egg substitute, sugar, milk and egg. Beat until smooth, 5-7 minutes. Pour 2 cups of batter into a small bowl; beat in melted chocolate. Pour plain batter into springform pan. Spoon chocolate batter on top of plain batter. Use a knife to swirl chocolate batter through plain batter to marbleize. Place springform pan inside a larger pan filled with 1 inch of water. Bake 45-50 minutes until edges of cake are light brown and center is nearly set. Cool on a wire rack for 30 minutes. Refrigerate overnight. Slice to serve.

Yield: 12 servings

Glenda Askew

Peanut Butter Chocolate Chip Cheesecake

CRUST:

1 1/4	cups finely crushed graham crackers	1/4	cup cocoa
1/3	cup sugar	1/3	cup butter, melted

Mix crumbs, sugar, cocoa and butter. Press into bottom of 9-inch springform pan.

FILLING:

3	(8-ounce) packages cream cheese, softened	2	teaspoons vanilla
1	(14-ounce) can sweetened condensed milk	4	eggs
1	(10-ounce) package peanut butter chips, melted	1	cup mini semisweet chocolate morsels

Preheat oven to 300°. Beat cream cheese in a large mixing bowl until fluffy. Gradually add milk and peanut butter chips. Beat until cream cheese is smooth. Add vanilla, then eggs, one at a time, beating well after each. Stir in mini chips and pour into crust. Bake 55-65 minutes or until center is set. Cool, refrigerate until ready to serve.

Yield: 8-10 servings

Carolyn McDonald

Bailey's Irish Cream Cheesecake

Nonstick vegetable oil spray	1/4 cup sugar
2 cups graham cracker crumbs	6 tablespoons butter, melted

Coat a 9-inch springform pan with oil spray. To make crust, combine crumbs and sugar in pan; add butter; blend with crumbs. Press mixture into bottom and 1-inch up side of pan. Bake at 325° for 7 minutes until light brown.

FILLING:

36 ounces cream cheese	1 cup Bailey's Irish Cream
1²/₃ cups sugar	1 tablespoon vanilla
5 eggs, room temperature	1 cup semisweet chocolate chips

Using electric mixer, beat cream cheese until smooth. Gradually add and mix in sugar. Beat in eggs, one at a time. Blend in Bailey's and vanilla. Sprinkle 1/2 of chips over crust. Spoon in filling; sprinkle with remaining chips. Bake cake at 325° for about 1 hour and 20 minutes until puffed, springy in center and golden brown. Cool completely before serving.

Yield: Serves 10-12   Linda Brown

♥ Easy Lemon Cheesecake

1 (14-ounce) can sweetened condensed milk or nonfat sweetened condensed milk	1 (6-ounce) can frozen lemonade, thawed
1 (8-ounce) container frozen whipped topping, thawed	2 (9-inch) prepared graham cracker pie crusts Cherry or blueberry pie filling (optional)

Mix milk, whipped topping and lemonade in a medium bowl. Pour into crusts. Chill 4-6 hours until set. Top with pie filling, if desired.

Yield: 12 servings   Anne Thurston

♣ Toffee Crunch Ice Cream Cake

1 (12-ounce) package butterscotch chips	6 cups crispy cocoa rice cereal
3/4 cup crunchy peanut butter	1/2 gallon chocolate chip or butter pecan ice cream, softened

In large saucepan melt chips and peanut butter; stir constantly. Stir in cereal; cool slightly. Reserve 1 cup for topping. In large bowl combine ice cream and 5 cups of cereal mixture. Spoon into ungreased 10-inch springform pan. Top with reserved cereal mixture. Freeze until firm. Cut into wedges to serve.

Yield: 16-20 servings

Peter Pumpkin Cheesecake

CRUST:

1½ cups graham cracker crumbs
⅓ cup almonds, ground
½ teaspoon ginger

½ teaspoon cinnamon
⅓ cup butter

Preheat oven to 425°. Combine all ingredients and press into springform cake pan. Bake 10 minutes. Remove from oven; set aside.

FILLING:

4 (8-ounce) packages
  cream cheese, softened
1¼ cups sugar
3 tablespoons maple syrup
3 tablespoons cognac
1 teaspoon ginger
1 teaspoon cinnamon

½ teaspoon nutmeg
4 large eggs,
  room temperature
¼ cup heavy cream
1 cup canned solid pumpkin
  (not pumpkin pie filling)

Beat cream cheese with mixer until smooth. Gradually add sugar, maple syrup, cognac, ginger, cinnamon, and nutmeg; beat well. Add eggs, one at a time, beating well after each. Add cream and pumpkin; blend well. Pour into prepared crust. Reduce oven temperature. Bake at 325° for 45 minutes.

TOPPING:

2 cups sour cream
¼ cup sugar

1 tablespoon maple syrup
1 tablespoon cognac

Preheat oven to 425°. Blend sour cream, sugar, maple syrup and cognac. Spread over cheesecake and bake 10 minutes. Allow cake to cool at room temperature; chill for about 3 hours before removing from pan to serve.

NOTE: *Optional garnishes, 1/4 cup almonds sautéed in 1 tablespoon butter or 12-16 MARZIPAN PUMPKINS (see index).*

Yield: 12-16 servings   Karen Morris

Mama's Hot Fudge Sauce

2 tablespoons butter
3-4 (1-ounce) squares
  unsweetened chocolate
2 cups sugar

⅛ teaspoon salt
1 (12-ounce) can evaporated
  milk
1 teaspoon vanilla

Melt butter and chocolate in saucepan. Add sugar, salt and milk; blend well. Cook over medium heat, stirring constantly until thick and smooth. Remove from heat; add vanilla. Store in refrigerator. To serve, reheat as needed.

Yield: About 2-3 cups   Betsy Knauf

Tiramisu
A delicious and authentic Italian recipe

WHIPPED CREAM:

1 pint heavy whipping cream	2 teaspoons vanilla
1/8 cup sugar	

With electric mixer, whip cream, sugar and vanilla on high speed until firm. Refrigerate until ready for use.

ZABAGLIONE:

4 egg yolks	1 cup mascarpone
4 tablespoons Marsala wine	cheese (optional)
4 tablespoons sugar	

In a double boiler, whisk egg yolks, wine and sugar together until a loose custard forms. Remove from heat and place pan in bowl filled with ice and continue to whisk until chilled. Whisk cheese into custard.

LADYFINGERS:

24 ladyfingers	2 tablespoons Kahlúa liqueur
2 cups espresso	Cocoa powder

Dip ladyfingers in a mixture of espresso and Kahlúa and layer in a shallow casserole dish. Combine Whipped Cream mixture and Zabaglione to make custard. Cover ladyfingers with a layer of custard. Alternate layers of ladyfingers and custard. Lightly sprinkle top with cocoa powder. Chill at least 2 hours or refrigerate overnight to improve flavor. Scoop out portions to serve.

NOTE: *Softened cream cheese may be substituted for mascarpone cheese (an Italian cream cheese), but flavor will be altered. The translation for tiramisu is "carry me up." After tasting this dessert, one may add "to heaven".*

Yield: serves 4-6

Anthony Vitellozzi
General Manager
La Cava Restaurant

Friendship Cake

1 (18.25-ounce) box yellow cake mix	4 large eggs
	2/3 cup vegetable oil
1 (3.4-ounce) package of banana cream instant pudding mix	1 cup chopped pecans
	2 1/3 cups *FRIENDSHIP BRANDIED FRUITS,* (Page 289) drained

Combine cake mix, pudding mix, eggs and oil. Mix well. Add pecans and fruits; stir well. Pour batter into a greased and floured Bundt pan. Bake at 325° for 1-1 1/2 hours, or until done.

Yield: 8-12 servings

Tiramisu Cake

1½ cups cold brewed coffee
5 tablespoons coffee liqueur or almond liqueur
¾ cup non-fat cottage cheese
1 cup mascarpone cheese
2 tablespoons skim milk

3 tablespoons powdered sugar
1 (8-inch) angel food cake, cut horizontally into 4 layers
2 ounces bittersweet chocolate, grated

In a bowl, combine coffee and 3 tablespoons of liqueur. In another bowl, beat cottage cheese until smooth; add mascarpone, skim milk, sugar and remaining 2 tablespoons liqueur. In 8x8-inch glass dish, tear two layers of cake into pieces; place in bottom of dish. Sprinkle half of coffee mixture over cake and top with half the cheese mixture. Tear last two layers of cake and place over cheese mixture. Sprinkle remaining coffee mixture over cake and spread with cheese mixture. Grate chocolate over cake and cover. Refrigerate 24 hours before serving.

Yield: 8 servings

Mrs. Edward H. Clement (Nancy)

Mother's Banana Pudding

¾ cup sugar
2 tablespoons flour
¼ teaspoon salt
2 cups milk

3 eggs, separated
1 teaspoon vanilla
6 bananas, sliced
1 (11-ounce) box vanilla wafers

Combine 1/2 cup sugar, flour and salt in top of double boiler. Stir in milk and cook over boiling water, stirring constantly until thickened. Cook uncovered 15 minutes more, stirring occasionally. Beat egg yolks and gradually stir into hot mixture. Continue cooking and stirring 5 minutes more. Remove from heat and add vanilla. In an 8x8-inch glass casserole dish (or if doubling recipe, in a 9x13-inch dish), alternately layer wafers, bananas and custard. Beat egg whites until stiff but not dry. Gradually add remaining 1/4 cup sugar and beat until stiff peaks form. Pile on top of pudding. Bake at 425° for 5 minutes.

Yield: 6-8 servings

Betsy Crowell

Buttermilk Coconut Pie

6 eggs, beaten
2 cups shredded coconut
1 cup buttermilk

1 cup sugar
2 (9-inch) unbaked pie shells

Combine eggs, coconut, buttermilk and sugar. Stir. Pour into pie shells. Bake at 325° for 40 minutes; or until tops are brown.

Yield: 2 pies (12-14 servings)

Carr Garner

Banana Pudding

3-4 **medium bananas, peeled,
sliced
Frozen lemon juice from
concentrate, thawed**
1 **(14-ounce) can sweetened
condensed milk**

1½ **cups cold water**
1 **(3.4-ounce) box instant
vanilla pudding mix**
2 **cups whipping cream,
whipped**
36 **vanilla wafers**

In a small bowl dip bananas in lemon juice and drain. In a large bowl, combine milk and water. Add pudding mix and beat well. Chill for 5 minutes. Fold in whipped cream. Spoon 1 cup of pudding mixture into a 2 1/2-quart glass serving bowl. Layer with 1/3 each of wafers, bananas and pudding mixture. Repeat layers twice, ending with pudding. Chill before serving.

Yield: 8 servings   Tami Nianouris

Rum Pudding

1 **(¼-ounce) envelope
unflavored gelatin**
¼ **cup boiling water**
2 **eggs, separated**

4 **tablespoons sugar**
½ **cup rum**
1 **cup whipping cream,
whipped**

Dissolve gelatin in boiling water; set aside to cool. Beat egg yolks with sugar in a bowl until pale in color. Add rum and gelatin mixture. When mixture starts to thicken, add the whipped cream. Beat the egg whites until stiff; fold into pudding. Pour into a 4-6 cup mold. Refrigerate at least 2 1/2 hours before serving.

Yield: Serves 4   Diana Potts

Miss Daisy's Boiled Custard

4 **cups whole milk**
4 **large eggs**
1 **cup sugar**

Dash of salt
1 **teaspoon vanilla**

In top of a double boiler, scald milk until almost boiling but do not boil. Beat eggs, sugar and salt in a separate bowl. Add hot milk in a thin stream, beating constantly until milk and egg mixture are well mixed. Return to top of double boiler, cook about 10 minutes, stirring frequently, until mixture thickens and coats a spoon. Do not overcook or mixture will curdle. Cool 10 minutes; stir in vanilla. Refrigerate. Serve in custard bowls, on cake, or with fruit. For a rich custard; substitute half and half for part of the whole milk.

Yield: 6-8 servings   Anne-Courtney Miller

♥ Ev's Banana Pudding

1	(6-ounce) package instant vanilla pudding mix
1	cup low fat milk
1	(16-ounce) carton low fat sour cream
3/4	teaspoon almond extract
1	(11-ounce) box vanilla wafers

3-4 bananas, sliced
1 (8-ounce) container frozen light whipped topping, thawed
1/2 (6-ounce) package frozen coconut for garnish

Beat pudding mix, milk and sour cream with electric mixer. Add almond extract and allow to set. In a glass dish, alternately layer wafers, pudding and bananas until filled, ending with pudding. Cover with whipped topping and sprinkle with coconut. Refrigerate. Chill well before serving.

NOTE: *This is a specialty of Evelyn Harrison.*

Yield: Serves 8-10   Sandy Lee

Marshmallow Fluff

15 graham crackers, crushed
1 pound miniature marshmallows
1 cup milk

1 (16-ounce) container frozen whipped topping, thawed
1 (16-ounce) can crushed pineapple, drained
1/2 cup finely chopped walnuts

Put 3/4 of crumbs in bottom of a 12x6-inch glass dish, save remainder for top of dessert. Microwave and stir marshmallows and milk until melted and blended. Cool. Combine whipped topping and pineapple. Mix all ingredients together; pour on top of crumbs in dish. Garnish with remaining crumbs and walnuts. Refrigerate overnight. Serve chilled.

Yield: 12 servings   Mrs. Dixie Nickell

Crème de Menthe Parfait
Simple and delicious

1 quart vanilla ice cream, softened
1 pint lime sherbet, softened
1/4 cup green crème de menthe

1/2 (8-ounce) container frozen whipped topping, thawed
Fresh strawberries and mint sprigs for garnish

Combine all ingredients in electric blender container. Process at medium speed until well mixed. Spoon into parfait glasses and place in freezer 3-4 hours. To serve, top with a fresh strawberry and sprig of mint.

Yield: 6 servings   Becky Reitz McKinley

Espresso Frozen Mousse
Decadent

MOUSSE:

4	teaspoons instant coffee	1	cup whipping cream, whipped
1	tablespoon hot water		
4	eggs, separated	1	tablespoon coffee liqueur
1/2	cup sugar		

Dissolve coffee in hot water and set aside. Beat egg whites until stiff. Gradually add sugar, beating until firm glossy peaks form. Fold in coffee mixture. Beat egg yolks until thick and lemon colored. Whip cream until stiff and blend in liqueur. Gently but thoroughly, fold together egg whites, yolks and whipped cream. Pour into a glass bowl, cover with plastic wrap and freeze.

CHOCOLATE SAUCE:

1/2	cup butter or margarine	1	cup powdered sugar
2 1/2	ounces unsweetened chocolate	1/3	cup milk

Melt butter and chocolate in top of double boiler over simmering water. Slowly add sugar alternately with milk. Cook for 30 minutes, stirring occasionally. Use immediately or refrigerate and then heat before serving.

TOPPINGS:

Whipped cream   Chopped pecans
Shaved chocolate

Before serving mousse, decorate by topping with warmed chocolate sauce, whipped cream, shaved chocolate and chopped pecans.

NOTE: *CHOCOLATE SAUCE doubles easily and keeps for weeks in refrigerator.*

Yield: 6-8 servings   Marie Fork

Kahlúa Chocolate Mousse

5	eggs, separated	3	tablespoons sugar
4	ounces semisweet chocolate chips	1/2	pint heavy cream
		1-2	tablespoons coffee liqueur

Beat egg yolks. Melt chocolate chips in top of double boiler. Add to beaten egg yolks and mix. In another bowl, add sugar to cream and whip until peaks form. Add whipped cream to chocolate mixture. Beat egg whites until stiff; fold into chocolate mixture. Add liqueur. Spoon into a bowl or stemmed glasses and refrigerate for at least 10 hours before serving.

Yield: 6-8 servings   Lesleigh Drye

Coffee & Fudge Ice Cream Pie

1	quart coffee ice cream, softened	1	(6-ounce) prepared chocolate cookie crust
1/2	(8-ounce) tub frozen whipped topping, thawed	1/2	cup fudge ice cream topping

Fold ice cream and whipped topping together and spread evenly into crust. Drizzle fudge topping over ice cream mixture. Freeze at least 8 hours before serving.

Yield: 6 servings

Lisa Ganem

Cheesecake Ice Cream

A requested recipe for Little League socials

4	eggs	2	bags ice
1	cup sugar		Electric ice cream freezer
4	teaspoons vanilla	1	large bag coarse rock salt
4	cups sour cream		

Mix eggs, sugar, vanilla and sour cream together. Pour into cylinder of ice cream freezer. Fill outside container 3/4 full of ice; add 1 cup coarse rock salt, layering ice and salt. Allow to stand several minutes before starting freezer on low speed. Turn slowly until a slight pull is felt. Then mix at triple speed for 5-6 minutes. Repack with ice and salt as needed. Let "ripen" several hours in freezer cylinder. Serve frozen.

NOTE: *This is my version of a recipe from a Julia Child's television show seen in the 1970's.*

Yield: 6-8 servings

Mrs. Eugene (Debra) McKinley

Toasted Pecan Balls

1	scoop vanilla ice cream	3	tablespoons hot fudge sauce
2	tablespoons finely chopped toasted pecans		

For each serving, roll scoop of ice cream in chopped nuts until well coated. Repeat process to make as many scoops as you will need and place in a plastic container. Freeze until ready to serve. To serve, heat your favorite hot fudge sauce. Place pecan ball in serving dish and top with hot fudge sauce.

Yield: 1 or more balls

Joanne Eichelberger

Nutty Eskimo Ice Cream Dessert

10   (3.5-ounce) or 14 (2-ounce) ice cream sandwiches

1/2 cup Kahlúa, chocolate or almond liqueur

1   cup crushed crispy peanut butter finger or toffee candy bars; or chocolate coated crispy rice baking pieces, crushed

2/3-3/4 cup chocolate syrup for ice cream

1   (8-ounce) container extra creamy, regular or lite frozen whipped topping, thawed

1   cup chopped pecans

1   (7.25-ounce) bottle chocolate magic shell (instant hardening) ice cream topping

Arrange sandwiches in a 11 3/4-x2 1/2-inch glass or re-usable foil pan. Drizzle half the liqueur on sandwiches. Turn sandwiches over. Drizzle with remainder of liqueur. Evenly sprinkle on crushed candy. Drizzle syrup over candy. Spread topping evenly over candy, covering to edge of dish. Sprinkle on nuts. Drizzle bottle of magic shell coating over topping. Tilt pan to evenly coat to edges of dessert. Freeze overnight until firm. Cut into squares to serve.

Yield: 10-12 servings

Flaky Two Crust Pie Pastry
A 4-H prize winning pie crust!

2   cups flour, sifted

1   teaspoon salt

2/3 cup plus 2 tablespoons solid vegetable shortening

5   tablespoons ice cold water

Place flour and salt in a mixing bowl. Add shortening; with a pastry blender cut in shortening until mixture is consistency of coarse crumbs. Sprinkle water over mixture, a tablespoon at a time. Mix lightly with a fork. Form dough into a ball with fingers. The secret to flaky crust is to handle dough as little as possible. Divide ball into 2 equal parts. Place 1 ball on lightly floured surface. Starting in the center, roll dough into a 11-12-inch circle. Place in a 9-inch pie pan and trim off excess. A decorative edge can be made by fluting dough or pressing top edge with tines of a fork. Repeat process for a second pastry shell or for a top crust for a filled pie. If baking shells prior to filling, bake at 450° for 12-15 minutes or until lightly browned.

NOTE: *For a SWEET NUT PIE PASTRY, add 1 tablespoon sugar and 2/3 cup finely chopped pecans or walnuts to basic recipe above. For a great CHEESE PIE CRUST for meat pies, add 2/3 cup grated cheddar cheese to basic recipe.*

Yield: Pastry for a 2 crust pie or 2 (9-inch) pie shells

Marvelous
Miniature Desserts

Dainty Desserts, Cookies for Pleasure;
Chewy Squares & Bars to Treasure

B
L
E
S
S
I
N
G
S

🧍 🎈 Crafty Mint Cookies
Stamp and design your own!

1 cup butter, softened	2 cups flour
1 cup white or pastel colored mint candies, finely crushed or pulverized	1 tablespoon white or decorative colored sugars

In a bowl, beat butter until fluffy. Add crushed candies to butter; blend well. Add flour. Mix well. Chill dough. Preheat oven to 300°. Place dough in a plastic zip-lock bag floured with powdered sugar; roll flat to a 9x9-inch square with a rolling pin. Chill. Leaving dough square in bag, cut and remove top layer of plastic bag. Sprinkle surface of dough with your choice of sugars and cut into 1 1/2-inch squares. Using assorted small cookie or canapé cutters (dipped in powdered sugar) or cookie stamps, press design on top of each square. Place cookies 1-inch apart on ungreased air-bake cookie sheet. Bake 18-22 minutes (do not overbake) until cookie bottoms are light brown. Cool.

Yield: 3 dozen

🧍 🎈 Cookie Candy Canes
Fun to make

1½ cup powdered sugar	1 egg
1 cup butter or margarine, softened	2½ cups flour
1 teaspoon vanilla	½ teaspoon red food coloring
1½-2 teaspoons almond extract or peppermint extract	½ cup crushed candy canes Powdered sugar for rolling cookies

Preheat oven to 375°. In a large bowl, mix 1 cup of the powdered sugar with margarine, vanilla, almond extract and egg. Stir in flour. Divide dough into 2 equal portions. Tint 1 portion with red food coloring. Chill dough. To make each candy cane, shape 1 teaspoon of uncolored dough into a 4-inch rope by rolling back and forth with hands on a flat surface, lightly floured with powdered sugar. Repeat the process with red dough. Lay 1 red and 1 uncolored rope side by side and twist together. Place on an air-bake cookie sheet. Curve the end of cookie to form cane hook. Bake 10 minutes or until lightly golden. Mix crushed candy and the remaining 1/2 cup powdered sugar and sprinkle over warm cookies. Remove from cookie sheet and store in cookie tin.

Yield: 4 dozen

🎈 Wonderful Chocolate Chip Cookies

1	cup soft butter or margarine	1	teaspoon baking soda
³/₄	cup sugar	¹/₂	teaspoon salt
³/₄	cup light or dark brown sugar	1	(12-ounce) package semi-sweet chocolate chips
1	teaspoon vanilla	³/₄	cup chopped pecans or walnuts
2	eggs		
2¹/₄	cups flour		

Preheat oven to 375°. Cream butter, sugar, brown sugar and vanilla. Add eggs and mix. Gradually add flour, baking soda and salt. Stir in chocolate chips and nuts. Drop by spoonfuls onto ungreased cookie sheet. Bake 7-10 minutes. Remove from pan and cool on rack.

NOTE: *Multi-colored candy coated chocolate baking bits or any other flavored chips may be substituted for chocolate chips.*

Yield: 6 dozen   Emily G. Cook

Cherry Truffle Tea Cake Cookies
A wonderful party treat

1¹/₂	cups powdered sugar	¹/₃	cup finely chopped maraschino cherries, drained (reserve juice)
2	cups butter or margarine, softened	¹/₄-¹/₂	teaspoon almond extract
3²/₃	cups flour		
¹/₄	teaspoon salt		

In a large bowl, cream sugar and butter until fluffy. Add flour and salt; stir until mixed. Combine cherries and almond extract with dough, kneading to blend. Cover and refrigerate for 30 minutes. Preheat oven to 350°. Shape dough into 1-inch balls and place on ungreased air-bake cookie sheet. Bake for 8-10 minutes, until done but not browned. Remove from cookie sheet quickly and cool slightly.

GLAZE:

¹/₄	cup powdered sugar	1¹/₄	teaspoon water
1	teaspoon reserved cherry juice	¹/₄	teaspoon almond extract

Mix sugar, juice, water and extract in a small bowl. With a spoon, drizzle glaze over each cookie.

NOTE: *For CHOCOLATE TRUFFLE NUT COOKIES, omit cherries and almond extract from cookie dough and omit glaze. Wrap small pieces of dough around each of 48 chocolate covered peanuts before baking. Bake as above. Glaze with a melted mixture of 1/4 cup chocolate chips, 1 tablespoon creamy peanut butter and 1 teaspoon vegetable shortening.*

Yield: 3 1/2 - 4 dozen

Butter Cookies

1 cup soft butter	1/2 teaspoon baking powder
1/4 cup powdered sugar	1/2 teaspoon vanilla
2 cups flour	

Cream butter and sugar. Add flour, baking powder and vanilla. Shape dough into 2 rolls; wrap in waxed paper. Refrigerate overnight. Preheat oven to 350º. Cut rolls into 1/4-inch thick slices and place on cookie sheet. Bake for 10 minutes.

ICING:

3 tablespoons butter	2 teaspoons vanilla
1 cup powdered sugar	Several drops milk

Mix butter, sugar, vanilla and milk to thin if needed. Spread on cooled cookies.

Yield: 2 dozen   Cindi Graham

🧍 🎈 Gingerbread Men

A holiday favorite for kids of all ages

1/4 cup butter	1/2 teaspoon cinnamon
1/2 cup brown sugar	1/2 teaspoon salt
1/2 cup dark molasses	1/4 cup water
3 1/2 cups flour	Raisins, candied cherries and
1 teaspoon ginger	cinnamon candies for
1 teaspoon baking soda	decorating
1/4 teaspoon ground cloves	

In a large mixing bowl, cream butter and sugar. Beat in molasses. Sift together flour, ginger, soda, cloves, cinnamon and salt. Add to butter mixture in 3 stages, alternating with water. Mix well. Chill dough for 1 hour. Preheat oven to 350°. Roll dough on a floured surface and cut out cookies with gingerbread men cookie cutters. Decorate with raisins, candied cherries, cinnamon candies, nuts, etc. Transfer to a greased cookie sheet and bake for 7-8 minutes.

NOTE: *To avoid breakage, small children may prepare cookies directly on a greased cookie sheet. Roll out dough, cut out cookies, remove excess dough, decorate and bake cookies, all on the same baking pan. Our family still loves to make gingerbread men for the holidays, even though "children" are the grown type.*

Yield: 12 medium size   Karen Busby

Christmas Cookies
Holiday cut - outs for children

1/2 cup butter, softened	3/4 cup sugar
1/2 teaspoon salt	2 eggs, well-beaten
1 teaspoon vanilla	2 1/2 cups flour, sifted

Cream butter, salt, vanilla and sugar with electric mixer on medium speed until light and fluffy. Add eggs and beat well. Add flour and mix well. Place in covered bowl and store in refrigerator overnight. Preheat oven to 350º. Remove about 1/3 of dough and roll out on lightly floured board to 1/4-inch thickness. Using cookie cutters that have been dipped in flour, cut out cookies. Place carefully on greased baking sheet. Bake for 8 minutes, or until lightly browned. Cool cookies on wire racks. Repeat procedure until all dough is used.

ICING:

1 (16-ounce) box powdered sugar Food coloring	Milk Cookie decorations (sprinkles, nonpareils, silver balls, etc.)

Mix sugar, food coloring and enough milk until consistency to spread on cookies (thin enough to spread easily and leaves no knife marks when icing sets up, but thick enough so it won't run). Spread on cooled cookies. Sprinkle with decorations while icing is soft. Let cookies sit several hours before storing in gift boxes.

NOTE: *If dough becomes too soft, refrigerate to chill. This recipe was created by my mother, Dorothy Bailey Ginn, for her children's Christmas cookies.*

Yield: 3 dozen   Tom Ginn

Holiday Fruit Cookies
A Christmas must!

1/2 cup shortening	1/4 cup buttermilk
1 cup brown sugar	1 cup raisins
1 egg (or 1/4 cup egg substitute), slightly beaten	3/4 cup pecans
	1 cup candied red and green cherries, cut in half
1 3/4 cups sifted flour	
1/2 teaspoon salt	1/2 cup coconut
1/2 teaspoon baking soda	

Cream shortening and sugar. Add egg. Sift flour, salt and soda into a bowl. Add milk to sugar mixture; then add flour mixture and blend well. Add raisins, pecans, cherries and coconut; mix, then chill. Preheat oven to 375°. Drop by teaspoonfuls onto greased cookie sheet. Bake for 13 minutes. Cool.

Yield: 4 dozen   Gloe Bertram

B
L
E
S
S
I
N
G
S

Hungarian Butter Horns
A delightful nut pastry

1	(1/4-ounce) package dry yeast	1/2	cup sour cream
2	tablespoons warm water	2	teaspoons vanilla
4	cups flour	3	egg whites
1/2	teaspoon salt	3/4	cup sugar
1 1/2	cups butter	1	cup ground pecans
3	egg yolks, beaten		Powdered sugar

Dissolve yeast in water. Sift flour and salt into mixing bowl. Cut in butter to make coarse crumbs. Blend in dissolved yeast, egg yolks, sour cream and 1 teaspoon of the vanilla. Dough will be quite stiff. Wrap in waxed paper and chill 1 hour. To make filling, beat egg whites until foamy. Gradually beat in sugar until stiff. Fold in nuts and remaining teaspoon vanilla and set aside. To make cookies, divide dough into 12 equal parts, each about the size of a 2-inch ball. Roll each part into a 6 to 7-inch circle on a board. Sprinkle with powdered sugar. Cut each circle into 6 wedges. Spread about a teaspoon of filling on each wedge. Beginning at wide edge, roll up pastry. Place pointed edge down onto lightly greased baking sheet. Bake in oven preheated to 375° for 12-15 minutes or until a light golden brown. Sprinkle with powdered sugar.

Yield: 6 dozen   Flora Lynn Abernethy

🎈 Lollipop Cookies

1	(32-ounce) roll refrigerated sugar or white chocolate chip cookie dough	1	(12-ounce) can buttercream frosting
			Food coloring (optional)
8	12-inch, or longer wooden sticks (without sharp points)	1/4-1/3	cup water or milk (optional)

Preheat oven to 350°. Slice cookie roll into 16 pieces. Place one slice on ungreased air-bake cookie sheet. Place stick end flat, centered on cookie. To form a 3-4-inch lollipop cookie, place another slice of cookie dough on top, pressing flat, sealing the two edges together. Repeat process, leaving a 3-inch space between cookies on pan. Bake for 10-15 minutes. Cool for 1 minute. Remove from pan, decorate as desired with frosting (tinted with food coloring if desired) or glaze cookies with a mixture of frosting thinned with water. Dry 4 hours or overnight.

NOTE: *Cookies may be formed into circle, heart, pumpkin, or egg shapes. Tie sticks with colorful ribbons. Attach gift tags and use as favors for children's parties, or present a gift bouquet to someone special of "long-stemmed cookie flowers" wrapped up in tissue in a florist box.*

Yield: 8 cookie lollipops

Melting Moments

1 **cup soft butter**	3/4 **cup cornstarch**
1/3 **cup powdered sugar**	1 **cup flour**

Cream butter and sugar. Add sifted cornstarch and flour. Mix well and chill 1 hour. Preheat oven to 350°. Roll into small balls and place on ungreased cookie sheet. Bake for 15-20 minutes. Cool on wire rack.

FROSTING:

1 **cup powdered sugar**	1 **tablespoon lemon juice**
1 **tablespoon melted butter**	1 **tablespoon orange juice**

Mix sugar, butter and juices. Frost cooled cookies.

Yield: 3 dozen   Mrs. Stuart (Annette) Snider

Grandmom Jinnie's Oatmeal Chocolate Chip Cookies

2 **cups flour**	1 1/2 **cups brown sugar**
1 1/2 **cups oatmeal**	3/4 **cup sugar**
1 **teaspoon baking soda**	2 **eggs**
1/2 **teaspoon salt**	1 **tablespoon vanilla**
1 **cup butter flavored vegetable shortening**	3/4 **(12-ounce) package chocolate chips**

Preheat oven to 350°. Thoroughly mix flour, oatmeal, baking soda and salt. In a separate bowl, cream shortening and sugars until fluffy. Add eggs and vanilla. Gradually add the flour mixture and chips. Drop by tablespoonfuls onto an ungreased baking sheet. Bake at 350° for 6-7 minutes. Cool.

Yield: 2 1/2 - 3 dozen   Karen Wood

● No Bake Oatmeal Cookies

1 **stick butter**	1/8 **teaspoon salt**
2 **cups sugar**	1/2 **teaspoon vanilla**
3 **tablespoons cocoa**	1/2 **cup peanut butter**
1/2 **cup milk**	3 **cups quick cooking oats**

Mix butter, sugar, cocoa, milk and salt in a saucepan. Bring mixture to a boil. Boil for 1 minute. Remove from heat; add vanilla and peanut butter. Stir in oats and mix well. Drop by spoonfuls onto waxed paper. Cool.

Yield: 2 1/2 - 3 dozen   Janie Golden

🔔 Oatmeal Party Cookies

4 cups brown sugar	4 teaspoons baking powder
4 cups sugar	1 teaspoon vanilla
1¾ cups solid vegetable shortening	⅛ cup water
1¾ cups margarine or butter	4 cups coconut
1 teaspoon salt	6 cups old fashioned oatmeal (not quick cook)
10 eggs	8-9 cups flour
4 teaspoons baking soda	

Preheat oven to 350°. Blend sugars, shortenings, salt, eggs, baking soda, baking powder, vanilla and water with an electric mixer. Add coconut, oats and flour; mix with hands. Using ice cream scoop as a measure, drop cookies on baking sheet and flatten to saucer size. Bake for 8 minutes or until light brown. Cool on pan a couple of minutes before removing.

NOTE: *Dough will keep overnight in refrigerator. Cookies freeze well.*

Yield: Over 12 dozen   Ruth Philpott

Orange Cookies

1 cup margarine	4 cups flour
2 cups sugar	1 cup sour milk
2 eggs	Juice of one orange
1 teaspoon baking soda	Zest of one orange
2 teaspoons baking powder	

Preheat oven to 375°. Cream margarine, sugar and eggs. Sift together baking soda, baking powder and flour. Stir dry ingredients into creamed mixture alternately with milk, orange juice and zest. Drop by teaspoonfuls onto greased cookie sheet. Bake for 15 minutes.

FROSTING:

1 (16-ounce) box powdered sugar	Zest of one orange
Juice of one orange	1 tablespoon melted butter

Mix sugar, juice, zest and butter until smooth. Spread frosting on cookies as they cool.

NOTE: *This was a favorite recipe of my husband's grandmother, who was born in 1885.*

Yield: About 3 dozen   Mrs. Eugene (Debra) McKinley

Oatmeal Tollhouse Cookies

A family favorite

1	cup solid vegetable shortening	1	teaspoon baking soda
3/4	cup sugar	1	teaspoon salt
6	tablespoons brown sugar	2	cups oatmeal
1	teaspoon vanilla	1	(12-ounce) bag chocolate chips
1/2	teaspoon water		Non-stick vegetable cooking spray
2	eggs		
1 1/2	cups flour		

Preheat oven to 350°-375°. Cream shortening, sugars, vanilla and water. Add eggs, one at a time. Sift together flour, baking soda and salt. Gradually add flour mixture to creamed mixture. Slowly stir in oatmeal and chips. For each cookie, spoon 1-1 1/2 tablespoons of dough onto a cookie sheet greased with non-stick vegetable cooking spray. Bake for 8-10 minutes. Watch closely, cookies brown quickly. Cool.

NOTE: *These have been THE favorite in our house for 25 years.*

Yield: 3 dozen   Marna Steinman

Peanut Butter Blossoms

Great treat for kids

1/2	cup sugar	1	teaspoon vanilla
1/2	cup brown sugar	1 3/4	cups flour
1/2	cup solid vegetable shortening	1	teaspoon baking soda
1/2	cup peanut butter	1/2	teaspoon salt
1	egg	24-30	chocolate candy kisses (optional)
2	tablespoons milk		Sugar for coating cookies

Preheat oven to 375°. Cream sugars, shortening and peanut butter in a large bowl. Add egg, milk and vanilla; beat well. Add flour, baking soda and salt. Beat on low speed with electric mixer. Shape dough into balls, using a teaspoonful for each. Roll balls in sugar and place on ungreased cookie sheet. Bake for 10-12 minutes. Top each cookie with a candy kiss, pressing candy down into cookie. Cool.

NOTE: *These cookies have gone to college many times and now they will be on hand for grandchildren. They keep well in a tin. To make Peanut Butter Cookies, omit chocolate kisses.*

Yield: 2-2 1/2 dozen   Marna Steinman

Crisscross Peanut Butter Cookies

B
L
E
S
S
I
N
G
S

1	cup butter or margarine	1	teaspoon vanilla
1	cup peanut butter	1	teaspoon allspice
1	cup sugar	2½	cups flour
1	cup brown sugar	1½	teaspoon baking soda
2	eggs	½	teaspoon salt

Preheat oven to 375°. Cream butter, peanut butter, sugars, eggs, vanilla and allspice. Add flour, baking soda and salt; mix well. Shape dough into 1-inch balls and place 2-inches apart on ungreased cookie sheet. Press cookies with a fork to make a crisscross pattern on top. Bake for 10-12 minutes. Cool slightly and remove from pan.

Yield: About 4 dozen   Robbin Curtis

Pineapple Puff Cookies

2	packages Anginetti cookies, split with a serrated knife	1	(8-ounce) carton frozen whipped topping, thawed
1	(8-ounce) package cream cheese	1	(20-ounce) can crushed pineapple, drained
3	tablespoons sugar		

Lay cookie bottoms side by side in a 9x13-inch pan, covering the bottom. Whip cream cheese and sugar until blended. Add whipped topping and pineapple. Blend until smooth. Drop by teaspoonfuls onto each cookie. Top with remaining cookie halves. Refrigerate one hour before serving.

NOTE: *Anginetti cookies are a "cream puff pastry-like" cookie.*

Yield: 40 cookies   Juli Anne Alfieri

🎄 🎈 Bird's Nest Macaroon Cookies

2	(8-ounce) cans or packages flaked coconut (not frozen)	1	(14-ounce) can sweetened condensed milk
	Few drops green food coloring	36	miniature jellybeans, assorted colors
2	tablespoons self-rising flour		

Preheat oven to 350°. In a mixing bowl, toss coconut with food coloring until tinted as desired. Stir in flour and milk, blending well. Spoon mixture into 1-inch mounds on a greased cookie sheet. Indent centers slightly. Bake 10 minutes. Remove from oven and top each "cookie nest" with 3 jellybeans. Cool.

Yield: 1 dozen

Ultimate Cookies

³/₄ **cup raisins**	2 **teaspoons grated orange peel**
3 **tablespoons orange juice**	1 **cup flour**
¹/₂ **cup soft butter**	1 **teaspoon baking soda**
³/₄ **cup sugar**	1¹/₂ **cups rolled oats**
1 **egg**	

Combine raisins and orange juice; let stand overnight. Preheat oven to 350°. Cream butter and sugar until fluffy. Beat in egg and orange peel. Mix flour and baking soda; stir into butter mixture. Add the raisins in orange juice and the oats. Mix well. Drop by teaspoonfuls 2-inches apart onto greased baking sheet. Flatten slightly. Bake 10-12 minutes. Cool.

GLAZE:

1 **teaspoon vegetable oil**	8 **ounces white chocolate baking chips**

Melt oil and chips over low heat. Dip cookies, one at a time, into mixture, covering about 1/3 of cookie. Place on waxed paper until glaze is set.

Yield: 2 1/2 dozen   Mary Eichelberger

● White Chocolate Cookies

1 **pound white chocolate**	1¹/₂ **cups crispy rice cereal**
1 **(12-ounce) jar crunchy peanut butter**	1 **cup roasted unsalted peanuts**

Melt chocolate in a double boiler. In a bowl, mix peanut butter, cereal and peanuts. Add melted chocolate and mix well. Drop by tablespoonfuls onto waxed paper to cool. Chill cookies in refrigerator if they do not harden at room temperature.

Yield: 3 1/2 dozen   Hannah Baker

Sugar Cookies

1 **cup margarine**	3 **cups flour**
1¹/₂ **cups sugar**	1 **teaspoon baking powder**
2 **eggs**	1¹/₂ **teaspoon vanilla**

Cream margarine and sugar. Add eggs and vanilla; beat well. Sift together flour and baking powder; add to creamed mixture. Chill dough. Preheat oven to 400°. Roll dough out thin, and cut into desired shapes. Bake 6-8 minutes or until lightly browned. Remove cookies immediately from pan. Cool.

Yield: 5-6 dozen   Jane Dutton

Apricot Bars
A real treat

CRUST:

1/2	cup soft butter	1	cup flour
1/4	cup sugar		

Preheat oven to 350°. Mix butter, sugar and flour until crumbly. Press crust into 8x8x2-inch pan. Bake for 25 minutes or until lightly browned.

FILLING:

1	cup dried apricots	1	cup light brown sugar
1/3	cup flour	1/2	teaspoon vanilla
1/2	teaspoon baking powder	1/2	cup chopped nuts
1/4	teaspoon salt		Powdered sugar
2	eggs, beaten		

Rinse apricots; cover with water in a saucepan. Boil 10 minutes; drain and chop. Set aside. Sift together flour, baking powder and salt. Beat eggs and brown sugar in separate bowl. Add flour mixture and mix well. Mix in apricots, vanilla and nuts. Spread over crust and bake at 350° for 30 minutes. Cool and cut into bars or squares. Roll in powdered sugar.

NOTE: *Freezes well. Best made with butter.*

Yield: 20   Ruth Walters Hanchette

Choco Chewy Scotch Bars
Rich, party time dessert

1	(12-ounce) package semi-sweet chocolate chips	2	eggs
1	(15-ounce) can sweetened condensed milk	2	cups flour
		1	teaspoon salt
1	cup plus 2 tablespoons butter or margarine	1	teaspoon vanilla
2 1/4	cups packed brown sugar	1/2	cup chopped pecans or walnuts

Over boiling water in a double boiler, melt chocolate pieces; add condensed milk and 2 tablespoons of the butter. Blend until smooth. Set aside. In medium saucepan, melt 1 cup butter. Add brown sugar and eggs. Mix well. Blend in flour, salt, vanilla and nuts. Mix well. Spread half of dough in greased and floured 9x13-inch (metal only) pan. Drizzle chocolate mixture over dough in pan. Dab top of chocolate mixture with remaining brown sugar dough. Swirl slightly with top of knife. Bake at 350° for 30-35 minutes until golden brown. Cool and cut into bars. Recipe may not be doubled; make two separate batches.

Yield: 48   Lollie Wesner Streiff

Cappuccino Almond Biscotti

So crunchy! Great with coffee

1	stick butter, softened	2½	cups flour
½	cup sugar	½	cup almond paste
¼	cup brown sugar	2	teaspoons baking powder
2	eggs	¼	teaspoon salt
1	teaspoon almond extract	½	cup chopped pecans
1-1½	tablespoons cappuccino flavored instant coffee	½	cup mini chocolate chips

Preheat oven to 350°. Cream butter and sugars until fluffy. Add eggs, extract and coffee powder. Beat well. In separate bowl, combine flour, almond paste, baking powder and salt. Blend in nuts and chips. Combine and blend flour and butter mixtures to form a dough. Lightly knead on floured surface; divide in half and shape into 2 (8x4x3/4-1-inch) oval loaves. Bake on uncoated air-bake cookie sheet for 40-45 minutes until firm. Remove from oven. Cool 10 minutes. On a cutting board, cut loaves crosswise into 3/4-inch thick slices. Place cut side up on cookie sheet. Bake at 350° for 10 minutes on each side. Cool; store in air tight container. May be frozen.

NOTE: *If desired, brush loaves with beaten egg and sprinkle with cinnamon-sugar before baking. For CHOCOLATE COATED BISCOTTI, dip half the biscotti in a large mug filled with melted chocolate or white chocolate baking morsels. Dry on wax paper.*

Yield: 24 biscotti

Chocolate Chip Cheese Loaves

A great spread for cookies and tea bread

3	(8-ounce) packages cream cheese, softened	1	tablespoon cinnamon
1½	cups semi-sweet chocolate chips	1¼	cups chopped pecans
1	cup powdered sugar, sifted	1	(7-ounce) milk chocolate candy bar, coarsely grated
			Gingersnaps

Combine cream cheese, chocolate chips, sugar and cinnamon, stirring until blended. Divide mixture in half. Spoon each half into a plastic wrap-lined 7 1/2x3-inch loaf pan. Wrap and chill 5 hours or until ready to serve. To serve, invert each loaf onto a serving plate and remove plastic wrap. Press pecans around sides of loaves. Sprinkle grated chocolate on top. Serve with gingersnaps.

Yield: 2 (2-cup) loaves   Laura Murph

Coconut Bars

1/2 cup butter or margarine	1 1/2 teaspoon vanilla
1 1/2 cups brown sugar	2 tablespoons flour
1 cup sifted flour	1/2 teaspoon baking powder
2 eggs	1 cup chopped pecans
1/8 teaspoon salt	1 cup shredded coconut

Preheat oven to 325°. Beat butter, 1/2 cup of the brown sugar and flour until well blended. Press into greased 8x8-inch pan. Bake for 20 minutes. Bars will be only partially done, do not brown. Beat eggs, salt, remaining cup of brown sugar, vanilla, flour and baking powder until light and fluffy. Add pecans. Spread batter over the partially baked crust. Sprinkle with coconut. Bake at 325° for 20 minutes until browned. Cool. Cut into squares. Freezes well.

Yield: 24   Gloe Bertram

Congo Squares

3/4 cup butter or margarine	2 1/2 cups flour
1 pound light brown sugar	1 teaspoon vanilla
2 eggs	1 (12-ounce) package
1/4 cup milk	chocolate chips
1/2 teaspoon salt	1 cup pecans, chopped
2 teaspoons baking powder	

Preheat oven to 325°. Melt butter. Using electric mixer, combine sugar with butter. Add eggs and beat. Add milk, salt, baking powder, flour and vanilla. Add chocolate chips and nuts. Spread mixture in well greased and floured 9x13-inch pan. Bake for 20-25 minutes. Cool, then cut into squares. Freezes well.

Yield: 15-20 squares   Daisy P. McDowell

Fudge Brownies

1 cup margarine	2 teaspoons vanilla
2 cups sugar	4 eggs
3/4 cup cocoa	1/2 cup chopped nuts (optional)
1 cup flour	

Preheat oven to 350°. Melt margarine. Add sugar, cocoa, flour and vanilla. Add eggs and mix well. Stir in nuts. Pour into a 9x13-inch greased pan. Bake for 20-25 minutes. Do not over bake. Cut into squares when cool. Freezes well.

Yield: 24 bars   Sally B. Bullock

Caramel Fudge Pecan Brownies

2	cups sifted flour	1	ounce semi-sweet chocolate
1/4	teaspoon salt	1/2	cup sugar
1/2	teaspoon baking powder	2	cups brown sugar
2	sticks butter	4	extra large eggs
4	ounces unsweetened chocolate	2	teaspoons vanilla
		2	cups toasted pecans

Preheat oven to 350°. Sift together flour, salt and baking powder. Place butter and chocolate in heavy saucepan over low heat. Stir occasionally until melted. Stir in sugars. Remove from heat before adding eggs one at a time. Blend in vanilla and dry ingredients. Fold in pecans. Line a 9x13-inch pan with foil. Melt small amount of butter in bottom of pan in the oven. Pour mixture into pan, spread and smooth top. Bake for 40-45 minutes until toothpick inserted in center comes out clean. Cool on rack. Place in refrigerator 1 hour or longer until brownies are firm. Cut into squares; serve.

Yield: 48 small or 24 large bars   Lucy Thurston Lowe

Delicious Brownies

1	cup sugar	1	teaspoon vanilla
1/2	cup margarine	2/3	cup flour
1/3	cup cocoa	1/2	teaspoon baking powder
1	teaspoon instant coffee	1/4	teaspoon salt
2	eggs	1/2	cup chopped nuts

Preheat oven to 350°. In medium saucepan combine sugar, margarine, cocoa and coffee. Cook and stir over medium heat until margarine melts. Cool 5 minutes. Add eggs and vanilla. Beat lightly by hand until combined. Stir in flour, baking powder and salt. Stir in nuts. Pour into a greased 9x9-inch pan. Bake for 20 minutes. Cool.

FROSTING:

3	tablespoons soft margarine	2-3	tablespoons milk
2	cups powdered sugar	1/2	teaspoon vanilla
1/4	cup cocoa		

Beat margarine until fluffy. Gradually add 1 cup of the powdered sugar and the cocoa. Beat well. Slowly beat in 2 tablespoons milk and vanilla. Slowly beat in remaining cup of sugar and add milk if necessary. Spread frosting on brownies and cut into bars to serve.

Yield: 16 bars   Carolyn Hood

Aunt Jemmie's Brownies
An old time family favorite

1 stick margarine, softened	1 (16-ounce) can chocolate
1 cup sugar	syrup
1 cup flour	Nuts (optional)
4 eggs	

Preheat oven to 350°. Mix all ingredients together. Place in 9x13-inch greased pan. Bake for 25 minutes.

ICING:

1½ cups sugar	1 stick margarine
⅓ cup milk	½ cup chocolate chips

Bring sugar, milk and margarine to a boil for 30 seconds. Remove from heat and add chocolate chips. Beat until chocolate is melted. Spread evenly over brownies and cut into squares.

NOTE: *Everyone asks for this recipe. It is absolutely delicious and is so easy.*

Yield: 24 bars   Teresa Williams

Melt in Your Mouth Bars

BOTTOM LAYER:

½ cup butter or margarine	1 cup flour
½ cup brown sugar	

Preheat oven to 350°. Combine butter, sugar and flour, blend until texture of coarse meal. Pat mixture in a buttered 9x9-inch pan. Bake 10 minutes or until slightly browned.

TOP LAYER:

1 cup brown sugar	2 tablespoons flour
1 teaspoon vanilla	2 eggs
½ teaspoon baking powder	¼ teaspoon salt
1 cup coconut	½ cup chopped nuts

Mix all ingredients together. Pour over bottom layer. Bake at 350° for 20-25 minutes or until brown. Cool, cut into bars.

Yield: 24 bars   Mary Ruth Arthur

Max's Brownies

1	cup vegetable shortening	1	cup flour
2	cups sugar	4	tablespoons cocoa
4	eggs	1	cup pecans, chopped
2	teaspoons vanilla		

Preheat oven to 325°. Mix shortening and sugar well. Add eggs and vanilla; mix. Add flour and cocoa; mix. Add pecans and mix. Spread batter in a 9x13-inch greased pan. Bake for 25-30 minutes. Cool. Cut into bars. Freezes well.

Yield: 24 bars   Mrs. Max Spear (Sara Ann)

Sensational Peppermint Patty Brownies

1½	cups butter or margarine, melted	1	cup cocoa
3	cups sugar	1	teaspoon baking powder
1	tablespoon vanilla	1	teaspoon salt
5	eggs	24	small (1½-inch) chocolate covered peppermint patties
2	cups flour		

Preheat oven to 350°. Grease a 9x13-inch baking pan. In large bowl stir together butter, sugar and vanilla. Add eggs, stirring until well blended. Stir in flour, cocoa, baking powder and salt; blend well. Reserve 2 cups batter; set aside. Spread remaining batter in baking pan. Arrange peppermint patties in single layer over batter, about 1/2 inch apart. Spread reserved batter over patties. Bake 50-55 minutes or until brownies begin to pull away from sides of pan. Cool completely in pan on wire rack. Cut into squares.

Yield: 36 bars   Ann Blankenship

Date Nut Bars or Balls

1	stick margarine	2½	cups frosted crisp rice cereal
1	cup sugar	1	teaspoon vanilla
1	egg	1	cup chopped nuts
1	(8-ounce) package chopped dates		Powdered sugar

Mix margarine, sugar, egg and dates in a Dutch oven. Cook over medium heat until boiling. Remove from heat and add cereal, vanilla and nuts. For bars, spread into an 8x11-inch dish; sprinkle with powdered sugar. Cut into bars to serve or shape mixture into balls; roll in powdered sugar, serve.

Yield: 24 bars or 24 balls   Linda Overcash

Lemon Squares

CRUST:

1 cup margarine	2 cups flour
1/2 cup powdered sugar	

Preheat oven to 350°. Cream margarine and sugar; add flour. To make crust, press into 9x13-inch pan. Bake for 20 minutes.

TOPPING:

2 cups sugar	6 tablespoons lemon juice
4 tablespoons flour	1/2 teaspoon grated lemon rind
1/2 teaspoon baking powder	Powdered sugar
4 eggs, slightly beaten	

Sift together sugar, flour and baking powder. Add eggs, lemon juice and rind; mix well. Pour over baked crust. Bake at 350° for 25 minutes or until lightly browned. Sprinkle with powdered sugar. Cut into squares when cool.

Yield: 24 squares   Pennie Martin

Mock Baby Ruth Bars

4 cups quick oatmeal	2/3 cup margarine, melted
1 cup brown sugar	1/4 cup creamy peanut butter
1/4 cup white corn syrup	1 teaspoon vanilla

Preheat oven to 400°. Combine oatmeal, brown sugar, corn syrup, margarine, peanut butter and vanilla. Mix well. Press mixture into greased 9x13-inch pan. Bake for 10-12 minutes.

TOPPING:

1 (6-ounce) package chocolate chips	1/2 (6-ounce) package butterscotch chips
	2/3 cup crunchy peanut butter

Melt chips; add peanut butter and mix well. Spread over warm bars. Cool; refrigerate several hours and cut into small bars.

NOTE: *I have made these for years for children's parties, picnics and cookouts. They freeze well.*

Yield: 36 bars   Gayle Smerznak

B
L
E
S
S
I
N
G
S

Dixies

2	sticks margarine, melted	2	cups flour
1	(16-ounce) box light brown	1/2	teaspoon salt
	sugar	1	teaspoon vanilla
2	eggs, beaten	1	cup chopped pecans

Preheat oven to 350°. Combine all ingredients and spread in a greased 9x13-inch pan. Bake for 30-40 minutes. Cut into squares while warm.

Yield: 24 squares   Peggy Blake

Shortcut Raspberry Shortbread

1	(18.5-ounce) package of	1	egg
	butter cake mix	1	(10-ounce) jar raspberry
1/2-3/4	cup finely chopped pecans		jam
1/4	cup butter, softened	2 1/2	teaspoons water (for
1	tablespoon powdered sugar		optional glaze)
	(plus 1/2 cup for optional	1/2	teaspoon almond extract
	glaze)		(for optional glaze)

Preheat oven to 350°. Grease and flour a 9x13-inch pan. Combine cake mix, pecans, butter, 1 tablespoon of powdered sugar and the egg in a bowl. Mix on low speed until crumbly. Press mixture on bottom of prepared pan. Spread with jam. Bake for 25 minutes, until edges are lightly golden. For *GLAZED RASPBERRY SHORTBREAD,* combine 1/2 cup powdered sugar, water and almond extract to make a glaze. Mix until smooth, drizzle glaze over warm shortbread. Cool. Cut into bars.

Yield: 36 bars

Chewy Bars

1	(18.25-ounce) box yellow	4	tablespoons flour
	cake mix	2	eggs
1/2	cup brown sugar	2	tablespoons soft margarine
1/2	cup chocolate chips	2	tablespoons light corn syrup
2	tablespoons water		

Preheat oven to 350°. Mix all ingredients in a large mixing bowl; beat for 3 minutes. Batter is very thick. Dampen a spatula with water to aid in spreading batter in a greased and floured 9x13-inch pan. Bake for 25-30 minutes. Cool in pan before cutting into squares. Freezes well.

Yield: 24 bars   Barbara Norman

Mom's Layer Cookies

1/2	cup margarine	1 1/2	cups flour
1	cup sugar	1/2	teaspoon salt
2	eggs, separated (reserve	1	teaspoon baking powder
	2 egg yolks and 2 egg whites)	1/2	teaspoon vanilla

Preheat oven to 325°. Cream margarine, sugar, 2 egg yolks and 1 of the egg whites. Add flour, salt, baking powder and vanilla. Pour mixture into greased 9x13-inch pan and set aside.

TOPPING:

1	reserved egg white	1	teaspoon vanilla
1	cup brown sugar		Chopped nuts (optional)

Beat remaining egg white until stiff. Gradually add sugar and vanilla. Spread topping over cookie dough. Sprinkle with chopped nuts, if desired. Bake for 25 minutes or until brown. Cut into squares to serve.

Yield: 24 squares   Arlene Duffala

Pecan Tassies

TART SHELLS:

1	cup flour	1/4	cup plus 3 tablespoons
1	(3-ounce) package cream		butter, softened
	cheese, softened		

Combine flour, cheese and butter. Blend well. Chill. Roll dough on a floured surface to 1/8-inch thickness. Cut out 24 mini tart shells using a 2 1/2-inch scalloped cookie cutter. Spray mini muffin tins with non-stick spray. Press dough rounds into the 24 (1 3/4-inch) muffin cups.

FILLING:

3/4	cup light brown sugar	1	tablespoon butter or
3/4	cup chopped pecans		margarine, softened
1	egg	1/8	teaspoon salt
		1	teaspoon vanilla

Preheat oven to 350°. Combine and blend ingredients. Fill shells 3/4 full. Bake 20 minutes, until brown. Loosen edges of tassies from muffin tins with knife while still warm; remove and cool.

NOTE: *For CHOCOLATE TASSIES, add 1 (1-ounce) square of baking chocolate, melted, to above filling. For ALMOND TASSIES, substitute a filling of 1 egg, blended with 1/2 cup sugar, 1 teaspoon almond extract and 1 cup almond paste. Fill each unbaked shell with 1 teaspoon filling before baking. For RASPBERRY TASSIES, blend 3 ounces strawberry cream cheese, 1 1/4 cups powdered sugar and 2 tablespoons seedless raspberry jam. Fill cooled shells that have been baked at 350° for 7-9 minutes. Chill.*

Yield: 20-24 tassies

Mini Banana Cupcakes

My kids love them!

¹/₂	cup solid vegetable shortening	1	tablespoon water
1	cup sugar	1³/₄	cup flour
1	egg, beaten	1	teaspoon nutmeg
1	cup mashed ripe banana (about 2 bananas)	¹/₂	teaspoon salt
1	teaspoon baking soda	1	teaspoon vanilla
			Powdered sugar (optional)

Preheat oven to 350°. In a bowl, cream shortening and sugar. Mix in egg and bananas. Dissolve baking soda in water and add to banana mixture. Slowly add flour, nutmeg and salt. Add vanilla. Spoon into tiny greased muffin tins. Bake for 12-15 minutes. If desired, roll cupcakes in powdered sugar.

Yield: 48 mini cupcakes   Susanne Pierce

Travel Cupcakes

4	squares semi-sweet chocolate	1¹/₃	cups sugar
2	sticks butter or margarine	1	cup cake flour
¹/₂-1	cup nuts	1	teaspoon vanilla
		4	eggs, beaten

Preheat oven to 325°. Melt chocolate and butter. Add nuts and stir. Combine sugar, flour and vanilla. Add to chocolate mixture and stir. Add eggs and stir again. Fill paper-lined muffin pans 1/2 full. Bake 25 minutes until shiny on top. Cupcakes will appear "mushy" and not done. Cool.

NOTE: *Called "travel cakes" because when they cool, you can put them in a bag and take on car trips. Kids love them!*

Yield: 24 cupcakes   Nancy Eason

Easy Mini Tartlet Shells

¹/₃	(20-ounce) roll slice and bake sugar cookie dough
	Granulated sugar

Preheat oven to 350°. Cut 12 (1/4-inch) thick slices from cookie dough roll. Halve each slice, roll into a ball and press onto bottom and sides of mini muffin tin cups that have been greased and sprinkled with sugar. Fill as desired before baking or bake shells until golden, cool, and then fill as desired.

Yield: 24 tartlet shells

● Merry Cheesecakes

1 cup flour	1/2 teaspoon vanilla
1/2 cup brown sugar	2 tablespoons milk
1/3 cup butter	2 tablespoons lemon juice
1/2 cup nuts	1 (8-ounce) carton sour cream
1 (8-ounce) package cream	(optional)
cheese, softened	1 (3.5-ounce) can shredded
1/4 cup sugar	coconut (optional)
1 egg	

Preheat oven to 350°. Blend flour, brown sugar and butter. Mix at slow speed for three minutes. Stir nuts into mixture. Reserve 1 cup of mixture for topping. Pat remainder into ungreased 8x8-inch pan for crust . Bake for 8-10 minutes. Blend cream cheese, sugar, egg, vanilla, milk and lemon juice well and spread over crust. Sprinkle with reserved crumbs and return to oven for 25-30 minutes or until brown. Cool completely before cutting into bars.

NOTE: *May also be topped with 1 (8-ounce) carton sour cream plus 1 (3.5-ounce) can coconut after baking.*

Yield: 24 bars   Debbie Spears

● Marbled Chocolate Cheesecake Cupcakes

1 (18.25-ounce) package devil's food chocolate cake mix, prepared according to package directions	1 egg
	1 (6-ounce) package chocolate chips
1 (8-ounce) package cream cheese	Chocolate or vanilla cream cheese frosting (prepared or homemade)
1/3 cup powdered sugar	

Preheat oven to 350°. Prepare cake mix; set aside. In a small bowl, mix cream cheese, sugar, egg and chocolate chips. Line 24-32 muffin tins with paper baking cups. Fill with cake batter. Spoon cheese mixture, into center of each cup, on top of chocolate batter. Bake for about 25-30 minutes. Cool and frost as desired.

NOTE: *To make MARVELOUS MARBLE CAKE, pour chocolate batter into 9x13-inch greased and floured pan. Randomly spoon cheese mixture on top of cake batter and swirl with knife to marbleize. Bake at 350° for 30-40 minutes. Cool. Frost cake with your choice of icing.*

Yield: 24-32 cupcakes or cake squares

Sweet Sensations
&
Neat Treats to Eat

Creamy Candies & Confections;
Crunchy Snacks & Nuts to Nibble

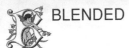
Easy Toffee Candy

B
L
E
S
S
I
N
G
S

10 cinnamon graham cracker
    squares
¹/₂ cup butter or margarine
³/₄ cup brown sugar

¹/₄ cup chopped pecans
1   (6-ounce) package
    semi-sweet chocolate or
    butterscotch pieces

Cover the bottom of a buttered 12x7-inch glass dish with crackers. Combine butter and brown sugar in a 4-cup glass bowl. Microwave on high for 2 minutes until butter is melted. Stir in nuts. Pour syrup mixture over crackers. Microwave on high 4-5 minutes until bubbly; top with chocolate bits. Cook 1 1/2 more minutes to soften chocolate. Spread chocolate evenly over top with spatula. Chill 30 minutes. Cut into bars or break into chunks with a knife.

NOTE: *For BUTTERSCOTCH TOFFEE, substitute butterscotch pieces. For CHOCOLATE ALMOND TOFFEE, omit pecans, chocolate pieces; substitute 12 (1/2-ounce) chocolate almond bars.*

Yield: 24 bars

Pecan or Peanut Brittle

1   cup white corn syrup
¹/₂ cup water
2   cups sugar
3-4 cups pecan halves or raw
    peanuts, shelled

    Scant teaspoon salt
1   teaspoon baking soda
¹/₂ inch stick paraffin
    Vegetable shortening

Bring syrup, water and sugar to boil in a heavy pot. Stir in nuts. Continue cooking over medium heat, stirring frequently until temperature on candy thermometer reaches 288°-290°. Remove from heat; stir in salt, soda and paraffin. Stir well. Immediately pour candy onto a well greased marble slab or baking sheet and spread, pull and stretch the candy out as thinly as possible with fingers greased with shortening. With spatula, quickly flip candy over. When cool, break into bite-size pieces. Store in covered tin.

Yield: 2 pounds   The Reverend James H. Foil, Jr.

Buttermilk Pralines

2   cups sugar
1   cup buttermilk
1   teaspoon baking soda

¹/₈ teaspoon salt
2   tablespoons butter
2   cups pecan halves

Cook sugar, milk, baking soda and salt over high heat for 5 minutes. Stir in butter and pecans. Cook 10 minutes until mixture forms a soft ball. Remove from heat; beat. Drop by spoonfuls onto waxed paper. Cool.

Yield: 4 dozen

Peanut Brittle

2	cups sugar	4	cups shelled raw peanuts
1	cup light corn syrup	1	teaspoon vanilla
1/2	stick margarine	1	tablespoon baking soda
1/2	cup water		

In a large saucepan on high, cook sugar, syrup, margarine and water together for 10 minutes until mixture spins a thread or candy thermometer reaches 293°. Stir often. Reduce heat to medium; add peanuts. Cook; stir until peanuts pop open and make a cracking sound. Add vanilla and baking soda. Stir rapidly; pour evenly onto a greased 11x17-inch baking sheet. Allow mixture to settle; do not smooth out. Cool. Break into pieces, store in airtight container.

Yield: 2 pounds   Bob Deal

Marguerites
Yummy! Quick treat

Saltine crackers	Butter or margarine
Large marshmallows	

Line a toaster oven tray with crackers. Place 1 marshmallow on each cracker and top each marshmallow with a dab of butter. Toast on medium heat. Remove from oven. Cool for 2 minutes. Enjoy!

Yield: Number desired   Allison Swaim

Creamy Mocha Fudge

1	(12-ounce) package semi-sweet chocolate chips	4	teaspoons instant coffee, dissolved in 1 tablespoon warm water or 1 tablespoon coffee-flavored liqueur
1	cup milk chocolate chips		
2	tablespoons milk	1	teaspoon vanilla
1	(14-ounce) can sweetened condensed milk	1	cup chopped nuts (optional)

Combine chips, milk, condensed milk, coffee liquid and vanilla in a heavy saucepan. Heat on low until chips are melted. Remove from heat; stir in nuts. Spread evenly in 8-9-inch square pan lined with foil. Chill 3 hours until firm. Turn out onto a cutting board; peel off foil. Cut into squares. Store in airtight container in refrigerator.

Yield: 2 pounds   Vickie M. Wallace

Butterscotch Pralines

So easy!

1	(3½-ounce) package butterscotch pie filling mix (not instant)	½	cup evaporated milk
½	cup brown sugar	1	tablespoon butter
1	cup sugar	1½	cups chopped pecans or walnuts

Combine pudding, sugars, milk and butter in a large saucepan, mixing well. Bring to a boil, stirring often. Stir in nuts; cook over medium heat, stirring occasionally, until candy reaches soft ball stage, 240° when measured with candy thermometer, about 4-5 minutes. Remove from heat. Beat with wooden spoon 2-3 minutes until mixture is creamy and begins to thicken. Quickly drop spoonfuls of mixture onto waxed paper to form individual candy patties. Cool completely before transferring to storage container.

NOTE: *For CHOCOLATE PRALINES or VANILLA PRALINES, substitute chocolate or vanilla pudding for flavor variety. Candy may be poured into an 8-9-inch square dish and cut into squares.*

Yield: 2 1/2 dozen   Judy Moore

Chocolate Almond Candy Cut - outs

A versatile recipe for parties or gifts

½	cup cocoa, unsweetened	1	(8-ounce) can almond paste
2	(1-pound) boxes powdered sugar	1½-2	ounces almond liqueur Plastic wrap
1	cup unsalted butter or margarine, softened		

Combine cocoa and sugar in a bowl. Blend butter and almond paste together and add to cocoa mixture. Add almond flavoring. Mix well by kneading candy dough with hands to form a large ball; chill. Roll out mixture to 1/4-1/2-inch thickness between two pieces of plastic wrap. Cut out desired shapes with miniature canapé or cookie cutters. Remove trimmings, re-roll, and cut out more candies until all dough is used. Place candies in a single layer on serving dishes. Cover with plastic wrap and chill until ready to serve.

NOTE: *A favorite recipe! May substitute almond extract to taste. I have used a heart shape cutter for bridal luncheons, tiny trees for Christmas and rabbits in the springtime. If rolled thick, candy resembles pieces of fudge. If rolled thin, it yields 75-100 dainty party candies.*

Yield: 2 pounds   Libby Gish

🎈 Holly Candy
A favorite kids holiday treat!

1	stick butter or margarine	2	teaspoons green food
30	large marshmallows		coloring
1	teaspoon vanilla	4¹/₂-5	cups corn flakes
			Red cinnamon candies

Melt butter in a double boiler; add marshmallows. Stir in vanilla and food coloring. Remove from heat and stir in corn flakes. Drop by spoonfuls onto waxed paper. Immediately add 4-5 red cinnamon candies to form "holly with berries".

NOTE: *Fingers and toes will be green, but tummies will enjoy. Kids love these treats and they are pretty for the Christmas cookie tray. Children can make easily with adult supervision.*

Yield: 16 candies

Karen Busby

🎈 Rocky Road
Everyone enjoys this Christmas candy

1	(12-ounce) package chocolate chips	1	cup peanut butter
1	(12-ounce) package butterscotch chips	1	(10¹/₂-ounce) package miniature marshmallows
		1	cup salted, dry roasted peanuts

Combine chips and peanut butter in large glass or plastic bowl. Microwave on high for 3 minutes, stirring once, until melted. Stir in marshmallows and peanuts. Spread in a 9x13-inch pan lined with foil. Refrigerate at least 2 hours. Cut into squares. Keep refrigerated.

Yield: 2 dozen

Mary Floyd

Candy Caramels

1	cup brown sugar	1	cup whole milk
1	cup sugar	1	cup butter
1	cup white corn syrup	1	cup chopped pecans
1	cup cream	2	teaspoons vanilla

Combine sugars, syrup, cream, milk and butter; bring to a boil on high heat. After mixture begins to boil, reduce to medium heat and stir occasionally. Cook until a small amount forms a hard ball when dropped into cold water, about 30-40 minutes. Remove from heat, add pecans and vanilla; pour into a well-greased 9x9-inch pan. When partially cold, mark and cut into 24-36 squares. Wrap in wax paper. Store in a cool place.

Yield: 24-36 caramels

Gloe Bertram

🔔 🎈 Cappuccino Party Mints

½ **cup cappuccino Italian style instant coffee powder**	1 **(8-ounce) package cream cheese, softened slightly**
1-2 **teaspoons boiling water**	2 **(1-pound) boxes powdered sugar**
2 **teaspoons almond extract**	

Make a paste by dissolving coffee powder in mixture of boiling water and almond extract. Blend paste into cream cheese; combine cream cheese mixture with sugar. Stir and knead until mixture is blended, smooth and forms a caramel color candy dough. Place mixture in a sealed ziplock bag to prevent drying and chill. Pinch off small pieces of dough and roll into dime sized balls, place on wax paper and press mints flat with fork tines. Set aside to dry or press mixture into cold candy molds, unmold and dry.

NOTE: *A no-cook candy, great for receptions. For CREAM CHEESE PARTY MINTS, omit coffee powder, water and almond flavoring. Add 1/4 teaspoon of peppermint oil and tint candy dough with a few drops of desired food coloring.*

Yield: 150-175 candies

🎈 Mini - Mac S'Mores

24 **vanilla wafers**	12 **chocolate covered peppermint patties**
½ **cup vanilla frosting, tinted red with food coloring**	12 **orange colored peanut shaped marshmallow candies**
¼ **cup flaked coconut, tinted green with food coloring**	6 **teaspoons white corn syrup Toasted sesame seeds**

Spread 12 vanilla wafers with red frosting (ketchup). Sprinkle on coconut (lettuce). Top with peppermint patty (burger). Compress peanut candies to form round "cheese slices". Top burger with "cheese" and remaining wafers. Brush syrup on tops of wafers; sprinkle on sesame seeds. Microwave the stacked burgers on high for 40 seconds. Compress; to flatten slightly. Microwave for 10 more seconds. Serve immediately.

Yield: 12 confections

🔔 White Chocolate Truffles

2 **cups vanilla milk chips**	2 **tablespoons amaretto**
¼ **cup sour cream**	**Powdered sugar**

Melt chips on low heat, stir constantly. Stir in sour cream and amaretto, blend well. Chill mixture 1 hour, stir often. Form into 1-inch balls; roll in sugar. Cover, store in refrigerator or freeze.

Yield: 4 dozen

No - Fail Fudge Icing or Fudge Candy

2	cups sugar	1/8	teaspoon salt
4	heaping tablespoons cocoa	1/4	cup butter, no substitution
1/2	cup milk	1	teaspoon vanilla
1/3	cup light corn syrup		

FUDGE ICING:
Blend sugar and cocoa well. Add milk; stir. Mix in syrup and salt, then add butter. Boil 5 minutes then add vanilla, stirring constantly while cooking. Remove from heat and stir until creamy and icing reaches a spreadable consistency. If mixture becomes too hard to spread, it may be thinned with evaporated milk. Makes enough icing to frost two 8-inch cake layers.

FUDGE CANDY:
Cook icing mixture a little longer until it reaches a thicker consistency. Spread mixture in a greased 8x8-inch pan; cool. Cut into 16 squares to serve.

NOTE: *This is a tried and true recipe for delicious icing or fudge.*

Yield: 2 cups frosting or
        16 squares candy   Mrs. D. A. Thompson (Atha)

Toasted Pecans

4	tablespoons cooking oil	1/2	teaspoon ground ginger
1 1/2	tablespoons Worcestershire	1/8	teaspoon hot sauce
1	teaspoon soy sauce	2	cups pecan halves

Preheat oven to 350°. Combine oil, Worcestershire, soy sauce, ginger and hot sauce in bowl. Stir in nuts. Pour mixture into glass casserole dish and bake for 30 minutes. Dry and cool on paper towels.

Yield: 2 cups   Mrs. Sanders Goodman (Judy)

🎈 🎈 Monkey Mix

3	cups mini cinnamon graham squares and crispy graham cereal	2	cups malted milk balls
		1 1/2	cups dried banana chips
		1 1/2	cup honey roasted peanuts

Combine ingredients in bowl. Toss. Store in covered container.

Yield: 8 cups

Cinnamon Buckeye Squares

2 sticks margarine	1 (16-ounce) box powdered
1½ cups crushed cinnamon	sugar
graham cracker crumbs	Non-stick cooking spray
2-2½ cups crunchy peanut butter	12 ounces chocolate chips

Melt margarine in microwave. Combine margarine with cracker crumbs in a medium size bowl. Blend 1 1/2-2 cups of peanut butter and the sugar. Mix thoroughly. Press mixture into a 9x13-inch pan, sprayed with cooking spray. Set aside. For topping, melt 1/2 cup peanut butter and chips in a glass dish in microwave. Spread mixture over cracker mixture in pan. Cool in refrigerator until you can neatly cut candy into 1-inch squares without crumbling the chocolate topping. Chill. May be frozen.

Yield: 100 squares

♥ ♥ Choco - Peanut Butter Sandwich Cookies

½ cup peanut butter	1 (16-ounce) box graham
1 (3.9-ounce) package instant	crackers
chocolate pudding, prepared	
according to package	
directions	

Combine peanut butter and 1/2 cup prepared pudding in a bowl. Spread on crackers, sandwich-cookie style. Eat immediately for a crunchy snack or freeze for a chewier snack.

NOTE: *This can be made with low sugar peanut butter and sugar-free, fat-free pudding for a healthier treat. Also makes a good PEANUT BUTTER SPREAD for fruits or PEANUT BUTTER CUPCAKE ICING.*

Yield: 20 cookies   Kay Paul

♥ Chocolate Cookie Cracker Squares

2 sticks margarine	1 (12-ounce) bag chocolate
1 cup brown sugar	chips
20 saltine crackers,	
approximately	

Line bottom of 9x12-inch baking dish with foil. Boil margarine and sugar for 3 minutes, stirring constantly. Spread mixture over crackers and bake at 400° for 4 minutes. Remove from oven and sprinkle top with chips. Spread softened chips evenly over crackers. Cool; cut into squares. Refrigerate.

Yield: 40 squares   Miriam L. Williams

🔔 🎈 Dirt Cake
Best dirt you'll ever eat!

2	(1-pound) bags cream-filled chocolate sandwich cookies	2	(3.9-ounce) boxes instant vanilla pudding
3/4	stick butter, softened	4	cups milk
1	(8-ounce) package cream cheese, softened	1	(8-ounce) carton whipped dessert topping, thawed
1 1/2	cups powdered sugar	6	gummy candy worms

Crush cookies (to make dirt) and set aside. Mix together butter, cream cheese and sugar. In a blender, mix pudding and milk. Mix cream cheese mixture with pudding mixture and whipped topping. Alternately with cookies, layer cream cheese mixture in a clean plastic or ceramic flower pot-shaped container, making 3 layers. Place candy worms in dirt and end with dirt on top. Refrigerate. Spoon into dessert dishes to serve.

NOTE: *To make a great table centerpiece, place plastic straws upright in cake. Stick a flower stem inside the straw. Remove straws and flowers before serving. Gummy candy worms are available at specialty candy counters or gourmet food shops. My grandsons request Dirt Cake for their birthdays every year.*

Yield: Serves 8-12   Wilburn Taylor

🎈 Snow Cream
Kids favorite!

1	egg white	1	teaspoon vanilla
1/2-3/4	cup sugar	1	quart fluffy white freshly fallen snow
1	cup milk		

In a bowl, beat egg white with electric beater until fluffy. Stir in sugar, milk and vanilla. Gently stir in snow. Spoon into dessert dishes. Serve at once.

Yield: 4 servings   Andi and Alex Steele

🎈 Doughnut Delights

4	cake or yeast doughnuts with small center hole	8	milk chocolate kisses with almonds, unwrapped
4	large marshmallows		

Split doughnuts and marshmallows in half horizontally. Place doughnuts, flat side down on grill or toaster pan. Place marshmallow halves, cut side down, over doughnut center holes. Grill or toast 2-3 minutes or until golden brown and marshmallows are soft. Immediately place and press chocolate kisses, point side down into marshmallows. Serve immediately.

Yield: 8 servings

♥ ♥ Handmade Ice Cream

1 **cup skim milk**	8 **cups ice cubes**
2 **tablespoons sugar**	1 **ziplock sandwich bag**
1/2 **teaspoon vanilla**	1 **(1-gallon) ziplock bag**
1 **cup table or rock salt**	

Combine milk, sugar and vanilla in a sandwich-size locking plastic bag; seal. In a gallon-size bag, combine salt and ice. Place milk-mixture bag into ice bag. Turn bag over and over for 6-7 minutes until ice cream is slushy.

NOTE: *For variety, add 1/4 teaspoon of other flavorings. We had fun making this ice cream in our 3rd grade science lab at Cabarrus Academy in Concord, NC.*

Yield: 1-2 servings   Sarah Bertram

♥ Frozen Pops

1 **(3-ounce) package any flavor fruit gelatin**	1 **cup sugar**
	2 **cups boiling water**
1 **(0.16-ounce) envelope any flavor unsweetened instant soft drink mix**	2 **cups cold water**
	24 **wooden popsicle sticks or plastic spoons**

Dissolve gelatin, instant soft drink mix and sugar in boiling water. Add cold water. Pour into ice cube trays, small paper cups or frozen pop molds. For handles, insert wooden sticks or plastic spoons at an angle in each ice cube section or mold. If desired, pops may be partially frozen before handles are inserted. Freeze until firm.

Yield: 20-24 servings   Arlene Duffala

♥ Microwave Caramel Corn

1/2 **cup margarine or butter**	1/2 **teaspoon baking soda**
1 **cup brown sugar**	3 **quarts popped corn**
1/4 **cup light corn syrup**	**(2 bags of microwavable**
1/2 **teaspoon salt**	**popcorn)**

Combine butter, sugar, corn syrup and salt in a microwave-safe bowl. Cook on high, about 3 minutes until mixture boils, stirring once or twice. Boil 3 more minutes. Add baking soda. Pour mixture over popcorn in a large (5-quart) microwave-safe bowl. Cook on high for 3 minutes, stirring once every minute, until well coated. Cool mixture on cookie sheet; break apart and store in airtight container.

Yield: 3 quarts   Helen Kichefski

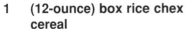
♥ Confection in a Bag

Great for college students

1	(12-ounce) box rice chex cereal	1	cup peanut butter
8	ounces peanuts	12	ounces chocolate chips
2	sticks butter	1	(13-gallon) plastic garbage bag
		1	(16-ounce) box powdered sugar

Mix the cereal and peanuts in a large bowl. Melt butter, peanut butter and chips slowly over low to medium heat. Pour peanut butter mixture over cereal mixture and stir until coated. Place mixture in a plastic kitchen garbage bag; add powdered sugar and shake until well coated. Store in airtight container.

NOTE: *Sometimes called "garbage" because it is prepared in a garbage bag. Great for sending to college students in ziplock bags.*

Yield: Serves a crowd   Mac and Wallace Duskin

♥ Salisbury Jumble

1	(12-ounce) package white chocolate chips	3	cups pretzel sticks
6	cups crispy corn cereal squares	2	cups pecan halves
		1	cup powdered sugar
		1	(2-gallon) plastic storage bag

Cook chocolate in microwave on high for 1 minute; stir. Heat 30 more seconds, until melted. Gently stir in cereal, pretzels and pecans; coat thoroughly. Place sugar in plastic bag. Add chocolate-coated cereal and pretzel mix. Toss until well coated. Store in airtight container in refrigerator.

Yield: 10 cups   Lisa Ganem

♥ Snick - Snack

Crunchy pick-up sticks!

1	(16-ounce) box mini cheese crackers	1	(10-ounce) bag small pretzels
1	(6-ounce) bag fish-shaped crackers	6	tablespoons butter
1	(1½-ounce) can potato sticks	4	teaspoons Worcestershire sauce
1	(11½-ounce) can mixed nuts	½	teaspoon seasoned salt

Empty crackers, potato sticks, nuts and pretzels into 9x13-inch roasting pan. Melt butter in large measuring cup. Stir in Worcestershire and salt. Pour over snack mixture, coating evenly. Bake at 250° for 45 minutes, stirring every 15 minutes. Cool. Store in air-tight container.

Yield: 10-12 servings   Susanne Pierce

Sugared Nuts

1 **cup sugar**	1 **teaspoon vanilla**
¼ **teaspoon salt**	2-3 **cups pecan halves**
1 **teaspoon grated orange rind**	**Wax paper**
6 **tablespoons milk**	

Combine sugar, salt, orange rind and milk in a 2-3 quart saucepan. Cook for 4-5 minutes or until candy reaches soft-ball stage, stirring frequently. Remove from heat; add vanilla and nuts. Stir a few minutes to coat nuts or until sugar becomes grainy. Turn out immediately onto wax paper. Separate nuts with fork.

Yield: 2-3 cups   Tom Ginn

Sugar Coated Peanuts

1 **cup sugar**	2 **cups raw peanuts, skins on**
½ **cup water**	

Dissolve sugar in water in saucepan over medium heat. Add peanuts. Continue to cook, stirring at 10 minute intervals, until peanuts are coated and no syrup remains. Quickly pour onto an ungreased cookie sheet and separate with fork.

NOTE: *May double recipe as these do not last long!*

Yield: 2 cups   Ruby Craig Long

❛ Cinnamon Tortilla Crisps
A crunchy treat!

1 **cup brown sugar**	1 **tablespoon cinnamon-sugar,**
1 **cup butter, softened, plus**	**plus extra for topping**
1 tablespoon melted butter	4-5 **(8-inch) flour tortillas**
for topping	

Preheat oven to 400°. Blend sugar, 1 cup of the butter and cinnamon-sugar. Spread each tortilla with mixture. Roll up each tortilla tightly. Place tortillas seam side down on non-stick cookie sheet. Brush tops with melted butter and sprinkle with additional cinnamon sugar. Bake for 15-20 minutes. Remove pan from oven and set aside for 5-10 minutes. Serve rolled tortillas while warm and crispy.

NOTE: ❛*CINNAMON CRISPY CUT-OUTS may be made by spreading above mixture on flour tortillas. Cut out desired shapes with cookie cutters and bake at 400° for 10 minutes. Cool slightly until crispy.*

Yield: 4-5 tortilla crisps or 12-20 cut-outs

Cinnamon - Sugar Pecans

1 egg white	1 cup sugar
1 tablespoon water	1 teaspoon cinnamon
1 pound pecan halves	1 scant teaspoon salt

Preheat oven to 325°. Mix egg white and water in a bowl. Add pecan halves and coat well. In a separate bowl, combine sugar, cinnamon and salt. Pour mixture over pecans; toss gently to coat. Place on a 10x13-inch cookie sheet with sides. Bake 40 minutes, stirring every 15 minutes. Cool.

Yield: 1 pound   Evelyn Ribelin

Praline Nuts

3 cups pecan halves	1/2 cup sour cream
1 cup brown sugar	1 teaspoon vanilla
1/2 cup sugar	

While making syrup, heat nuts on baking sheet in oven preheated to 200°. Combine sugars and sour cream in heavy saucepan. Cook over medium heat, stirring until sugar is dissolved. Continue to cook without stirring, until temperature on candy thermometer reaches 238° or until a soft ball forms when a small amount of mixture is dripped in cold water. Remove from heat; add vanilla and heated pecans. Stir gently until nuts are coated; turn out onto wax paper and quickly separate with a fork. Allow to dry.

Yield: 3 cups   Donna Yale

Oriental Cashew Crunch

Everyone loves it!

1 (16-ounce) package oat squares cereal	1/3 cup oil
	3 tablespoons soy sauce
1 (3-ounce) can chow mein noodles	1 teaspoon garlic powder
	1 teaspoon onion powder
1 cup cashews or peanuts	

Heal oven to 250°. Combine cereal, noodles and peanuts in a 9x13-inch pan. Set aside. Combine oil, soy sauce and powders in a small bowl. Quickly pour over cereal mixture and stir to coat evenly. Bake 1 hour, stirring every 20 minutes; cool. Store in sealed plastic bags or containers.

Yield: 10 cups   Dorothy Garrison

🔔 Chocolate Truffles
A sweet sensation!

30	ounces unsweetened chocolate	1	(16-ounce) box confectioner's sugar
5	sticks butter		Cocoa
1/2	pint heavy cream		Cinnamon

Melt chocolate and butter in top of a double boiler. Add cream and stir. Continue stirring and mix in sugar. Cover and refrigerate mixture for 12 hours. In a bowl, mix enough cocoa and cinnamon for coating truffle balls; set aside. Make balls by rolling a teaspoonful of cold truffle mixture in hands. Dip balls in cocoa mixture to coat. Place on trays or baking sheets; refrigerate 1 hour.

CHOCOLATE GLAZE:

30	ounces sweetened chocolate	2	ounces peanut oil

Melt chocolate in top of double boiler. Add oil to chocolate and blend with spoon. Remove pan from heat and cool mixture to the touch, but not hard. Dip balls in chocolate and place them on a wire rack to let excess glaze drip off. Chocolate will harden at room temperature in 15-20 minutes. Refrigerate truffles. Remove truffles from refrigerator two hours before serving, and allow them to return to room temperature. Serve.

Yield: 100 truffles

Charlie Broome
Broom & Foster Catering

🔔 🎈 White Chocolate Cinnamon Crunch

2¹/₂	cups cinnamon toast crunch cereal squares	1	(24-ounce) bag white almond bark or vanilla candy coating chunks
2¹/₂	cups frosted whole wheat oat cereal, doughnut shaped		

Mix cereals and distribute in layer on 10 1/2x15 1/2-inch jellyroll pan. Cook almond bark on high in microwave 2 minutes. Remove from oven; stir. Cook 3-4 minutes, stirring every 30-40 seconds until melted. Pour over cereal mixture; quickly stir to coat. Flatten mixture with rubber spatula. Cool to harden. Break into small pieces or chunks. Store in ziplock bag.

Yield: About 50 pieces

Pantry Potpourri

Buffet Food Bars, Gifts with Lids,
Edible Crafts for the Kids;
Preserves & Condiments, in a Dish;
Spicy Pickles & Jams to Relish

🧑 🎈 Toasted Rainbow Art

THE CANVAS:
Whole slices of sandwich bread or bread shapes cut out with cookie cutters

EDIBLE PAINT MEDIUMS:
Sweetened condensed milk
Milk or evaporated milk
Frozen orange juice concentrate, thawed
Whipped butter

THE TOOLS:
Muffin tin
Seasonal cookie cutters
A new or clean artist paint brush
A spatula or pastry brush
Colorful puffed alphabet or fruit cereal (optional)

EDIBLE PAINT COLORS:
Assorted food colors
Assorted colors of flavored fruit gelatins

TO MAKE EACH COLOR FOR PAINTING WITH A BRUSH: Mix 1/3 cup of milk or orange juice concentrate in a muffin cup with 2-3 tablespoons of gelatin or a few drops of selected food colors. Stir until blended. Using a paint brush, decorate bread with different colors for initials, simple shapes, designs or a "multi-colored rainbow." Toast in oven for about 5 minutes. Serve hot.

TO MAKE EACH COLOR FOR SPREADING WITH A SPATULA: Substitute 1/3 cup whipped butter for the milk or orange juice concentrate; mix as above and spread on bread. Decorate with cereal if desired. Toast in oven about 5 minutes. Serve hot.

Yield: A lot of fun!

Mom's Shortcut Apple Butter
A really good and quick version

5	pounds Granny Smith apples (or other cooking apple), peeled, cored and sliced	1/4	teaspoon ground cloves
3	cups water	3	cups sugar
3	cups brown sugar	1	(1.75-ounce) box Sure-Jell
1	tablespoon ground cinnamon	1/4	teaspoon nutmeg
		6	(1-pint) sterilized canning jars with lids

Combine apple slices and water in a large Dutch oven. Bring to a boil. Reduce heat; cook 20-25 minutes until tender. Mash apples and stir in remaining ingredients. Bring mixture to a boil. Cook 2 minutes, stirring constantly. Quickly pour mixture into hot sterilized jars, filling to 1/4-inch from the top. Wipe rims; cover with metal lids. Process sealed jars in boiling water bath for 5 minutes. Cool.

Yield: 6 pints

Kaye Hirst

♣ ● Peanut Butter Edible Play Dough

Children can eat what they create

1	(18-ounce) jar creamy peanut butter
6	tablespoons honey

1/4	cup non-fat powdered milk
4-5	teaspoons cocoa (optional)
1 1/2	cups powdered sugar

Assortment of: chocolate covered raisins, crunchy chocolate coated rice baking bits, or miniature chocolate chips, jelly beans, M&M's, marshmallows, malted Easter egg candies, colored decorative sprinkles, gummy candies, nuts, wheat germ, toasted coconut, chopped dates, frosted rice or other cereals to blend into or decorate dough

In a bowl, blend peanut butter and honey; gradually add milk, cocoa (if desired) and sugar. Knead mixture well with clean hands until it is smooth and sticks together, and reaches the consistency of commercial play dough. Store mixture in refrigerator in air-tight container or ziplock plastic kitchen bag until ready to use. This is a great activity for creative play. On a clean surface, children can mold or roll dough, sculpt hand prints, animals, or happy faces or cut out cookie cutter shapes. Decorate as desired. For *PEANUT BUTTER COATED GRAPES,* mold dough around seedless green grapes and roll in chopped nuts, graham cracker, cookie or cereal crumbs.

Yield: 4 1/2 cups   Libby Gish

Chunky Pickled Pineapple

A festive and colorful holiday treat

1	(20-ounce) can pineapple chunks in heavy syrup, drained, syrup reserved
1/2	cup apple cider vinegar
2	cinnamon sticks, broken into thirds

3/4	cup sugar
1/2	teaspoon ground mace
2-3	teaspoons red cinnamon candies
1 1/2	teaspoons corn syrup

In a small saucepan, combine reserved pineapple juice, vinegar, cinnamon sticks, sugar, mace, cinnamon candies and corn syrup. Simmer on low heat for 15-20 minutes. Add pineapple chunks; bring mixture to a boil. Reduce heat; cook for 10 more minutes to reduce liquid, stirring often. Cool. Refrigerate overnight in a covered jar. Remove pickled pineapple from spices and liquids and serve in a crystal dish.

NOTE: *For PICKLED PEACHES, substitute whole or halved canned peaches in heavy syrup for the pineapple in syrup. Substitute brown sugar for the sugar, and add 1/2-3/4 teaspoon allspice and 3-4 whole cloves. Proceed as above.*

Yield: 2 cups

🎄 🎈 Pounds of Cake Fun

1   (10.25-ounce) fresh or frozen pound cake, thawed and cut into
    desired shapes to make the following:

POUND CAKE CROUTONS:

³/₄ inch thick slices of pound cake	1 cup brown sugar
	1 cup butter or margarine
	2-3 teaspoons cinnamon sugar

Preheat oven to 250°. Thinly spread a mixture of the sugars and butter on 1 side of sliced cake. Cut into 3/4-inch cubes or decorative shapes with tiny cookie cutters. Place on ungreased air-bake cookie sheet. Toast for 20 minutes or until golden. Use as dessert garnishes or layer between mousses, puddings, or ice cream for *INDIVIDUAL DESSERT TRIFLES.*

Yield: 25-50 croutons

POUND CAKE KABOBS:

1¹/₂ inch cubes of pound cake
1   (3-ounce) jar currant jelly, melted
2   cups sweetened condensed milk (optional)

1   (12-ounce) can orange-pineapple concentrate, thawed (optional)
1   (7-ounce) package finely shredded coconut

Dip cake cubes in melted jelly, milk or juice. Roll in coconut; thread onto skewers. Grill or toast until golden brown.

Yield: 36 cubes

POUND CAKE S'MORES:

1   (1-inch) thick slice pound cake
5   mini-marshmallows

³/₄ teaspoon mini-chocolate chips

Make a horizontal slit or pocket in cake slice. Fill pocket with a mixture of marshmallows and chips. Bake or grill until golden or mixture has melted.

Yield: 1 serving

POUND CAKE COOKIE CUT-OUTS:

¹/₂ inch thick slices of pound cake cut with cookie-cutters
1   (12-ounce) can chocolate or vanilla frosting

Decorative cake sprinkles or colored sugar crystals or M & M's

Frost and decorate toasted or "unbaked" cookie-cut-outs.

POUND CAKE PETIT FOURS:

10 (2-inch) cubes of pound cake, crusts trimmed

Flavored frosting of choice for icing, or melted for a glaze

Frost or glaze sides and top of cake cubes as desired. Serve in individual paper baking cups.

Yield: 16

Cake in a Jar

Bake a cake for someone special!

Non-stick vegetable cooking spray
6 (1-pint) clean, wide-mouth canning jars with lids
1 (18.35-ounce) box spice cake mix
4 eggs
1 cup apple butter (10-ounce jar) or canned pumpkin pie mix (not solid-pack pumpkin)

²/₃ cup oil
1 (3.9-ounce) package instant chocolate pudding mix
¹/₃ cup chopped dates, raisins, or chocolate chips (optional)
³/₄ cup chopped pecans (optional)

Spray non-stick cooking oil in the interior surfaces of all jars. Preheat oven to 325°. Place cake mix, eggs, apple butter or pumpkin pie mix, oil, pudding mix, dates and nuts if desired in a mixing bowl. With electric mixer, beat stiff batter, mixing thoroughly. Fill each jar half full with 1 cup of batter. Place open jars, evenly spaced on a pizza pan. Bake about 1 hour and test for doneness. Do not over bake. Remove from oven. Cool. Cover tops of jars with plastic wrap. Compress cakes slightly and screw on lids. Store, sealed at room temperature for 2-3 days. Refrigerate for longer storage. When ready to serve, slide out cake by inverting and tapping on jar bottom. Loosen edges gently with knife. Slice to serve.

NOTE: *Applesauce or water may be substituted for apple butter. Reduce cooking time to 45 minutes. Experiment with a variety of cake mixes and puddings. If desired, attach the recipe, a bow and a personalized gift tag, and share with a friend.*

Yield: 6 cakes in jars

Granola Crunch

A cereal, snack or ice cream topping

3 cups oats
1 cup shredded coconut
1 cup chopped nuts
¹/₄ cup honey

¹/₄ cup melted butter
1¹/₂ teaspoons cinnamon
¹/₂ teaspoon salt
²/₃ cup raisins

Combine all ingredients except raisins. Spread in ungreased 9x13-inch pan. Bake at 350° for 25-30 minutes, stirring every 10 minutes. Remove from oven; stir in raisins. Cool. Store in refrigerator.

NOTE: *For flavor variety, other dried fruits may be added.*

Yield: 6 cups   Dorothy Collin Grubb Horne

 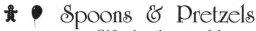 Spoons & Pretzels

Gifts by the mugful

10 ounces milk chocolate, almond bark or white chocolate candy coating cubes or chips; or candy melt wafers in assorted pastel colors and flavors	10 plastic spoons 10 pretzel rods Oil-based food colors or flavorings (optional) Crushed peppermint candy (optional)

Place chocolate in a ziplock plastic bag and float bag in a hot water bath (double boiler fashion) in kitchen sink. Stir chocolate, replacing hot water often until melted or melt in microwave on high for 2-3 minutes stirring every 30 seconds until smooth. Keep warm. Add a few drops of food coloring or flavoring, if desired. Knead bag to mix well. Dip spoon bowls or pretzels into melted chocolate. Place pretzels or spoons (bowl side up) on wax paper lined pan in refrigerator or freezer until firm. Wrap individually with plastic wrap; place bundle in a decorative mug. Tie gift tag and ribbons to mug handle. Pretzels are fun to eat! Use spoons to stir hot chocolate or coffee. Spoons and pretzels may be double dipped in alternate colors of chocolate after first layer hardens, or drizzle on the chocolate by squeezing it through a tiny snipped off corner of plastic bag, creating a pastry tube.

NOTE: *For CHOCOLATE PEPPERMINT SPOONS or CHOCOLATE PEPPER-MINT PRETZELS, sprinkle on crushed peppermint candy before chocolate hardens.*

Yield: 10 spoons or pretzels

Cream Chantilly

1 cup heavy whipping cream, chilled 1/4 cup powdered sugar	1 teaspoon vanilla or almond extract

In a metal or glass bowl, beat cream with electric mixer, gradually adding sugar until soft peaks form. Fold in flavorings. Blend well. Serve under, or on top of fruits or desserts.

NOTE: *For SOUR CREAM CHANTILLY, add 1 cup sour cream to basic recipe. For CREAM CHEESE CHANTILLY, blend 3-ounces cream cheese with 1/4 cup sugar; fold in whipped cream and 2 tablespoons Amaretto. For other flavoring options, add 2 tablespoons of one of each of the following: powdered cocoa, cinnamon sugar, honey, syrups or flavored liqueurs.*

Yield: 2-3 cups

Whole Cranberry Sauce

1	pound fresh cranberries
2	cups sugar
1/4	teaspoon finely grated lime zest

1	teaspoon finely grated orange zest
1	tablespoon lime juice
1/4	cup fresh orange juice
3/4	cup water

Combine all ingredients in a heavy saucepan. Bring to a boil. Reduce heat; simmer for 10 minutes or until berries pop open. Skim foam off surface. Cool mixture. Spoon into a container and refrigerate before serving.

NOTE: *Lime juice and zest add sharpness to the flavor.*

Yield: 8 servings   Betty Little

Cranberry Orange Chutney

4	cups cranberries
2	cups sugar
1	cup unpeeled, chopped apple
1	cup fresh orange sections
1/4	cup orange juice

1/2	cup raisins
1/4	cup English walnuts, chopped
1	tablespoon vinegar
1/2	teaspoon cinnamon

Combine all ingredients in a large pan. Bring to a boil; reduce heat and simmer for 5 minutes or until berries begin to burst. Cool and spoon into small clean glass jars or serve portions in a glass dish. Keep refrigerated.

NOTE: *This is so good with muffins, biscuits and bread. A great gift to share with a new neighbor.*

Yield: 5 cups   Stella Gillespie

♥ Homemade Mayonnaise

1	cup sugar
2 1/2	tablespoons flour
1	teaspoon dry mustard
1	cup white vinegar

4	eggs or equivalent egg substitute, beaten until foamy
1	cup hot water

In a 2-quart saucepan, mix sugar, flour and mustard. Stir in vinegar, eggs and water. Cook over medium heat, stirring constantly with wooden spoon until thickened. When cool, refrigerate in glass jar or airtight container.

NOTE: *This is excellent for potato or macaroni salad. Recipe may be halved.*

Yield: 3 cups   Mildred D. Venable

Unbeatable Beets
Great for Picnics

1	cup sugar	1	(15.5-ounce) can sliced
1	cup white vinegar		beets, drained
1/2	cup salad oil	1	white onion, thinly sliced

Bring sugar, vinegar and oil to a boil; cool. Pour cooled liquid over beets and onions in a bowl. Chill 2 hours. Serve as a salad.

Yield: 1 quart   June Eshelman

Sweet & Sour Pickles

5	large cucumbers, unpeeled and sliced	1	teaspoon celery seed
5	medium onions, sliced	1	teaspoon turmeric
1/4	cup salt	1/4	teaspoon pepper
2	cups white vinegar	6	(1-pint) sterilized canning
4	cups sugar		jars with lids

In a large container, cover cucumbers and onions with salted water and refrigerate for 1 hour. In a 6-quart pot, bring vinegar, sugar, celery seed, turmeric and pepper to a boil; add drained cucumbers and onions. Bring to a boil; remove from heat. Let stand to cool. Pour into jars and seal. Refrigerate.

Yield: 6 pints   Jan Broaddus Lewis

Hap's Quick Garlic Dill Pickles

4	pounds (3-4-inch) pickling cucumbers	1	small whole red pepper
6	cups water	16	garlic cloves, peeled, split
4 1/2	cups apple cider vinegar	16	heads fresh dill
6	tablespoons pickling salt	7-9	(1-pint) sterilized and hot canning jars with lids

Wash cucumbers and remove blossom end. In a 3-quart non-corrosive saucepan, combine water, vinegar, salt and red pepper. Boil. Place 2 pieces of garlic and 1 head of dill in each pint jar. Firmly pack cucumbers upright in jars, leaving a 1/2-inch head space. Top with 2 additional pieces of garlic and 1 head of dill. Pour hot vinegar mixture over cucumbers, leaving 1/2-inch head space. Carefully run a non-metallic utensil down and around inside of jars to remove trapped air bubbles. Wipe jar tops and threads clean. Place lids on jars; screw bands on firmly. Process in boiling water in a canner for 10 minutes. Store in cool, dark place to age for 6 weeks before using.

Yield: 7-9 pints   Hap Roberts

Watermelon Rind Pickles

7	pounds cubed watermelon rind, trimmed well (all pink pulp and peelings removed)
1	cup pickling lime
1	gallon water, plus 1 quart
1	quart white vinegar
5	pounds sugar

1/2	teaspoon oil of cloves
1/2	teaspoon oil of cinnamon or 3 cinnamon sticks
	Green food coloring
10	(1-pint) glass jars and lids, sterilized

In a large enamel pot, mix pickling lime in 1 gallon of water. Soak cubed rinds overnight in pickling mixture until crisp. Remove cubes; rinse well. Make a syrup by dissolving vinegar and sugar in 1 quart of water over medium heat. When syrup comes to a boil, add rinds and cook gently for 15 minutes. Add cinnamon and cloves. Let mixture stand overnight. Remove rinds from syrup. Heat syrup to boiling, return rinds to the pot and let rinds soak in mixture overnight. Repeat procedure for 3 days. On the fourth day, add a few drops of food coloring and stir into mixture. Pour pickles with syrup into hot jars and seal.

NOTE: *The Black Diamond variety of watermelon has a thick rind and works best for these pickles.*

Yield: 10 pints

The Reverend James H. Foil, Jr.

Pickled Squash
Colorful, crunchy and delicious!

2/3	cup salt
3	quarts water
1 1/4	pounds (4 cups) thinly sliced small (1 1/2-2-inch diameter) yellow summer squash
1 1/4	pounds (4 cups) thinly sliced small (1 1/2-2-inch diameter) zucchini squash
2 1/2	cups sugar

2	cups white vinegar
2	teaspoons mustard seeds
1 1/2	teaspoons celery seeds
2	medium onions, thinly sliced
2	green bell peppers, seeded, thinly sliced
1	(4-ounce) jar sliced pimento, drained

Dissolve salt in 3 quarts water in a large bowl; add squash. Submerge squash in salt water by placing a dinner plate on top to hold it down. Let stand, covered, 3 hours, then drain. Bring sugar, vinegar, mustard seeds and celery seeds to a boil in a large stock pot. Stir until sugar dissolves. Add squash, onions, peppers and pimento; return to a boil. Remove pot from heat and cool pickles. Store in airtight containers in refrigerator up to 2 weeks or place boiling hot mixture in sterile glass canning jars and seal with new lids.

Yield: 1 1/2 - 2 quarts

Carol Freed

B
L
E
S
S
I
N
G
S

Steve's Pickled Okra

4¹/₂	pounds small (2-3-inch) fresh okra pods, rinsed well	1	teaspoon dill seed
6	(1-pint) sterilized canning jars with lids	¹/₂	teaspoon mustard seed
		1	quart 5% white vinegar
¹/₄	teaspoon garlic powder	1	cup water
¹/₂	teaspoon celery seed	¹/₂	cup pickling salt
¹/₈	teaspoon cayenne pepper	6	teaspoons sugar or saccharin tablets

Cut off okra stems, (do not pierce pods or okra juices will be lost; pack okra in jars. Combine garlic, celery seed, pepper, dill and mustard seeds; evenly sprinkle in jars. In a pan, boil vinegar, water, pickling salt and sugar 5 minutes; pour over okra in jars. Seal; process jars in boiling water bath 10 minutes. Let sit 30 days before using.

NOTE: *May omit salt, but if so, increase amount of vinegar used.*

Yield: 6 pints   Dr. Steve Thurston

Snazzy Jezebel Sauce

1	(18-ounce) jar peach preserves	6	tablespoons creamy horseradish sauce
1	(16-ounce) jar apple jelly	¹/₂-1	tablespoon freshly ground white pepper
5	teaspoons honey-Dijon mustard	1	cup cranberry sauce (optional)

Mix ingredients in medium bowl. Use sauce to accompany turkey, pork, ham or beef, or pour over a block of cream cheese and serve with crackers as an appetizer, or spread on biscuits filled with sliced ham or turkey. Keeps several days in refrigerator.

NOTE: *For CRANBERRY JEZEBEL SAUCE, add jellied cranberry sauce.*

Yield: 4 1/2 - 5 1/2 cups

Crock Pot Apple Butter

4	pounds apples, peeled	1	tablespoon cinnamon sugar
¹/₂	cup apple cider vinegar	1	teaspoon ground nutmeg
2¹/₂	cups sugar	1	cup raspberry jam (optional)
1¹/₂	cups brown sugar		

Cook cored and sliced apples and vinegar on high 6 hours in 4-quart covered crock pot. Stir in sugars and nutmeg. Cook covered on low 4 hours. Add jam last hour if desired for *RASPBERRY APPLE BUTTER*. Cool. Keeps in refrigerator 1 week.

Yield: 6 cups

Chili Relish

50	medium to large tomatoes	6	cups apple cider vinegar
1/2	cup hot peppers, chopped or ground	2	teaspoons cinnamon
1	cup onion, chopped	2	teaspoons ginger, fresh or crushed
3	green bell peppers, chopped	2	teaspoons cloves
3	red bell peppers, chopped	2	teaspoons nutmeg
5	cups sugar	12	(1-pint) sterilized canning jars with lids
1/2	cup salt		

Remove tomato skins after dropping washed tomatoes into a pan of boiling water to loosen. Soak until skin begins to blister. Remove from hot water and place in cold water. When cool to the touch, gently peel and core tomatoes. Use food processor to chop tomatoes. Put tomatoes in a large pot and add remaining ingredients. Boil for 3 hours on medium heat. Stir often. Pour into canning jars. Screw on lids and submerge jars in simmering water for 10 minutes. After processing, sandwich jars between layers of towels to cool.

Yield: 12 pints   Hap Roberts

Tomato Pineapple Relish

2	cups or 1 (28-ounce) can tomatoes, undrained	2	tablespoons white or apple cider vinegar
1	(1.75-ounce) box Sure-Jell	1/2	teaspoon ground cinnamon
1 1/2	cups or 1 (13.5-ounce) can crushed pineapple, undrained	1/2	teaspoon ground allspice
		1/4	teaspoon ground cloves
2	teaspoons Worcestershire sauce	5 1/2	cups sugar
		1	stick paraffin, cut into pieces
		8	(8-ounce) glass jars with lids

Place tomatoes in a blender container. Process very briefly, leaving some tomato chunks in mixture. Mix Sure-Jell, pineapple and seasonings with tomatoes. In a saucepan, bring mixture to a hard boil, while stirring. Add sugar. Bring to a full rolling boil; boil hard for 1 minute, stirring constantly. Remove from heat and skim off foam. Stir and skim foam for 5 minutes. Ladle relish into small glass jars that have been washed in hot cycle of dishwasher. Melt paraffin in a glass jar, sitting in a pan of boiling water. Pour melted paraffin over top of relish to seal jars. Refrigerate after opening. Serve with pork, turkey or chicken.

Yield: 8 jars   Mimi Carlton

Howard Moore's Quick Hot Salsa

2   (10-ounce) cans Ro-Tel Italian
    diced tomatoes and green
    chiles, drained
1   (14½-ounce) can diced
    tomatoes, drained
½   small white onion, chopped

1   bunch cilantro, chopped
3   fresh jalapeño or serrano
    peppers, cut, seeds removed
    and chopped
    Juice of 1 fresh lime

Dice tomatoes into smaller chunks if desired. In a bowl, combine tomatoes, onion, cilantro, peppers to taste and lime juice. Refrigerate overnight. Serve with Mexican tortilla chips.

NOTE: *Use caution when handling peppers to avoid skin and eye irritation.*

Yield: 4 cups   Sophie Kivett

Seasoning Salt
Great Christmas gift

1½ cup coarse sea salt
1   (2.3-ounce) bottle cracked
    pepper

1   tablespoon minced fresh
    garlic or bottled ground
    garlic cloves
2   tablespoons powdered
    ginger

Mix all ingredients and store in an airtight container. Use mixture sparingly as a seasoning on meat, poultry, salads or stir fry. Seems to keep well without refrigeration.

Yield: 2 cups   Camille King Reische

Savory Walnut Topping
Adds crunch to vegetables or salads!

¼   cup margarine or butter
½   cup walnuts, coarsely
    chopped
1   cup soft bread crumbs

¼   teaspoon crushed dill weed,
    rosemary or oregano
    (or other desired herbs)
1   clove garlic, finely minced

Melt margarine in medium skillet. Add nuts, crumbs, herbs of choice and garlic. Stir until lightly toasted. Sprinkle over cooked vegetables or salads. Store in air-tight container in refrigerator.

Yield: 1 cup

FOOD WEB SITES

www.fatfree.com
www.guiltless.com
www.healthychoice.com
www.vegweb.com
www.fabulousfoods.com
www.epicurious.com
www.goodcooking.com
www.ilovepasta.org/pasta.html
www.seafood.com
www.eatright.org
www.peanutbutterlovers.com
www.rmc.com/wrap
www.thelovechef.com
www.campbellsoup.com
www.flyingnoodle.com
www.tpeaks.com
www.snydersofhanover.com
www.family.com

FOOD WEB SITES

www.fritolay.com
www.starchefs.com
www.birdseye.com
www.spiceguide.com
www.foodallergy.org
www.egb.org
www.kitchenlink.com
www.cyberkitchen.com
www.cappucino.com
www.wetravel.com/lowfat
www.dietcontrol.com
www.landolakes.com
www.mealsforyou.com
www.whymilk.com
www.cookinglight.com
www.snax.com
www.shawguides.com/cook
www.calstrawberry.com/recipes

HOT LINES

Beef Industry Council 1-800-922-2373
Food Allergy Network 1-800-929-4040
Nutrition Hotline for American Dietetic Association. 1-800-366-1655
USDA Meat & Poultry Hotline 1-800-535-4555
FDA Seafood Hotline. 1-800-FDA-4010
National Fluid Milk. 1-800-WHYMILK
Pork Hotline 1-800-937-PORK
Yeast Baking Hotline. 1-800-227-6202
Calcium Information Center. 1-800-321-2681
Sodium Information Hotline. 1-800-622-3274
National Cholesterol Education Program 1-800-575-WELL

EQUIVALENTS AND CONVERSIONS

Granules (Pinch/Dash) . $1/8$ teaspoon
Liquid (Dash) . . . . 2-3 drops
3 teaspoons . . . . 1 tablespoon
1 tablespoon . . . . $1/2$ fluid ounce
2 tablespoons . . . . 1 fluid ounce
4 tablespoons ($1/4$ cup) 2 fluid ounces
$5^1/3$ tablespoons . . . . $1/3$ cup
8 tablespoons ($1/2$ cup) . . . . 4 ounces
12 tablespoons ($3/4$ cup) . . . 6 ounces
16 tablespoons (1 cup). . . . 8 ounces
1 cup . . . . $1/2$ pint

2 cups . . . . $1/2$ quart
2 pints . . . . 1 quart
4 cups (1 quart) . . . . 32 ounces
8 cups (2 quarts) . . . . 64 ounces
2 quarts. . . . . $1/2$ gallon
4 quarts . . . . 1 gallon
1 quart . . . . 32 ounces
1 quart. . . . . .946 liters
1 liter. . . . 1 quart + $3^1/2$ tablespoons
1 pound . . . . 16 ounces

419

INGREDIENT YIELDS

FRUITS

Apple or Orange	1 medium	1 cup, chopped
Apples	1 pound	3 medium-sized
Bananas	1-2	1 cup, sliced or mashed
Blueberries	1 pint	2 cups
Coconut	8 ounces	2^1/$_2$ cups
Cranberries, Fresh	1 pound	4 cups cranberries or 1 quart cranberry sauce
Dates	8 ounces	1^1/$_2$ cups, chopped
Grapes	2 pounds	160 grapes
Lemon	1 medium	2 teaspoons zest + 2 tablespoons juice
Lemons (4)	1 pound	1 cup juice
Lime	1 medium	1 teaspoon zest + 1^1/$_2$ -2 tablespoons juice
Limes (6-8)	1 pound	^{1}/$_2$ cup juice
Orange	1 medium	2 tablespoons zest + ^{1}/$_2$ cup juice
Oranges (3-4)	1 pound	1 cup juice
Pears or Peaches	4 medium	2 cups, sliced
Pineapple	1 medium	2 cups, cubed
Plums	6 medium	2^1/$_2$ cups, halved
Raspberries	1 pint	1^3/$_4$-2 cups
Strawberries	1 pint	2 cups, sliced

VEGETABLES

Asparagus (12-15 spears)	1 pound	3^1/$_2$ cups, cut
Beans, Dried	1 cup	2^1/$_4$ cups, cooked
Beans, Green	1 pound	3 cups, cut into pieces
Broccoli or Cauliflower	1 pound	2 cups florets
Cabbage, Head	2 pounds	9 cups, shredded or 4-5 cups, cooked
Carrot	1 medium	^{1}/$_2$ cup, sliced or ^{1}/$_3$ cup grated
Carrots (6-7)	1 pound	3^1/$_2$ cups, sliced; 2 cups, grated
Corn	2-3 ears	1 cup cut kernels
Cucumbers	1 medium	1 cup, sliced
Garlic	1 clove	^{1}/$_2$ teaspoon, finely chopped
Lettuce, Head, Iceberg	1 pound	6 cups torn pieces
Lettuce, Leaf	1 pound	8 cups torn pieces
Lettuce, Romaine	1^1/$_2$ pounds	12 cups torn pieces
Mushrooms	1 pound	4 cups, chopped; 6 cups, sliced
Okra (22-28 pods)	1 pound	5 cups, cut
Olives	15 large; 36 small	1 cup, chopped
Onions, Green	2 medium bulbs	1 tablespoon, chopped
Onions (4 large)	1 pound	4 cups, sliced; 2 cups, cooked
Peas, Frozen	1 (10-ounce) box	2 cups, cooked
Peas, Shelled	1 pound	1 cup
Pepper, Bell	1 medium seeded	1 cup, chopped
Potatoes, Sweet	1 (15-ounce) can	2 cups, mashed
Potatoes, Sweet or White	1 pound	3 medium potatoes
Potatoes, Sweet or White	3 medium	3 cups sliced or grated 2^1/$_4$ cups, diced; 2 cups mashed
Pumpkin, Solid Pack	1 (16-ounce) can	2 cups, mashed
Pumpkin or Winter Squash	1 pound	1 cup, cooked
Spinach, Fresh	1 pound	6 cups, raw; 1^1/$_2$ cups, cooked
Spinach, Frozen	1 (10-ounce) box	1^1/$_2$ cups, cooked
Squash, Summer	1 pound	3^1/$_2$ cups, sliced; 2 cups, grated
Tomatoes (3-4)	1 pound	3-4 cups, chopped 2 cups, cooked

INGREDIENT YIELDS

BREADS & GRAINS

Bread, Loaf, Sliced	1 pound	16-22 slices
Bread, Dry or Toasted	4 slices	1 cup fine crumbs
Bread, Fresh	2 slices	1 cup soft crumbs
Cookies, Chocolate Wafer Shortbread Cookies	18-19	1 cup crumbs
Crackers, Graham	14 (2$\frac{1}{2}$ x 2$\frac{1}{2}$) or 7 (5 x 2$\frac{1}{2}$) inches	1 cup crumbs
Crackers, Ritz or Saltine	28 Ritz, 28 saltines	1 cup crumbs
Cornflakes	3 cups	1 cup crushed crumbs
Flour	1 pound	4 cups
Noodles	8 ounces	4 cups, cooked
Rice, Long Grain, Brown or Converted; Grits	1 cup, uncooked	3-4 cups, cooked
Gingersnaps	15	1 cup crumbs

MEATS

Bacon, Cooked Crisp	8 slices	$\frac{1}{2}$ cup, crumbled
Beef Meats, Chopped	1 pound	3 cups, cooked
Beef Meats, Ground	1 pound	2 cups, cooked
Chicken, Whole Fryer	3$\frac{1}{2}$ pounds	2 cups, cooked, cubed
Chicken, Whole Hen	5 pounds	4 cups, cooked, cubed
Chicken, Boneless Parts	$\frac{1}{2}$ pound	1 cup
Crabmeat, Fresh	1 pound	3 cups, cooked
Crab, in Shell	1 pound	$\frac{3}{4}$-1 cup, flaked
Scallops, Fresh	1 pound	3 cups, cooked
Shrimp, Raw, Jumbo	1 pound	10-15 shrimp
Shrimp, Raw, Medium	1 pound	25-30 shrimp
Shrimp, Raw, Small	1 pound	30-35 shrimp
Shrimp, Raw	2 pounds	1 pound, shelled, cleaned, cooked
Coconut	1 medium	4 cups, shredded
Nuts (Pecans/Almonds)	1 pound in shells	2 cups, shelled
Nuts, Shelled	4 ounces	1 cup, chopped

DAIRY

Butter, 1 Stick	$\frac{1}{4}$ pound ($\frac{1}{2}$ cup)	8 tablespoons
Cheese, Cheddar, Swiss, American, Parmesan	1 pound	4 cups, shredded
Cream, Heavy Whipping	1 cup, ($\frac{1}{2}$ pint)	2 cups, whipped
Ice Cream	1 quart	4 (8-ounce) servings
Milk, Evaporated, Chilled	1 (5$\frac{3}{4}$-ounce) can	2 cups, whipped
Milk, Evaporated, Chilled	1 (8-ounce) can	3 cups, whipped

MISCELLANEOUS

Chocolate Chips	6 ounces	1 cup chips
Chocolate	1 (1-ounce) square	3 tablespoons, chopped, grated or melted
Gelatin, Plain	1 packet	Congeals 2 cups liquid
Sugar	1 pound	2 cups granulated 2$\frac{1}{3}$ cups brown 3$\frac{3}{4}$ cups confectioners or 100 cubes
Marshmallows	1 cup, packed	10 large or 100 miniature
Marshmallows	12-ounce bag	40 large, 400 miniature
Marshmallow creme	7-ounce jar	2 cups creme

HANDY COOKING SUBSTITUTIONS

INSTEAD OF:	USE:
1 Cake Compressed Yeast	• 1 package active yeast
1 Cup Granulated Sugar	• 1¾ cups confectioners; ¾ cup light corn syrup or honey
1 Cup Honey	• 1 cup light corn syrup or ½ cup frozen fruit juice concentrate, thawed
1 Cup Corn Syrup	• 1¼ cups granulated sugar + ⅓ cup water; boiled to a syrup
1 Cup Maple Syrup	• 1 cup dark corn syrup
1 Cup Brown Sugar	• 1 cup white sugar + 3 tablespoons of molasses
1 Teaspoon Sugar	• 1 (¼ gram) 12.3 mg saccharin tablet; or 1 tablet or 1 packet of aspartame
1 (7-ounce) Jar Marshmallow Creme	• 40 standard marshmallows, or 400 mini; melted
2 Tablespoons Flour	• 1 tablespoon cornstarch or tapioca
1 Cup Cake Flour	• 1 cup less 2 tablespoons all-purpose flour
1 Cup Self-Rising Flour	• 1 cup all-purpose flour + ½ teaspoon baking powder + ¼ teaspoon salt
1 Teaspoon Baking Powder	• ½ teaspoon cream of tartar + ¼ teaspoon baking soda
1 Cup Bread Crumbs	• ¾ cup cracker crumbs, 1 cup cornflakes, or ⅔ cups rolled oats
1 Cup Butter (16 Tablespoons)	• 1 cup margarine; or ⅞ cup vegetable oil or shortening
1 Cup Melted Shortening	• 1 cup vegetable oil
1 Cup Yogurt	• 1 cup sour cream/buttermilk
1 Cup Crème Fraîche	• ¾ cup sour cream + ¼ cup milk
1 Cup Sour Cream	• 1 cup sour milk or evaporated milk + 1 tablespoon lemon juice; or 1 cup low-fat cottage cheese, pureed + 2 tablespoons skim milk
1 Cup Whole Milk	• ½ cup evaporated milk + ½ cup water
1 Cup Espresso, Brewed	• 1 cup brewed double-strength coffee
1 Cup Heavy Whipping Cream	• 1 cup evaporated or evaporated skim milk chilled in freezer; = 2 cups, whipped
1 Cup Heavy Cream, Whipped	• 2 cups frozen whipped dessert topping, thawed
1 Cup Ricotta Cheese	• 1 cup cottage cheese, pureed
1 Pita Bread	• 1 flour tortilla
1 Cup Chopped Pecans	• 1 cup regular oats; toasted until crunchy at 350°
1 Cup Pine Nuts	• 1 cup chopped almonds/walnuts
1 (1-inch) Vanilla Bean	• 1 teaspoon vanilla extract
3 (1-ounce) Squares of Semi-Sweet Baking Chocolate	• ½ cup semi-sweet chips
1 (1-ounce) Square Unsweetened Chocolate	• 3 tablespoons cocoa + 1 tablespoon butter, oil or margarine
1 (1-ounce) Square Chocolate	• 2 tablespoons chocolate chips
1 ounce Semi-Sweet Chocolate	• 1 ounce unsweetened chocolate + 1 tablespoon sugar
1⅓ Cups Fresh Strawberries, Sliced	• 1 (10-ounce) box frozen strawberries in liquid
1 Cup Dried Currants	• 1 cup raisins or chopped dates
1 Cup Pears, Chopped	• 1 cup apples, chopped
Juice of 1 Orange	• ⅓-½ cup pasteurized orange juice
2 Tablespoons Orange Zest, Grated	• 2 tablespoons of orange marmalade or dried orange peel or 3 teaspoons orange extract
Juice of 1 Lemon	• 2 tablespoons frozen lemon juice from concentrate, thawed; or 1½ teaspoons lemon extract
1 Teaspoon Citrus Zest	• 2 tablespoons fresh juice, 1 teaspoon dried zest or ½ teaspoon extract
1 Teaspoon Lemon Juice	• ½ teaspoon white vinegar
1 Tablespoon Balsamic Vinegar	• 1 tablespoon red wine vinegar + 2 teaspoons sugar, or 1 tablespoon sherry vinegar
1 Cup Wine/Sherry	• apple cider or juice, white grape juice or dry vermouth or champagne
1 Cup Rice Wine	• 1 cup dry sherry

HANDY COOKING SUBSTITUTIONS

INSTEAD OF:	USE:
¼ Cup Marsala Wine	• ¼ cup of sherry, sweet white wine, or dry white wine + 1 tablespoon of brandy
2 Tablespoons Brandy	• ½ teaspoon brandy extract + 2 tablespoons water
½ Cup Rum	• ½ cup brandy or cognac
1 Teaspoon Black Pepper	• 1 teaspoon paprika or white pepper
¼ Teaspoon Chili Powder	• ¼ teaspoon cayenne pepper or 6-8 drops of hot pepper sauce
1 Tablespoon Worcestershire Sauce	• 1 tablespoon steak sauce
¼ Cup Soy Sauce	• 1½ tablespoons Worcestershire sauce + 1½ tablespoons water
2 Teaspoons Worcestershire Sauce	• 2 teaspoons soy sauce + dash of cayenne pepper
1 Tablespoon Prepared Mustard	• 1 teaspoon dry mustard + 1 tablespoon vinegar
1 Tablespoon Fresh Grated Horseradish	• 1-2 tablespoons prepared or cream style horseradish
1 Cup Barbecue Sauce	• 1 cup ketchup + 1-2 tablespoons Worcestershire sauce
1 Cup Ketchup/Chili Sauce	• 1 cup tomato sauce + ½ cup sugar + 2 tablespoons vinegar + dash of allspice, cloves, onion powder
1 Tablespoon Tomato Paste	• 1 tablespoon ketchup
1 Cup Tomato Puree	• ½ cup tomato paste + ½ cup water
2 Cups Tomato Sauce	• 1 (6-ounce) can tomato paste + 1 cup water
1 Cup Tomato Juice	• ½ cup tomato sauce + 2 tablespoons sugar + 1 tablespoon vinegar + ⅛ tablespoon ground cloves
1 Cup Canned Tomatoes	• 1⅓ cups chopped fresh tomatoes, simmered 10 minutes
1 Cup Rice, Regular, Uncooked	• 1 cup wild, converted, or brown rice
1 Pound Mushrooms, Fresh	• 3 cups freeze-dried, rehydrated (for pizzas, etc.) or 1 (8-ounce) can sliced mushrooms
Few Drops Hot Pepper Sauce	• dash of cayenne or red pepper
3 Tablespoons Red Bell Pepper, Chopped	• 2 tablespoons chopped pimentos, or 1 tablespoon sweet red pepper flakes
1 Medium Onion (⅓ Cup Chopped)	• ⅓ cup frozen, chopped onion (thawed) or 2 tablespoons dried minced onion flakes rehydrated in ice water
1 Tablespoon Chives, Chopped	• 1 tablespoon chopped green onion tops
1 Garlic Clove	• ¼-½ teaspoon bottled ready-to-use minced ground garlic; or garlic juice or ¼ teaspoon garlic salt; or ⅛ teaspoon garlic powder
Parsley, Fresh	• Leafy celery tops (for soups/stews)
1 Cup Fresh/Canned Beef or Chicken Broth	• 1 bouillon cube; or 1 teaspoon powdered broth or concentrate dissolved in 1 cup boiling water
Proscuitto	• Wafer thin slices of cured Smithfield or Virginia ham
Pepperoni Slices	• Salami slices
Chicken, 1 Cup Diced	• 1 (5-ounce) can boned chicken
1 Tablespoon Fresh Herbs	• 1 teaspoon dried leaf; ½ teaspoon crushed, ⅓ teaspoon ground or ½ teaspoon herb salt (reduce salt in recipe)
1 Teaspoon Italian Spice	• ¼ teaspoon each (basil, oregano, rosemary, thyme) + dash of cayenne
1 Teaspoon Poultry Seasoning	• ¾ teaspoon sage + ¼ teaspoon thyme
1 Teaspoon Chervil	• 1 teaspoon tarragon/parsley
1 Teaspoon Sage	• 1 teaspoon thyme
1 Teaspoon Oregano	• 1 teaspoon marjoram
1 Tablespoon Ginger	• ⅛ teaspoon powdered ginger; or 1 tablespoon candied ginger, rinsed in water, chopped
1 Teaspoon Pumpkin Pie Spice	• ½ teaspoon cinnamon + ¼ teaspoon ginger + ⅛ teaspoon each allspice and nutmeg
1 Teaspoon Ground Mace	• 1 teaspoon ground nutmeg
1 Teaspoon Allspice	• ½ teaspoon cinnamon + ⅛ teaspoon cloves + ¼ teaspoon nutmeg
1 Teaspoon Apple Pie Spice	• ½ teaspoon cinnamon + ¼ teaspoon nutmeg + ⅛ teaspoon allspice + dash of ginger & cardamom

HEALTHY TIPS & HINTS

INSTEAD OF	USE
Frosted Cakes or Pound Cakes	• Modify the ingredients or use angel cakes or sponge cakes, or meringues topped or filled with fruits.
Ice Cream with Fudge Sauce	• Frozen yogurt, non-fat ice cream, fat free fudge toppings, fruit sorbets, sherbets or ice milk.
Whipped Cream	• Freezer chilled & whipped evaporated skim milk, lite whipped topping or "airy" topping in aerosol cans.
Cream Cheese	• Low fat or neufchatel cream cheese or blended cottage cheese (for cheesecakes)
2 Crust Pies Made with Shortening	• 1 crust pies, crumb crusts, or cobbler toppings, made with light vegetable oil or margarine.
Whole Milk Products, Cream & Cheese	• Skim milk, 1-2% lowfat milk, reduced fat sour cream, yogurt, cream cheese and non-fat powdered creamer.
Processed Cereal, Bread, Flour & Rice	• High fiber cereals, oatmeal, bran, whole grain bread, whole wheat flour & brown rice.
1 cup Butter	• 1 cup margarine or $7/8$ cup vegetable oil.
1 whole Egg	• 1 tablespoon egg based salad dressing.
1 large Egg	• 2 egg whites or 3 tablespoons egg substitute.
Egg Based Croissants, Breads & Noodles	• Hard rolls, wheat, rye, pita breads or rice or pasta.
Sugar or Honey	• Artificial sweeteners or concentrated fruit juices.
Carbonated Beverages, & Regular Caffeinated Tea/Coffee	• Use diet drinks, punch made with diet sodas, and decaffeinated tea/coffee.
Chocolate Baking Squares	• Flavor foods when possible with chocolate syrup, fat free fudge topping or pudding.
High Sodium Diet	• Eliminate; or reduce intake by $1/2$ or use lite soy sauce, lite salt and low salt crackers.
Seasoning Foods with Butter & Salt	• Herbs, lemon pepper, mustard, horseradish, vinegar, Worcestershire, garlic and onions.
Yellow Cheese like Cheddar	• Reduce the amount by $1/2$, or use cheeses made with skim milk or reduced fat Swiss or Parmesan cheese.
Buttered Breads	• Dip bread in olive oil or use reduced fat spreads.
Frying Foods	• Bake, steam, grill, broil or stir fry.
Oil Packed Tuna, Smoked, Canned, Cured or Salted Meats	• Water packed tuna, salmon or fresh meat, fish, poultry or ham.
Fried Crumbled Bacon	• Imitation or bottled bacon bits with 50% less fat.
Cream Based Soups or High Sodium Bouillon	• Low sodium soups, bouillon and broth based soups.
Cream Based Pasta Sauces like Alfredo	• Sauces prepared with low fat milk products, fresh tomatoes or vegetables.
High Fat Bacon, Lunch Meat, Hot Dogs, Ground Beef or Sausage	• Turkey products, ground turkey or lean ground beef or vegetable breakfast patties.
Dark Meat Poultry with Skin	• Light meat, skinned chicken, turkey.
Fatty Meats like Pork Chops or Steaks	• Fat trimmed & fat drained meats or leaner meats like tenderloin.
Margarine, Oil or Butter when Baking Cakes, Cookies, Breads, or Brownies	• Substitute equal portions of applesauce, mashed banana, prune or fruit puree or "fat free bottled fruit based replacement for oil".

- Read package labels carefully for food nutrient contents.
- Use naturally flavored fruit spread, frozen fruits & juices without added sugar.
- Extend meat casseroles with low calorie vegetable like mushrooms.
- Use non-stick pans for cooking or grease pans with non-stick vegetable cooking spray or sauté foods in small amount of olive oil, flavored vinegar, wine, garlic or fat free broths instead of "meat" fats or butter.
- Decrease intake of "animal fats"; use polyunsaturated fats like corn, olive or safflower oil.
- Avoid foods preserved with sodium or high in sodium, like canned sauerkraut, canned vegetables, pickles, olives, ketchup, chili, sauce, and barbecue sauce.
- If necessary, chill soups, sauce & gravies to solidify fats; then skim & remove fat.
- Use reduced-fat butter, salad dressing & mayonnaise products.
- Try replacing $1/2$ of oil (in some recipes) with juice or water.
- Avoid high cholesterol foods like liver & organ meats.

INDEX

427

431

D

E

H

I

J

K

L

M

439

ॐ

SALADS, SALAD DRESSINGS & TOPPINGS
Congealed or Frozen

Fruit

Meat, Poultry & Seafood

Pasta, Potato & Rice

Vegetable

T

Hymn of Promise

In the bulb there is a flower; in the seed, an apple tree;
In cocoons, a hidden Promise: butterflies will soon be Free!
In the cold and snow of winter there's a Spring that waits to be,
Unrevealed until its season, something God alone can see.

There's a song in every silence; seeking words and melody;
There's a dawn in every darkness, bringing hope to you and me.
From the past will come the future; what it holds a mystery,
Unrevealed until its season, something God alone can see.

In our end is our beginning; in our time, infinity;
In our doubt there is believing; in our life, eternity.
In our death, a resurrection; at the last a victory,
Unrevealed until its season, something God alone can see.

Words and music by Natalie Sleeth

®1986 by Hope Publishing Company, Carol Stream, Illinois 60188
Reprinted with permission under license # 5699

ALPHA & OMEGA STAINED GLASS WINDOWS

The second First Presbyterian Church building was completed in 1892.
When it was demolished, two beautiful stained glass windows were saved.
Several years later, two of our faithful church women, Mrs. Lillian Heitman
and Mrs. Elizabeth Hurley paid to have the windows structurally installed in
the new church, which was built in 1969. The windows can be seen today
on the church exterior and from both interior stairwells leading to the
church balcony. The center of the window designs feature, and represent
THE ALPHA and THE OMEGA, THE BEGINNING and THE END.

THE ALPHA – THE BEGINNING

THE OMEGA – THE END

The Alpha, the first letter of the Greek alphabet, and The Omega, the last
letter of the Greek alphabet, are used in the Old Testament and The New
Testament to express the eternity of God, as both the beginning and the
end. Both the Greeks and the Hebrews used these letters of the alphabet
as numerals.

*Color photographs of the stained glass windows were reproduced for the title page
 of this book.

BLENDED BLESSINGS

Please Make Checks Payable and Mail to:

FIRST PRESBYTERIAN CHURCH WOMEN
308 West Fisher Street
Salisbury, North Carolina 28144

Please Mail Blended Blessings Cookbook to:

– PLEASE PRINT –

_____ _____ _____
First Name   MI   Last Name

_____ _____ _____ _____
Street Address or Post Office Box Number   City   State   Zip Code

(_____)_____ – _____
        Telephone Number

Please Do Not   Please Send _____ Copies   @ $20⁰⁰ *each*

Send Cash   *Postage & Handling*   @ $3⁰⁰ *each*

Sorry, No CODs   TOTAL AMOUNT ENCLOSED **$** _____

ORDER FORM

BLENDED BLESSINGS

Please Make Checks Payable and Mail to:

FIRST PRESBYTERIAN CHURCH WOMEN
308 West Fisher Street
Salisbury, North Carolina 28144

Please Mail Blended Blessings Cookbook to:

– PLEASE PRINT –

_____ _____ _____
First Name   MI   Last Name

_____ _____ _____ _____
Street Address or Post Office Box Number   City   State   Zip Code

(_____)_____ – _____
        Telephone Number

Please Do Not   Please Send _____ Copies   @ $20⁰⁰ *each*

Send Cash   *Postage & Handling*   @ $3⁰⁰ *each*

Sorry, No CODs   TOTAL AMOUNT ENCLOSED **$** _____

ORDER FORM

Notes

Bibliography

RECIPES INTO TYPE
A Handbook For Cookbook Writers and Editors, By Joan Whitman and Delores Simon. 1993 By Harper Collins Publishers

THE COMPLETE GUIDE TO SUCCESSFUL PUBLISHING
How To Create, Print, Distribute, and Make Money Publishing Books. By Avery Cardoza 1995 By CARDOZA PUBLISHERS

FOOD LOVER'S COMPANION
Comprehensive Definitions of Over 4000 Food, Wine, and Culinary Terms By Sharon Tyler Herbst 1995 Barron's Educational Series, Inc.

THE SELF-PUBLISHED COOK
How To Write, Publish, and Sell Your Own Cookbook, Marilyn M. Moore 1995, Wooden Spoon Kitchen Inc.

TIPS ON TYPE
By Bill Gray, 1983 By Van Nostrand Reinhold Company Inc.

PRECISION TYPE FONT REFERENCE GUIDE
The Complete Font Software Resource For Electronic Publishing By Leff Level, Bruce Newman and Brenda Newman 1995 By Precision Type Inc.

A DICTIONARY OF THE BIBLE
By William Smith, L.L.D. Thomas Nelson. Thomas Nelson Publishers